Amos—The Prophet and His Oracles

Research on the Book of Amos

M. DANIEL CARROLL R.

Westminster John Knox Press
LOUISVILLE • LONDON

To my mother
· EDIT RODAS CARROLL ·

who imparted an insatiable thirst for learning,
modeled a passion for teaching,
and bequeathed to me a deep love for my Latin American heritage
in "la tierra de la eterna primavera"—Guatemala

Scripture quotations are from the New Revised Standard Version of the Bible, copyright © 1989 by the Division of Christian Education of the National Council of the Churches of Christ in the U.S.A., and used by permission.

Book design by Sharon Adams
Cover design by Night and Day

First edition
Published by Westminster John Knox Press
Louisville, Kentucky

This book is printed on acid-free paper that meets the American National Standards Institute Z39.48 standard. ∞

PRINTED IN THE UNITED STATES OF AMERICA

02 03 04 05 06 07 08 09 10 11 — 10 9 8 7 6 5 4 3 2 1

Cataloging-in-Publication Data can be obtained from the Library of Congress.

ISBN 0-664-22455-5

Contents

Preface

My interest in the book of Amos was kindled in Guatemala. As a seminary student, I had begun to read about theological trends in Latin America that were trying to respond to the pressing economic needs and social injustice of that long-suffering region. This literature would often appeal to the prophets of the Hebrew Bible in order to ground their demands for change in a powerful word from God. Shortly after graduation my wife and I moved to Central America, where I was to teach at an evangelical seminary in Guatemala City.

This was a homecoming of sorts for me. I am half-Guatemalan (my mother is Guatemalan, hence my second surname is Rodas), and I had spent quite a bit of time there as a boy. Now, though, it was all being processed differently: as a seminary professor trying to teach students from all over the Americas about God, the Bible, and Christian living in a manner that would be relevant and authentic to that context. So I turned to the eighth-century prophet for guidance.

My doctoral research at the University of Sheffield revolved around the book of Amos, and since that time this ancient text has served as the testing ground to explore how orientations drawn from other disciplines, such as literary theory, anthropology, sociology, and ethics, might illuminate the study of the Bible. Ultimately, all of the insights gained are designed to help draw Amos and the Hebrew Bible into a closer dialogue with the realities of the modern world, especially Latin America. Biblical studies for me have always been *for* something, not an end in themselves or a scholarly exercise divorced from the very stuff of life. To try to bridge the gap in the academy between traditional approaches and more directed ones is not always easy, and there can be distrust (even disdain) from each side of the divide toward the other. Hopefully, the days of such scholarly apartheid are numbered.

My hope is that this introduction to Amos research might serve to promote further study of this prophetic text. This volume is divided into two parts. The first part begins with two essays that present the history of Amos research. The initial essay takes the reader from the second half of the nineteenth century to about the year 1990; the second brings the survey up to the present and closes with some thoughts concerning where research might head in the future. It is difficult to try to distill the huge amount of research that has been done into a readable and truly representative survey. I encourage the reader to mine the endnotes, where other sources and details, which would have made the essays too cumbersome, are mentioned and discussed. The third essay of this initial part is not a sustained historical overview, but rather a presentation of what many would label "readings from the margins"—that is, interpretations of the book since 1990 by minority groups within the West and from the perspective of the Two-Thirds World.

Part two consists of four bibliographies that cover commentaries, monographs, and articles on every aspect and part of the book. These are designed to be comprehensive, not exhaustive, listings of sources for further study. The last bibliography is an annotated listing of all doctoral dissertations on Amos completed between 1985 and 2000.

David Orton was the one who introduced me to this project. Carey Newman, my initial editor at Westminster John Knox Press, and Dan Braden have been a great help and a joy to work with in the race to meet publishing deadlines. I would like to thank the library staff at Denver Seminary for their untiring help, expressed always with a gracious smile, in finding obscure references. A special word of thanks goes to Zola Hill, the one in charge of interlibrary loans, who was able to secure all sorts of sources from around the world for a professor so focused on this one Minor Prophet.

My wife, Joan, and two sons, Matthew and Adam, have been patient again with the long nights and weekends at my desk at home. But, in the end, I dedicate this book to my mother, Edit Rodas Carroll. It was she who gave me a love of books and the classroom, as well as nurtured my Guatemalan roots. These are things that define in so many ways who I am and my vocation in life. *Mamá, desde lo más profundo de mi corazón, te agradezco por el rico legado que me has dado: por tu persona, por tu ejemplo en tantas esferas de la vida, y por el orgullo que siento por mi 'guatemalidad.'*

Thanksgiving, 2001

Abbreviations

AB	Anchor Bible
AcAn	*Acta Antiqua*
ACEBT	*Amsterdamse Cahiers voor Exegese en bijbelse Theologie*
AGJU	Arbeiten zur Geschichte des antiken Judentums und des Urchristentums
AJA	*American Journal of Archaeology*
AJSL	*American Journal of Semitic Languages and Literatures*
AnOr	Analecta Orientalia
ASTI	*Annual of the Swedish Theological Institute*
AOAT	Alter Orient und Altes Testament
ATANT	Abhandlungen zur Theologie des Alten und Neuen Testaments
ATD	Das Alte Testament Deutsch
ATLA	American Theological Library Association
AusBR	*Australian Biblical Review*
Auss	*Andrews University Seminary Studies*
AzTh	Arbeiten zur Theologie
BAR	*Biblical Archaeology Review*
BASOR	*Bulletin of the American Schools of Oriental Research*
BAT	Die Botschaft des Alten Testaments
BBB	Bonner biblische Beiträge
BBET	Beiträge zur biblischen Exegese und Theologie
BBR	*Bulletin for Biblical Research*
BEATAJ	Beiträge zur Erforschung des Alten Testaments und des antiken Judentums
BeO	*Bibbia e Oriente*
BEvT	Beiträge zur evangelischen Theologie
BHS	*Biblia hebraica stuttgartensia*, ed. K. Elliger and W. Rudolph. Stuttgart: Deutsche Bibelstiftung, 1981
Bib	*Biblica*

BibFe	*Biblia y fe*
BibInt	*Biblical Interpretation: A Journal of Contemporary Approaches*
BibLeb	*Bibel und Leben*
BibOr	Biblica et orientalia
BIOSCS	*Bulletin of the International Organization of Septuagint and Cognate Studies*
BKAT	Biblischer Kommentar: Altes Testament
BL	*Bibel und Liturgie*
BMik	*Beth Mikra*
BN	*Biblische Notizen*
BolTeol	*Boletín Teológico*
BR	*Bible Review*
BRT	*The Baptist Review of Theology/La Revue Baptiste de Théologie*
BSac	*Bibliotheca sacra*
BT	*The Bible Translator*
BTB	*Biblical Theology Bulletin*
BTF	*Bangalore Theological Forum*
BTS	*Bible et Terre Sainte*
BV	*Biblical Viewpoint*
BVC	*Bible et Vie Chrétienne*
BWANT	Beiträge zur Wissenschaft vom Alten und Neuen Testament
BZ	*Biblische Zeitschrift*
BZAW	Beihefte zur Zeitschrift für die alttestamentliche Wissenschaft
CB	*Cultura bíblica*
CBQ	*Catholic Biblical Quarterly*
ConBOT	Coniectanea Biblica, Old Testament
CR:BS	*Currents in Research: Biblical Studies*
CuadTeol	*Cuadernos de teología*
CurTM	*Currents in Theology and Mission*
DBAT	*Deilheimer Blätter zum Alten Testament und seiner Rezeption in der Alten Kirche*
DBSup	*Dictionnaire de la Bible, Supplément*
DJD	Discoveries in the Judaean Desert
DosB	*Les Dossiers de la Bible*
DTT	*Dansk teologisk tidsskrift*
EBib	Études bibliques
EgT	*Église et Théologie*
EI	*Eretz Israel*
EstBíb	*Estudios bíblicos*
ETL	*Ephemerides theologicae lovanienses*
ETR	*Études théologiques et religieuses*

EvT	*Evangelische Theologie*
ExpTim	*Expository Times*
FAT	Forschungen zum Alten Testament
FO	*Folia Orientalia*
FOTL	Forms of the Old Testament Literature
FRLANT	Forschungen zur Religion und Literatur des Alten und Neuen Testaments
Greg	*Gregorianum*
GTJ	*Grace Theological Journal*
HAR	*Hebrew Annual Review*
HBT	*Horizons in Biblical Theology*
HDR	Harvard Dissertations in Religion
Hen	*Henoch*
HervTS	*Hervormde teologiese studies*
Hor	*Horizons*
HS	*Hebrew Studies*
HSM	Harvard Semitic Monographs
HTR	*Harvard Theological Review*
HSS	Harvard Semitic Studies
HUCA	*Hebrew Union College Annual*
IBS	*Irish Biblical Studies*
IEJ	*Israel Exploration Journal*
Int	*Interpretation*
ITC	International Theological Commentary
Iter	*Actual name of a journal out of Venezuela*
ITQ	*Irish Theological Quarterly*
JANESCU	*Journal of the Ancient Near Eastern Society of Columbia University*
JAOS	*Journal of the American Oriental Society*
JBL	*Journal of Biblical Literature*
JETS	*Journal of the Evangelical Theological Society*
JITC	*Journal, Interdenominational Theological Center*
JJS	*Journal of Jewish Studies*
JLT	*Journal of Literature and Theology*
JMEOS	*Journal of the Manchester University Egyptian and Oriental Society*
JNES	*Journal of Near Eastern Studies*
JNSL	*Journal of Northwest Semitic Languages*
JSOT	*Journal for the Study of the Old Testament*
JSOTSup	*Journal for the Study of the Old Testament, Supplement Series*
JQR	*Jewish Quarterly Review*
JR	*Journal of Religion*

JRT	*Journal of Religious Thought*
JSS	*Journal of Semitic Studies*
JTS	*Journal of Theological Studies*
JTSA	*Journal of Theology for Southern Africa*
Jud	*Judaica*
KAT	Kommentar zum Alten Testament
KJV	King James Version
KTU	*Die Keilalphabetischen Texte aus Ugarit*, ed. M. Dietrich et al. AOAT 24/1. Neukirchen-Vluyn: Neukirchener Verlag, 1976
LAI	Library of Ancient Israel
Leš	*Lešonénu*
LVitae	*Lumen vitae*
LW	*The Living Word*
LXX	Septuagint
MT	Masoretic Text
MUSJ	*Mélanges de l'Université Saint-Joseph*
NAC	New American Commentary
NEB	New English Bible
NedTTs	*Nederlands theologisch Tijdschrift*
NGTT	*Nederduitse gereformeerde teologiese tydskrif*
NIV	New International Version
NKJV	New King James Version
NKZ	*Neue kirchliche Zeitschrift*
NorTT	*Norsk Teologisk tidsskrift*
NovT	*Novum Testamentum*
NRSV	New Revised Standard Version
NT	New Testament
NTS	*New Testament Studies*
NZSTR	*Neue Zeitschrift für systematische Theologie und Religionsphilosophie*
OBO	Orbis biblicus et orientalis
OBT	Overtures to Biblical Theology
OPTT	*Occasional Papers in Translation and Textlinguistics*
Or	*Orientalia*
OrAnt	*Oriens antiquus*
OT	Old Testament
OTE	*Old Testament Essays*
OTG	Old Testament Guides
OTL	Old Testament Library
OTS	*Oudtestamentische Studiën*
OTWSA	*Ou Testamentiese Werkgemeenskap in Suid-Afrika*

PEQ	*Palestine Exploration Quarterly*
PSB	*Princeton Seminary Bulletin*
PSV	*Parola, spirito e vita*
R&T	*Religion & Theology*
RB	*Revue Biblique*
REB	Revised English Bible
REJ	*Revue des Études Juives*
RelSRev	*Religious Studies Review*
ResQ	*Restoration Quarterly*
RevExp	*Review and Expositor*
RevistB	*Revista bíblica*
RevQ	*Revue de Qumran*
RevScRel	*Revue des sciences religieuses*
RevT	*Revista teológica*
RIBLA	*Revista de Interpretación Bíblica Latinoamericana*
RivB	*Rivista biblica*
RSO	*Rivista degli Studi Orientali*
RSR	*Recherches de science religieuse*
RSV	Revised Standard Version
RTP	*Revue de théologie et de philosophie*
RV	Revised Version
SAT	Die Schriften des Alten Testaments in Auswahl
SBJ	La Sainte Bible, traduite en français sous la direction de l'École Biblique de Jérusalem
SBLDS	Society of Biblical Literature Dissertation Series
SBLEJL	Society of Biblical Literature Early Judaism and Its Literature
SBLMS	*Society of Biblical Literature Monograph Series*
SBLSP	*Society of Biblical Literature Seminar Papers*
SBLSymS	Society of Biblical Literature Symposium Series
SBS	Stuttgarter Bibelstudien
SBT	Studies in Biblical Theology
SBTS	Sources for Biblical and Theological Study
ScEs	*Science et esprit*
ScrB	*Scripture Bulletin*
ScrHier	*Scripta hierosolymitana*
SEÅ	*Svensk Exegetisk Årsbok*
SHR	Studies in the History of Religion
SJOT	*Scandinavian Journal of the Old Testament*
SJT	*Scottish Journal of Theology*
SOTSMS	Society for Old Testament Study Monograph Series
SR	*Studies in Religion/Sciences religieuses*

ST	*Studia theologica*
SWBA	Social World of Biblical Antiquity
SwJT	*Southwest Journal of Theology*
TB	Theologische Bücherei
TBl	*Theologische Blätter*
TBT	*The Bible Today*
TEV	Today's English Version
TGl	*Theologie und Glaube*
ThX	*Theologia Xaveriana*
TLZ	*Theologische Literaturzeitung*
TOTC	Tyndale Old Testament Commentaries
TQ	*Theologische Quartalschrift*
TRu	*Theologische Rundschau*
TSAJ	Texte und Studien zum antiken Judentum
TSK	*Theologische Studien und Kritiken*
TTE	*The Theological Educator*
TTZ	*Trierer theologische Zeitschrift*
TynBul	*Tyndale Bulletin*
TZ	*Theologische Zeitschrift*
UF	*Ugarit-Forschungen*
VCaro	*Verbum caro*
VD	*Verbum domini*
VF	*Verkündigung und Forschung*
VSp	*Vie spirituelle*
VT	*Vetus Testamentum*
VTSup	Supplements to *Vetus Testamentum*
WBC	Word Biblical Commentary
WMANT	Wissenschaftliche Monographien zum Alten und Neuen Testament
WO	*Die Welt des Orients*
WuD	*Wort und Diest*
ZAH	*Zeitschrift für Althebräistik*
ZAW	*Zeitschrift für die alttestamentliche Wissenschaft*
ZDPV	*Zeitschrift des deutschen Palästina-Vereins*
ZTK	*Zeitschrift für Theologie und Kirche*
ZWT	*Zeitschrift für wissenschaftliche Theologie*

PART I

Essays on Amos Research

1

A History of Amos Research:
From Wellhausen until 1990

INTRODUCTION

The book of Amos holds a unique place among the canonical prophetic literature. Its place as the first written prophetic text, the brief biographical revelations of a call and its impressive visions, and the enduring power of the message of the man from Tekoa have continually brought this text into the center of many of the broader concerns of investigation into prophetism in general. A number of years ago James Mays aptly remarked:

> Amos is the first of the writing prophets, and so the point of departure for the study of the prophetic movement and its literature. His book is the testing ground for every thesis about the nature of prophecy and its developing history. Prophets there had been before him, but his oracles are the earliest direct evidence for what a prophet said, so that those who preceded him must be seen somewhat in the light of the given of his book, and his successors in the prophetic calling are approached with the knowledge that he has already been in the field. Moreover, his preaching is direct, clear, simple—deceptively so. His vocabulary is relatively small, his concerns specific, and his message seems as plain as his style. Here, surely, is a prophet one can read and understand.[1]

David Petersen more recently has voiced the same sentiment:

> Amos and the scholarship devoted to it offer a microcosm of work on prophetic literature. Virtually every method or perspective available has been exercised on these nine chapters. As a result, no prophetic book has a bibliography comparable in size to that on Amos.[2]

It is possible to trace research into Amos, therefore, in parallel with the trends and interests that have driven the study of the prophets as persons, their words, and the composition of the books that now bear their names. This correspondence will be evident as I review in this essay scholarly work on Amos since the end of the nineteenth century.

The review of studies on Amos in this first essay is in no way exhaustive, but rather attempts to be representative of the most important currents in research and of those scholars who have had the most impact in the field from the closing years of the nineteenth century until about 1990. My breakdown of the history of Amos research into three periods must be appreciated as a suggestion of approximate divisions, as trends overlap and work off of each other in mutual fashion. My purpose is to present a general, but trustworthy, picture that can prove insightful to those intending more extensive study of this prophetic book. The survey essay in the next chapter will cover research from the early 1990s until the present and also will offer projections about the future.

Those who desire to pursue Amos research until 1990 are well served by a number of helpful survey articles,[3] a formal bibliography,[4] and by several recent monographs that offer detailed summaries of research and extensive bibliographies.[5] Each of these sources, of course, reflects the particular priorities of its social and academic context and so allows one to take the pulse, as it were, of scholarly concerns over time.

THE PROPHET AS A CREATIVE RELIGIOUS GENIUS

This opening section of inquiry will focus on three interrelated principal topics of scholarly investigation from the mid-1880s through the first decades of the twentieth century: the appearance of a different understanding of faith in the God of Israel among the eighth-century prophets, the interest in ecstasy, and the desire to recover the very words of these spokespersons for God from the prophetic books.

Amos as a Religious Innovator

Any examination of theories about the evolution of the beliefs and religious practices of Israel finds a natural starting point with the nineteenth-century German Old Testament scholar Julius Wellhausen. In his epoch-making *Prolegomena to the History of Israel*, the first edition of which was published in 1878, Wellhausen articulated a reconstruction of the history of the religion of Israel that would largely define scholarly comprehension of the development of the people's religion for years to come as well as forever change the appreciation of the biblical presentation of that faith. This reconstruction of

Israel's religion, of course, necessarily also affected the understanding of the nature of prophetism. In Wellhausen's view, and in contradistinction from what is found in the pages of Scripture, the classical (or canonical) prophets—of whom Amos was the first—predated the Mosaic covenant and the law. In other words, the actual historical sequence contradicted the biblical presentation.[6] At least two components of this perspective are especially pertinent to this discussion.

To begin with, the strident ethical demands of these divine spokespersons could no longer be taken as grounded in the lists of Pentateuchal statutory and institutional stipulations; instead, they now were taken to be the reflection of universal moral principles. What is more, the message of the prophets was envisioned as primarily a call to social justice, with direct access to God coming only in the doing of righteousness. Consequently, the prophets adamantly opposed the misguided rituals of the people and would have denied the efficacy of the intricate and mediated cult as it is now presented in Exodus to Deuteronomy. Indeed, the move to a formal cult system, with all of its rites and personnel, actually signified a degeneration of the faith of Israel, a loss of a more personal relationship with God.[7] Thus, through the work of Wellhausen and others, a breach had been driven between the prophets and sacrificial religion.

A second observation springs from the first. The appeal to and proclamation of fundamental moral principles also meant that in the prophets' day Yahweh could not be conceived solely within the limits of a theology of a national patron deity. In their preaching, the God of Israel was to be recognized as the God of every nation who would judge all of humanity in accordance with the requirements of his character of justice.[8]

This combination of moral demand and geographical transcendence was in some measure discontinuous with Israel's earlier beliefs. Even though in the prophetic teaching the God of Israel was the same God as that of the ancient fathers of the nation, the understanding of the nature of his person and demands received a fresh orientation. In this theological development the prophet Amos, as the initial canonical prophet, had a special role to play: "Amos was the founder, and the purest type, of a new phase of prophecy."[9] With him came the inchoate steps toward a universalism, founded upon what this German scholar would call "ethical monotheism." The prophets expanded Israel's understanding of their Deity and so ultimately would help lay the theological foundation that would later help preserve that monotheistic faith by placing it beyond the sociopolitical vicissitudes and fatal final destiny of the nation.

At this juncture Wellhausen's almost poetic description of the appearance of the prophet Amos merits citation:

Under King Jeroboam II, two years before a great earthquake that served ever after for a date to all who had experienced it, there occurred at Bethel, the greatest and most conspicuous sanctuary of Jehovah in Israel, a scene full of significance. The multitude were assembled there with gifts and offerings for the observance of a festival, when there stepped forward a man whose grim seriousness interrupted the joy of the feast. It was a Judaean, Amos of Tekoa, a shepherd from the wilderness bordering on the Dead Sea. Into the midst of the joyful tones of the songs which with harp and tabor were being sung at the sacred banquet he brought the discordant note of the mourner's wail. For over all the joyous stir of busy life his ear caught the sounds of death: "the virgin of Israel has fallen, never more to rise; lies prostrate in her own land with no one to lift her up." He prophesied as close at hand the downfall of the kingdom which just at that moment was rejoicing most in the consciousness of power, and the deportation of the people to a far-off northern land.[10]

A short while later Wellhausen would repeat this view of the prophet Amos with more detail in his brief commentary on the Minor Prophets. For instance, the introduction to his observations on 4:4–14 reads:

This passage no longer applies to those of high position in the capital, but rather to the people as a whole, perhaps to a feast gathering. *The sin of the people is the cult*—that is, the false estimation itself, the illusion, that through it Yahweh could be sought and found and connected with Israel. Of a foreign service or illicit practices Amos says nothing. He does not take Bethel, Gilgal, and Beersheba as idolatrous sanctuaries, but rather as the glorious places for the cult of Yahweh. . . . The more zealously and grandiosely they pursue the cult, the more they offend Yahweh. He had clearly and repeatedly made known their offense, but the tragedy is that they did not then turn from this, but rather still continued to be attached to the false way, simply offering more sacrifices and gifts.[11]

At 5:24 he says: "The old antithesis: no cult, but rather justice!"[12] The violation of the divine ethical imperative allows no hope for restoration beyond the judgment. In Wellhausen's oft-quoted phrase: "Roses and lavender instead of blood and iron."[13]

Several elements of this position concerning the prophetic (and hence Amos's) assessment of Israelite worship continued to have a profound influence on Old Testament studies. Discussion on the significance of the cult and its relationship to divine ethical demands would persist for many years after the appearance of Wellhausen's volume. In broad terms, scholars continued to underscore the idea that the ethical emphasis and universalism of Amos was somewhat of a new view birthed by the prophet Amos, but differences surfaced vis-à-vis the conceptualization of the details of the historical-religious reconstruction. Some—whether speaking of prophetism in general[14] or as commentators on Amos in particular[15]—continued to maintain a sharp opposition between the theology of Amos and the ideology and practices of the cult as celebrated by Israel in the prophet's day.[16] Other scholars could agree with the notion of the priority of the moral, without at the same time holding that the prophet desired the dismissal of everything cultic.[17] Still others held that the theme of justice was certainly central to the message of Amos but disagreed that the prophet was the creator of an ethical monotheism, since Amos appealed to theological and historical antecedents within Israel and assumed a sense of basic right and wrong in all peoples.[18] In any case, the perception of Amos as the champion of the marginalized gained prominence. He, along with the other eighth-century prophets, was seen as a harbinger of the higher ethics of the Christian faith and a precursor to the social gospel of the early twentieth century.

Amos as an Ecstatic

Another avenue of investigation that dominated scholarly interest in this time period was the desire to arrive at the uniqueness of the prophets by probing their inner life. This was an attempt to describe the nature of their communion with God and the subsequent communication of the divine revelation to the people of Israel. The crucial term in these discussions was "ecstasy"—that is, the supernatural overpowering of the prophets in the reception of Yahweh's message and the divine compulsion to transmit this word against the sins of Israel. For some scholars this uncommon encounter with God was tied into the ethical monotheism that the prophets preached: that prophetic conviction was ultimately grounded in an intense, personal experience with Yahweh.

The best-known pioneer of this approach was G. Hölscher, who proposed a theory of the development of prophetism in *Die Propheten*.[19] He was by no means the first to show interest in prophetic inspiration and ecstasy,[20] but with his work the topic captured special attention. Hölscher joined comparative evidence from surrounding cultures with psychological theory to propose an explanation of prophetic ecstasy. He believed that the phenomenon originated in pre-Israelite Syria and Asia Minor and was then taken up by Israel's early prophets. Certain characteristics, he believed, continued to mark prophetism, even though there were changes over time in terms of its magnitude and manifestations.[21]

Scholarly debate focused primarily on four points. First, were ecstasy's beginnings to be limited to early Palestine and Asia Minor, or was the phenomenon more global (both throughout the ancient Near East and in modern religious experience)? Second, although all acknowledged certain bizarre activity in early prophetism (e.g., 1 Sam. 10:5–13, 18:10, 19:20–24), was the ecstasy mentioned later in Israel's history (e.g., 1 Kgs. 18:25–29; cf. 2 Kgs. 9:11; Hos. 9:7; Jer. 29:26) to be limited to false or non-Yahwistic prophets? In other words, did the classical prophets, with their developed socioethical messages, demonstrate in any way some of the same ecstatic behavior? Third, was the label "ecstasy" best applied to the reception of the divine word, to its delivery to an audience, or to the whole process from the special encounter with God to the divinely empowered communication? Lastly, could the meaning of the term be related to the etymology or to a particular verbal stem of the verb "to prophesy" (*nb'*)? Such concerns were still occupying large portions of intro-ductory texts on prophetism even during those days in which the idea of ecstasy had lost much of its appeal.[22] One of the last to seek more far-ranging ancient and modern parallels and to attempt to nuance its meaning and so demonstrate its relevance for the study of prophetism was Lindblom.[23]

The prophet Amos, as the first of the canonical prophets and as one who concentrated on the ethical, marked for many the change from ecstatic phe-nomena to a more rational and controlled prophetism. Nevertheless, some did hold that Amos in some fashion was an ecstatic, too.[24] For instance, in regard to the vision of the basket of fruit in 8:1–3, Robinson writes:

> It would seem that we have here a suggestion as to one of the ways in which ecstasy took hold of the Prophet. He might be looking fixedly at a certain object, and its name, revolving in his mind, would bring home to him the substance of what he was to say. The dazed condi-tion which often springs from such a fixed gaze would thus merge gradually into the actual experience of the ecstasy itself.[25]

Lindblom also sought to establish some kind of solid link between Amos and the earlier ecstatic *nĕbî'îm*. In his mind, some discontinuities and developments within prophetism had inevitably taken place, but Amos was still to be con-sidered an ecstatic. Lindblom enumerated those items that he felt would qual-ify this prophet as an ecstatic:

> It is clear that the difference between Amos and the earlier nabis was not a radical one. He was connected with them by many ties. In tradi-tion he was regarded as a prophet. Amaziah called him a seer, *hōzêh*. "Seer" and "prophet" were at the time identical. His activity was described as "prophesying," i.e., his appearance and his actions were those of a nabi. The redactor of the Book of Amos calls its contents "words which he saw," i.e., prophetic revelations. Amos himself rep-resents Yahweh's command at the moment of his call this way: "Go, speak as a prophet to my people Israel." When he says, "When the Lord Yahweh speaks, who can but prophesy?" (iii. 8), he no doubt has in mind himself and his personal experiences. His messages frequently have the form of oracles, introduced by the usual oracle formula: "Thus says Yahweh." They were based on revelations from God. As

divine words they were regarded as having effective power. Amaziah said that the land was unable to endure all his words. The feeling of divine constraint and compulsion is expressed in his words: "When the lion roars, who does not fear? When the Lord speaks, who can but prophesy?" (iii. 8). A series of real visions received by Amos is preserved in tradition. A real vision is always based upon ecstasy of one form or another.[26]

Many could agree with much of this list of observations about the ministry of the prophet Amos; nevertheless, eventually few scholars came to classify these items under the rubric of "ecstasy." One commentator strongly opposed such a suggestion:

> Although Amos can see visions, yet evidence is entirely absent that the primitive or lower kind of *ecstasy*, which was the distinguishing feature of earlier "prophecy," was part of Amos' equipment. . . . If prophets in the line begun by Amos received at times, in an abnormal state, their message, or their first "call," the "ecstasy" seems to have been almost entirely of a high order, having its analogy somewhat in that of the Christian mystic; it is difficult to understand how it could be compared with that which is common in a primitive religion. Nor does there seem to be sufficient evidence to conclude that their messages were *delivered* in ecstasy.[27]

More tellingly, this same scholar quotes Hölscher himself to substantiate the profound change that had taken place within prophetism by the time of Amos's appearance:

> In all this, the words of Amos stand out as ecstatic speech—but what a distance from the older prophetic ecstasy! No stammered, half-intelligent sounds, but distinct announcement of divine truths. All external expedients, all exaggerated behaviour has disappeared before manifest spirtualisation.[28]

By the mid-1960s interest in ecstasy had diminished. It would surface again, though, years later within the very different conceptual framework of cultural anthropology approaches (see below).

The Ipsissima Verba of Amos

A third important issue was the effort to isolate within the received biblical text the very words of the prophets and so recuperate their fundamental message. This recovery of the prophetic revelation was thought to be very important, because these words would represent the essence of their unusual personal experience with God as well as the unadulterated call to the spiritual and ethical faith demanded by Yahweh.

There were two fundamental theoretical perspectives on how to identify the original words of the prophets and then reconstruct the process of the composition of the canonical books. These distinct means of argumentation were sometimes coordinated and utilized together. The first approach returned to the theme of ecstasy. The style and parameters of prophetic speech were defined in accordance with that prophetic experience: the intense meetings with God provided just short, symbolic messages, which were then communicated verbally rather than written down. In other words, the prophets were above all else orators and poets, not authors. Gunkel makes this view clear:

> Originally, the prophets were not writers, but became such towards the end of their history. They were originally orators, as can be seen from the expression "Hear!" with which their speeches begin. We must try and imagine their sayings being uttered orally, and not as they stand on paper, if we are to understand them. . . . We must not imagine that their manner of delivery, especially in the case of the older prophets, was as deliberate as that of modern preachers, and in fact the comparison between prophets and preachers (and even more between them and teachers) has greatly hindered our understanding.[29]

And again: "Of its nature, enthusiastic inspiration speaks in poetic form, and rational reflection in the form of prose. Consequently, in form the prophetic 'speech' was originally a poem."[30] This view, accordingly, would hold any prophetic oracle to be unavoidably brief, and, in the case of the juxtaposition of several oracles, no necessary coherence between them was to be expected. Robinson states:

> To each of these [i.e., prophetic utterances] we may give the name "oracle," understanding by that term the message given at any one time and through any one ecstatic experience. There is no reason to believe that this experience was commonly of long duration. . . . In any case it seems clear that the oracle itself—that is, the words in which the message was enshrined, was almost always short, and consisted of a few sentences which would drive home the point in unforgettable fashion. Further, it would seem that the oracle was always cast in poetic form, that it was, in fact, a short poem of the characteristic Hebrew type. It is this fact which enables us to ascertain something of the structure of the prophetic books. The Hebrew was not reflective, and the ecstatic experience tended to produce emotional expression rather than logical consistency. The result is that one does not look in the individual oracle for more than one dominant idea. It is not a reasoned process of thought that is attempted. The prophetic oracle is rather an effort to bring home a single truth in arresting language and striking phrases.[31]

In accordance with this point of view, with the passing of time these poignant words from God, which had been proclaimed on any number of separate occasions, would have been recorded and then collected by a prophet's disciples.[32] Still later, this collection would have been supplemented by additional material. The task of the exegete, therefore, was to isolate those first poetic sayings in order to *truly* hear the voice of the prophet.

The second perspective offered a different rationale for singling out the authentic oracles. This approach paralleled the literary-critical viewpoint prevalent at that time within Old Testament studies in general and within Pentateuch research in particular. Here the focus was on demarcating the first written sources, which later would have been expanded. Philosophically, these scholars held that the chronologically earlier—that is, the original revelations—were inherently superior to the subsequent additions. In other words, the necessity of trimming back the existing text to uncover the original words of the prophets was still paramount:

> Nowhere is it more necessary to distinguish sharply between the actual words of an author and those that have been added by later writers than in the case of Amos and Hosea. . . . Care has been taken, therefore, to keep separate the quite considerable portion of material (ascribed by tradition to these authors) which may confidently be treated as of later origin.[33]

Harper explains that Amos left his oracles in writing to his disciples. To get back to these initial oracles, which are now interlaced with several succeeding layers of secondary material, Harper appeals to the poetic character of prophetic speech. This, he believes, was of a consistent strophe length and meter and so can be retrieved by the careful study of the text. The nature of the primary poetic level is delineated in detail and serves to introduce his exposition of the text.[34] Wolfe takes the same tack, but does so in a more dramatic tone that exhibits an unbounded confidence in the critical method and the sensibilities of "discerning scholarship":

> Inasmuch as Amos and Hosea were master poets, a number of secondary additions issue their own condemnation by reason of poor poetic quality or even prose style. The interpolations also frequently show variations (in person, number, case, tense, word usage, vocabulary, etc.) which set them off from the context into which they are placed. In these, and other numerous ways, stylistic and grammatical, the secondary passages usually bear witness against themselves.
>
> Faced with this condition of the prophetic productions, the biblical scholar has been confronted with a formidable challenge. This is the project of restoring these writings to something approaching the original forcefulness and beauty they possessed as they left the lips of these prophets. Marvelous restorations are carried on these days in all branches of art. Why cannot the same be done with these masterpieces of literary and religious art? . . . As with the art critics and their

restored paintings, it has been a thrilling adventure to remove the secondary accretions here and there, repair the damage to the text caused
by careless scribes, and see these writings re-emerge, after all the centuries, to display once more their original grandeur and again speak
their powerful messages.[35]

In sum, each of these three topics of research—ethical monotheism, ecstasy,
and the quest for the ipsissima verba of the prophets—in its own way sought
to discover the locus of the prophetic genius, whether by basing it on a transcendent moral content, an incomparable encounter with the divine, or the
rhythmic patterns of a sublime message. New trends, however, were emerging, some of which were presented as direct alternatives to these scholarly
views.

LOCATING THE PROPHET
SOCIALLY AND THEOLOGICALLY

In sharp contrast to some scholarly opinion that the prophets eschewed ritual
in order to champion a more pure ethical ideal, new directions in research that
gathered force in the 1920s began to suggest that the prophets—or at least
some of them—were intimately connected with cultic institutions. This new
orientation was part of a broader movement to better understand the setting
of the prophets and their messages within the social life of Israel. This interest was pursued in two distinct, but sometimes related, tracks. The first focused
more on certain comparative material from the surrounding cultures of the
ancient Near East and a selection of biblical passages and terminology; the second grounded its arguments primarily in theories about specific literary forms
and the traditions embedded within the prophetic books.

The New Year Festival Theory and Prophetic Labels

While commenting on 1 Sam. 10, Hölscher in passing had suggested a connection between some of the prophets and the cult.[36] Gunkel, too, noticed
commonalities between the prophetic literature and the Psalms, such as the
use of liturgical language in some of the prophets (e.g., Joel), the polemics
against ritual and the concern for social justice in several psalms that also are
prevalent in the prophets, and the appearance of oracular speech (the divine
"I") in certain psalms that looked like prophetic utterances. In his mind, and
in line with the scholarly view at the time that many of the psalms were to be
dated relatively late, the implication of these observations was that the
prophets had influenced the cult.

An important development, which would alter the direction of future study, came with Sigmund Mowinckel's landmark work, *Psalmenstudien*.[37] The crucial change in outlook was Mowinckel's reversal of Gunkel's conviction that the prophetic writings had often preceded the production of the psalms. This different appreciation of the relationship grew out of this Danish scholar's reconstruction of the history of prophetism in Israel. He believed that a prophetic link with the cult could be substantiated early in Israel's existence in the seer's pronunciation of divine oracles of curse and blessing at the sanctuaries. The seer, in other words, performed a prophetic function. Once in Canaan, Israel had appropriated the charismatic form of the ecstatic *nĕbî'îm*, who in time organized themselves into prophetic guilds and assumed the role of those ancient seers.[38] The giving of oracles (characteristically of weal) continued to play an important part in the cultic setting, as the prophets would respond to appeals to the Deity by the people, the king, and other individuals (e.g., Pss. 60, 82, 110). Some prophets, he believed, probably had composed a number of the psalms.

The premier cultic setting for Mowinckel was an annual New Year Festival, in which he envisioned a symbolic reenthronement of Yahweh in a ceremonial drama with the participation of the king. The festival, he believed, ultimately had its roots in the Babylonian *Akitu* festival.[39] This rite also entailed the renewal of Israel's covenant with their God, with the attendant proclamation of promises of blessing and threats as well as the demand for adherence to covenant obligations. One of the complex of foundational "festal myths" celebrated at these festivals would have been the victory of Yahweh over his and Israel's enemies. Mowinckel suggested that the Oracles against the Nations in Amos (chaps. 1–2) may have had their origin in such a cultic setting.[40]

Mowinckel distinguished the prophets at the sanctuaries (especially the temple in Jerusalem) from those in the prophetic guilds and the "free reform" or canonical prophets (who could be very critical of the cult), but other scholars soon extended the category of "cult prophet" to include either every or most of the biblical prophets. Haldar, for instance, broadened the data base for coupling the prophets with the cult by arguing for similarities with the ancient Near Eastern phenomena of divination and ecstasy. More specifically, he connected the seer-priest in Israel with the Mesopotamian *bārûm* and the prophets with the *muḫḫûm*. Unlike most scholars, he denied any disjunction between the earlier prophets and the writing prophets.[41] A less extreme and more carefully articulated view was put forth by Aubrey Johnson. In his understanding of prophetism, the prophets were members of the official cultic personnel—once again, this would have been true especially in Jerusalem[42]—and occupied themselves with the giving of oracles and offering intercession at the sanctuaries. Theirs was the task of promoting the welfare of the nation by communicating

the will of Yahweh to the people. The classical or canonical prophets, therefore, had not lashed out at the cult as such, but rather had spoken out against
those who abused their vocation by giving false oracles while claiming to speak
for Yahweh.[43]

The studies by Haldar and Johnson mention Amos only briefly. For Haldar the designations *nōqēd* (Amos 1:1) and *bôqēr* (7:14) prove "him to have
belonged to the cult staff."[44] The first term he defines in accordance with a
specific interpretation of a phrase in an Ugaritic text (*KTU* 1.6.vi.55), which
links certain shepherds to a sanctuary: *rb khnm rb nqdm* ("chief of the priests,
chief of the shepherds"). Haldar relates the second label (*bôqēr*) to the Hebrew
verb *biqqer* (piel of the root *bqr*) and to divination. Johnson cites Amos 3:7 as
an illustration of the personal contact with Yahweh, which would have been
the basis for the prophetic oracular function in the cult.[45]

Several scholars, whose research was more directly concerned with Amos,
also contended that Amos had some sort of relationship with the cult or a sanctuary. Bič argued that the term *nōqēd* in 1:1 revealed that the prophet was a
hepatoscoper—that is, one who inspected the livers of sacrificial animals in
order to interpret oracles.[46] On the basis of the use of this term in the aforementioned Ugaritic text, Kapelrud proposed that Amos had been a high-
ranking cult official, who was in charge of the temple herds (cf. *KTU* 4.68.71;
2 Kgs. 3:4). In addition, with Mowinckel, he related the prophet's message
about the day of the Lord to the New Year Festival.[47]

Lindblom reacted against the idea that the terms *nōqēd* and *bôqēr* meant that
Amos was a formal member of a sanctuary staff, but on other grounds did feel
that the prophet had been attached to a group of sanctuary prophets at Bethel
for a brief period and that Amaziah had addressed him as such.[48] Watts disagreed, too, with categorizing Amos as a cult prophet per se, if by so doing
there was any hint of participation in divination. In his view, Amos appeared
regularly at the sanctuaries—especially at the New Year Festival of covenant
renewal—to deliver his messages. His ministry as a mediator and spokesperson, in other words, had been carried out within the context of the cult, even
if Amos himself was not a cult prophet.[49] Others questioned the interpretation
of the Ugaritic data, in particular the meaning of the term *nōqēd*.[50] The significance, even the very existence, of a New Year Festival as envisioned by
Mowinckel and others came increasingly into question.[51]

The Prophet within Form and Tradition Criticism

Interest in a cultic background for the prophets (and thus Amos) arose from other
quarters as well. Early in the twentieth century scholars began to try to probe
behind the hypothetical documents postulated by source criticism with different

methods called form criticism and tradition criticism.[52] The former developed first, with the discipline of tradition history appearing somewhat later. Though distinct, these approaches are interrelated by a shared concern to comprehend the preliterary history (i.e., the origin and development) of biblical texts.

Form criticism focuses on certain terminology and ideas, which are set in definite conventional literary structures and genres (*Gattungen*), and attempts to discern the possible social and institutional settings (the *Sitze im Leben*) in ancient Israel that might have given rise to those forms now within the biblical documents. From this perspective, these forms would have originally been oral compositions, which only at a later time were put into writing. Tradition criticism in theory studies the progression from oral through written transmission evident between the stages highlighted by form and source criticism. Like form criticism, tradition criticism is concerned about the social contexts in which the biblical materials were created and handed down and also underscores the prominence of the oral over the written.[53]

An important consequence of the form- and tradition-critical approaches was the conviction that, in contradistinction from previous scholarship, the prophets were heirs, transmitters, and developers of earlier communal and national theological convictions and expressions (such as liturgies). In other words, their creative genius did not lay in a break with the past in an anticultic ethical monotheism but rather was displayed in the recontextualization, as it were, of older forms and beliefs into new situations. Importantly for our discussion, at this juncture in Old Testament studies form and tradition criticism linked the prophets to the Israelite cult, which both rooted in an ancient covenantal theology.[54] Even though at that time there was a widespread *theological* coordination of the prophets in general (and Amos in particular)[55] with cult and covenant, I will narrow attention to specific trends within form-critical and tradition-historical studies of Amos.

First, scholars have long had a special interest in identifying the most characteristic and foundational genre of prophetic speech. For many the earliest form was the judgment speech. It has been recognized that these oracles usually consist of two parts: the threat or announcement of judgment (*Drohwort*) and the reproach or reason for that declaration (*Scheltwort*). Research on the genre has debated several issues, such as the adequacy of scholarly terminology, whether these two aspects were originally separate or go intrinsically together, and whether both are a divine revelation or the second a (human) prophetic reflection.[56] Our concern is not to rehearse opinions on these details but instead to concentrate particularly on the proposed *Sitz im Leben* of the prophetic accusations.

Although significant work on the judgment speeches in Amos appeared as early as 1926,[57] several studies particularly stand out in the discussion about the relationship between the oracles of Amos and the cult. In 1950 Würthwein published a long essay entitled simply "Amos-Studien," in which he argued that Amos indeed had been a cult prophet.[58] His position was grounded in the widely held supposition that the prophets at the sanctuaries were prophets of weal (*Heilsnabi*), who delivered messages that would have denounced the enemies of Israel and proclaimed blessing for the nation (e.g., the Oracles against the Nations in Amos 1–2). In time, however, Amos's vocation had been dramatically altered. This change in perspective and calling, Würthwein believed, could be traced through the visions in chapters 7–9: from the task of intercession on behalf of Israel evident in the first two visions (7:1–6), Amos is moved to an obligation to announce judgment in the final three (7:7–9; 8:1–2; 9:1–4). Just as the initial call had thrust him into the prophetic office (7:14), through another direct intervention of Yahweh Amos now had become a prophet of woe (*Unheilsnabi*).[59] This change in the tone and content of his message would explain the motivation behind the confrontation with Amaziah: Amos had now stepped outside the proper boundaries for a cult prophet at the central sanctuary (7:10–17). In light of this reconstruction of the ministry of Amos, it could no longer be said that the prophet was either against all ritual or that he stood against the prophets in general (cf. 2:11–12; 3:7).[60] In addition, Würthwein argued that Amos's denouncing of Israel was based on early preexilic amphictyonic laws[61] and a covenant.

In a subsequent elaboration of the idea that Amos was a cult prophet, Reventlow disallowed the dichotomy between the two kinds of prophets that Würthwein had postulated.[62] In Reventlow's view, the cultic prophets interceded on the people's behalf as well as delivered oracles of both woe and weal. This breadth of activity is evident in Amos's ministry. Reventlow went beyond earlier studies to suggest further that much of the material in the book of Amos had specific liturgical settings: the Oracles against the Nations reflected a cursing ceremony against foreign enemies,[63] and the original context of 4:6–11 and 9:13–15 was to be found within the blessing and cursing rituals of a covenant feast. A few years later Brueggemann could agree with Reventlow's connection between 4:6–11 and the covenant curses of Lev. 26 and suggested that the passage reflected a covenant renewal festival. He did not think, however, that Amos had held a cultic office;[64] for Crenshaw, these verses suggested a "liturgy of penance."[65]

Another avenue of support for the position that the message of Amos was grounded in covenant theology and thus connected to some sort of covenant ritual came from research into ancient Near Eastern suzerain-vassal treaties of the second millennium B.C.E.[66] Special appeal was made to the form of a covenant lawsuit (the *rîb*), in which the superior within the agreement chastises the vassal for breach of covenant and then enumerates curses for that disobedience. The prophets were said to have consciously patterned their words to reflect such an arrangement between Yahweh and his people; at the same time, this background material also was cited to defend the idea that the concept of covenant within Israel would have been an early and natural perspective rather than a late development within the history of their religion. This perspective was applied to the prophet Amos, who by means of such a lawsuit would have attacked the monarchy and the nation for having violated the Sinai covenant and invoked the appropriate covenant curses.[67]

Reactions to the characterization of Amos as a cult prophet and to the conviction of a prophetic covenant theology were varied. Several critics raised the issue of the authenticity of several passages utilized in some of the argumentation that Amos had officially ministered at a sanctuary.[68] There was the doubt, too, about whether the use of cultic language by Amos required that he be a cult prophet. Farr commented that he may well have been simply "an intelligent layman who took his religion seriously, attending the services in the temple and at other shrines."[69] In addition, many scholars attacked both the biblical data and the use of the ancient Near Eastern material that had been marshaled to expound a covenant theology for the classical prophets. The coupling of various forms and terminology with an ancient covenant were considered to be tenuous, and the concept itself was once again pushed forward in time to be contemporaneous with (or even later than) the eighth-century prophets.[70] Nevertheless, the explanation of the words of Amos against the treaty background has been championed by some recent commentators,[71] and others continue to argue for the importance of covenant ideas for the book's message and assume the antiquity of covenant ideas.[72]

Yet another response to the covenant emphasis was the presentation of an alternative social context for Amos to that of the cult: wisdom.[73] After a period of neglect, wisdom literature began to generate more scholarly interest in the 1930s. This was sparked in part by archaeological finds (such as the Egyptian Wisdom of Amenemope), which, on the one hand, pointed to a prominence of wisdom thought prior to the exile and hence to its possible influence on pre-exilic prophetic ideas[74] and, on the other hand, suggested that comparable groups of wisdom teachers within the royal court and scribal schools might have existed in Israel as they had elsewhere in the ancient Near East.[75] Terrien subsequently proposed that Amos had drawn from the language and several literary forms of wisdom in communicating his message.[76]

The identification of Amos's intellectual and spiritual background (*geistige Heimat*) with wisdom was most carefully articulated by Wolff. Building on Terrien's work, which had linked the graded numerical sequence (3/4) of the Oracles against the Nations in chapters 1 and 2, the didactic questions of 3:3–8, and certain vocabulary (e.g., "the right" in 3:10) to wisdom, he expanded the data base of wisdom influence to include still more forms (the woe cries of 6:1, 3–6; 5:18–20; and perhaps 5:7, 10; the exhortation speeches [*Mahnrede*] of 4:4–5; 5:4–6, 14–15) and themes (such as the concern for the poor and the condemnation of extravagant lifestyles).[77] Wolff specified Amos's milieu as that of the older, more rural, ethical clan wisdom in contradistinction from that of the royal circles.[78]

This point of view, however, also came under severe scrutiny. A number of scholars have questioned the notion of clan wisdom as the framework for the preaching of Amos and have given other explanations for each point of Terrien's and Wolff's hypotheses.[79] As in the cases of the cult and covenant, advocates of a very circumscribed intellectual and social background have tended to overstate their case and have ignored or inadequately handled contrary data. Research has increasingly come to the conclusion that the prophet probably appealed to the variety of extant theological traditions available to him to communicate the divine will to Israel.[80]

In sum, these attempts to reconstruct the institutional and social context of the prophet Amos on the basis of parallels drawn from the rituals and literature of the surrounding cultures and by more textually focused critical methods illuminated many biblical details and succeeded in offering fresh perspectives on the man from Tekoa. In the end, however, it was recognized that these approaches had yielded theories of varying strengths and weaknesses. This frustration would lead scholars to pursue more sure results by other means or would suggest to some that such an enterprise must be abandoned for alternative interests.

THE QUEST FOR WHAT LIES BEHIND, WITHIN, AND IN FRONT OF THE TEXT

As this heading implies, I will subdivide this final section of the essay, which covers research from the late 1960s and early 1970s to about 1990, into three parts. Each of these foci concentrates on a particular dimension of the study of the prophetic literature.

Behind the Text

The phrase "behind the text" refers to those approaches that concentrate on some sort of historical reconstruction—whether that be by trying to trace the compositional growth and redaction history of the book of Amos, to uncover archaeological data to elucidate textual particulars, or to explain the complexities of the actual world of the eighth-century prophet on the basis of social theory.[81]

Proposals about how this prophetic book came to be continued in the line of form and tradition criticism. Pride of place in this kind of textual approach belongs to the commentary by Wolff. In his introduction Wolff presents a survey of the various speech forms in the book of Amos,[82] and the exposition of each pericope is prefaced by the discussion of its "Form" and "Setting." Building upon an earlier piece by Schmidt as well as his own criteria for distinguishing and dating phrases and pericopes, Wolff proposes a six-stage formation of Amos.[83] Three of these strata, he believes, can be traced to the eighth century (the very words of Amos in chaps. 3 and 4; the "literary fixation" of the Oracles against the Nations and the visions; and the "old school of Amos"); to these were added the Bethel redaction of the Josianic reform of the seventh century, an exilic Deuteronomistic redaction, and the postexilic words of restoration. Wolff presents this hypothetical reconstruction with confidence. While he can say "the initial phases [of the transmission] are the most difficult to ascertain," just a few lines later he will declare that these layers can be separated out "with a high degree of probability."[84] Wolff posits that the redactional efforts of those who actualized the prophecy of Amos were motivated by the conviction that the divine revelation continued to have power and relevance across the centuries:

> On the whole, therefore, the uniquely sombre message of Amos concerning the end of Israel remains unmistakably audible through all layers of tradition. To be sure, the old school of Amos modified it in one instance with the cultic expectation of salvation (5:14–15). The Bethel-exposition and the Deuteronomistic redaction recognize the new relevance of the words of Amos in the seventh and sixth centuries. Only the postexilic theology adds, briefly but distinctly, that Yahweh's sentence of death is not his last word.[85]

Several commentators and detailed studies, to a lesser or greater degree, assumed Wolff's reconstruction of the genesis of Amos.[86] At the same time, the creative role of the redactors of the various stages of the book's composition began to draw greater attention. Although Wolff spoke of the setting of his hypothetical redactors and the reasons for their additions, other scholars were more aware of literary and lexical interconnections between the various passages within the text and tried to elaborate more comprehensive theories regarding the growth of Amos at the hands of redactors with intentional theological and political agendas.[87] For some, this redactional work also had pastoral and theological implications for today. Coote, for example, states:

> Each stage of recomposition represents an interpretation of Amos's words, and thus an actualization of them, a reading and understanding of them that makes them real and important in a new and different present. Without these successive actualizations, the words of Amos

would soon have been forgotten. These actualizations are earlier ana-
logues of our own interpretation of Amos by which we make it meaningful to us. The life of the word in the community of faith depends on
continuously reactualizing the word. To say the recomposers of the
book of Amos may not meaningfully do so is to imply that we may not.
To say that they may, and to take them seriously at it, allows us to see
ourselves in direct continuity with the persons and communities of
faith that read Amos so actively that they rewrote him as they read. Our
Scriptures *came into being in the process of interpretation*.[88]

The most elaborate presentation came from a cooperative project headed
by Koch.[89] In a very extensive analysis, Koch prioritizes the structure of the
text as we now have it, yet without discounting editorial activity. He divides
the book into four principal parts (chaps. 1–2; chaps. 3–4; 5:1–9:6; 9:7–15).
Introductory and closing formulae and the hymnic passages are especially
highlighted in the exposition of the coherence of the larger units and of the
book as a whole. Some studies concentrated on particular sections within the
text instead of encompassing the entire book. Fritz and Gosse, for instance,
tried to coordinate the Oracles against the Nations with the Deuteronomistic
History; each, however, drew different conclusions from the data regarding
whether and how each corpus might have influenced the other and what the
dates of the individual oracles might have been.[90]

During the same period of this concern to elucidate the *literary prehistory* of
Amos, archaeological discoveries were providing an ever-growing amount of
information that could help clarify the *concrete historical realities lying behind the
prophetic message*. Evidence came from a wide spectrum of social life,[91] but new
data concerning the religious beliefs and practices of Israel dominated scholarly publications and debates. Standing stones, altars and cult stands, terra-
cotta figurines, seals, and other religious paraphernalia had been discovered
throughout the length and breadth of Palestine.[92] Two finds particularly stand
out, both of which have profoundly affected the scholarly understanding of
popular religion in eighth-century Israel and, therefore, can impact the interpretation of the message and ministry of the prophet Amos as well.

One area of research had to do with the *marzēaḥ* feast. This was apparently
a celebration sponsored by wealthy fraternal associations, documentation for
which covers several centuries and a wide geographical area. Opinions differed
over the possible religious significance of these banquets. In addition, there
were the spectacular finds at Kuntillet ‘Ajrud in the eastern Sinai and at Khirbet el-Qôm, which is near Hebron in Judah. At Kuntillet ‘Ajrud paintings and
inscriptions on two pithoi (large storage jars) created a stir, as scenes apparently depicting religious motifs were juxtaposed with lines pronouncing a
blessing in the name of "Yahweh of Samaria and his asherah." At Khirbet

el-Qôm another inscription also communicated a blessing in the name of "Yahweh and his asherah."

Discussion has revolved around a set of interrelated issues.[93] First, the figures and their activity in the pictures had to be identified, and the words and syntax of the inscriptions needed to be deciphered and properly translated. These efforts often have gone hand in hand with attempts to categorize the various religious movements within ancient Israel. Scholars have tried to distinguish the "official Yahwism" of the state apparatus from "popular" faith;[94] questions surfaced concerning the (foreign or indigenous) sources and development of any "heterodox" elements; and the nature of the prophetic critique of the eighth century vis-à-vis these various religious expressions had to be formulated. This archaeological data concerning the *marzēaḥ* and Kuntillet 'Ajrud and Khirbet el-Qôm many times became part of the basis of broader hypotheses regarding the rise of Yahwistic monotheism.

This essay will not offer any decisions regarding this evidence or the evolution of Yahwism. Rather, what is important for my purposes here is to point out the impact this material has had on the study of Amos. Some scholars readily incorporated this information into the interpretation of the book. To begin with, the term *mirzaḥ* actually appears in 6:7. King noted the parallels between the description of the feast in 6:4–7 and what had been discovered about the *marzēaḥ* elsewhere.[95] Barstad took the evidence still further and postulated that the prophetic diatribe against the feast appears as well at 2:7b–8 and 4:1 and incorporated this interpretation into his view that the primary goal of the prophet Amos had been to counteract Baalism and promote the worship of Yahweh alone.[96] Others recognized the presence of the *marzēaḥ* feast and its religious connotations but did not conjecture that the prophet's overriding concern was to attack religious aberrations.[97] Still others focused on the social ramifications of the celebration in 6:4–7 but did not concern themselves with (or perhaps were unaware of) its religious implications.[98]

The data from Kuntillet 'Ajrud and Khirbet el-Qôm have underlined the complexity of the nature of religion in eighth-century Israel, and this information can be related indirectly to Amos research. I say "indirectly" in the sense that it can inform the discussion of certain passages, especially 5:25–26 and 8:14. Scholars have disagreed over whether these verses point to other deities and, if so, whether these words could have come from the prophet himself. Wolff and others would admit references to other divinities but date these lines later than the ministry of Amos,[99] while some argue that the worship of other deities beside Yahweh can be situated within his time frame.[100] There are two other means of linking these finds with the message of the book of Amos. Some propose taking *'ašmâ* ("guilt") in 8:14a to be a pejorative allusion to a female deity;[101] other scholars emend the text to read either "Ashima" or

"A/asherah."[102] In addition, the term *'ašmâ* in 8:14 is in construct with "Samaria." The notion of a local manifestation and worship of the Deity echoes the inscriptions at Kuntillet 'Ajrud. All of these options can establish a clearer connection with the scholarly debate over the religious contexts at Kuntillet 'Ajrud, Khirbet el-Qôm, and elsewhere.

A third type of research into Amos that attempts to get "behind the text" has come from anthropological and sociological approaches.[103] Attempts to utilize the social sciences in Old Testament studies go back over a hundred years. One well-known example is Max Weber's *Ancient Judaism*, which attempted to reconstruct Jewish history and the emergence of the Jews as a "pariah people." Within his scheme Amos was one of the classical prophets that had evolved from the "free *nebiim*." These were, in Weber's opinion, intellectuals and political ideologues who opposed the professionalization of the army, the bureaucratization of the state, the violation of the values of Israel's nomadic past, and the concentration of wealth and power in the urban centers.[104]

The last quarter of the twentieth century, however, has witnessed the use of the social sciences with an increased theoretical sophistication. Two avenues of study have been of special importance in Amos research. The first appeals to cultural anthropology and cross-cultural comparisons; the second works at reconstructing the socioeconomic system that was the target of the prophet's harsh denunciation. I will deal with each in turn.

In his *Prophecy and Society in Ancient Israel* Robert A. Wilson explores the social dimensions of prophecy.[105] He believes that the term "intermediary" is the best label to cover the range of prophetic activities and to facilitate the search for parallels within contemporary religious communities around the globe that might exhibit phenomena similar to that of the Old Testament. The interest in the social requires that one be attuned to the expectations and models for intermediation for both the (aspiring and accomplished) prophets and their audience. The calling by a deity, experiences with the divine, certain behavioral characteristics, and acts of power are but some of the necessary components for the social acceptance of prophets and for them to function effectively. It is within this kind of theoretical framework that the issue of ecstasy resurfaced (also note Overholt, below).

Wilson also differentiates between central and peripheral intermediaries. Broadly speaking, the former would be those who promote the maintenance of the existing social construction of reality; the latter stand outside those structures, seek more radical social change, and question the various legitimations of the status quo.[106] Coupling his cultural analogies with form- and tradition-critical approaches, Wilson presents a hypothetical picture of each prophet's social location, ministry, and message. Amos is tentatively classified as a Northern peripheral prophet from Judah.[107]

Another scholar who employs cultural anthropology and cross-cultural parallels is Thomas Overholt.[108] He draws his comparisons from several Native American prophets of the eighteenth and nineteenth centuries. In his paradigm, the prophetic process necessitates three actors: a deity, a prophet, and an audience. These three relate to one another in complex ways. This dynamic includes one or more revelations, the proclamation of the divine message, feedback, and supernatural corroboration of the prophet's call and ministry. The feedback has two dimensions—that between the prophet and the deity, and that between the prophet and the recipients of the message. The basis and nature of the audience's reaction is contextually determined. That is, within their sociocultural and historical setting people acquire a set of expectations as to what a prophet should look like, do, and say. Divine confirmation can strengthen the audience's perceptions and evaluation and can be made manifest in several ways (such as trances, visions, and miracles). From this perspective, prophets cannot base their authority only on claims of personal encounters with God. Public acknowledgment and some sort of institutional support (or rejection), too, are foundational for allowing the exercise of their ministry and for determining its success. Overholt applies these phenomenological insights to several passages in Amos that allude to the reception of the prophet's person and message (2:11–12; 3:8; 7:10–17).

Sociological approaches that attempt to reconstruct the socioeconomic world that the prophets so vigorously condemned have received a major impetus from the work of several scholars, especially Norman Gottwald. His general thesis is that the prophets reacted against the change from the communitarian ideals and social structure of early Israel to a tributary mode of production, which arose with the monarchy and led to unjust social relations of production and the unequal distribution of wealth.[109] Other scholars, appealing to a different theoretical construct, explain the mechanisms of oppression within the framework of what is labeled "rent capitalism."[110]

Rent capitalism is a system in which rural peasants are in many ways at the mercy of political and economic urban elites. As they fail in their struggle to subsist and support their families, these peasants fall into debt. They are forced to seek credit for tools and seed, and eventually can lose their patrimonial land to creditors. According to some of this persuasion, in addition to this development in ancient Israel, with the shift in the sociopolitical structure to a centralized monarchy, prebendal domain whereby land and privileges are granted to state officials as rewards for loyal service became more common and extensive. These various factors would have given rise to more extreme social stratification and to latifundialization. The end result was an oppressive social and economic system, which exploited those without power.

Among the several social theories applied to the world described in the book of Amos,[111] this perspective of rent capitalism has been championed by

Coote and Lang.[112] This suggestion, however, has not gone unchallenged. Dearman believes that the notion of envisioning a capitalistic economy for eighth-century Israel is anachronistic and argues that such a view fails to recognize the intrusive role of the state in ancient economies (in contrast to private entrepreneurs in a more open-market system) and the impact of other important external, international factors—political, economic, and military.[113] After criticizing the rent capitalism hypothesis for lack of sufficient substantiating data, Fleischer alternatively proposes a progressive impoverishment of the nation due to population growth, inheritance problems, and other changes brought about by the development of the monarchy.[114]

Nevertheless, these criticisms and disagreements are not meant to convey the idea that sociological approaches are without value. Scholarship in general is enriched by a host of intriguing possibilities for understanding the prophetic milieu and message. What was being called for was greater theoretical clarity and more careful utilization of these sorts of tools. At the same time, though, in the general time period under discussion other scholars were pursuing a second avenue of interest. Increased attention was directed at the received text of the Old Testament. The goal was not necessarily to "get behind it" by various kinds of reconstructions (whether by form or tradition criticism, archaeology, anthropology, or sociology), but rather "to move within the text" in order to grasp better its structure and inner workings.

Within the Text

Several factors served to stimulate scholars to turn from more traditional critical methods to investigate other means of textual study. First, on the basis of their historical research, some contended that most of the book of Amos could be confidently connected to the prophet of the eighth century.[115] Therefore, there was no need to try to separate out possible redactional layers. In other words, the textual phenomena had explanations other than those that had been put forth in some critical approaches. Andersen and Freedman argued that the apparent inconsistencies that scholars had taken as evidence of multiple redactions could be better interpreted as referring to discrete stages in the prophet's career.[116] This conviction was reinforced by a renewed attention to literary structures, a sensibility that could appreciate more artistry and less disjunction in the final form of the text.

> If we finish with a reluctance to disregard any part of the book as "certainly not Amos," it is partly because we have come to the conclusion, after working through the whole business many times and weighing all the arguments, that there are no compelling reasons against accepting most if not all of the book as possibly, indeed probably (we can never say "certainly") Amos'.

> We have two main reasons for deviating from traditional criticism on these points. First is the cumulative demonstration of the *literary coherence* of all of these diverse ingredients in the whole assemblage, which is more than an assemblage; it is a highly structured unity. Second is the diverse and divergent (even apparently contradictory, sometimes) points of view we account for as reflecting successive phases in the prophet's career, which underwent quite substantial changes in inner perception and declared messages.[117]

Not all scholars, however, have contended for focusing on the received text because of biographical considerations. For example, from the perspective of canonical criticism Childs argues for the primacy of the final form for very different reasons. On the one hand, and in contradistinction from the aforementioned scholars, he could agree with critical studies that postulate a complex prehistory of that final form: "Historical critical research has demonstrated convincingly, in my judgment, that the present form of the book of Amos has been reached only after a lengthy history of development."[118] Nevertheless, at the same time, unlike those methods that purpose to unravel a hypothetical redaction history, "the goal of canonical interpretation is to discern in the final composition how the message of Amos was appropriated and formed to serve as authoritative scripture within the community of faith."[119] He believes that in ancient Israel there had been a conscious process by which the various oracles—whatever their provenance—were put together and shaped to endure as an ever-relevant message. In other words, this prophetic book ascribed to Amos is not to be taken as simply the written testimony of the past, which is locked in to a specific time and place. Childs chides Wolff's work of historical and literary reconstruction as marked by "speculation," as "counter" to what the text is trying to communicate, and finally (along with much of critical method) as doomed by "theological bankruptcy" in its attempt to make the text meaningful to the believing community today.[120]

Besides these two orientations informed by particular historical perspectives or by a commitment to the Old Testament as part of the Scripture of the Christian church, several trends within general literary theory, which called for closer readings of the final form of texts, began to be utilized within Old Testament studies. Approaches guided by rhetorical criticism, formalism, and structuralism began to pay closer attention to patterns and literary techniques in every segment and level of the biblical text. Even though many of these publications dealt with narratives in the Pentateuch and in the historical literature (such as the books of Samuel and Kings), some scholars did turn their attention to the prophetic material.[121] Amos research was also the beneficiary of these new studies.

More literary readings of Amos ranged from studies of smaller units to that of the book as a whole.[122] Chávez published a compendium of a wide assortment of literary techniques found in the book.[123] Gese pointed out the text's penchant for series of five items, while Limburg demonstrated the tendency for heptads (i.e., series of seven).[124] Utilizing insights from classical rhetoric, Gitay analyzed 3:1–15 as a single, carefully crafted unit designed to make a powerful appeal to the prophet's audience.[125] Landy discussed the skillful interconnectedness and emotional impact of the language in the five visions and the accompanying "interludes" (7:10–17, 8:3–14) in chapters 7–9.[126]

De Waard and others discerned a chiasm spanning 5:1–17, as well as shorter concentric structures within that same section.[127] De Waard and Smalley even suggested that the entire book could be organized as a chiasm, whose center lay at 5:8 ("Yahweh is his name")—the very same climax as that of the chiasm of 5:1–17.[128] Wendland also believed that chiasms are prominent in Amos, but he criticized de Waard and Smalley's efforts to apply such a structure to the entire text as somewhat forced.[129] Working from the very different theoretical base of archetypal criticism associated with Northrop Frye, Ryken concentrated on the general tone (rather than on an exegetical study of the text) of the prophet's attack on the institutions and society of Israel to categorize the genre of Amos as "the major work of informal satire in the Bible"[130] that utilizes "a rhetoric of subversion."[131]

Still another level at which to analyze the received text was to locate Amos within what has been called "the Book of the Twelve"—that is, within the Minor Prophets as a literary unit in their current canonical order. House proposed that this "Book" exhibits a general thematic coherence and a "comic" plot line, which moves from an indictment of sin, to the announcement of punishment, and then to a resolution with the restoration of Israel.[132] Amos is located in the section that enumerates the rebellious acts of Israel and of the other nations. In its canonical sequence, then, it specifies the sins of the nations alluded to in Joel (even as its focus on Edom serves as a transition to Obadiah), while also underscoring the covenantal disobedience described in Hosea.

In sum, different interpretive interests and methodological considerations changed the center of attention from the various kinds of historical considerations that might lie behind the book of Amos to the present shape of the prophetic text itself. This cursory review demonstrates the potential contributions to a new appreciation of this prophetic book that literary approaches had begun to offer. While some were limited to more structural insights on texts of various lengths, others pursued issues of character and plot development.

In Front of the Text

The last several decades of the twentieth century also witnessed the rise of a number of ways of studying the Bible that were committed to placing the context, needs, and rights of certain groups into the foreground and exploring the interaction that takes place between the text and readers (and communities of readers). This was a commitment not to limit research simply to deciphering new background information or to discovering literary styles and structures. More important was what happened "in front of the text"—that is, in the impact of the text upon readers and in their appropriation of that text.

The variety of approaches that can be placed within this perspective do not accept the notion of a hypothetical objective stance by the reader vis-à-vis the text or that of a rootless, autonomous text that can transcend time and space. Consequently, certain presuppositions of classical critical methods and of more recent literary studies as practiced by some scholars were judged to be inadequate and naive at best (and conscious hegemonic enterprises that continue to monopolize the academic guild and faith communities at worst) in their attempts to mine the text for timeless universals, to bring to light information related to the background or the production of that text, or to uncover interesting literary elements. Those who underscored what is "in front of the text" saw the proper—and, more crucially, the ethical—goal of the study of the Bible as moving beyond some sort of theological, historical, or literary reconstruction of the text. It was not, however, that these criticized methodologies were in and of themselves totally counterproductive. The crucial evaluative factor lay in the purpose of their use in biblical studies. The Bible was to be proactively and intentionally engaged from and for a particular agenda. Under this rubric one could place the various liberation theologies and other alternative approaches from the Two-Thirds World.[133]

The book of Amos has always drawn the attention of those stirred by the exploitation of the weak.[134] Time and time again the text has been made more relevant to new contexts by substituting places, people, and ethical issues that have been considered to be equivalent or parallel to those of the ancient text. Amos has been used to combat violations of a more singular nature, such as racism,[135] or utilized to try to move the conscience of believing communities in a more general way.[136]

The concern for justice and the prophetic denunciation of oppression has resonated in a special way in liberation theology within the Two-Thirds World. The prophets in general, of course, have always provided an important biblical foundation for liberation theologians' denunciation of social injustice and the announcement of a better tomorrow.[137] Speaking out of the Latin American context in her *Bible of the Oppressed*, Tamez tried to develop a theology of justice based on the study of nine Hebrew roots related to oppression.[138] This analysis, she argued, demonstrates that the exploitation by the powerful occurs at both national and international levels in ways that violate the dignity and very personhood of the poor. Several verses in the book of Amos are cited as examples (note the verbs in 4:1, *'āšaq, rāṣaṣ*; 6:14, *lāḥaṣ*).

For his part, Miranda utilized source and tradition criticism to ascertain what he believed to be the original, and hence, authentic message of the prophets. This he construed as the forceful demand for social justice. The book of Amos figures in two parts of his presentation. First, Miranda cites 5:21–25 to highlight Yahweh's view of Israel's rituals. It will not do to hold that God desires merely a reform of the cult that would require a more sensitive attitude to the needy. The conviction of the prophet Amos, Miranda explained, is more radical: "What he says can be summarized in this way: *I do not want cultus, but rather interhuman justice.*"[139] Indeed, Yahweh is unknowable apart from participation in acts of justice.[140] Second, the sharp rejection of the nation of Israel by Yahweh, therefore, is to be understood as grounded in the violation of this moral imperative (he mentions Amos 2:4–8; 3:9–11; 5:11; 8:4–14).[141] Based on his critical criteria, Miranda said that the call for justice in the prophets, which also was made explicit in the Old Testament laws, was not based on a covenant theology (which he holds to be no earlier than the seventh century). The mandate goes back to the exodus, the most dramatic divine intervention in history on behalf of the exploited, and ultimately to the character of Yahweh himself.[142]

In several publications the Argentine liberationist Old Testament scholar Severino Croatto has articulated a hermeneutical perspective that is depen-dent in many ways on Ricoeur and other literary theorists.[143] He reasoned that the potential of sacred oracles to continue to generate meaning is evident in the redactional reworking of earlier layers of the biblical material, which he takes to be subsequent appropriations of the text by later communities of faith. According to Croatto, this activity is exemplified in the book of Amos. On the one hand, he postulated that Amos 9:11–15 was a postexilic addition designed to alter the condemnatory tone of the original prophetic diatribe of the rest of the book. In other words, this intentional canonical reshaping would show that the earlier text had acquired a new significance in a new context and that its declaration of the end of Israel was no longer considered to be Yahweh's final word.[144] This sort of expansion of the prophetic books, whereby a message of judgment is subsequently supplemented by one of restoration, exhibits a pat-tern he felt also should have been repeated in the quest for justice in his own country during the 1980s: the Argentine military, who apparently had been responsible for the death and disappearance of thousands of innocent victims, must submit to due process of law before there could be any talk of pardon or reconciliation. The good news of reconciliation must follow the proper exe-cution of judgment, not bypass or supplant it, even as the hope passage of Amos appeared only after the actual experience of the wrath of God.[145] The rereading of texts and the canonical formation of the Bible in the past, then, are akin to the theological and hermeneutical exercise that continues to this day. Pablo Andriñach also appeals in part to Ricoeur to establish the theoretical foundation of his study of Amos, but his analysis follows a structuralist approach.[146] The fundamental binary opposition that he develops throughout the book is oppression-justice, and this focus serves then as the basis of his hermeneutical move to critique areas of ideology, cult, praxis, and *concientización* in Latin America today.

In a full-length study of the book, Milton Schwantes draws parallels between the context and message of the prophet and the situation of "total terror" that the poor and oppressed in Latin America endure in their day-to-day existence.[147] He declares this connection with modern realities in dramatic fashion:

> Amos spoke and speaks. He comes from experiences of long ago and arises in those of today. His context lodges itself in our context.
>
> It behooves us then to embrace the words that our God has had reach us through this biblical text. And it falls to us to live in continual protest against the pain that is laid upon our Latin American peoples.
>
> Therefore, let us listen to Amos, bowed down and reverent before the text but unsubmissive and irreverent before the hangmen.[148]

According to Schwantes's understanding of Amos's background, one can locate him among the rural poor, who survive by doing several jobs and seasonal work. His chapter discussions of a portion of the prophetic text are either introduced or closed by quotations from Latin American activists. As is often the case with other liberationist biblical studies, this work is grounded in critical approaches to the text. In fact, Schwantes dedicates an entire chapter to explaining the book's redactional history.[149]

Because of a lack of acquaintance with the broad spectrum of biblical studies being produced in the Two-Thirds World, many in the West sometimes have a limited perspective that reduces discussions of contextual approaches to liberation theology. Yet a more informed look at the theological reflection that has gone on in Latin America over the last few decades, for instance, makes clear that this restricted perspective does not do justice to those of certain evangelical persuasions or of more traditional Roman Catholic convictions, which also have wrestled with the pressing socioeconomic and political needs.[150] An example of a context-sensitive evangelical work on Amos is the commentary by the Ecuadorian Washington Padilla. In his introduction Padilla declares:

> Amos is one of the most relevant books of the Bible for the situation of the poor countries of the world today, as it deals with one of the most burning issues of the twentieth century: social injustice as the specific manifestation that the sin of idolatry assumes in society, and the justice that God demands as the expression of true devotion to him, the true God.[151]

he adds:

> The relevance of the message of Amos for the spiritual, political, and social problems and conditions of today's world is undeniable. It is significant that in our effort to contextualize this message for today we have had no difficulty in finding parallels—while maintaining the proper distance—between the situations, sins, and truths that we encounter in this ancient biblical document and the news that we read every day in the newspapers.[152]

Padilla's discussion of each section of the prophetic text is followed by extensive comments on the violence, class tensions, economic inequalities, and distorted images of Yahweh that have characterized Latin American life for the last five hundred years.

It is evident that exegetical methods were now envisioned to be answerable to very concrete, social obligations. Biblical research was not to be considered an academic pursuit for personal gain and academic acclaim. Scholars were to use their training to serve the needs of suffering humanity. The task of working what was "in front of the text" was to be the final objective of the work that had been done "behind" and "within" the book of Amos.

CONCLUSION

This survey of a century of Amos research charts the shifting points of interests of scholars in the person of the prophet Amos and in the book that bears his name. Each area of study in its own way has contributed to a fuller understanding of the phenomena of prophetic activity and of the message of this one who claimed to speak for Yahweh. Scholars have probed the prophet's experience of the divine and the social setting and cultural backdrop of Amos's ministry, as well as investigated with detailed precision the text itself. In addition, the demands of the modern world also have pressed scholars to see how their work might prove relevant in a constructive way for those who unfortunately live in exploitative circumstances.

In light of this rich and varied research, one could say that scholars now can articulate their views regarding this eighth-century prophet more knowledgeably than ever before. Nevertheless, at the same time, my comments in each major section of this essay have also made clear that every phase of study and kind of approach has lacunae and also raises new questions. It is not surprising, therefore, that research into Amos has not diminished. The next essay will highlight studies that have been done since 1990 and will offer projections as to where Amos research might go in the future.

2

The State of Amos Research:
Present Trends and Projections
into the Twenty-first Century

The book of Amos continues to generate scholarly interest. Since 1990, a full-length introduction to Amos research has appeared,[1] and entire issues of journals have been dedicated to this prophetic book.[2] R. F. Melugin has written a detailed survey of Amos research that covers the last twenty years,[3] and H. O. Thompson has provided a comprehensive annotated bibliography.[4]

The purpose of this essay is to bring the survey of Amos research begun in the previous chapter up to the present day and to make some prognostications as to where it might continue to develop in the coming years. Following the layout of the final section of that last essay, my discussion will be divided into three major parts that will summarize approaches that focus on what is behind, within, and in front of the text. This breakdown is designed in part to demonstrate that studies today in some measure are continuing past trends.

RECONSTRUCTING WHAT LIES BEHIND THE TEXT

To investigate what is "behind" the text is to probe various different directions of research: theories concerning the literary history of the received text, the findings of archaeology, and possible explanations from the social sciences for the more systemic issues driving the prophetic critique. This first section will deal with each of these three areas in turn.

The Literary Prehistory of the Book of Amos

Some scholars remain dedicated to trying to ascertain the trajectory and development of the various layers of textual material that eventually led to the

canonical book of Amos.[5] Over the last number of years the hypothetical
redactors have been ascribed an increasingly greater creative role in the shaping of the biblical texts. They are not envisioned simply as editors working in
a mechanical way to piece together originally independent prophetic oracles
with new additions. To the contrary, scholars envision them as astute theologians with a high level of literary skill and theological sophistication.[6] Perhaps
the most prolific and influential scholar of this persuasion to attempt a literary reconstruction of Amos, both in its constituent parts as well as in regard
to the book as a whole, has been Jörg Jeremias. He has published essays on different sections of the book of Amos, several of which have been gathered in a
recent collection.[7] The results of his work inform his commentary on Amos.[8]

Jeremias believes that the historical Amos proclaimed the end of Israel,
a fate deserved because of its failure to live out properly its responsibility as
the people of God. The difficult challenge for the critical scholar today, he
says, is to try to sift through the redactional accretions and work back to the
prophet's original message (he considers the vision accounts to be the earliest material). On the one hand, the received text of Amos does have a certain
priority, since it is the Scripture of the Christian church. Nevertheless,
Jeremias is convinced that tracing the redactional trajectory can offer insights
into a living text that was modified over time and reappropriated for new
situations by later believers in Yahweh. Because the community of faith must
continually contextualize its Scripture, research into that process of compilation can become a constructive theological and pastoral enterprise to orient this ongoing need. Jeremias lays out the nature of that process as he
envisions it:

> To be sure, Amos' message . . . can be recovered only through com-
> plicated, and in many instances only hypothetical, reconstruction. The
> book of Amos by no means reflects this message directly, but repre-
> sents rather the precipitate of this message's history of reception and
> influence; it was not transmitted as a result of any historical interest in
> past history, but rather was written down and at the same time con-
> tinually updated on the basis of its meaning for an ever new and chang-
> ing present.[9]

Jeremias posits several steps in the growth of the book: an original collection from chapters 3–6, flanked on either side by five authentic oracles against
the nations (chaps. 1–2) and the five vision reports (7:1–9:4). Subsequent redactions occurred before and after the fall of Jerusalem (the Josianic and Deuteronomistic material) and in the postexilic period (9:7–15). In general terms, the
impact of the process on the earliest edition was that the pointed attack on certain circles of the elite was broadened to include the entire nation.[10]

Two unique aspects of Jeremias's thesis that stand out are his attention to the literary qualities of the canonical text and his argument that Hosea and Amos need to be read together. A good illustration of his sensitivity to the synchronic is his treatment of 5:1–17, a favorite passage of final form studies that is often heralded as a stellar example of the book's inherent literary quality because of its neat chiastic structure. While he acknowledges that many critics have missed the literary artistry of this text and therefore unnecessarily emended and rearranged verses according to other criteria, Jeremias, too, defends a redactional history behind its present form.[11] He holds that three originally separate sayings (vv. 2–3; vv. 4–5; vv. 7, 10–12, 16–17) and other early material were supplemented in the exilic-postexilic period (vv. 5ab, 6, 8–9, 13), but he also supposes that from the beginning there existed a basic ring structure. Subsequent additions were designed to fill out and expand that first chiasm.

The other special contribution by Jeremias is his attention to intertextual details, whether between pericopes within the book or between Amos and other prophetic texts—specifically, between Amos and Hosea. Examples of the conscious connections between passages within Amos would include, for instance, those between the Oracles against the Nations and the visions and between 8:4–7 and 2:6–7.[12] In regard to the affinities between Amos and Hosea, Jeremias argues that influences flowed in both directions.[13] He finds echoes of Amos 4:4 and 8:14 in Hos. 4:15, while Hos. 8:14 sounds like the standard judgment formula found in the Oracles against the Nations. Jeremias feels that here one can see evidence of Hosea's Judean readers applying Amos's denunciation of Israel to Judah after the fall of Samaria, but before Josiah's destruction of Bethel. At the same time, Jeremias proposes that the book of Amos was influenced by Hosea, since thematic dependence on Hosea is visible, he holds, at Amos 2:6–8; 3:2; 5:25; 6:8; and 7:9. This mutual influence would indicate that the prophets' disciples wanted these two prophetic messages to be read conjointly as a single divine word for the people of God. This cross-pollination, as it were, would have occurred before the exile (i.e., before the Deuteronomic standardization of all of the prophetic materials), but at different times in the case of each collection. Jeremias postulates that the book of Amos from its very initial stages drew upon an original edition of Hoseanic texts, whereas at least parts of the book of Hosea were fixed before the insertion of Amos-like lines.

Several other scholars have put forth their own hypotheses concerning the redactional history of the book of Amos. In his 1996 monograph, *Studien zur Redaktion und Komposition des Amosbuches*, Rottzoll argues for twelve redactional stages.[14] Although he does build on some of Jeremias's positions (e.g., that chaps. 1–2 and 7–9 were the frame for chaps. 3–6), Rottzoll presents a much more complex picture of subsequent redactional activity. Of note is

Rottzoll's view that the entire book of Amos is shaped as a chiasm, with the concentric structure of 5:1–17 as its centerpiece. He even organizes his exposition of Amos accordingly, with each of his chapters working step by step from the outer sections of that overarching ring composition in toward the core passage. As in the case of Jeremias, Rottzoll does not see synchronic analysis as mutually exclusive of diachronic concerns. He, too, understands the elaboration of many of the literary patterns to be later in the history of the development of the finished text.

Very different approaches are offered by Loretz and Peckham. Loretz attempts to place the composition of Amos against the background of ancient Near Eastern prophecy.[15] He observes that it has not been uncommon for scholars to point out correspondences between the terminology and worldview of Israel's prophets and those of its neighbors. What they have neglected, however, is the important fact that the prophetic oracles of the surrounding cultures are not preserved in anything like the "book" form of Israelite prophecy. Loretz believes that the gathering of prophetic oracles into these collections was a postexilic phenomenon. He also is careful to differentiate between the historical Amos and the canonical work that now bears his name. This distinction is apparent in terms of Amos's use of the Law. The phrase *lex post prophetas* would have been quite applicable to the prophet himself and the message he spoke in the eighth century, but, in contrast, the book of Amos presupposes the Pentateuchal laws.[16] Loretz calls the book of Amos a "midrashic" composition, whose goal was to explain the Assyrian invasion of Israel and the later defeat of Judah.

Unlike most critical scholars, Peckham argues that Amos (and the rest of the Hebrew Bible for that matter) was from the very beginning a written work.[17] The book as we now know it was produced in two primary stages. He would describe the first edition of Amos's words in this way: "Amos wrote a long narrative poem filled with repeated forms, refrains, catalogs and listlike chants and declamations. Each part of the poem is a collection of rhetorically similar sayings, a canto with its own rhythm and beat building in a crescendo of insistent sound."[18] The four original cantos would have been: I (1:1a–2:16), II (3:1–5:7), III (5:10–6:13), and IV (7:1–8:10). A later revision, both literary and theological, which apparently knew of the Deuteronomistic History, Isaiah, Ezekiel, Obadiah, and Joel, separated these cantos with the insertion of new material and added literary connections between them.[19]

In addition to those scholars who have proposed a redactional process for the entire prophetic book, others have produced studies on specific passages. For instance, Williamson and Clements have written detailed analyses of the encounter between Amos and Amaziah at Bethel (7:9/10–17) and its relationship to the third vision report (7:7–8).[20] Their conclusions are quite different.

The location of 7:9–17, Williamson believes, cannot be adequately explained by saying that the passage follows chronologically in the life of Amos after the three visions (thereby explaining his expulsion from the North) or by appealing to a catchword principle, which would bind 7:10–17 to 7:9 ("Jeroboam"/"by the sword," vv. 9, 11). Williamson argues instead that 7:9–17 was inserted deliberately as a unit at this juncture by a Deuteronomistic editor. In line with the emphasis of the Deuteronomic "school" on the prophetic role in warning the people of God of the consequences of violating Yahweh's moral law (note, e.g., Deut. 18:18–19; 2 Kgs. 17:13, 23; 21:10–15; 24:2), this passage would have been placed here to demonstrate that the rejection of the prophet Amos confirmed the judgment of inescapable doom that would befall Israel.[21]

Clements takes a different tack. He distinguishes verse 9 as a distinct redactional level from 7:10–17. The former would have been added to 7:7–8 after 745 B.C.E. and the rise of Assyria, while the latter sometime between 722 and 701 B.C.E. Both supplements would have served basically the same purpose. Each was a redactor's interpretation of how the rather obscure prophetic prediction of divine judgment in 7:7–8 had actually been worked out in the political history of the nation. On the one hand, 7:9 took the warning pictured by the weapon in Yahweh's hand[22] as fulfilled with the termination of Jeroboam's dynasty; 7:10–17, on the other hand, saw the vision confirmed by the death and exile wrought by the Assyrian invasion and the destruction of the Northern Kingdom.

Another section of Amos that has received attention is the Oracles against the Nations. Niemann begins his reconstruction with the Israel oracle, without which the others, he says, would not make sense.[23] He envisions a three-stage process. The first, around 720 B.C.E., would have included the Damascus, Ammon, and Israel oracles; the second, after 586, involved the insertion of the Gaza and Edom oracles between the Damascus and Ammon oracles. The last phase completed the set with the oracles directed at Tyre, Moab, and Judah. This final arrangement was designed to provide a sense of comprehensiveness to the theological and historical focus of the older collection by a geographical framework, which moved from an outer ring (Damascus-Gaza-Tyre-Edom) to an inner circle (Ammon-Moab-Judah-Israel).

Niemann mentions the possibility of the mutual influence between the oracles and the vision reports.[24] The oracles apparently presuppose Amos's understanding of his mission as one to announce judgment, a change in self-perception manifest in the visions. The oracles and the visions, therefore, are to be read in conjunction, informing each other. He suggests that, if these two sets of material had been at one time a single composition (possibly going back to Amos himself), the visions at that stage might have preceded the Oracles against the Nations. This arrangement would have been changed to the present order, when they were combined with chapters 3–6.

The Book of the Twelve

This survey of redaction-critical approaches can serve as a bridge to another topic that has become the focus of quite a bit of scholarly research: the composition of the Book of the Twelve (i.e., the Twelve Minor Prophets read as a unit). This is not a totally novel topic, but the high level of interest is quite recent.[25] Even newer commentaries have begun to incorporate hypotheses of the composition of the book of Amos within a broader theory about the literary history of the Twelve.[26] What is happening for the first time in a significant way is the placement of theories of the prehistories of individual prophetic books within the larger framework of the redaction of the entire corpus of the Minor Prophets.

Jeremias concludes his discussion of the connections between Amos and Hosea by mentioning two possible implications for the development of the Book of the Twelve.[27] To begin with, if the first edition of Hosea does indeed predate that of Amos (even though the historical prophet ministered after Amos), then the placement of Hosea before Amos in the collection of the Minor Prophets might find a ready explanation. Second, the multiple links between these two books proves to him that the Minor Prophets were never conceived of as twelve separate and disconnected entities but rather always as part of a larger whole.

Aaron Schart, a student of Jeremias, has taken this hypothesis of an intertwined origin for the books of Hosea and Amos as the foundation for a more intricate theory concerning the composition of the Twelve.[28] Schart coordinates his analysis of the literary evolution of Amos with that of the Twelve by identifying parallels between the redactional layers of each. He postulates that the earliest stages of Amos (the collection of speeches in chaps. 3–6 and then the first edition of chaps. 1–9) were expanded by a Deuteronomistic layer and that this redaction was part of a broader effort to produce a Deuteronomistic corpus (Amos + Hosea, Micah, Zephaniah). Nahum and Habakkuk are related because of their *maśśā'* superscriptions, and they supplemented that initial group of four. A salvific redaction (Amos 9:11, 12b, 13a, 14–15) brought the addition of Haggai and Zechariah 1–8 (and perhaps much of Zech. 9–13), while Joel and Obadiah were part of an even later eschatological stage (Amos 9:13aβ,b; 4:9). Jonah and Malachi were the final texts annexed to the collection.

While the starting point for both Jeremias and Schart is Amos, other scholars do not give the book such a prominent place within their hypotheses about the composition of the Twelve. One of the more ambitious projects has been that of Nogalski. Even though he mentions a number of features, like quotations, allusions, motifs, and framing devices, the most important criterion for his theory is the catchword principle:[29]

> Intertextual work in the Twelve must recognize that catchwords play
> a significant role in the literary logic of the Twelve as both an order-
> ing principle and a logical principle in light of significant evidence that
> catchwords recur consistently across neighboring writings and that
> many of these catchwords have been deliberately (redactionally)
> implanted into existing texts to highlight these connections. In addi-
> tion, catchwords also reach across non-adjacent writings in the Twelve,
> thereby serving as potential guides to any reading strategy.[30]

He argues for two multivolume collections: a Deuteronomistic (Hosea, Amos,
Micah, Zephaniah) and a Haggai–Zechariah 1–8 corpus. These each predate
the appearance of the Book of the Twelve. The incorporation of these six into
the larger corpus did not entail expansions in nearly the same degree as Nogalski thinks is evident in the other six books. Important for his reconstruction is
a "Joel layer," which brought the first two collections together and added
Nahum, Habakkuk, Malachi, Joel, and Obadiah. While the first three of these
five had probably existed as independent texts, Joel and Obadiah were probably intentional theological creations based upon and simultaneously intercon-
necting the entire corpus. Jonah and Zechariah 9–13 were the last to be
included.

His comments on Amos attempt to explain the nature of the relationships
between Joel, Obadiah, and Amos.[31] Nogalski believes that Joel 4:15 (Eng.
3:15) takes up Amos 1:2. The Oracles of the Nations, in other words, were
used as a model for the last chapter of Joel. At the same time, according to his
critical reconstruction of the literary history of Amos 9:11–15, Joel 4:18 (Eng.
3:18) is cited in Amos 9:13 (the promise of abundance). Amos 9:12a (the eschatological judgment upon the nations), on the other hand, is a summary of, and
anticipates, Obad. 17–21. Amos 9:12a, 13 are canonical markers, therefore,
that point in two opposite directions—one back to Joel, the other forward to
Obadiah. This kind of interconnectedness (along with other similarities
between Joel and Obadiah) hints at the strong possibility that Joel and Obadiah entered the Twelve at the same time, probably during the postexilic
period.

Jones, while appreciative of much of Nogalski's work, brings the Septuagint
(LXX) and 4QXII[a] into the discussion and on the basis of that evidence has to
question some of Nogalski's conclusions. Differences in the order of the Minor
Prophets in these collections suggests that at one time there could have been
three versions of the Twelve in circulation, of which the Masoretic Text (MT)
was the last to be formed. He dedicates considerable space to Amos 9:12, in
part because of its importance for Nogalski's argument.[32] In Jones's view, the
disagreement between the LXX and the MT of 9:12 is not due to a scribal mis-
reading by the LXX; instead, he argues that the LXX reflects a different

Hebrew *Vorlage*, which the MT emended to establish a connection between Amos and Obadiah. The Masoretic version would have moved Joel, Obadiah, and Jonah from their original location in the LXX to their present position.

While each of these scholars has labored in his own way to understand how the Book of the Twelve took shape over time,[33] others, while assuming a redactional history, nevertheless have focused on a synchronic reading of the Twelve. Here one can include the work of van Leeuwen and Sweeney.[34] Van Leeuwen endeavors "to detail certain techniques by which the scribes added hermeneutical patches at key junctures, arranged and stitched together previously existing works, all to shape this prophetic scroll into a theological whole."[35] The fundamental issue, he feels, for the redactor(s) of the Twelve was theodicy, an effort to explain Yahweh's decision to destroy Israel and then Judah. Exodus 34:6–7, with its juxtaposition of mercy and justice, serves as "the base text" for the theological shaping of the first six books of the Twelve. While making the common observations about the similarities between certain verses in Joel, Amos, and Obadiah, van Leeuwen proposes that Joel and Obadiah were placed on either side of Amos at a later date to respond to the theological problem of the devastating judgment announced in Hosea and Amos. Joel communicates that repentance (something Israel did not do) can lead to restoration and so vindicates the severe sentence (and the grace) of God. Obadiah puts the destruction of the Northern and Southern Kingdoms within the broader perspective of a universal, eschatological judgment and the future exaltation of the people of God.

Sweeney also offers a synchronic reading of the Twelve, for both the MT and LXX.[36] That the purpose of each Book of the Twelve differs, he argues, follows logically from the different order of the prophetic books. As with several other scholars, the placement of Joel in the MT is key:

> Joel defines the Leitmotif of the Masoretic form of the Book of the Twelve, i.e., Jerusalem will be threatened by the nations and the natural order will be threatened by the forces of chaos, but YHWH will step in to deliver Jerusalem and creation from that threat on the Day of YHWH when the forces of the nations and chaos are defeated and subsumed to YHWH 's sovereignty at Zion.[37]

In line with the MT's concentration on Jerusalem, the present form of the book of Amos is designed to highlight the divine decree of judgment upon the cult at Bethel and the monarchy of the Northern Kingdom, both illegitimate, and so urge the faithful to seek Yahweh in Jerusalem and under Davidic rule.[38]

A final kind of approach to the Book of the Twelve offers a synchronic reading, but without exploring the possibility of a history of redaction as relevant to that enterprise.[39] The most prominent scholar of this perspective is Paul

House. He is aware and appreciative of the other approaches to the Twelve, but his aim is to ascertain a coherent reading of the canonical order of these texts. House divides the Twelve into a fundamental three-part structure: covenant and cosmic sin (Hosea–Micah), covenant and cosmic punishment (Nahum–Zephaniah), and hope for restoration (Haggai–Malachi). These divisions are not meant to imply that these are the exclusive themes of each part, but rather that these headings reflect the main points of the prophetic message. More recently House has written on the character of God that is disclosed within this scheme. In the book of Amos, God is portrayed as the sovereign judge and creator.[40]

The Archaeological Background to the Book of Amos

In addition to the preliterary history of the received text, there is the aspect of the material remains that also "lie behind the text." The most complete utilization of archaeology to interpret the book of Amos is found in Shalom Paul's commentary in the Hermeneia series. Both the comments themselves and the footnotes are a mine of information about pertinent ancient Near Eastern material. Good examples of the contribution of his expertise to the exposition of the text are his discussions of 5:26, 6:7, and 8:14.[41] In each case he provides a great amount of detail regarding ancient religious practices and beliefs. Paul's commentary is obviously very different from the classic form- and tradition-critical work by Wolff (1977) in the same series, a fact that the editor readily acknowledges.[42]

Other scholars have offered work of more limited scope to help illuminate Amos's cultural setting. For example, Campbell and Freedman and Welch present shorter, chapter-length studies on relevant topics—fittingly in a *Festschrift* dedicated to Philip King, the author of an archaeological commentary on several eighth-century prophets.[43] Campbell believes that a fruitful avenue to explore in order to ascertain the targets of the prophetic invective has been the excavation of domestic dwellings.[44] The results can help shed light on the nature of the social life that Amos denounces. An early study that claimed to have substantiated inequalities on the basis of an investigation of dwellings was the excavation of Roland de Vaux at Tirzah (Tell el-Far'ah North), Stratum II. Though many have criticized that work, Campbell believes that this French archaeologist's point was well taken. Campbell focuses on another site: Shechem, Field VII, Stratum VII—more particularly, House 1727. A reconstruction of these remains seems to point to a two-story structure of select building materials, which would have been destroyed by the invading Assyrian army in the eighth century. This dwelling could very well indicate the existence of a social stratum of the well-to-do beyond the limited confines of the royal court. In other words, in the outlying towns there also would have been those who were quite probably taking advantage of less fortunate neighbors. For their part, Freedman and Welch try to discern allusions to the earthquake mentioned in 1:1 in other passages in the book of Amos, as well as capture the impact of earthquakes in general upon the ministry of other prophets.[45]

Several other items of archaeological interest for Amos research that were touched on in the last essay continue to garner attention. To begin with, scholars still debate the significance of the *marzēaḥ* feast in Amos 6:3–7 (and possibly at 2:8; 4:1). Did this ceremony have religious connotations, and was it related to any sort of veneration of the dead? Schmidt denies any connections to such a cult in the passage. In his view, biblical references to preexilic mortuary rites actually describe later practices that have been read back into these earlier textual settings.[46] Other scholars, however, do argue for an early cult of the dead, of which the *marzēaḥ* would have been a manifestation.[47]

Second, the burgeoning literature on a/Asherah often makes at least passing reference to the enigmatic phrase '*ašmat Šōmĕrôn* ("the guilt of Samaria") in Amos 8:14. The question that is raised is whether these words can be translated or emended in such a way so as to be accepted as evidence for a cult to the goddess or to another deity in ancient Israel.[48] Of course, scholarly discussion about the *marzēaḥ* and the a/Asherah is often part of more comprehensive hypotheses about the rise of monotheism and the nature of popular religion in ancient Israel.[49]

Finally, a textual detail that has generated more scrutiny has been the term '*ănāk* in 7:7–8.[50] Debates revolve around the precise meaning of this Akkadian loanword and its significance in the context of the third vision. Although in the last few decades the trend has been to translate '*ănāk* as "tin," Williamson and Hoffmeier have argued for a return to the more traditional view, which takes this word to denote "lead" (or some alloy) and so to be a reference to a plumb line.[51] Williamson begins with a thorough review of the different interpretations of this hapax legomenon, but for a variety of reasons rejects the interpretation of "tin." He links this passage to the work of Deuteronomistic editors, who underscored the consequences of rejecting the prophets' warnings of judgment. He feels that the comparison of Amos to a plumb line would picture in a graphic way the ideal of a prophet found in Deut. 18:18–19 (i.e., Amos himself embodied the standard of obedience), while the confrontation of 7:10–17 exemplifies the disregard of the prophetic message. To Williamson's focus on lexical issues Hoffmeier adds evidence from Egypt.[52] In addition to presenting pictographic illustrations of plumb lines for architectural use and a brief overview of some pertinent linguistic parallels, Hoffmeier notes the association of plumb lines with scales—specifically with the divine balance that weighs the life of the dead in terms of the practice of justice. Could not these lines, asks Hoffmeier, have been part of a dramatically enacted prophetic parable in which Amos demonstrated that Israel and its leaders had been found guilty when their actions were tested by Yahweh's divine standards?

Social Science Approaches to the Book of Amos

A third way of "getting behind the text," beyond the literary and archaeological, appeals to the social sciences. Here the aim is to attempt to reconstruct social realties, systems, institutions, and movements in dimensions that more traditional historical approaches are usually ill equipped to do. Scholars have utilized a variety of orientations (such as functionalist and cultural materialist) and a plethora of models in order to better understand the ancient world. This diversity increasingly has forced the practitioners in the field to be more methodologically self-conscious and articulate.[53]

Within Amos studies, Carroll R. has pointed out with the most detail some of the problems and limitations of social science approaches to this prophetic book.[54] He mentions two basic issues that can radically affect the quality of the research: the actual expertise of the biblical scholar in the social science selected as the analytical tool, and the availability of reliable data (both within and outside the text). From this line of questioning, Carroll R. moves on to propose a consideration of sociologist W. G. Runciman's discussion of the four tasks required for constructing a rigorous social science study.[55]

Runciman's first step is *reportage*, a depiction of the actions, attitudes or context to be investigated, which would be acceptable to the agents under study and other observers. The second is *explanation*. This is the attempt to construct a reasonable and successful account (especially in contradistinction from rival conceptual models) for what is presented under reportage. A third aspect is *description*. This is not reportage, as the purpose at this juncture is to ascertain a conceptualization of what life is truly felt and understood to be like, which both the agents and the researcher would deem accurate and authentic. The last phase is *evaluation*, by which what is researched is judged to be good or bad. At each step it is important to keep distinct the researcher's point of view from that of the agents themselves.[56] What has often happened in social science approaches within biblical studies is that these essentially distinct components of a social theory model are either confused or bypassed. The resulting hypothetical constructs, therefore, can be muddled or skewed.

This critique, however, in no way implies that one abandon the effort to put the social sciences to good use in the examination of the book of Amos. On the contrary, Carroll R. himself turns to interpretive anthropology, whose best-known spokesperson has been Clifford Geertz.[57] Carroll R.'s primary interest has been to explore the nature of religious life reflected in the world of the text of Amos. He has devoted attention to the concepts of religion in general and popular religion in particular. Differing from other demographic and sociological approaches to popular religion, this perspective appreciates the formal and informal symbols, values, behavior, and rituals that are shared across generational, socioeconomic, and gender boundaries—those "webs of significances," to use Geertz's famous phrase, which provide some level of coherence within any cultural setting. The resulting picture of religion described (and denounced) by Amos, therefore, can be much more complex and self-destructive than many might think.

Izabela Jaruzelska has published several social science studies of the book of Amos, but her work has not been readily accessible to a large English-speaking audience.[58] Her desire is to push beyond the simple dichotomy of rich versus poor that occasionally appears in some Amos research. Utilizing what she calls a society-as-a-whole orientation and the socioeconomic theory of ownership, as well as data drawn from the biblical text and archaeology, Jaruzelska endeavors to examine the status of royal officials in eighth-century Israel and the control of the means of production and labor that came under the prophet's critical scrutiny. She differentiates several types of officials within the government bureaucracy (such as those responsible for exacting taxes) and tries to reconstruct the impact of their lifestyles and policies upon the broader populace.

Another kind of social science approach turns from the world that is being described through the text to the text itself as a social artifact. These studies can be placed under the rubric of what is known as ideological criticism.[59] The issue here is the production of texts as sociotheological, even political, literature within particular ancient contexts. Ideological criticism also brings to the fore the researcher's own ideology vis-à-vis the text, but that dimension will be dealt with in the third major section of this essay.

J. David Pleins looks at the multiple, and sometimes conflicting, ethical visions that find expression in the biblical materials and tries to locate them socially and historically.[60] His discussion of Amos reviews those passages that deal with injustice and the abuse of the poor in Israel's agrarian-based economy (e.g., 2:6 and 8:4–6; 2:8a; 5:11–12; 3:12, 15; 6:4). Through Amos, Yahweh condemns the exploitative legal and economic structures, as well as the Canaanite urban values that had permeated and adversely influenced social life. The prophet offered no systemic analysis of Israel's ills, just announced the nation's ruin and exhorted the people to seek the face of God.[61] Pleins's section on Amos is part of his chapter on the Minor Prophets, whose purpose was to emphasize (although in different ways) "the justice question." The impact of this ethical thread can be felt as one moves across that collection of prophetic oracles. A properly informed critical appreciation of this material, he says, will sense the important role of the redactors in the growth of these books and the interrelationships between them in their present canonical shape:

> In the ebb and flow of the waters of this righteous stream, we hear some provocative answers regarding how to live out that collective call to justice. We also hear words of warning spoken to the society that fails to heed this call. Furthermore, in the writing, transmission, and reading of these words, we see this tradition-under-construction offering a hermeneutical model for bringing past prophecies into active dialogue with radically changed circumstances and institutional realities.[62]

Pleins's conviction is that an appreciation of the diversity within the Hebrew Bible will enable readers to better appropriate the biblical traditions today. For him an ideological approach is a constructive ethical task. As will be seen later, other scholars are not so sanguine about what the text has to offer.

READING WHAT LIES WITHIN THE TEXT

While some have directed their efforts at inquiring into the various dimensions behind the text, the number of those scholars who deal with the text-as-it-is has been increasing. Of course, reasons for studying the final form do vary. It is interesting to observe that even a few who have acquired a reputation for their work in form and redaction criticism are less sanguine today of these approaches than in the past. Melugin, for example, explicitly singles out Wolff's theory of the composition of Amos as an illustration of composition theories that stretch meager evidence too far, and encourages more concern for synchronic readings.[63] This feeling that some redaction work is built on too tenuous a foundation is echoed by others. Gowan states:

> My work on the prophets has led me to question both of these assumptions [i.e., of biographical and redactional reconstructions] and to set aside every effort to recover the "historical Amos," focusing instead on the book of Amos, or what may also be called the Amos tradition. The first assumption fails because of the scarcity of explicit evidence about the life of Amos, which should call for scholarly caution. I see no reason to be as skeptical as some scholars are, but I am skeptical of all efforts to deduce from the words of the prophets what their personal experiences may have been or clear standards as to what they could or could not have said. The book of Amos may all have come from him, may be mostly his with a few later additions, or may have been heavily redacted. Each of these opinions may be found in the work of able scholars, but we cannot demonstrate that any one of them is true or false, and since that is the case, some might be driven to the skeptical

conclusion that we cannot be sure that any of these words are the very words of Amos.

I prefer to think of this conclusion as cautious rather than truly skeptical, however. It is probably far less important to know exactly what the man Amos said than many have assumed . . . the lives and religious experiences of the prophets seem to have been a subject of little or no interest to the Israelites who collected and produced the final editions of this material. The incidents from the lives of the prophets that are contained in these books quite clearly have been pre-served because they contain a message from God to Israel, and not because the prophets lived such interesting lives.[64]

In addition to those who have grown impatient with certain critical approaches, there are others who will testify to the theological coherence of the book as proof of its general authenticity and as the rationale for studying the book as a whole. Gerhard Pfeifer believes that the prophet would have been able to write and thus transcribe much of what we now have in the book. He analyzes the relationship between its rhetoric and theology with a method he has labeled *Denkformenanalyse*.[65] For Pfeifer, the theology of the book revolves around the multiple descriptions of the person and actions of Yahweh. Niehaus and Bramer, on the other hand, propose a pervasive theology of covenant, communicated in the genre of a covenant lawsuit, in order to explain how every part of the book is interrelated.[66] Shalom Paul's conviction of accepting almost all the text as authentic is based more on historical factors. Careful historical study, he believes, would eliminate most critical objections. With few exceptions, he sees no cause to question parts of the book as not orig-inating with the prophet.[67]

The aim of this part of my essay, however, is not to survey arguments for the authenticity of the book of Amos, but rather to highlight developments in literary approaches to the received text. The scholars that have just been men-tioned are aware of some of the literary qualities of the text, but their efforts are not designed to be primarily literary readings per se. Paul, for instance, points out heptads in the text and certain chiastic structures. His greatest con-tribution in terms of literary sensitivity has been his widely cited analysis of the Oracles against the Nations. He describes this set of oracles as carefully linked together by a concatenation of catchwords and phrases.[68]

Since 1990 there have been quite a variety of literary studies published on the book of Amos.[69] I divide the discussion into three parts. First are those studies that have concentrated on structural schemes. Dempster argues for an intentional arrangement of the names of God, a patterning that helps disclose the outline of the book (1:1–2:16; chaps. 3–6; 7:1–9:6; 9:7–15) and serves to underline theologically the identity and nature of Yahweh.[70] Steinmann posits that the Oracles against the Nations exhibit several interlocking patterns (geographical, linguistic, political) that reveal anything but a haphazard collection of words against the enemies of Yahweh.[71] O'Connell also turns to these Oracles.[72] While acknowledging that recognition of the N/N+1 (that is, 3/4) pattern is commonplace, he attempts to extrapolate this speech form to include the entire book. Not only does O'Connell find evidence of this arrangement throughout the text, he also would suggest that there is a concomitant "telescoping pattern of development" after 2:16, whereby the final member of a particular 3/3+1 sequence functions as a transition to the next on at least three occasions.

One tendency that has become especially prominent within this kind of approach is the notion that the book of Amos, in its parts and as a whole, exhibits chiasm (alternatively called symmetric, inverted, palistrophic, ring, or concentric patterns). As mentioned in the preceding essay, the existence of this kind of structure in 5:1–17 was heralded in the 1970s and 1980s by scholars such as Jan de Waard.[73] Since that time, others have produced more detailed and comprehensive chiastic designs for Amos. Two that deserve special mention are David Dorsey and Roland Meynet, both of whom have written on Amos yet also have published volumes encompassing the entire Hebrew Bible.[74]

Dorsey underscores the use of heptads (he lists twenty-three) in conjunction with the chiasms as the most striking literary features of the book.[75] He envisions a chiasm of seven sections for the prophetic text (with its center at 5:1–17), as well as smaller symmetric units within this larger framework (i.e., in 3:1–15; 5:1–17; 5:18–6:14; and 8:4–9:15). He feels that this pattern is ubiquitous in the biblical material (and the ancient Near East) and serves to enhance its beauty, coherence, and power.[76] Meynet has coauthored a detailed work on the book of Amos with Pietro Bovati.[77] They classify their approach as *rhétorique biblique* in contradistinction to *rhétorique classique*. They hold that the latter is based more on Greco-Latin criteria and terminology than inherent within the biblical text itself;[78] "biblical rhetoric" is heavily characterized by parallelism and concentric constructions. They propose the book of Amos to be chiastic, in both its three larger sections (1:3–2:16; 3:1–6:14; and 7:1–9:15) and its smaller parts (which they call "sequences"). The creative and extensive use of different fonts makes it possible for them to enhance the visual presentation of interrelated words and phrases within each inverted structure and the connections that cut across the book as a whole. In a more recent volume Meynet traces the historical development of scholarly awareness of this "biblical rhetoric" over the last couple of centuries and then gives a detailed exposition of its presuppositions and features. Multiple examples from the book of Amos appear in his methodological discussion.[79]

A second category of literary approach does not limit its attention so acutely to textual structures. These studies do incorporate structural observations but also probe the theological conundrums that are communicated through these structures and a host of literary wordplays, metaphors, and nuances.[80] In an article that distills much of his doctoral thesis, Karl Möller reconceptualizes Wolff's category of *Auftrittsskizzen*, the objection-response interaction between a prophet and his audience transmitted onto the pages of a prophetic book (he uses this of Hosea), into a rhetorical strategy of the compilers of Amos.[81] In other words, his view of this format is not so much historical and biographical as literary. This strategy he describes as "the presentation of a prophet in debate" and was intended to motivate its hearers and readers to learn from the fate of fallen Israel and so respond appropriately to the prophetic word. He substantiates his proposal with a reading of Amos 3, the doxologies, and 7:10–17.

Paul Noble has published a series of articles on the book of Amos over the last decade. Each of these in its own way attempts to demonstrate the advantages of a synchronic approach over against some limitations of diachronic studies.[82] Several grapple with an issue that has been much debated throughout the history of Amos research: Was the prophet's declaration of judgment final and without possibility of escape, or was it the case that the prophet warned his people of destruction in hyperbolic fashion while at the same time giving them glimpses of hope if they turned in repentance to Yahweh? Based on his close readings of the Oracles against the Nations, chapters 3–6, and 9:1–10, Noble argues that the answer to that question is less than clear and that it is full of tensions.[83] It will not do to eliminate one of the options to attain a neat and tidy message. The eschatological message of hope at the end of the book is well integrated into the rest of the prophetic text, even as it makes the whole more complex and paradoxical. More recently, Noble has offered a synchronic study of Amos 7–8 in order to demonstrate that these chapters are a structural and thematic unit.[84] The narrative that follows the third and fourth vision has the same function: to illustrate the sin and thus justify the pronouncement of disaster upon Israel communicated in the preceding vision.

James Linville proposes to bring to light the profound subtleties and ambiguities of the text.[85] His detailed readings attempt to display the book's inherent—and deliberate—polysemy. He considers that various readings are possible and plausible at any one time and that these interact with each other and reveal themselves to be more or less viable as the reader progresses through the book. Expectations are met or frustrated in the ongoing encounter with the metaphors, irony, and structure. Unlike Noble, however, Linville does have a concern for specifying the historical context and purpose for the text. He argues that the book of Amos reflects a literary world created by scribes in the postmonarchic period, which has been projected back into the experiences of the eighth-century prophet to try to deal with their own questions about prophecy and faith.

A third category of literary approach, poetics, has a bit of a different focus. While appreciating and utilizing observations of methodological orientations similar to the first two (i.e., structure and literary art), poetics develops with more emphasis other features such as plot, point of view, and characterization. This sort of approach has often been identified with scholars such as Robert Alter, Meir Sternberg, Harold Fisch, and Adele Berlin. M. Daniel Carroll R. has applied the insights of poetics to the book of Amos.[86] Beginning with his doctoral thesis, later published as a monograph, he has endeavored to present careful readings of different parts of the prophetic text. The goal has been to grasp the characterization of the nation and leaders that is portrayed within the world that is the Northern Kingdom in the book. The entirety of Israel, along with all of its institutions and social mores, merits Yahweh's pronouncement through the prophet of imminent and devastating destruction. What surfaces in these readings is a deeply religious construction of reality, with multiple intersecting interests and complicity in self-deluding, and finally fatal, misconceptions about life and the Deity by every sector of the population.

A feature that distinguishes Carroll R.'s work from other scholars is that he complements his poetics with contributions from other disciplines, like cultural anthropology, the sociology of knowledge, virtue ethics, and other elements of literary theory.[87] He finds these to be useful tools, as he does not want to divorce literary readings from either the realities of ancient Israel or those of the world today. Ultimately, Carroll R.'s desire is to engage the readings of Amos with modern life. They are to be readings hopefully of a "responsible reader," of one engaged with the challenges of daily social existence. Carroll R.'s primary interlocutor in that effort has been Latin America—in particular Guatemala.

This commitment to put the book of Amos into meaningful dialogue with the contexts of modern readers and their communities is a helpful transition to the final major section of this essay. For the sphere of Amos research that looks to the relevance of this text, what is of paramount concern is the nature and impact of the interaction between it and its various audiences.[88]

IN FRONT OF THE TEXT AND INTO THE WORLD

The book of Amos has continued to grip the imagination of those seeking to establish justice in the world today. The preceding essay described how, especially in the decades of the 1970s and 1980s, Amos was an important text for liberation theology. Since 1990, liberation theology has not commanded the same high profile it once did. There are various reasons for this, but that discussion lies beyond the purposes of this chapter.[89] These "readings from the margins," however, do continue to appear all over the globe. Sadly, many scholars in institutions of the First World are uninformed about work on the prophetic material being done by minority communities within their own countries and in different parts of the world. My third essay provides excerpts of interpretations from African American, Hispanic American, feminist, womanist, ecological, African, and Latin American perspectives.

Of course, it would not be fair to limit interest in the social and ethical to liberationist or minority circles. Several other Old Testament scholars from across the theological spectrum recently have published lay-oriented commentaries on Amos, each of which provides ample suggestions concerning its ongoing relevance at personal, ecclesial, and broader social levels: Donald Gowan,[90] Bruce Birch,[91] and Allen Guenther.[92] Gary Smith has published a commentary in the NIV Application Series. The discussion of each passage is divided into three parts: in "Original Meaning" the author summarizes the fruit of his textual work; in "Bridging Contexts" more transcendent principles are sought to help carry the implications of the biblical material over to the modern world; the last section seeks to explore more specifically the "Contemporary Significance." What is interesting in the case of Smith is that he published a more traditional commentary on the book of Amos over a decade earlier. Undergirding his reflections for today, therefore, is a solid exegetical foundation.[93] Amos, in other words, is clearly not a dead text.

CONCLUSION: WHERE DOES AMOS RESEARCH GO FROM HERE?

Where might Amos research go in the future? At the beginning of the first essay I said that developments in Amos studies have paralleled research on the prophets in general. Naturally, this will continue. But what might that broad statement imply for this prophetic book in particular? The three-part breakdown of "behind the text," "within the text," and "in front of the text"—some of which have subcategories—has served as a heuristic device to encompass the multitude of methods that have been utilized to study the book. Those fundamental divisions will be maintained here.

Scholars naturally tend to gravitate to one or more of these three orientations or emphases, according to their interests and training. It is not possible to say that any one of the three (or one of the methods listed under them) embodies *the* paradigm that will take the field. One should not say, as Ferdinand Deist has, that a newer set of questions and approach are replacing an older, "dominant" model.[94] From his point of view, this change was to be led by methods informed by the social sciences and the "new archaeology." In the

past others have trumpeted the rise of literary approaches as signaling a dras-
tic paradigm shift. Surely Robert P. Gordon is correct: "The current phase of
prophets study is, therefore, a multifaceted one, and it is difficult to imagine
the discipline ever again being hogged by a single dominant approach as was
the case for large areas of biblical scholarship in the era of the historical-
critical *solus*."[95] It is best to speak of alternative paradigms, the number of
which seems to be multiplying. Sometimes these are easily distinguishable,
each with their own set of projects and researchers. At other times, however,
boundaries are crossed, and the results of these multidisciplinary efforts profoundly enrich the entire enterprise. What trends can be envisioned in each of
the three general areas in the investigation of the book of Amos? Let me briefly
mention a few that seem to be more prominent.

Behind the Text

It is safe to say that redaction studies are growing increasingly complex. Part
of the reason for this is that the "text" under study is expanding. Now some
link the redaction of Amos to the growth of the Book of the Twelve. New questions arise, new data have to be considered, and composition theories have to
be more all-encompassing. This newer area of research has been generating
quite a bit of activity, so at least in the short term one should expect more such
hypotheses to emerge.[96]

Another factor leading to increased complexity in redaction theories comes
from a very different quarter. Comparative information from ancient Near
Eastern prophecy also is being brought to bear by some on these discussions,
especially in regard to the move from oral performance to the actual writing
down of prophecy.[97] Redaction questions, then, could become more contextually informed and rely less on scholarly ingenuity divorced from more solid
historical controls.

Continuing study of the lives and messages of prophets elsewhere in the
ancient Near East should also shed more light on the theology and genres of
the words of one like the prophet Amos.[98] In addition, as discoveries into the
various types of religious phenomena in Syria-Palestine come to light and
fresh paradigms are put forward to explain their meaning and significance, our
understanding of the prophet's denunciation of the cultic practices of eighth-
century Israel can only become more lucid and exact.

Attempting to forecast where social science approaches might go in the
coming years is a more difficult task. On the one hand, the call for greater
methodological precision and self-awareness will be more insistent. Scholars
will have to be more careful in their proposals and should expect a level of edu-
cated critique that might not have been possible before. On the other hand,

the direction of some of this kind of research might depend in part on a new set of global influences. In the past, certain scholars—not all, of course—probed the depths of social theory to serve a social cause, such as the liberation of the poor in the Two-Thirds World. The social sciences facilitated the exploration of both ancient and modern socioeconomic realities in order to get at the text's ethical message. Will the changes in the world's economic and political arrangements occasioned by the collapse of the Soviet Union and the disillusion worldwide with much of socialism redirect social science research into different areas (e.g., ecology and ethnicity)? If so, to what extent and how? For others, the motivation to use the social sciences has been simply one of historical interest to attain a more comprehensive vision of the past. Whatever the agenda, new research in a wide variety of areas will be relevant and beneficial to Amos research.

Within the Text

Literary approaches will continue to appear and should provide fresh appreciation of the book of Amos. The question in search of an answer, however, is whether over time some types of approaches might lose their appeal and value, while others come more to the fore. How many new literary patterns still lie undetected, waiting to be uncovered by those studies that focus solely on textual structures? Perhaps those studies that incorporate other dimensions of literature (such as plot, characterization, point of view) and utilize diverse literary theories to explore the history and nature of text reception, the nature of metaphor, and the like represent the long-term future of literary orientations.

Of course, if theories of redaction multiply, so might literary readings of all kinds as well, as they are applied to the different composition layers to explain their purpose and cohesion. It also bears mentioning that entry into this field by certain scholars who had specialized in other critical approaches and so have unique lenses to read the text could generate creative work in many directions along the wide spectrum of literary approaches.[99]

In front of the Text

The book of Amos has always engaged the contexts within which it has been read. The end of the twentieth century witnessed its appropriation by fresh voices around the world seeking a life free from social, economic, political, or gender oppression: liberation theologies, feminism, womanist views, and concerned evangelicals. The harsh realities of human existence, sadly, guarantee that Amos will continue to be a source of encouragement to those who denounce evil and hope for a qualitative difference in their day-to-day life.

What remains to be seen is the impact of the conviction that the book is in some way ideologically flawed, even harmful. Can such a text continue to speak with the same power as in the past? If not, what might be its impact? How will such approaches interface with those who might share similar contextual concerns in the modern world but are more inclined to accept the text in its totality as a word from God?

In sum, it is hard to do anything more than give vague ideas about where Amos research is headed. The future seems bright, even if its paths only will become clearer as the twenty-first century unfolds.

3

Reading Amos from the Margins:
The Impact of Context
on Interpretation Since 1990

INTRODUCTION

The book of Amos has always held an attraction for approaches seeking theological warrant for significant sociopolitical, economic, and cultural change. The ongoing harsh realities of oppression and exploitation—of whatever sort—all around the world continue to sustain in powerful ways the motivation to engage the book of Amos, even as they have over so many centuries. What often distinguishes these sorts of readings is a self-conscious "reading *as*" or "reading *from*" more marginalized groups rather than from the perspective of more classical scholarship. These are intentionally situated approaches, which argue that the study of the biblical text cannot be a strictly academic exercise. The prophetic word, as it were, must move outside its pages either to capture or perhaps even to repel its readers, either to inspire them or to make them cast doubts upon its voice. These important angles on reality and faith come to the text from the very difficult stuff of life, and it behooves the broader Christian community to listen to them in order to probe further the depths of the Bible's message and impact. Hermeneutical issues, quite naturally, abound and continue to spark debate.[1] Those who deal with the biblical text in this way also wrestle with defining the appropriate role of the scholar vis-à-vis these readings "from below"[2] and are aware now more than ever of what sometimes has been an unfortunate historical legacy of the imposition of destructive interpretations of the Bible upon subjugated peoples in the past.[3]

The final subsection ("In front of the Text") of the first essay surveyed a number of these sorts of approaches to the book of Amos up to about 1990, with a special focus on liberationist and nonliberationist studies from Latin America. This chapter carries these concerns forward from 1990 to the present. Happily, in recent years researchers have been provided with a wide array of helpful source material. Several collections offer a spectrum of readings from different ethnic, gender, and theological points of view and from various parts of the globe that can serve to introduce those readers who might be accustomed to more traditional approaches to alternative kinds of discourse.[4] Still other volumes concentrate on specific regions of the world, such as Africa or Latin America.[5] My focus, of course, will be on work done on Amos.

This chapter is divided into two parts. The first presents readings from what we call the "First World"—that is, from North America and Western Europe. The second shifts to the "Two-Thirds World" (or "Third World") with offerings from Africa and Latin America. The format differs from the previous two essays in that the primary goal is to feature exemplary and extensive citations of this new manner of handling the prophetic text rather than to provide a detailed summary discussion of research. This shift in presentation is designed to give readers the opportunity to become acquainted firsthand with these perspectives, since pragmatically it must be admitted that few courses on the book of Amos or introductions to Amos research do much more than allude to these studies in the footnotes—if they even mention them at all. I hope that this chapter can fill this void somewhat and encourage those who have been taken by this prophetic text to continue to pursue on their own the surprising echoes of its words.

READINGS FROM THE FIRST WORLD

The many kinds of readings that have arisen within North America and Western Europe and that strive to read on behalf of specific communities or groups are rich in their diversity. Many times the call for responsible biblical work is born out of the deep desire to redress wrongs suffered because of race or gender and legitimated by certain interpretations. What is more, this cross-examining of interpretations has led some to begin to take the additional step of postulating that the text itself might have ideological blind spots (whether conscious or not) inherent within its pages. Not all would push their questioning this far, but the phenomenon is not uncommon, as the following excerpts will attest.

I begin, however, with selections that take the merit of the socioeconomic critique in the message of the book of Amos at face value. One of the ways people assimilate and make a text their own is to restate it in their own words and to locate themselves within it. This kind of rewriting can come from anywhere on the theological spectrum. The following two pieces try to imagine what the prophet might say if he were living in the United States at the end of the twentieth century. They voice wide-ranging ethical concerns, but with confidence both claim the prophetic mantle for today. The first comes from an interesting volume edited by Alice Ogden Bellis that records reactions to the messages of the Twelve by students seeking to capture the spirit of the text in a way authentic to their particular background.

> The voice of the Lord is clear:
>   It is heard throughout the world.
> When the voice of the Lord is heard,
>   everything that has breath is subject to it.
> Thus says the Lord:
>   For three transgressions of Iraq and for four,
>   punishment will come;
>   because they have destroyed the Kurdish people
>   by denying them land, food, and dignity.
>   So I will send a fire on the hills and valleys of Iraq
>   and I will turn my hand against them, says the Lord God.
> Thus says the Lord:
>   For three transgressions of Libya and for four,
>   punishment will come;
>   because of the terrorism they have inflicted on the innocent.
>   So I will send a fire on the deserts of Libya
>   and I will turn my hand against them, says the Lord God.
> Thus says the Lord:
>   For three transgressions of Haiti and for four,
>   punishment will come;
>   because they have not fed the children
>   and they have sent them into exile on the sea.
>   So I will send a fire on the shores of Haiti
>   and I will turn my hand against them, says the Lord God.
> Thus says the Lord:
>   For three transgressions of South Africa and for four,
>   punishment will come;
>   because they have cherished those who are white
>   and abhorred those who are black.
>   So I will send a fire on the cities of South Africa
>   and I will turn my hand against them, says the Lord God.
> Thus says the Lord:
>   For three transgressions of the United States and for four,
>   punishment will come;
>   because you have been the great hypocrites of the earth:
>   putting your moralistic finger and expounding your pious rhetoric
>   while you commit the same atrocities as the other nations.
> Hear these words, you people that call yourselves "number one"
>   among the nations:
>   Your status is due to the oppression of other nations:
>   You force them to grow crops that they cannot eat,

You sell infant formula to them so their children will not grow,
  You care only for the security of countries that benefit your
    own security. . . .
You say that South Africa determines the value of people by the color of
  their skin. But the quality of health, safety, and standard of living
  is determined by an insidious, festering racism that permeates your
  communities.
Alas for those who hoard their wealth and eat and sleep with no concern
  for their responsibility in the community.
I am the Lord your God who made a covenant with you.
  Like a patient mother, I have loved and cared for you.
  Like a patient teacher, I have taught you to love one another.
I demand justice.
  I demand mercy.
My anger at the destruction of the creation
  is full of fury, says the Lord your God.[6]

In a similar manner, Joel Drinkard has rewritten the entire book of Amos.
The following excerpt is his reconceptualization of Amos 3:1ff.

Hear this word which the LORD has spoken against you,
O people of America, against the whole family whom I have raised
up in North America:
  You and you especially have I blessed
    out of all the families of the earth;
  therefore I will punish you all the more
    for your iniquities.
Does any effect happen without a cause?
Does a gun fire unless the trigger is pulled?
Does a light come on unless the switch is thrown?
Does an animal fall into a trap where there is no trap?
Does a rabbit spring from his box when nothing has sprung the trigger?
Does God punish without giving the opportunity for repentance?
When a lion roars, how can we not be afraid?
When lightning flashes, how can we but fear?
When God speaks, who can but prophesy?

Hear this word, you who fill your television with violence or spoofs
of violence,
  yet cannot understand why your children become violent—
  They become what they see, and what they see accepted by their role
    models.
Woe to you who fear the escalating arms race,
  yet demand high power rifles for your sport,
    and automatic assault rifles as your constitutional right.
  "Guns don't kill," you piously proclaim,
    as you sell another Saturday night special.
  Tell that to the children in Stockton.

How long, O Lord, how long?
> How long will the nation continue to offer freely
> > to any taker automatic assault rifles?
> How long will a people let the National Rifle Association lobby
> > determine public policy?
> How many more schools in Stockton, California?
> > How many more Post Offices in Edmond, Oklahoma?
> > How many more Standard Gravures in Louisville, Kentucky?
> > How long, O Lord, how long?[7]

African American Perspectives

From these more general utilizations of the prophetic book, this section now turns to its appropriation by a particular community. A fitting place to start is to listen to the towering figure of Martin Luther King Jr., who played an invaluable part in raising African American consciousness in the United States and in forcing an entire nation to begin to face the realities of its racism. In a famous commencement address given at Lincoln University in Pennsylvania on June 6, 1961, this powerful spokesperson for human dignity and the rights of the downtrodden appealed with his characteristic eloquence to the prophet Amos as he drove home words that continue to inspire decades later:

> I know sometimes we get discouraged and sometimes disappointed with the slow pace of things. At times we begin to talk about racial separation instead of racial integration, feeling that there is no other way out. My only answer is that the problem will never be solved by substituting one tyranny for another. Black supremacy is as dangerous as white supremacy. . . . God is interested in the freedom of the whole human race and in the creation of a society where all men can live together as brothers. . . .
>
> And so, with all of these attitudes and principles working together, I believe we will be able to make a contribution as men of good will to the ongoing structure of our society and toward the realization of the American dream. And so, as you go out today, I call upon you not to be detached spectators, but involved participants, in this great drama that is taking place in our nation and around the world.
>
> Every academic discipline has its technical nomenclature, and modern psychology has a word that is used, probably, more than any other. It is the word *maladjusted* . . . there are certain things within our social order to which I am proud to be maladjusted and to which I call upon all men of good will to be maladjusted.
>
> If you will allow the preacher in me to come out now, let me say to you that I never did intend to adjust to the evils of segregation and discrimination. I never did adjust myself to religious bigotry. . . . And I call upon all men of good will to be maladjusted because it may well be the salvation of our world lies in the hands of the maladjusted.

So let us be maladjusted, as maladjusted as the prophet Amos, who in the midst of the injustices of his day could cry out in words that echo across the centuries, "Let justice run down like waters and righteousness like a mighty stream." Let us be as maladjusted as Abraham Lincoln, who had the vision to see that this nation could not exist half slave and half free. Let us be as maladjusted as Jesus of Nazareth, who could cry out, "Love your enemies. Bless them that curse you. Pray for them that spitefully use you."

I believe that it is through such maladjustment that we will be able to emerge from the bleak and desolate midnight of man's inhumanity to man into the bright and glittering daybreak of freedom and justice. That will be the day when all God's children, black men and white men, Jews and Gentiles, Catholics and Protestants, will be able to join hands and sing in the words of the old Negro spiritual, "Free at last! Free at last! Thank God almighty, we are free at last!"[8]

Even as many years ago Martin Luther King Jr. could call on Amos to side with the oppressed in that long road to a different society and way of life, so J. Deotis Roberts also brings the prophet into his own experience to speak against racism today. He relates some thoughts quickened by a trip to the Midwest, and in doing so Roberts recalls and reconsiders the implications of King's efforts:

A black pastor pointed to Amos as a prophet of justice. Amos knew only the wrath of God. The minister wanted to know if the black church should take Amos more seriously. It was his impression that the church is a "do-nothing" institution simply because it is paralyzed by "love." . . . There is a moral honesty in Amos that is essential for exposing the seriousness of our inhumanity. Black Theology needs a heavy dose of Amos.

The God of Amos is "an angry God." Amos is a man of the people; he is a "folk" prophet. The masses have been exploited by priests and politicians just as blacks have been. Amos is a prophet of social justice. . . .

Those who exploit the poor and mete out violence to the needy and underprivileged, sleep "upon beds of ivory" (Amos 6:4), possess "winter" and "summer" houses (Amos 3:15). They "sell the righteous for silver, and the needy for a pair of shoes" (Amos 2:6). This speaks of punishment, desolation, darkness, and judgment. . . .

Recently as I rode with friends through the city of Indianapolis, I noticed a sign over a tractor company: God Bless America. This reminded me of the "God and Country" romance going on. The friendship, developing into a national scandal, between Billy Graham and Richard Nixon illustrated this trend. The Honor America program on July 4, 1970, in which Billy Graham was a chief star, attempted to ignore all the injustices at home and abroad in which this county was so deeply involved. It wanted to sprinkle holy water on "unholy" America. . . . The unholy alliance is most deadly because of the power controlled by those involved together with the insensitivity to evil. . . .

But unless we are to fall victim to the Marcionite misunderstanding of God, the God of Amos must also be the God of Hosea. The God of justice is also the God of love and mercy. . . .

One observes in Martin Luther King Jr., this blend of justice and love. Amos and Jesus are prophetic models for King. A worthy understanding of the Christian God and God's moral requirements must include justice and mercy, judgment and forgiveness. . . .

Dr. King, I believe, had a sound grasp of biblical ethics—one that will win in the long run. It is my understanding that he leaned too far, at first, toward love as an ethical norm. . . . But, because the shadow of Amos, the prophet of justice, forever haunted him, King never allowed love to become sentimentality. The later King, when confronted with Black Power, became more and more like Amos. He became more militant and thus even love became a means to racial injustice. He was pushed by the logic of events to the very edge of violence. . . . He insistently made the point that his program was the only alternative to violence, thus perhaps unwittingly contributing to the racial fears that breed violence.[9]

Hispanic American

The African American community is not the only minority community that has sought guidance or encouragement from the book of Amos. Others do as well, and it is now possible to hear more voices within the increasingly multicultural world that the United States and Western Europe are becoming.

As the Hispanic population in North America continues to grow and its percentage of the general populace increases, their profile at the lay level within historic Protestant and evangelical denominations and especially within the Roman Catholic Church has become more prominent. At the same time, Hispanic theological reflection also has begun to acquire a hearing.[10] Their (multiple) cultural backgrounds and peculiar experiences, as members either of long-standing minority communities or of very recent immigrant groups, can lead to fresh and distinct insights into the biblical text. This very diverse set of communities that make up the Hispanic population also appeals to Amos, but perhaps in a different way and for different reasons than have African Americans. At least in the excerpt that follows, the prophet is not so much a model of denunciation as an example of a clever undermining of the powers.

García-Treto has explored how the prophet's confrontation with Amaziah parallels patterns of "improvisational performance" ("riffing") common in Caribbean (and African American) culture, where words are toyed with in order to redefine power relations.[11] García-Treto begins by voicing his agreement with the theoretical proposition that a reader's interpretive strategies are determined to a large extent by the community with which that reader identifies. The first step in the interpretive enterprise, therefore, is to identify the group within which and for which the text is read.

> In order to sketch a reading of Amos 7.10–17, I would like to specify more precisely the interpretive community of this particular reader, a community largely congruent with, but partly different from, that of the general class of academic biblical scholars active at this time in North America. Because of my ethnic background, cultural allegiance, personal history and experience and numerous other factors, I see myself—and others see me—as a Hispanic-American. I find myself in sympathy with Justo González's recent plea for a conscious effort on the part of Hispanics to read the Bible "in Spanish," that is, a reading of people—whether biblical scholars or unsophisticated folk—who read the Bible "as exiles, as members of a powerless group, as those excluded from the 'innocent' history of the dominant group." That reading will approach the Bible as a political book.[12]

By "political" García-Treto means that his reading will look at the dynamic of the construct of prestige and privilege between the characters within the pericope. Thus he seeks to discern echoes of "riffing":

> I would read Amos's reply to Amaziah first as a series of "riffs" on the latter's use of *ḥōzeh* as what I have called "an ironic trope on *nābî*'." Amos pointedly ignores the term *ḥōzeh* but launches into a "riff"—or a variation, if you will—in which he denies his "*nābî*hood"—"I am not a *nābî*', nor the son of a *nābî*'," apparently going Amaziah one better in denying his own status, at the same time that he turns Amaziah's irony inside out by embracing the lack of status and title which the priest's ironic *ḥōzeh* had implied. He doesn't stop "riffing," however, but launches next into a series of self-identifications as a rustic which can be read as yet another quick-witted elaboration on Amaziah's attack. Amos goes on apparently agreeing with Amaziah's implication that he does not belong where he is—"I am a herdsman, and a dresser of sycamore trees," also claiming that the Lord found him "following the flock". . . . Amos seems in effect to be telling Amaziah, "I am *anything but* a prophet! I am nothing but a cowboy, a clodhopper, a sheep-kicker!" The rhetorical, performative strategy of seeming to agree with the one who "puts you down" in order to "put him on" is what appears to be at work here, rather than an otherwise awkward attempt on Amos's part to present some sort of *curriculum vitae* as a "self-justification speech." The real impact of this parodic self-deprecation appears immediately, however, when Amos reveals to Amaziah that the latter's attack on him in fact has gone right through Amos to impinge on the One behind him. "*Yahweh* took me from following the flock,

and *Yahweh* said to me. . . ." The repetition of Yahweh's name, which appears here for the first time in the exchange between priest and prophet, is the turning point in the power game in which the two have been engaged. . . .

Amos does not slink away defeated. The "alternative imagination" he represents in fact wins the day, in a performance that decenters and overwhelms Amaziah, more importantly, a performance that persuades the reader that ultimate power, far from being "a monopoly of throne and temple," remains with Amos's God.[13]

Feminist and Womanist Approaches

From a focus on race and class, this section turns to the contributions of women. Feminist scholars offer insights grounded in their gender, and womanists present a perspective informed by gender and race. In both cases, the reader is alerted to issues that approaches whose attention is primarily on race and class might miss.

In her *Introduction to the Old Testament: A Feminist Perspective*, Alice L. Laffey lists several pertinent themes in the Latter Prophets that, from a feminist perspective, demand consideration.[14] These books in her opinion exhibit patriarchy and hierarchy. A redeeming value of this literature, however, is the prophetic concern for the victims of injustice, which is suffered by women and men alike. Such critiques of the Prophets, and of the Bible in general, have generated different appreciations by feminist scholars of the nature of biblical authority. Some hold that the feminist lens should lead to the reinterpretation of problematic texts; others believe that only those parts of the biblical corpus that censure patriarchy or that manifest liberating themes are worthy of appropriation; still others argue that the entire Bible is irredeemable because of its destructive attitudes toward women.

A mixed assessment of the book of Amos is voiced by several feminist scholars. For example, Judith Sanderson in *The Woman's Bible Commentary* criticizes the text's apparent blindness to the sad condition of poor women, who have always made up the majority of the disenfranchised and defenseless. In other words, she questions how the poor are "gendered" in Amos.[15] How well can a male truly grasp the plight of oppressed women? Looking at the other end of the socioeconomic scale, Sanderson wonders if the description of the wealthy women of Samaria as "cows of Bashan" also might not point to a patriarchal perspective and thus, not surprisingly, be an exaggerated and unfair characterization.

> Amos specifically condemned wealthy women for oppressing the poor (4:1) but failed specifically to champion the women among the poor. Yet both the analogy of modern times and the witness of the Bible itself strongly suggest that women were disproportionately represented

among the poor in Israel. The modern feminization of poverty is evident in statistics showing that women suffer disproportionately from poverty with all of its ramifications: inadequate but high-cost housing, low and unstable salaries, poor nutrition, and the struggle to care for children with too few resources. The recurring concern throughout the Bible for widows, often linked with the fatherless and resident aliens, as exemplifying the most vulnerable and exploited segment of society . . . shows that other biblical writers were aware of the plight of at least one group of women—those who had no man to provide for them financially and legally. Yet no word has survived that would indicate that Amos demonstrated any such awareness of the special sufferings and exploitations of women. . . . In addition, Amos's sweeping condemnation of wealthy women must be approached with suspicion. Again, both the analogy of modern times and the witness of the Bible itself show that patriarchal thinking enables the power and sinfulness of women to be greatly exaggerated. Far too often in both biblical texts and the interpretive tradition, women, whether literal or metaphorical, are scapegoated or even seen as personifying evil. . . . While it is especially common to blame women for sexual sins, Amos and Isaiah (Isa. 3:16–4:1) both broadened the picture of their culpability.[16]

She does work to be evenhanded with the text and recognizes that it would not be right to say that the book exhibits no concern at all for the suffering of unfortunate women. A case in point is 1:13.

Some scholars find the motive [for ripping open the pregnant women in 1:13] in a determination either to decrease the next generation of enemy soldiers or to emasculate the fathers ritually. While such theories are plausible, it is interesting that they focus the attention entirely on the males, whether unborn sons or fathers, and ignore the slaughter of the mothers. Yet throughout history it has been commonplace for soldiers to lash out at women in uncontrolled acts of violence including rape, sexual mutilation, and murder. Specifically, in ancient times conquered women were customarily raped and carried off as booty; women already pregnant were butchered on the spot, as were small children who could not make the journey. While they were unfortunately not extraordinary acts, Amos considered the Ammonites' atrocities against pregnant women at least worthy of God's judgment of conquest and exile.[17]

All of these observations, though, do not disqualify the book of Amos from any positive input into modern realities. To the contrary, modern readers, who have access to feminist perspectives along with more precise systemic analyses, can utilize this prophetic text as a constructive starting point:

Women today are building on the kind of insight that Amos showed and developing a more consistent critique of society than is evident in the book named for him. This more thoroughgoing analysis leads to a more specific and a more structural sense of justice than was possible in Amos's day. . . . Such an understanding will enable Amos's vision to speak to this generation of women and men alike and will flesh out that vision more profoundly than Amos himself was in a position to do.[18]

In a volume that is part of a series entitled "A Liberation-Critical Reading of the Old Testament," Carol J. Dempsey dedicates a chapter to Amos.[19] She begins with this attention-grabbing line: "Resplendent with a variety of rhetorical forms expressive of a polished, impassioned, dynamic, and didactic style, the book of Amos captures the imagination of its readers with its straightforward, 'in your face' message."[20] Nevertheless, while appreciative of much of its championing of social justice, Dempsey is deeply suspicious of the text's ideology—perhaps more suspicious than Sanderson. In her mind, in spite of its positive contributions, it reflects a hierarchical worldview in regard to power, class, and gender. For example, commenting on the Aram pericope (1:3–5), which is the first of the so-called Oracles against the Nations, she says:

> In vv 3–5 God is portrayed as "warrior god" who has "power over" injustice and "power over" other peoples. As "warrior god," God promises to deal with injustice by "conquering" the enemy, the perpetrator of injustice. This image of the "warrior god" and its association with the notion of power and having "power over" is due, in large part, to a gender-specific portrayal of and metaphor for God. In the ancient world, and in many circles today, God was and is imagined as a male deity. Furthermore, the historical and cultural times of the prophets were marked by countries in conflict with each other, with Israel being no exception. Consequently, experiences and ideologues of war shaped and informed Israel's self-understanding and self-expression. Therefore, it is not surprising that the "warrior of warriors" would be a male God whose might would make right by avenging the enemy. Lastly, this image of God having power over a non-Israelite country also comes from Israel's self-understanding that its God is the true God who is "ruler over all."[21]

This critical judgment of Amos, tempered with an acknowledgment of its constructive possibilities, also surfaces among womanist scholars. Renita Weems is appreciative of Amos's straightforward attack on privilege, especially within an Old Testament—and an academic guild!—that she feels are not always so discriminating. The belief in special election can lead to destructive attitudes and behavior toward others; it should rather encourage a sense of responsibility. The prophet's critique, therefore, continues to serve as a model for today, where parallel forces are at work.

> Invariably, the way Israel understood the particularity of that election, that is its particular relationship to its god, would influence the way

Israel viewed reality, constituted itself, ordered society, shaped social
and political institutions, narrated history, and reacted to its environment. . . . Some of that conduct, defined in liberation circles as patriarchal and oppressive, took the form of sexual discrimination, ethnic
discrimination, religious repression, territorial expansionism, and
economic exploitation. Therefore, any critique that aims to challenge
the theological and cultural assumptions and biases of the biblical
mindset must begin with an analysis of what it means and meant for
Israel to claim to be elected. . . . The premise here is simple: until criticism takes seriously the biblical peoples' pervasive belief in their election and their understanding of what it meant to be elected, . . . then
we have not begun to resist the ideological foundation of the patriarchal world order, its ordering of society and its view of a select few in
society in relation to the cosmos and the rest of the world. If, indeed,
patriarchy is described as a system of exploitation wherein "a few men
have power over other men, women, children, slaves, and colonialized
people," then we cannot afford to limit our examinations to, say, gender oppression alone. As the victims of "a simultaneity of oppression,"
the question women of color must continuously pose of the dominate
scholarship, and of our own scholarship, is whether any one analysis—
gender, class, racial/ethnic—is sufficiently comprehensive to do justice to the complexity of patriarchy. I think not.

Fortunately the Bible has canonized within itself some of its most
ardent critics. For example, the book of Amos is a model dissenting
voice to what appears to have been the prevailing way of thinking
about Israel's divine election. The intense social justice emphases of
the book of Amos are frequently noted. More attention, however,
should be given to the manner in which the prophet sternly criticizes
Israel's election traditions, or more accurately, the manner in which
the prophet criticizes the hegemonic interpretation of what it meant
to be God's elect people. To this rural prophet who was outside the
dominant interpretative circle, Israel's election did not give it special
priority over others. . . . To Amos, election did not mean preference.
It certainly did not mean that Israel's every social, political or religious
impulse and formulation automatically found favor with God. Evi-
dently, whatever it meant to be elected by God, argues Amos, brought
with it grave responsibility for the wholeness of society. The prophecy
of Amos is one of a number of voices in the canon that counters those
cultural structures in ancient Israel designed to legitimate and defend
the systematic exploitation of the powerless. These counter-cultural
voices, however oblique they may be, deserve our attention.[22]

Ideological Critique

It is evident that feminist and womanist scholarship, at least in the sources just
cited, are a bit reticent to acquiesce too easily to a Bible they feel in some fashion
discriminates against women. David Clines takes that hermeneutic of suspicion

yet one step further. His negative assessment is directed at not only the prophetic text itself, but also at those who comment on it. Clines is intolerant of scholars (and he quotes liberally from several commentators), who (in his view) inexcusably accept the book's biased ideology without question and mimic its values.[23] For Clines, what makes this sort of scholarship particularly pernicious is that readers of their commentaries are not trained to be more careful critics. So, he accuses, the biblical text can continue to hold its grip over a credulous public. What is needed, he feels, to remedy this state of affairs is "metacommentary."

> Metacommentary, what is that? Let me try this formulation: When we write commentary, we read what commentators say. When we write metacommentary, we notice what commentators do. . . .
>
> Well, the main thing they do but do not say is not say what they don't say. . . . So, since we innocent members of the public, who go on laying out good money on commentaries, need protection against those commentators who are failing to tell us what it is they are failing to do, it becomes an urgent public duty to create a neighborhood watch committee of metacommentators who will tell us how we are being shortchanged. . . .
>
> Metacommentating Amos myself, I propose noticing some of the things commentators do. First, they adopt the view of the text regarding the social and economic situation in ancient Israel. Secondly, they adopt the ideology of the text regarding the existence of God and the authenticity of the prophetic vocation. Thirdly, they conceal from their readers that this is what they are doing.[24]

Not to engage the text and question it, Clines says, is to ignore consciously or to consent naively to the author's ideological agenda, along with its theological expression and justification.

> In short, it would be uncritical of us to simply accept Amos's analysis of his society, to simply buy the ideology of the text. Somehow we must distance ourselves from the prophetic voice, and recognize that the prophet's is only one voice in his community. The prophet, and the text, have a corner to fight, a position to uphold, and we for our part need to identify that position, and to relativize it, not so as to discard it but only so as to give it its proper due. But, hardly surprisingly, most of the books about Amos simply take Amos's point of view for granted.[25]

In other words, to offer in commentary the book's perspective as the only true analysis and viable evaluation of the state of affairs in ancient Israel and to propound its view of God as the correct one—and to do so without question or doubt—for Clines is unacceptable, even insidious.

> But once they start commentating on Amos they accede to Amos's simple moral defeatism. Not one of them has the courage—or the

intellectual capacity—to extract himself (they are all males) from the ideology of the text and to pronounce judgment upon the prophecy. To be sure, the future *was* very much as the prophecy says—whether it predicted it or wrote about it in hindsight. Things *were* awful, for rich and poor alike. But it is even more awful to ascribe the destruction of a state and the forcible deportation of its citizens to an avenging God. If that is how a believer finds himself or herself impelled to conclude, that it is a terrifying thing to fall into the hands of the living God, the metacommentator can respect that. But to affirm it casually, to pretend that it is unproblematic—*that* is not scholarly, it is not even human.[26]

Ecology

The final type of reading in this first section on new perspectives from the First World voices ecological concerns. Thus far, the variety of approaches has been quite broad, moving from more racial and class to gender issues to a point of view that questions the whole interpretive enterprise. This last perspective is quite different, yet suspicions about the text linger.

It is obvious that the book of Amos does not deal directly with God's commitment to or human responsibility for nature. Nevertheless, some have drawn indirect application from Amos to issues of ecology. The following excerpt is from a discussion that in general focuses more on liberation and feminist issues. As noted earlier, and as will become evident in this excerpt, many from this persuasion would question the ideological and theological point of view of Amos. The text that serves as the occasion for the following comment is Amos 4:1.

> Because a majority within Israelite society were herders and farmers, many metaphors come from the natural environment. In its own social world context, comparing the Samarian women to the cows of Bashan would, for its hearers and early readers, perhaps, communicate nothing more than a comparison between pedigree cows and well-kept women. . . . "It was common to compare human qualities to animal qualities; whether the application was positive or negative depended upon the context."
>
> When heard in the context of a contemporary technological society that has health and ecological concerns and sensitivities, this metaphor takes on a new nuance. The comparison is heard as derogatory, inferring that the women were "fat and unacceptable." Moreover, referring to a person as an animal is to be guilty of diminishing the human, if viewed hierarchically, because an animal is considered to be of lesser value than a human being. Interlocked in diminution is the eco-ethical issue of speciesism, "the assumption that animals are inferior to human beings and do not warrant equal consideration and respect."[27]

READINGS FROM THE TWO-THIRDS WORLD

In other parts of the world, where injustice weighs heavily upon the general population, the book of Amos also continues to encourage those who claim to follow Yahweh to press for social change. Interestingly, the level of suspicion argued by First World scholars does not find an echo in the Two-Thirds World. Both its message and the short vignettes of the prophet, in which Amos boldly stands up to the high priest and the king, serve as motivations for the same kind of courageous stance before oppression today. The second part of this chapter directs its attention to the text's contextualization in two major regions, first to Africa and then to Latin America.

Africa

It is interesting to note how theological reflection in Africa has sometimes drawn inspiration and insights from Latin American liberation theologians. While cognizant of differences in history and circumstances, there have been both formal and informal interchanges of thought and method between the two continents.[28] Those in the First World, who might have some acquaintance with biblical studies out of Africa, usually have their frame of reference limited to work of ecumenical Protestants from the Republic of South Africa. In an attempt to broaden this exposure, I cite a piece calling for reform in Nigeria from a Roman Catholic clergyman.

> One problem that beckons on Human Promotional experts in Nigeria is that of injustice and corruption which would make the Prophet Amos, the Patron Saint of Social Reformers, turn many times over in his grave. . . .
> In this venture, we should be inspired by, among others, the Patron Saint of Justice, Fairplay and social Reformers, Prophet Amos. Guided by this prophet's inspirational and theological perspicacity, we should show in a concrete, if academic way our solidarity with the poor of the Lord. . . . We must do it now, since any problem involving injustice in any of its forms must be considered urgent, for: justice delayed, is justice denied.[29]

At the end of his article Owan mentions some liberationist priests, several of whom ministered in Latin America, as exemplars, who stand as testimonies of self-sacrifice for what he feels are the moral demands of the Christian faith. The appreciation of those from Latin America, however, is not a blanket one. It is clear that this cleric has opted for the ways of nonviolence and for respect for the hierarchy of the Roman Catholic Church.

Amos, our Patron Saint of social reformers that we should really be, motivates us to be the voice of the voiceless that he was, the conscience of the Nation that he was. . . . He has been called the Oscar Romero (remember the murdered Archbishop of San Salvador, who championed the cause of the poor of his land) of the 8th century Israel. We would as Nigerians easily localize this idea by calling Amos, the Olumbumi Okogie of the 8th century. But if Amos' fire was Romero's, and Amos' zeal and bravado is still Archbishop Okogie's, these virtues can still be ours, challenged by the cause of our down-trodden masses.

Finally, those who are priests and religious leaders may not really cast off their clerical garbs like Father Camilo Torres who declared that "revolutionary action is a Christian priestly struggle" and went and joined, yes, literally joined the poor guerrilla fighters of Colombia. . . . We may not be as hasty as Father Fernandon Cardinal [sic] in drawing neat battle lines and dumping even our religious leaders with the oppressors . . . their liberation should not only be from sin, not only to freedom, but for the cause of Human Promotion in all of its ramifications. . . . Struggle must continue![30]

Latin America

The allusion to Latin America can serve as a helpful transition to a presentation of some Latin American studies. Over the last three decades biblical studies committed to social change from that part of the world have come primarily from the pen of liberationists. The first essay detailed the contributions from the 1970s to the late 1980s of prominent Old Testament liberationist scholars, such as Tamez, Miranda, Croatto, and Schwantes. Although no work by a Latin American specifically dedicated to Amos has appeared in the last several years, the European Haroldo Reimer has published a monograph that investigates the ethical message of the book and appeals directly to the value of Latin American liberationist perspectives.

Reimer begins his work on Amos by contrasting German academic approaches with what can be found in some of the base communities of Latin America.[31] European scholars (and here he parades a series of prominent names), while they have debated whether the prophet Amos offered any hope to Israel as a nation or to segments within that society, have missed some of the socioeconomic dimensions of the book and of ancient Israelite society. In contrast, the poor, he says, can be more qualified and legitimate hermeneuticians of the biblical text. They and liberation theologians are better situated to discover its true power. As other liberation scholars have done, Reimer uses critical tools in his own textual work to recover what he believes to be the original message of the prophet. The result of this exegesis is that he finds a sweeping condemnation of all of Israelite society, even of other peasants who exploit the more unfortunate among them. The only hope for the nation lies in the restoration of justice at the town gates (cf. 5:15). He has published a helpful synthesis of his work in a Latin American journal, and offers a succint summary at the beginning of that article. The goal of his research, he says, is to

> make clear that the agents of the oppression and exploitation suffered by the Israelite peasants and denounced by the prophet Amos are, on the one hand, persons structurally connected to the tributary state (the army, the priests of the official temples, the king, and the royal court). Within this orbit of relationships, the mechanisms are temporary forced labor and the collecting of tribute in kind, and the army and the priests function as the coercive agents. On the other hand, the oppression and exploitation also occur in the social and economic relationships among Israelites of the same class or category, without the intervention of the tributary state. Abusing the institution of justice at the gate, some poor Israelites can enrich themselves, thus becoming exploiters and oppressors of people of the same social category.[32]

As I explained in the first essay, not all who champion Amos as a text for social change write from the perspective of liberation theology. Several scholars of evangelical convictions have also written on this prophetic book with an eye to its relevance for Latin American society. For example, Humberto R. Cassanova has presented a study of the issue of justice in the book of Amos based primarily on historical and lexical data. He closes his article with an exhortation that seems to hit at the evangelical tendency sometimes to ignore the harsh realities of social existence or overspiritualize life with God:

> Now, it also has been established that God hates corruption and exploitation. Each one of the texts that has been analyzed rises up like an accusation and condemnation of all the atrocities that it mentions, or proceeds to sentencing by God, who promises to execute his punishment against any government and people who in general have violated his covenant in the most cruel way. This occurs because in Scripture religion and a relationship with God are inconceivable in cultic or fetish terms. Communion with, and service and devotion to, God are defined above all else as a total commitment of the believer to justice and truth; these are understood in terms of the normative concepts of the torah, and not according to any natural ethic or tribal tradition. Both our inspiration for justice as well as the definition we give to it should come from the Scriptures and faith. . . .
>
> Therefore, it does not matter how much I feel God in my heart. The Lord will be with me only to the degree that his presence is mediated through action according to his will, as "since *only in this way* will Yahweh God Almighty be" truly with us. When human beings begin to hate evil and love the good, this will be the clearest signal that their *profession of faith* is real, that it is the fruit of the work of God in their hearts, changing their unceasing inclination toward sin for a new life

of justice and holiness. Justice and holiness should arise from our faith,
just as true faith should become concrete in incarnated justice and in
lived-out truth.[33]

M. Daniel Carroll R. has written extensively on the book of Amos and has
consistently attempted to interface a literary reading of the text (although one
informed by historical and sociological studies) with issues pertaining to Latin
America in general and to Guatemala in particular. Different publications have
contextualized different parts of Amos to those contexts. The following
excerpt and the next are juxtaposed purposely. Both deal with the hope passage, 9:11–15, and build off of the recognition that these descriptions appear
to be a conscious reversal of the destruction pictured earlier in the book. The
first was written before the signing of the peace accords in Guatemala in late
December 1996, while that country was still in the midst of a civil war that had
lasted over thirty years. The second appeared after that agreement, as Guatemala was beginning to try to rebuild its infrastructure and civil society after
the formal end of the conflict.

> The world of the book of Amos, I believe, can trigger reflection on the
> different expressions of Christian faith within Central America.
> Within that textual world, Yahweh stands over against the use of his
> person for the military convictions and hubris of Israel. In the mod-
> ern context we need to let the text challenge us to ask, "How has Yah-
> weh been utilized to legitimate postures of violence and identified with
> particular political persuasions or regimes in our world?"
>   At the same time, in Central America where many feel compelled
> to take options, we wrestle with the question of whose side might Yah-
> weh be on. With claims on God from across the political spectrum, I
> wonder if the best we can say in light of this text is that Yahweh is
> *within our history* and that he is committed to the destruction of *all*
> regimes of war and *all* military pretense. Could we not entertain the
> possibility that Yahweh is permitting the tearing down of *our* warlike
> world and allowing our self-destruction, because of the commitment
> of some to causes (of the Right or the Left) which conscript Yahweh
> in order to justify their cause and political aspirations. In the reality of
> the book of Amos there are no heroes or martyrs, just the ugliness of
> war, the wailing in the streets, and the suffering of guilty and innocent
> alike. Maybe it must be so with us.
>   But the text will not allow the reader to forget the hope of another
> reality: 9:11–15 offers a vision of peace and reconstruction. Do our
> theologies in Central America proclaim peace, a peace like that in the
> textual world that is a negation of the present and that makes no sense
> apart from the horrors of today's realities? Is the God of the churches
> ultimately a God of peace? How do we, can we, contribute to national
> reconstruction during and beyond the political negotiation process?
> How can the churches participate in an alternative future that must be

built upon the ruins of conflict? Can we speculate on mediations of the future? What shape would these take? How should the Church nurture a people of peace? How can the Church's liturgy stimulate worshippers to consider and embrace peace? Questions arise abruptly and starkly in the search for a viable theology and the incarnation of Christian virtue and vision.

A literary reading of the prophetic text such as the one offered here may not solve all the hermeneutical, theological and ethical issues that arise within our Central American context. But it can invite the reader to live the tension of war and peace, and not evade it by the dating of passages as early or late or by simply opting for the peace tradition within its message. I submit that a pacifist position should consider this *literary tension* between Yahweh Lord God of Hosts and the God of peace and between judgment and hope. Perhaps the deity is to be experienced in that very tension, which is the reality of everyday life of the Church in Central America in its pilgrimage to a different future.[34]

This next piece appeared in 1999. The situation in Guatemala had changed, but now the pressing need was to try to process theologically what it might mean to rebuild the country after so many years of war.

> For those who have lived in a country at war, the movement of language between phrases saying all will die to others suggesting the survival of some makes perfect sense. "War is hell": bodies lying everywhere (6:9–10, 8:2–3), people mourning in the fields of battle (5:1–2, 16–17), the poor scratching out a living against all odds (2:6–8; 4:6–9; 5:11–13; 8:4–6), while others in the capital city drink and dine in comfort (4:1; 6:4–6)—all these descriptions of the prophetic text of Amos are not uncommon pictures in Guatemala's recent past, where hundreds of thousands have been killed, orphaned, widowed, exiled or displaced, whereas others seem to live as if untouched by the conflict.
>
> In such a situation of extreme loss, a few words which speak of rebuilding ruins, accompanied by general descriptions of peace and plenty, such as those of 9:11–15, are vague enough not to promise anything too specific but concrete enough to make the horror endurable. The brief hope passage, in other words, whatever the final decision on historical authenticity, ideologically coheres with a war context. Yet, and this is the point of the title of my article, in Guatemala we live now between the time of war and the actualization of hope. Literarily, the people live "between the lines," somewhere between 9:10 and 9:11.
>
> If one stands in that seam between despair and expectation one can look forward to the hope passage or back to the descriptions of the earlier part of the book. To look back, or to read from back to front in the Hebrew text (from left to write as it were), is to remember the experiences of want and war.[35]

The closing paragraphs of the article sum up how the text can generate a different appreciation of this juncture in this Central American country's history.

These images of politics and economics, however, lie beyond Guatemala's grasp. They are goals and hopes that can energize in the present, because they speak meaningfully and realistically to the here and now. The challenge is thinking through how to actualize these images triggered by the text into daily life at all levels of existence.

Guatemala now lives "between the lines," in that space between historical memory and a new reality. In the "meantime" the Christian Church can participate in both activities: healing wounds and working toward peace. One must never forget that living between the lines should not be a place to dig roots; it is but a stop in the journey from what was to a different tomorrow. After all, Amos does end with 9:11–15.[36]

CONCLUSION

The summaries of Amos research presented in these three essays have been rather sweeping in scope—broad in their coverage of trends and in their historical review. This third essay is unique among the three in its effort to offer creative readings of the text of Amos to those who might be interested in expanding their appreciation of its power to include these newer frontiers of theological and biblical reflection. The collections of this sort of biblical work mentioned at the beginning of this chapter present readings of different texts from across the canon. In contrast to that more "vertical" approach, as it were, I have endeavored a more "horizontal" view by considering readings of one book. There is value in looking at the same text over and over again with different lenses: Amos can become a steady and constant dialogue partner in the quest for meaning and relevance in regard to the Bible, faith, and God.

Ideally, all the disparate ways of studying this prophetic book mentioned in these essays can make a contribution to that never-ending pilgrimage. To ignore any of them, for whatever reason, is to turn our backs on a serious grappling with the text and to the text's voice at that point in time. It is to say, "Do not prophesy!" (Amos 2:12); it is to settle too easily for settled interpretations and their secure social (and scholarly!) arrangements (7:12–13). May the lion's roar continue to shake the foundations of all of our fortresses!

PART II

Bibliographies for Amos Research

4

Introductory Works, Commentaries, and Monographs

1. Bibliographies

1.1. Scholarly bibliographies specifically of the book of Amos

"Annotated Bibliography of Amos." *BV* 27, no. 2 (1993): 55–82.

> Extensive comments on 62 commentaries and other works, both academic and more lay oriented. Classifies them under the two broad headings, "conservative" and "critical." The latter label is used "because some authors in the *Critical* group may be theologically conservatives, but still they express skepticism about significant portions of Scripture" (p. 55).

Pigott, Susan M. "Amos: An Annotated Bibliography." *SwJT* 38, no. 1 (1995): 29–35.

> A survey of several general introductions, monographs, and commentaries on Amos published in English since the mid-1960s. The choice of sources summarized demonstrates a concern to service those with interests and expertise ranging from the scholarly to the pastoral and lay levels.

Thompson, Henry O. *The Book of Amos: An Annotated Bibliography*. ATLA Bibliographies 42. Lanham, Md.: Scarecrow Press, 1997.

> A comprehensive annotated bibliography, arranged alphabetically by author, of primarily English works produced since World War II. Includes a listing of dissertations on Amos. Indexes according to journal, author, biblical reference, and subject.

van der Wal, Adri. *Amos: A Classified Bibliography*. Applicatio 3. 3d ed. Amsterdam: Free University Press, 1986.

> A bibliography of approximately 1,600 titles of books and articles published from 1800 to 1986. The book is divided into two parts: the first is a listing of works according to topic (pp. 1–82); the second is organized by chapter and verse (pp. 82–266).

> Note the sources listed below under "Critical Surveys and Introductions" (3) that survey studies on the book of Amos. Many monographs and commentaries on

Amos also provide extensive bibliographies. Worthy of special mention are those in Hans Walter Wolff, *Joel and Amos*, trans. W. Janzen, S. D. McBride Jr., and C. A. Muenchow (Hermeneia; Philadelphia: Fortress, 1977); Douglas Stuart, *Hosea–Jonah* (WBC 31; Waco: Word, 1987); Shalom M. Paul, *Amos: A Commentary on the Book of Amos* (Hermeneia; Minneapolis: Fortress, 1991); and Gerhard F. Hasel, *Understanding the Book of Amos: Basic Issues in Current Interpretations* (Grand Rapids: Baker, 1991). Wolff and Paul catalog their bibliographies according to several categories (pp. 358–71 and 299–367, respectively). Stuart provides a lengthy bibliography in his introduction (pp. 274–82), as well as a list of sources before his exposition of each pericope. Hasel lists over 800 publications produced between 1969 and 1990 (pp. 121–66). For works published before 1903, see the bibliographies in W. R. Harper, *A Critical and Exegetical Commentary on Amos and Hosea* (ICC 18; Edinburgh: T. & T. Clark, 1905), clxv–clxvi and clxxvii–clxxxi.

1.2. Annotated bibliographic sources on the Old Testament for those in ministry

Ministers and students who might not have ready access to scholarly bibliographies of OT studies may find in the following sources a less daunting initial orientation to sources in Amos studies:

Childs, Brevard S. *Old Testament Books for Pastor and Teacher*, 85. Philadelphia: Westminster, 1977.
Goldingay, John, with additions and editing by M. Branson and R. Hubbard. *Old Testament Commentary Survey*, 44–45. Madison: Theological Student Fellowship, 1981.
Longman, Tremper, III. *Old Testament Commentary Survey*, 148–51. 2d ed. Grand Rapids: Baker, 1991.

2. Concordances

Andersen, Francis I., and A. Dean Forbes. *A Synoptic Concordance to Hosea, Amos, Micah*. Computer Bible 6. Wooster, Ohio: Biblical Research Association, 1972.

Andersen, Francis I., and A. Dean Forbes. *Eight Minor Prophets: A Linguistic Concordance*. Computer Bible 10. Wooster, Ohio: Biblical Research Association, 1976.
Designed to supersede the 1972 concordance. Improves on the earlier effort in layout quality, analysis, and categorization, and broadens the extent of that work to include eight prophetic books. Subdivides the data into 32 different syntactical and grammatical categories.

Pfeifer, Gerhard. *Hebräische Wortkonkordanz zum Amosbuch*. Frankfort am Main: Peter Lang, 1998.
A listing of all of the basic lexical forms in the book of Amos (Pfeifer enumerates 638), along with their inflected forms and the verses in which they appear. Closes with two charts that provide the word count for each chapter and verse and for the book as a whole (pp. 85–86).

Thompson, J. David. *A Critical Concordance to the Septuagint Amos*. Computer Bible 80. Lewiston: Edwin Mellen, 2000.
Offers various kinds of word frequency counts. The actual concordance is

divided into two parts: a forward word list and a reverse word list. The latter is alphabetical, according to the last letters of words, in order to link terms by person, number, gender, case, tense, and mood.

van der Wal, Adri, and Eep Talstra. *Amos: Concordance and Lexical Surveys*. Applicatio 2. Amsterdam: Free University Press, 1984.

> This book is divided into two parts. The first is a comprehensive concordance of nouns, verbs, articles, and prepositions (pp. 11–104); the second is a listing of the frequency of all the lexemes in the major literary units in Amos (pp. 105–35) proposed by van der Wal in "The Structure of Amos," *JSOT* 26 (1983): 107–13.

3. Critical Surveys and Introductions

3.1. Articles

Craghan, John F. "The Prophet Amos in Recent Literature." *BTB* 2, no. 3 (1972): 242–61.

> A survey, with ample bibliography, of several key topics of Amos research: the composition of the book, Amos's vocation and relationship to the cult and wisdom traditions, and the prophet's appropriation of Israel's historical traditions.

House, Paul. "Amos and Literary Criticism." *RevExp* 92, no. 2 (1995): 175–87.

> After an introduction to literary approaches (House favors a formalist perspective), surveys some recent works on Amos. Closes with a personal perspective on the structure, plot, and characterization within the book of Amos.

Hyatt, J. Philip. "The Book of Amos." *Int* 3, no. 3 (1949): 338–48.

> Designed to serve as a general introduction to the study of this prophetic text. Not a survey of scholarship, but rather a summary of the content and message of the book. Closes with a brief annotated bibliography of works on the prophets in general and on Amos in particular.

Kelley, Page H. "Contemporary Study of Amos and Prophetism." *RevExp* 63, no. 4 (1966): 375–85.

> Surveys developments in prophetic studies and their impact on Amos research. Topics include the shift from source-critical to tradition-historical and form-critical approaches, the cult, ecstasy, and the development of the prophetic office. Footnotes provide a good bibliographic source of scholarship at the time of writing.

Köhler, Ludwig. "Amos-Forschungen von 1917 bis 1932." *TRu* 4, no. 4 (1932): 195–213.

> Surveys the works (from commentaries and monographs to articles) on Amos of sixteen scholars during the stipulated time period, including Balla, Cripps, Horst, Marti, Sellin, and Weiser. The foil throughout is Cramer's *Amos, Versuch einer theologischen Interpretation* (1930).

Mays, James L. "Words about the Words of Amos: Recent Study of the Book of Amos." *Int* 13, no. 3 (1959): 259–72.

> Surveys several trends in Amos research before arguing that the prophet is best seen as grounding his message in the covenant instead of being the creator of a

new religion of universal justice. An appreciation of this foundation, he believes, helps orient the interpretation of the oracles of imminent doom, the calls to repentance, and the prophetic evaluation of the cult.

Melugin, Roy F. "Amos in Recent Research." *CR:BS* 6 (1998): 65–101.
A very thorough and well-informed survey of the breadth of different approaches to the study of the book of Amos published in the last two decades. Discussion covers commentaries, monographs, and significant articles from European, North American, and Latin American scholars.

Roberts, J. J. M. "Recent Trends in the Study of Amos." *ResQ* 13, no. 1 (1970): 1–16.
Reviews the cultic interpretation given to the prophet Amos—particularly by Würthwein—along with the critiques brought by other scholars to that perspective. Roberts appreciates the new insights but believes that the position has been overstated.

van der Woude, A. S. "Three Classical Prophets: Amos, Hosea and Micah." In *Israel's Prophetic Tradition* (Festschrift P. R. Ackroyd). Edited by R. Coggins, A. Phillips, and M. Knibb, 32–57. Cambridge: Cambridge University Press, 1982.
Deals primarily with discussions in the decades of the 1960s and 1970s concerning the theological influences behind the message of the prophet (pp. 34–43). Closes by questioning the fruitfulness of some of the debates about the redaction history of the book.

Watts, John D. W. "Amos: Across Fifty Years of Study." *RevExp* 92, no. 2 (1995): 189–93 (reprinted in idem, *Vision and Prophecy in Amos*. Expanded anniversary edition, 117–22. Macon, Ga.: Mercer University Press, 1997).
An autobiographical chronicle of the author's interest in Amos studies over the length of his scholarly career.

3.2. Books

Auld, A. G. *Amos*. OTG. Sheffield: JSOT Press, 1986.
The author is skeptical about the possibility of recovering with a high degree of certainty the prophet's own self-understanding concerning prophetic activity. The second half of this book is dedicated to exploring the message of the prophetic text from a critical perspective.

Hasel, Gerhard F. *Understanding the Book of Amos: Basic Issues in Current Interpretations*. Grand Rapids: Baker, 1991.
Separate chapters deal with important topics of Amos studies, such as the history of research, the prophet's call and origin, the influence of Israel's theological traditions, the composition of the book as a whole and of key sections (e.g., the Oracles against the Nations), and the prophet's social concern and eschatology. Extensive footnotes and bibliography (pp. 121–66).

Martin-Achard, Robert. *Amos: L'homme, le message, l'influence*. Publications de la Faculté de Théologie de l'Université de Genève 7. Geneva: Labor et Fides, 1984.
Surveys scholarly discussions in separate chapters on the person of the prophet, his message, theological underpinnings, the visions, and the relationship between Israel and the nations. An important contribution to Amos research is

the survey of how this prophetic text has been appropriated by subsequent communities—from Qumran to the modern era (pp. 161–271). Bibliography of cited works (pp. 278–301).

Wolff, Hans Walter. *Amos the Prophet: The Man and His Background*. Translated by F. R. McCurley. Philadelphia: Fortress, 1973.
> On the basis of particular literary forms and themes Wolff argues that the context of the prophet and his message is to be found within clan wisdom, instead of against the background of the cultic and legal traditions.

3.3. Journal issues dedicated to Amos include: RevExp 63, no. 4 (1966); TBT 19, no. 5 (1981); BV 27, no. 2 (1993); RevExp 92, no. 2 (1995); SwJT 38, no. 1 (1995); DosB 59 (1995); TTE 52, no. 1 (1995).

4. Representative Listing of Dictionaries and Encyclopedias

"Amos." In *Dictionary of Biblical Imagery*. Edited by L. Ryken, J. C. Wilhoit, and T. Longman III, 21–23. Downers Grove, Ill.: InterVarsity Press, 1998.

Budde, Karl. "Amos." In *Jewish Encyclopedia*. Edited by I. Singer et al., 1:530–33. New York: Ktav, n.d.

Gehman, Henry Snyder. "Amos; Amos, The Book of." In *New Westminster Dictionary of the Bible*. Edited by H. S. Gehman, 38–40. Philadelphia: Westminster, 1970.

Haran, Menahem. "Amos." In *Encyclopaedia Judaica*. Edited by C. Roth and G. Wigoder, 2:879–89. Jerusalem: Keter; New York: Macmillan, 1971.

Harrison, R. K. "Amos." In *Zondervan Pictorial Encyclopedia of the Bible*. Edited by M. C. Tenney, 1:143–50. Grand Rapids: Zondervan, 1975.

Hiebert, Robert J. V. "Amos, Theology of." In *Evangelical Dictionary of Biblical Theology*. Edited by W. A. Elwell, 17–21. Carlisle, U.K.; Grand Rapids: Baker, 1996.

Honeycutt, Roy L. "Amos." In *Holman Bible Dictionary*. Edited by T. C. Butler, 45–48. Nashville: Holman, 1991.

Horn, Siegfried H. "Amos; Amos, Book of." In *Seventh-Day Adventist Bible Dictionary*, 39–41. Washington, D.C.: Review and Herald, 1960.

Jones, Barry A. "Amos." In *Eerdmans Dictionary of the Bible*. Edited by D. N. Freedman, 56–57. Grand Rapids: Eerdmans, 2000.

Kapelrud, A. S. "Amos; Amosbuch." In *Biblisch-historisches Handwörterbuch*. Edited by B. Reicke and L. Rost, 85–87. Göttingen: Vandenhoeck & Ruprecht, 1962.

Krause, Martin. "Amos; Amosbuch." In *Reclams Bibellexikon*. Edited by K. Koch et al., 33–34. Stuttgart: Philipp Reclam, 1992.

Markert, L. "Amos; Amosbuch." *Theologische Realenzyklopädie*. Edited by G. Krause and G. Müller, 2: 471–87. Berlin: de Gruyter, 1978.

Monloubou, L. "Amos." In *DBSup* 8 (1972). Edited by L. Pirot et al. 706–24. Paris: Létouzey et Ané, 1928–1993.

Monloubou, L., and F. M. Du Buit. "Amos." In *Dictionnaire Biblique Universel*, 29–30. Paris: Desclée, 1984.

O'Brien, J. Randall. "Amos; Amos, Book of." In *Mercer Dictionary of the Bible*. Edited by W. E. Mills, 25–27. Macon, Ga.: Mercer University Press, 1990.

Reinecker, Fritz. "Amos." In *Lexikon zur Bibel*. Edited by H. Haag, 82–83. Wuppertal: R. Brockhaus, 1994.

Robertson, James. "Amos." In *International Standard Bible Encyclopedia*. Edited by J. Orr, 1:120–25. Grand Rapids: Eerdmans, 1939.

Robertson, James, and Carl Armerding. "Amos." In *International Standard Bible Ency-clopedia*. Edited by G. W. Bromiley, 1:114–17. Rev. ed. Grand Rapids: Eerdmans, 1979.

Rosenbaum, S. N. "Amos." In *Dictionary of Biblical Interpretation*. Edited by J. H. Hayes, 1:30–34. Nashville: Abingdon, 1999.

Smart, J. D. "Amos." In *The Interpreter's Dictionary of the Bible*. Edited by G. Buttrick et al., 1:116–21. Nashville: Abingdon, 1962.

Smith, Gary V. "Amos: Theology of." In *New International Dictionary of Old Testament Theology and Exegesis*. Edited by W. A. VanGemeren, 4:373–77. Grand Rapids: Zondervan, 1997.

Steinmuller, John E., and Kathryn Sullivan. "Amos; Amos, Book of." In *Catholic Biblical Encyclopedia—Old Testament*, 62–64. New York: Joseph F. Wagner, 1956.

Thomson, J. G. S. S. "Amos." In *The New Bible Dictionary*. Edited by J. D. Douglas, 32–33. Grand Rapids: Eerdmans, 1962.

Thomson, J. G. S. S. and J. A. Motyer. "Amos." In *The Illustrated Bible Dictionary*. Edited by J. D. Douglas and N. Hillyer, 1:44–45. Leicester: InterVarsity; Wheaton, Ill.: Tyndale, 1980.

Tucker, Gene M. "Amos, the Book of." In *HarperCollins Bible Dictionary*. Edited by P. J. Achtemeier, 31–32. Rev. ed. San Francisco: HarperCollins, 1996.

Willoughby, Bruce E. "Amos." In *Anchor Bible Dictionary*. Edited by D. N. Freedman, 1:203–12. Garden City, N.Y.: Doubleday, 1992.

5. Commentaries

5.1. Surveys of Commentaries

Bulkeley, Tim. "The Long and the Short of It: Two Recent Commentaries on the Book of Amos." *JSOT* 51 (1991): 119–21.
A review and comparison of the commentaries by F. I. Andersen and D. N. Freedman (1989) and J. H. Hayes (1988).

Clines, David J. A. "Metacommentating Amos." In *Of Prophets' Visions and the Wisdom of Sages* (Festschrift R. N. Whybray), ed. H. A. McKay and D. J. A. Clines, 142–60. JSOTSup 163. Sheffield: Sheffield Academic Press, 1993.
A biting critique of recent commentators of the book of Amos, who uncritically accept the ideology of the text and then endorse it in their expositions.

Mowvley, Harry. "Which Is the Best Commentary? XVI. Amos and Hosea." *ExpTim* 103, no. 12 (1992): 364–68.
Surveys the major commentaries in English of this century. Categorizes discussion according to the degree of technicality and intended audiences of each.

Watts, John D. W. "Commentaries on Amos: A Review." *RelSRev* 7, no. 2 (1981): 128–32.
A review of the commentaries by Mays (1969), Rudolph (1971), and Wolff (1969; Eng. 1977).

5.2. Commentaries within Broader Single-Volume Commentaries or Multivolume Sets

Achtemeier, Elizabeth. "Amos." In *Minor Prophets*, 1:165–236. New International Biblical Commentary. Peabody, Mass.: Hendrickson; Carlisle, U.K.: Paternoster, 1996.

A section-by-section commentary based on NIV. The primary task of this commentary is to reflect on the theological meaning of the canonical text. Within the comments words and phrases of the biblical text are highlighted in bold. More technical discussions appear in the "Additional Notes," which appear at the end of each section. Offers a general bibliography on all of the prophetic books (pp. 371–72).

Alonso Schökel, Luis, and José Luis Sicre Díaz. "Amos." In *Profetas. Comentario*. Edited by L. Alonso Schökel et al., 2:951–93. 2d ed. Nueva Biblia Española. Madrid: Cristiandad, 1987.
    Begins with an introduction to the book of Amos (pp. 951–60). Comment is generally on short pericopes but is quite detailed; includes observations on Hebrew text and literary features. This second edition closes the section on Amos with a bibliography of resources published since the first edition (1980).

Amsler, Samuel. "Amos." In E. Jacob, C. A. Keller, and S. Amsler, *Osée, Joël, Abdias, Jonas, Amos*, 157–247. 2d ed. Commentaire de l'Ancien Testament 11a. Geneva: Labor et Fides, 1982.
    Begins with short introduction and substantial bibliography (pp. 159–66). Detailed and informed comments, with technical issues of translation and textual variants appearing in the footnotes. The comments themselves focus on interpreting the text, whereas interaction with other scholars is also put in the footnotes. Stresses the polemical quality of the prophet's message.

Anderson, B. W. "Amos." In *The Eighth Century Prophets: Amos, Hosea, Isaiah, Micah*. Proclamation Commentaries. Philadelphia: Fortress, 1978.
    Comments on these four prophets are interwoven around discussions of what the author believes are their most important themes (such as judgment, the relevance of the future in the present, and social justice). Exposition of specific passages from Amos appear primarily in chapters 1–4. Concludes with "Index of Prophetic Preaching Themes" (pp. 109–11).

Asurmendi, Jesús M. "Amós." In *Amós y Oseas*, 4–30. Cuadernos Bíblicos 64. Navarra, Spain: Verbo Divino, 1993.
    Handbook format designed for the informed layperson. Comments on specific blocks of text are interspersed with inset discussions of key issues of Amos research, study questions, and points for theological reflection.

Asurmendi, Jesús M. "Amos." In *Les livres des prophètes*. Edited by J. M. Asurmendi, J. Ferry, and A. Fournier-Bidoz, 2:179–204. Paris: Bayard/Centurion, 1999.
    After a brief introduction (pp. 181–86), comments only on a select group of passages. Comments tend to be relatively brief and general, with occasional links to the NT. Labels itself a "pastoral commentary."

Barré, Michael L. "Amos." In *The New Jerome Biblical Commentary*. Edited by R. E. Brown, J. A. Fitzmyer, and R. E. Murphy, 209–16. New York: Geoffrey Chapman, 1990.
    Begins with a brief bibliography of significant works and an introduction that deals with basic issues of background, theology, and structure. Discussions are concise but surprisingly detailed and are laced with allusions to scholarly debates and extra bibliographic data.

Birch, Bruce C. "Amos." In *Hosea, Joel, and Amos*, 163–259. Westminster Bible Companion. Louisville: Westminster John Knox, 1997.
     This series is based upon NRSV and is expressly designed to be guides for the laity. The exposition of the pericopes of this prophetic text seeks to explore how it might inform the worship and social conscious of Christians today.

Canney, Maurice A. "Amos." In *A Commentary on the Bible*. Edited by A. S. Peake, 547–54. New York: Thomas Nelson & Sons; London: T. C. & E. C. Jack, 1920.
     A brief but thorough commentary that interacts throughout with the scholarship of its time. Does not hesitate to present technical observations on text-critical, translation, and background matters.

Carroll R., M. Daniel. "Amos." In *Eerdmans Commentary on the Bible*. Edited by J. W. Rogerson and J. D. G. Dunn. Grand Rapids: Eerdmans, forthcoming.
     Offers a literary reading of final form of the text, at the level of both larger passages and shorter pericopes. Attempts to incorporate insights from recent social science approaches into the exposition of the book's demand for justice and its socioethical critique of ancient Israel.

Chisolm, Robert B., Jr. "Amos." In *Interpreting the Minor Prophets*, 69–108. Grand Rapids, Zondervan, 1990.
     Exposition of larger units of the text with attention to literary structure of the final form. Closes with a section on the theology of the book.

Coggins, Richard James. "Amos." In *Joel and Amos*, 70–162. New Century Bible Commentary. Sheffield: Sheffield Academic Press, 2000.
     Based on the final form of the text, primarily as translated in NRSV. Admirably incorporates points of modern scholarly debate within discussions of passages. Attention in this verse-by-verse commentary is given more to interpretive details of textual particulars than to literary structures. Considers the possibility that some of the condemnations are exaggerated, designed for rhetorical effect.

Craigie, Peter C. "Amos." In *The Twelve Prophets*, 1:120–94. Daily Study Bible. Philadelphia: Westminster, 1984.
     Designed as a companion to the NT Daily Study Bible series of W. Barclay. Based on RSV. Although not overtly academic, does allude to scholarly discussions. Not a verse-by-verse analysis, but rather deals with pericopes in order to offer a practical and theological orientation to the book of Amos for Christian readers.

Deane, W. J., and Edgar Henry. "Amos." In *Pulpit Commentary*. Edited by H. D. M. Spence and J. S. Exell, 4:i–vii, 1–199. Reprint, Maclean, Va.: Macdonald Publishing Co., n.d.
     The discussion of each portion of the text is divided into two parts: the exposition (Deane) and homiletics (Henry). The latter contains homiletical suggestions and observations as well as actual homilies by various others. Closes with an index of the topics of the homiletics section of each of the chapters of Amos (pp. 197–99).

Deissler, Alfons. "Amos." In *Zwölf Propheten*, vol. 1: *Hosea, Joel, Amos*, 89–136. Die Neu Echter Bibel 4/4. Würzburg: Echter, 1981.

Part of a Roman Catholic series. Very brief introduction to the Minor Prophets with bibliography (pp. 5–6). Amos section also has a brief introduction and bibliography (pp. 89–93). The layout of the commentary places the biblical text and cross-references on the top of the page, with comments below (occasional observations on the Hebrew text and ancient versions appear between). Comments are on pericopes and are not overly detailed, although they do weave in critical observations.

Dines, Jennifer M. "Amos." In *Oxford Bible Commentary*. Edited by J. Barton and J. Muddiman, 581–90. Oxford: Oxford University Press, 2001.
A brief introduction indicates the main scholarly questions and options. The commentary itself offers a section-by-section close reading of the canonical text as, finally, a Second Temple product with a coherent theological outlook despite tensions. Although based on NRSV, it highlights significant Hebrew vocabulary to enable readers to grasp something of the original text.

Dorsey, David A. "Amos." In *The Literary Structure of the Old Testament: A Commentary on Genesis–Malachi*, 277–86. Grand Rapids: Baker, 1999.
More of a literary analysis of the larger sections of the prophetic text than a commentary. Sees overall structure of the book as a seven-member chiasm that is itself characterized throughout by "the prolific use of sevenfold structuring." This volume opens with an extensive introduction on the author's literary approach (pp. 15–44).

Driver, S. R. "Amos." In *The Books of Joel and Amos with Introduction and Notes*, 93–239. Cambridge Bible for Schools and Colleges. Rev. ed. Cambridge: Cambridge University Press, 1915.
An introduction to the book (pp. 93–124) is followed by extensive comments on diverse exegetical items in the biblical text (pp. 125–226). A section entitled "Additional Notes" provides eight excurses on background issues and theological terms (pp. 227–40). The English translation is that of the Cambridge Paragraph Bible. Still helpful. The first edition appeared in 1897.

Duhm, Bernhard. "Amos." In *The Twelve Prophets: A Version in the Various Poetical Measures of the Original Writings*. Translated by A. Duff, 53–80. London: Adam and Charles Black, 1912.
Begins with a general introduction to prophetism (pp. 3–52). Not a commentary, but rather a translation of the text (pp. 53–80). Passages that are deemed to be secondary appear in a different letter type.

Finley, Thomas John. "Amos." In *Joel, Amos, Obadiah*, 105–338. Wycliffe Exegetical Commentary. Chicago: Moody, 1990.
The exegetical discussion of each passage concludes with a section entitled "Additional Notes," which deals in more detail with particular lexical problems and other technical issues. Assumes the authenticity of the text. The commentary on Amos closes with excurses on the hymnic passages and the social concerns of the book (pp. 329–38).

Fosbroke, Hughell E. W., and Sidney Lovett. "The Book of Amos, Introduction and Exegesis." In *The Interpreter's Bible*. Edited by G. A. Buttrick, 6:761–853. Nashville: Abingdon, 1956.

The introduction, which is lengthy for a commentary of this sort (pp. 763–76), and the exegesis are provided by Fosbroke. The exposition, which is much briefer than the exegesis, is by Lovett. The layout of each page juxtaposes KJV and RSV at the top, while the exegesis appears in the middle and the exposition at the bottom. Interestingly, the exegesis and exposition differ on the authenticity of 9:8–15.

Gabelein, A. C. "Amos." In *The Annotated Bible: The Holy Scriptures Analyzed and Annotated*, 5:117–39. New York: Our Hope; Glasgow: Pickering & Inglis; Sydney: Christian Workers Depot, 1911.
Brief exposition designed for the layperson. Offers occasional connections to the NT and strives to present lessons for the faith and day-to-day life of the Christian. Theological framework based on classic dispensationalism (cf. comments on 9:11–15).

Gowan, Donald E. "Amos." In *New Interpreter's Bible*. Edited by L. E. Keck et al., 7:339–431. Nashville: Abingdon, 1996.
Focuses on the final form of the text with attention to insights from form-critical and rhetorical analysis. The discussion of each passage is divided into four parts: Overview, the juxtaposition of NIV and NRSV translations, Commentary, Reflections. The "Overview" surveys scholarly debates and structural items; "Reflections" connects the ideas of the passage with the rest of the Bible and Christian theology. The essence of the message of Amos is said to be the announcement of the end of God's people.

Gressmann, Hugo. "Amos." In *Die älteste Geschichtsschreibung und Prophetie Israels (von Samuel bis Amos und Hosea) übersetzt, eklärt und mit Einleitung versehen*. Edited by Hugo Gressmann et al., 323–59. SAT 3/1. 2d ed. Göttingen: Vandenhoeck & Ruprecht, 1921.
Places commentary on Amos within the discussion of the history of Israel, after the discussion of 2 Kgs. 14:23–29 (Jeroboam II). The translation of each pericope is followed by a brief section of comments. Within the translation, material deemed to be secondary is presented in a different type size.

Guenther, Allen R. "Amos." In *Hosea, Amos*, 228–370. Believers Church Bible Commentary. Scottdale, Pa.: Herald, 1998.
Designed for the layperson. Reads text as a literary whole. Each section includes an outline, an exposition of the passage, theological reflections, and an attempt to relate the OT to the mission of the church today. Closes with a helpful series of studies on pertinent issues of theology and ancient Near Eastern backgrounds (pp. 372–402).

Guthe, Hermann. "Amos." In *Die heilige Schrift des Alten Testament*. Edited by E. F. Kautzsch and A. Bertholet, 4:30–47. 4th ed. Tübingen: Mohr, 1923.
Presents translation, with passages deemed to be inauthentic in a different type size. General notes to introduce sections and pericopes, and more detailed and technical notes below translation. Older German script may be hard to read for some.

Harper, William Rainey. *A Critical and Exegetical Commentary on Amos and Hosea*, c–cxl, clxiv–clxxviii, 1–200. ICC 18. Edinburgh: T. & T. Clark, 1905.

A very technical commentary, with an emphasis on textual and lexical issues. Extensive introduction (pp. c–cxl, clxiv–clxxviii). Exegesis of each passage is preceded by a review of the readings of the ancient versions and followed by surveys of certain debated items. Both of these discussions appear in a smaller type size. Reflecting scholarly concerns of that day, Harper is especially concerned to try to identify the original words of the prophet. Dated, but still very valuable.

Hauret, Charles. "Amos." In *Amos et Osée*, 7–126. Verbum Salutis, Ancien Testament 5. Paris: Beauchesne, 1970.
   Commentary on pericopes instead of verse-by-verse. Not too detailed, yet does include occasional footnotes that demonstrate interaction with Amos research. Closes with a bibliography that is subdivided into several categories, with some of the commentaries listed with brief annotations. Includes subject and author indices (pp. 269–76).

Holland, Martin. "Amos." In *Die Propheten Joel, Amos und Obadja*, 87–231. Wuppertaler Studienbibel: Altes Testament. Wuppertal: R. Brockhaus, 1991.
   After the introduction (pp. 87–94), commentary divides into three parts: the words of Amos (1:1–6:14), the visions (7:1–9:4), and the epilogue (9:5–15). Provides a translation with notes, exegesis of passages, and discussion of teaching from a Christian perspective. Each section followed by a summary list of the major points. Not supportive of several scholarly critical reconstructions (note discussion of Wolff, pp. 91–93).

Hubbard, David Allan. "Amos." In *Joel and Amos: An Introduction and Commentary*, 87–245. TOTC. Downers Grove, Ill.: InterVarsity Press, 1989.
   Substantial introduction (pp. 87–123) followed by exposition based on RSV. Sees the covenantal relationship as foundational to the prophetic message. Thorough and up-to-date exegesis with a sensitivity to literary issues and theological implications.

Hyatt, J. Philip. "Amos." In *Peake's Commentary on the Bible*. Edited by M. Black and H. H. Rowley, 617–25. New York and London: Nelson, 1963.
   Replaces the original commentary of the same title of the turn of the century. Attempts to continue in the tradition of the earlier volume in conveying the results of current biblical scholarship in non-technical language. Comments based on RSV. Volume begins with a wide-ranging series of introductory articles for the OT (pp. 1–174). Each paragraph is numbered (in a system encompassing the entire volume). Quite detailed for a contribution to a one-volume commentary.

Keil, Carl Friedrich. "Amos." In idem and F. Delitzsch, *Biblical Commentary on the Old Testament*, vol. 10: *The Twelve Minor Prophets*, 233–336. Translated by J. Martin. Reprint, Grand Rapids: Eerdmans, 1967.
   Originally published 1882. A classic exposition of the text, whose exegesis of the Hebrew text is still helpful though dated. A short introduction (pp. 233–39) concludes that Amos was a poor shepherd, who carefully composed the entirety of the book.

King, Philip J. "Amos." In *The Jerome Biblical Commentary*. Edited by R. E. Brown, J. A. Fitzmyer, and R. E. Murphy, 245–52. Englewood Cliffs, N.J.: Prentice-Hall, 1968.

This commentary places the prophets in what is deemed to be their historical order. Accordingly, Amos is the first canonical prophet to be commented on and follows introductory articles on the prophetic literature and Hebrew poetry (pp. 223–37 and 238–44, respectively). Offers a short introduction (pp. 245–46) and comments on each pericope.

Kraft, Charles F. "Amos." In *The Interpreter's One-Volume Commentary on the Bible*. Edited by C. M. Laymon, 465–76. Nashville: Abingdon, 1971.
Very brief introduction (p. 465). Provides succinct comments (moderately critical) of each short pericope.

Lehrman, S. M. "Amos." In *The Twelve Prophets*. Edited by A. Cohen, 80–124. 2d ed. Soncino Books of the Bible. London: Soncino Press, 1948.
Hebrew text with Jewish Publication Society translation appears in the upper half of each page, with concise notes below. The notes deal only with particular individual words or phrases. Textual variants in some verses appear in a smaller font between the notes and the biblical text. Takes rabbinic tradition into account. Written expressly from a Jewish perspective.

Limburg, James. "Amos." In *Hosea–Micah*, 79–126. Interpretation. Atlanta: John Knox, 1988.
Exposition in this series is based on RSV, with an eye to communicating the results of historical and theological study in a relevant way. After a survey of the entire book, the author discusses only those sections of the text that he feels would be of special value for teaching and preaching. He highlights those dealing with social ethics and empty ritual.

Maclaren, Alexander. "Amos." In *Exposition of Holy Scripture*, 6:143–76. Reprint, Grand Rapids: Baker, 1974.
Treatment of only five selected passages (3:3; 4:4–13; 5:14–15; 6:1–8; 8:1–14). Reflections on these verses aim to draw lessons for the individual Christian and the Christian church.

Marsh, John. "Amos." In *Amos and Micah: Introduction and Commentary*, 25–75. Torch Bible Commentaries. London: SCM, 1959.
First part is a general introduction to prophetism (pp. 9–21). Although explicitly designed for the lay reader (p. 7), it does express a moderately critical stance on occasion: even if a passage does not go directly back to the historical prophet, all of the book is ultimately grounded in the tradition of an "Amos-community" (note, e.g., his comments at 6:2 or 9:11–15). General comments on individual verses or on short pericopes.

Marti, Karl. "Amos." In *Dodekapropheten*, 144–227. Kurzer Hand-Commentar zum Alten Testament 13. Tübingen: Mohr (Siebeck), 1904.
An introduction (pp. 144–54) precedes the technical verse-by-verse commentary. A celebrated early critical work. Before the discussion of each pericope a short section deals with issues of a more general nature, which includes historical, critical, and literary data.

Martin-Achard, Robert. "The End of the People of God: A Commentary on the Book of Amos." In idem and S. Raul Re'emi, *God's People in Crisis: A Commentary on the Book of Amos and a Commentary on the Book of Lamentations*, 1–71. ITC. Edinburgh: Handsel; Grand Rapids: Eerdmans, 1984.

Part of a series designed to communicate the theological message and contemporary relevance of the biblical text. Written from a critical perspective, at the same time it assumes the unity of the Bible and continually seeks to link the prophetic word with NT passages.

McComiskey, Thomas E. "Amos." In *Expositor's Bible*, vol. 7: *Daniel, Minor Prophets*. Edited by F. E. Gabelein et al., 267–331. Grand Rapids: Zondervan, 1985.

The introduction (pp. 269–77) assumes the authenticity of the whole book, with the possible exception of 7:10–17, which could have come from the hand of a disciple. As in the case of the rest of this series, the modern translation that forms the basis of the exegesis is NIV. The exposition of each pericope is followed by a brief section entitled "Notes," which focuses on specific technical discussions.

McKeating, Henry. "The Book of Amos." In *The Books of Amos, Hosea and Micah*, 12–70. Cambridge Bible Commentary. Cambridge: Cambridge University Press, 1971.

Begins with a short, general introduction to the eighth-century prophets (pp. 1–11). Based on NEB. More technical text-critical observations and options appear in footnotes. Provides helpful comments on specific particulars in each verse.

Melugin, Roy F. "Amos." In *Harper's Bible Commentary*. Edited by J. L. Mays et al., 720–25. San Francisco: Harper & Row, 1988.

Mentions general critical position concerning the composition of the book in the introduction, but comments interpret primarily the "completed text" (p. 720). Is most attentive to literary dimensions and imagery instead of focusing on historical issues.

Melugin, Roy F. "Amos." In *Asbury Bible Commentary*. Edited by E. E. Carpenter and W. McCown, 735–49. Grand Rapids: Zondervan, 1992.

While the introduction says that the "material in Amos, for the most part, was originally delivered orally and later written down and preserved by an ongoing group of disciples" (p. 736), comments do not allude to critical issues but rather focus on the final form of the text. Seeks to highlight structure and imagery in the exposition of the principal points of the book's major sections.

Menezes, Rui de. "Amos." In *The International Bible Commentary: A Catholic and Ecumenical Commentary for the Twenty-First Century*. Edited by W. R. Farmer, 1132–41. Collegeville, Minn.: Liturgical Press, 1998.

Moderately critical, comments on large sections of the final form of the prophetic text. Cites ideas and explicit quotations of Amos found in other canonical and apocryphal books and Catholic liturgy. Divides the body of the book of Amos into two primary parts: International Justice (1:3–2:16), Internal Justice (3:1–9:10).

Mowvley, Harry. "Amos." In *The Books of Amos & Hosea*, pp. 3–91. Epworth Commentaries. London: Epworth, 1991.

Part of a series renewing the Epworth Preacher's Commentaries of the 1950s and 1960s. Based on REB. Exposition demonstrates acquaintance with scholarly debates and occasionally offers theological applications for Christians today. Contains excurses on "the Word of the Lord," "Honest" (i.e., "righteous"), "Life," and "the Day of the Lord."

Myers, Jacob M. "Amos." In *The Books of Hosea, Joel, Amos, Obadiah, and Jonah*, 97–149. Layman's Bible Commentary 14. Atlanta: John Knox, 1959.
Commentary is based on RSV. The introduction (pp. 97–102) says that the purpose of the book of Amos was to preserve the word of the prophet, and that his message was basically to announce judgment of Israel. Sees most of the book as authentic; alludes to critical perspectives in nontechnical fashion in accordance with the purpose of the series. Comments on pericopes instead of verse-by-verse.

Niehaus, Jeffrey. "Amos." In *The Minor Prophets: An Exegetical and Expository Commentary*, vol. 1: *Hosea, Joel, and Amos*. Edited by T. E. McComiskey, 315–494. Grand Rapids: Baker, 1992.
Argues that this prophetic book consistently reflects the pattern of the covenant lawsuit and utilizes covenant vocabulary (pp. 317–28). Follows the format of the series: (a) the discussion of each pericope is preceded by two columns of English translation—the first is the author's own, the second is NRSV; (b) each page is divided into two parts: the top section is an exegesis of the Hebrew text; the bottom offers a fuller exposition of the exegetical observations.

Ogilvie, Lloyd J. "Amos." In *The Communicator's Commentary*, vol. 20: *Hosea–Jonah*, 261–364. Dallas: Word, 1990.
The author, editor of the series, offers what he deems most helpful to expositors of the biblical message: some technical commentary in a readable (sometimes conversational) style, outlines of the passages, applications, and illustrations from contemporary life. Utilizes NKJV.

Osty, Émile. "Amos." In *Amos, Osée*, 7–60. 2d ed. SBJ. Paris: Cerf, 1960.
The introduction (pp. 9–19) is followed by the translation of the Hebrew text into French and notes. The translation appears on the top part of each page, with the comments in the form of footnotes below. The occasional observation on a textual variation from the ancient versions is located between the two. Holds that Amos's poor life in the desert has marked his life and message with fiery independence and an abhorrence of luxury.

Padilla, Washington. "Amós." In *Amós–Abdías*, 9–201. Comentario Bíblico Hispanoamericano. Miami: Editorial Caribe, 1989.
Exposition of the text with the express purpose of attempting to contextualize extensively the prophetic message into the realities of modern Latin America. Contends that the book denounces an idolatry (i.e., a perverse understanding of Yahweh) manifest in injustice and oppression. Contextualizing discussions are highlighted against a blue background.

Pusey, E. B. "Amos." In *The Minor Prophets with a Commentary. Explanatory and Practical and Introduction to the Several Books*, 1:223–341. Reprint, Buffalo: William S. Hein, 1986.
Introduction to the life and message of Amos (pp. 223–32) followed by detailed verse-by-verse comments. Discussions interact with the NT, the Church Fathers,

and nineteenth-century scholars. Reads the prophetic text from an overtly Christological perspective.

Ries, Claude A. "Amos." In *The Wesleyan Bible Commentary*. Edited by C. W. Carter, 3:609–35. Grand Rapids: Eerdmans, 1969.
> Includes a translation of each portion of the biblical text before its exposition, so not much space is available for the exposition itself. Comments are brief and general. Concludes with one-page bibliography (p. 635).

Rinaldi, Giovanni. "Amos." In *I Profeti minori*, 1:121–218. La Sacra Bibbia. Turin: Marietti, 1953.
> The first half of this volume is an introduction to prophetism (pp. 3–120). After a brief introduction to the book of Amos (pp. 123–31) the commentary juxtaposes the text in Italian and Latin on facing pages. Beneath each are technical notes on the corresponding translation and detailed observations on the passage. Comments interact extensively with Amos research and allude also to relevant ancient Near Eastern data. An interesting addition are the photos that close out the book, two of which are of twentieth-century threshing instruments (cf. 1:3).

Rosenberg, A. J. "Amos." In *The Book of the Twelve Prophets*, 1:114–71. New York: Judaica Press, 1991.
> Provides Hebrew of biblical text and of rabbinic commentators. Translation and most comments are drawn primarily from Rashi, although also cites other rabbinic sources (e.g., Ibn Ezra, Redak). An appendix (pp. 242–54) provides a discussion based on these sources rather than simply quotations.

Rudolph, Wilhelm. "Amos." In *Joel–Amos–Obadja–Jonah*, 93–292. KAT 13/2. Gütersloh: Gerd Mohn, 1971.
> An important, moderately critical commentary. Helpful introduction to the book of Amos, with lengthy bibliography (pp. 95–108). Very detailed, with extensive discussions on text-critical matters and lengthy interaction with other scholarly opinions. Often taken as a foil for the commentary by H. W. Wolff, now translated and appearing in the Hermeneia series (see below).

Ryan, D. "Amos." In *A New Catholic Commentary on Holy Scripture*. Edited by R. C. Fuller, L. Johnston, and C. Kearns, 693–701. Rev. ed. Nashville: Nelson, 1975.
> A significant revision of *A Catholic Commentary on Holy Scripture* (1953), based on RSV. Throughout the volume each paragraph in the introductory articles and commentaries is given a number in order to facilitate cross-referencing. Comments are brief, but substantial, and reflect an acquaintance with scholarship.

Ryken, Leyland. "Amos." In *A Complete Literary Guide to the Bible*. Edited by L. Ryken and T. Longman III, 337–47. Grand Rapids: Zondervan, 1993.
> Proposes to look at this prophetic book under the literary genre of "satire," which exposes and condemns human folly and vice. Although the ultimate aim is positive—i.e., to generate change in the reader—the technique is bitingly condemnatory. Believes that Amos is the best example in the Bible of "informal satire," with a greater interest in the message than in comprehensive literary art.

Sanderson, Judith E. "Amos." In *The Women's Bible Commentary*. Edited by C. A. Newsome and S. H. Ringe, 205–9. Louisville: Westminster John Knox, 1992.
> A feminist approach to the prophetic text. Although she praises the prophet for
> championing the poor, Sanderson wonders why he does not single out women
> as particular objects of concern (as they are often "disproportionately repre-
> sented among the poor") and asks whether the criticism of wealthy women (in
> 4:1) might not represent a certain patriarchal bias.

Sellin, E. "Amos." In *Das Zwölfprophetenbuch übersetzt und eklärt*, 144–225. KAT 12/1.
Leipzig: A. Deichert, 1922.
> A lengthy introduction (pp. 144–60) precedes the verse-by-verse commentary.
> An important early critical work; note that words and clauses considered sec-
> ondary are put in a separate typeset from the rest of the translation. Technical,
> with treatment of ancient versions, meter, and interaction with other scholarly
> sources.

Sgargi, Giorgio. "Amos." In *Gioele, Amos, Abdia*. Edited by G. Sgargi, xviii–lxxxviii,
101–256. Biblia, I libri della Biblia interpretati dalla grande Tradizione: AT 32–34.
Bologna: EDB, 1998.
> The extensive introduction begins with a listing of textual variants and conjec-
> tures for the Masoretic, Septuagint, Peshitta, and Vulgate and gives the tenden-
> cies of the Targum (pp. xviii–xxix) before giving an orientation to the ten
> commentators who will be cited in the rest of the volume (pp. xxxi–lxxxvi). A
> verse-by-verse presentation of the Hebrew text follows (pp. 102–256), which
> compares a standard Italian translation with the versions and Targum, as well as
> offering observations of these commentators from over the centuries—from the
> early church through the medieval era and Reformation until modern times.

Smith, Billy K. "Amos." In *Hosea, Joel, Amos, Obadiah, Jonah*, 89–129. Layman's Bible
Book Commentary 13. Nashville: Broadman, 1982.
> Popular commentary, based on RSV. Comments on larger sections of the biblical
> text, instead of on shorter pericopes or individual verses. No discussion of critical
> issues, but does offer a good level of exposition for lay readers (although without
> attempting to contextualize the prophetic books' messages to the modern world).

Smith, Billy K. "Amos." In B. K. Smith and F. S. Page, *Amos, Obadiah, Jonah*, 23–170.
NAC 19B. Nashville: Broadman, 1995.
> This series is presented as being in continuity with the American Commentary
> of the end of the nineteenth century and is aimed primarily at ministers and stu-
> dents. The exposition is based on NIV but also consistently refers to the Hebrew
> text. Discussions of scholarly debates and technical issues refer only to English
> language sources.

Smith, Gary V. "Amos: The End Has Come!" In *The Prophets as Preachers: An Introduction to the Hebrew Prophets*, 47–65. Nashville: Broadman & Holman, 1994.
> Designed as textbook for classroom use. Smith's approach, which utilizes com-
> munication theory and the sociology of knowledge (pp. 5–45), proposes to inves-
> tigate the dynamics of how the prophets attempted to transform Israel's way of
> thinking and living. Explains the skill of the prophet in announcing that Israel
> was soon to be severely judged.

Smith, Gary V. "Amos." In *Hosea, Amos, Micah*, 203–418. NIV Application Commentary. Grand Rapids: Zondervan, 2001.

    Follows the three-division discussion format of the series: Original Meaning, Bridging Contexts, Contemporary Significance. In the introduction Smith argues that the prophet is trying to confront and expose the erroneous, self-deceptive worldview and lifestyle of Israel. Offers applications at various levels: the individual believer, the church, and society in general. Smith has published several studies on Amos, so the reader can be confident of a careful exegesis undergirding these applications.

Smith, George Adam. "Amos." In *The Book of the Twelve Prophets*, vol. 1: *Amos, Hosea, Micah*, 55–216. Rev. ed. London: Hodder and Stoughton; New York: Harper & Brothers, 1928.

    This revised edition takes into consideration advances in critical studies of the prophets since the first edition's appearance in 1896. Argues that Amos's ultimate goal was to combat a false religion that saw Yahweh as primarily a nationalistic god and that trusted in the efficacy of ritual. For the prophet there could be no separation of justice from the character of God and the kind of life demanded of Israel. Weaves into the textual discussions lessons for Christian faith in the modern world.

Smith, George Adam. "Amos." In *The Expositor's Bible*. Edited by W. R. Nicoll, 4:456–94. Grand Rapids: Eerdmans, 1947.

    Not a verse-by-verse commentary. Discussions build on the textual data to explore issues related to Israel's religious life. Occasional footnotes deal with more technical points of the Hebrew text and LXX. Grounds the message of the prophet especially on a strong moral sense. Dedicates much space to critical discussions, which he couples with a reverent respect for the divine authority behind the text.

Smith, Ralph L. "Amos: An Introduction and Commentary." In *Broadman Bible Commentary*. Edited by C. J. Allen, 7:81–141. Nashville: Broadman, 1972.

    Part of a series designed for ministers and laypersons. Based upon RSV. The introduction focuses primarily on the theology of the book (pp. 81–88). Balances exegesis and the occasional more technical observations with more fundamental exposition. Does mention critical positions in discussions of particular passages.

Snaith, N. H. "Amos." In *Amos, Hosea, and Micah*, 11–51. Epworth Preachers' Commentaries. London: Epworth, 1956.

    Part of a series designed to communicate the essential message and relevance of the biblical text. As Snaith holds that prophetic oracles were originally short, the exposition is of short pericopes, with an eye toward explicating difficult words, phrases, and key theological ideas.

Stuart, Douglas. "Amos." In *Hosea–Jonah*, 273–400. WBC 31. Waco: Word, 1987.

    Provides broad introduction with lengthy bibliography (pp. 274–95). Argues that the prophets consciously based their message on the Mosaic covenant and applied its blessings and curses to their contexts (pp. xxxi–xlii). In accordance with the series format, discussion of each pericope follows the sequence: bibliography, translation, notes, form/structure/setting, comment, and explanation. The notes explain particulars of the translation; the comment and explanation offer fuller exposition, with the latter occasionally probing theological implications.

Sunukjian, Donald R. "Amos." In *The Bible Knowledge Commentary: An Exposition of the Scriptures by Dallas Seminary Faculty.* Edited by J. F. Walvoord and R. B. Zuck, 1:1425–52. Wheaton, Ill.: Victor, 1985.
Introduction and commentary from a dispensational perspective, designed for the layperson. Basic exposition of the English text based upon NIV.

Sweeney, Marvin A. "Amos." In idem et al., *The Twelve Prophets,* 1:189–276. Berit Olam. Collegeville, Minn.: Liturgical Press, 2000.
The introduction surveys recent theories on the redaction of the Book of the Twelve (pp. xv–xlii). Attempts to provide a synchronic literary analysis of this prophetic book. Proposes that the text argues for the destruction of Bethel and advocates the reunification and restoration of all Israel around the proper worship of Yahweh in Jerusalem and the Davidic monarchy.

Unger, Merrill F. "Amos." In *Unger's Commentary on the Old Testament,* 2:1773–1811. Chicago: Moody, 1981.
Brief, lay-oriented comments on each verse; based on KJV. Dispensational orientation evident at 9:11b. Begins with a short introduction (pp. 1773–74), no bibliography.

Vawter, Bruce. "Amos." In *Amos, Hosea, Micah, with an Introduction to Classical Prophecy,* 20–22, 29–75. Old Testament Message 7. Wilmington, Del.: Glazier, 1981.
Begins with a general introduction to prophecy (pp. 9–20). Comments are not very technical nor verse by verse, but rather offer quite brief observations on pericopes. Critical positions concerning the authenticity of passages are alluded to. Although one of the aims of the series is to be "theological" (p. 8), this purpose is not well reflected in the comments.

Vázquez, Bernardino. *Dios es justo y fiel: Oseas–Habacuc,* 41–68. Estudio Bíblico ELA. Puebla, Mexico: Ediciones las Américas, 1994.
Part of a series of lay-level commentaries designed to accompany a quarterly study of the Bible. Amos is presented in three lessons. Comments interspersed with charts, as well as with applications to modern Latin American evangelical church context.

Ward, James M. *Amos and Isaiah: Prophets of the Word of God,* 17–140. Nashville: Abingdon, 1969.
The preface states that Ward endeavors to explore the theology and ethics of the prophet for relevant lessons for today. Passages are assigned and treated under three categories: "Word of the Prophet—Word of the Lord," "The Righteousness of God and the Righteousness of Man," and "The Book of Amos and Israelite Worship." Integrates scholarly issues and debates into the discussions of these broader concerns.

Ward, James M. "Amos." In *Amos–Hosea,* 1–49. Knox Preaching Guides. Atlanta: John Knox, 1981.
Exposition of a general sort designed to offer ideas for communicating biblical themes and prophetic demands to a modern audience.

Weiser, Artur. "Amos." In *Das Buch der zwölf kleiner Propheten*, vol. 1: *Die Propheten Hosea–Micha*, 127–206. ATD 24. 2d ed. Göttingen: Vandenhoeck & Ruprecht, 1979.
 Weiser also wrote a significant one-volume critical commentary on this prophetic book (see below). This volume begins with a very brief introduction to the Book of the Twelve, with bibliography (pp. 8–10). Detailed comments, with more technical issues and scholarly interaction relegated to the footnotes. Reorders text in some places and thus the comments accordingly (note on chaps. 7–9, pp. 180–206). Older German script might prove difficult to read for some.

Wellhausen, Julius. "Amos." In *Die kleinen Propheten übersetzt und erklärt*, pp. 67–96. 4th ed. Reprint, Berlin: de Gruyter, 1963.
 Opens with the author's translation of the Minor Prophets. The comments on individual verses and pericopes are brief, sometimes exceedingly so. The overall tenor of the observations reflects Wellhausen's views on Israelite religion and prophetism.

Winton, George B. "Amos." In *Pleaders for Righteousness: Studies in the Prophecies of Amos and Hosea*, 32–138. Leadership Training Series. Nashville: Cokesbury, 1928.
 Part of a series aimed at Christian workers, of which each volume is made up of twelve chapters. Each chapter ends with questions for discussion. In this volume six of the twelve pertain to Amos; the first is a general introduction to prophetism. The chapters are arranged topically. The prophet spoke out against the evils of social life and a corrupt religion.

Wolfe, Rolland Emerson. "Amos." In *Meet Amos and Hosea, the Prophets of Israel*, 3–69. New York: Harper & Brothers, 1945.
 Its stated goal is to popularize the findings of critical scholarship. Argues that the prophet, who was later perhaps imprisoned and executed, condemned the nation for its failure to live according to the divine demand for an ethical religion.

Wolff, Hans Walter. "Amos." In *Joel and Amos*, 87–335. Translated by W. Janzen, S. D. McBride Jr., and C. A. Muenchow. Hermeneia. Philadelphia: Fortress, 1977.
 Now a classic in Amos research. A detailed commentary utilizing form, tradition, and redaction criticisms. Known for its position that the prophet's message found its home within clan wisdom and for Wolff's theory of a six-stage compositional history. Analysis of each pericope is preceded by a bibliography and observations on text-critical issues. Closes with a lengthy bibliography (pp. 358–71) and indices of passages, Hebrew words, subjects, and authors.

5.2. Single-Volume Commentaries

Andersen, Francis I., and David Noel Freedman. *Amos: A New Translation with Introduction and Commentary*. AB 24A. Garden City, N.Y.: Doubleday, 1989.
 A massive commentary full of exegetical, literary, and historical details. In addition to the extensive and wide-ranging introduction at the beginning (pp. 1–178), which includes a lengthy bibliography, each of the four major sections of the exposition is preceded by another introductory discussion of primarily literary matters. Argues for the authenticity of most of the book and understands the various parts of the book to reflect different stages in the ministry of the prophet. Closes with indices of subjects, authors, Hebrew words, and scriptural references (pp. 927–79).

Bič, Milos. *Das Buch Amos*. Berlin: Evangelische Verlagsanstalt, 1969.

Offers only a brief introduction (pp. 5–14), and discusses the text more on a pericope than a verse-by-verse format. In Amos studies Bič is known for his article on the notion that the term *nōqēd* in 1:1 means that Amos was a hepatoscoper (*VT* 1, no. 4 [1951]:293–96); not surprisingly Bič provides a lengthy discussion of the book's superscription (pp. 15–21).

Bovati, Pietro, and Roland Meynet. *Le livre du prophète Amos*. Rhétorique biblique 3. Paris: Cerf, 1994.

Not a commentary in the traditional sense. Claims to be a new genre of commentary that systematically applies rhetorical analysis to a prophetic book. The authors see the book as a whole and its constituent parts as following concentric patterns. Each of these are presented in charts with a variety of font styles to highlight interconnections. The primary theological theme is the justice of God.

Bovati, Pietro, and Roland Meynet. *La fin d'Israël: Paroles d'Amos*. Lire la Bible 121. Paris: Cerf, 1994.

A condensation of the more extensive *Le livre du prophète Amos*. The title is taken from Amos 8:2.

Budde, Karl. "Zu Text und Auslegung des Buches Amos." *JBL* 43 (1924): 46–131; 44 (1925): 63–122.

Though appearing in journal form, these two articles are a commentary on the entire book, expositing the Hebrew text. The first part goes through Amos 6; the second covers Amos 7–9.

Carbone, Sandro P., and Giovanni Rizzi. *Il libro di Amos, lettura ebraica, greca e aramaica*. Bologna: Dehoniane, 1993.

Separate introductory chapters on the textual data, tendencies, and ideas of the MT, LXX, and Targum. The bulk of the volume presents these three versions in parallel columns with notes that point out the similarities and differences between them. The conclusion summarizes findings and attempts to discern the reasons for divergences.

Cramer, Karl. *Amos, Versuch einer theologischen Interpretation*. BWANT 3/15. Stuttgart: Kohlhammer, 1930.

An analysis of theological and exegetical issues (over 20 chapters on distinct topics) rather than a verse-by-verse commentary. Topics include: the vocation of Amos; the belief in election; the prophet as revolutionary, demagogue, or reformer; the Law; and whether Amos had any hope for the future. Holds to the importance of covenant in the message of the prophet. Concludes with a helpful summary list of findings (pp. 213–15).

Cripps, Richard S. *A Commentary on the Book of Amos*. Limited Classical Reprint Library. Reprint, Minneapolis: Klock & Klock, 1981.

Preface to the second edition (pp. xvii–xxxix) provides an update of prophetic and Amos research since the publication of the 1929 edition. Lengthy introduction (pp. 1–110) is followed by detailed exegesis of each verse that focuses on individual words and phrases. "Additional Notes" on items in each chapter (pp. 279–324) and four excurses (pp. 325–48) fill out the exposition. In addition to the general topical index, Cripps presents indices of the ancient documents and Hebrew terms.

de Waard, Jan, and William A. Smalley. *A Translator's Handbook on the Book of Amos*. Helps for Translators. New York: United Bible Societies, 1979.
Designed to aid translators of Amos around the world, the detailed exposition of each pericope explores options of interpretation that might affect the clear communication of the message of the text into different languages and contexts. Utilizes RSV and TEV as the primary foils for discussion. Appendix argues for chiastic structures throughout the book (pp. 189–214). Provides a glossary of technical exegetical and linguistic terms (pp. 266–70).

Doorly, William J. *Prophet of Justice: Understanding the Book of Amos*. New York: Paulist, 1989.
A popularization of scholarly research (specifically the work of Robert Coote). This lay-oriented commentary is geared to making the prophet's message of socioeconomic justice applicable to the modern world.

Edghill, Ernest Arthur. *The Book of Amos with Notes*. Westminster Commentary. 2d ed. London: Methuen, 1926.
Because of the premature death of the author, an introduction is provided by G. A. Cooke (pp. xi–xxv), who also edited and revised the notes. The discussion of each pericope is preceded by an introductory section of varying size that summarizes what follows and probes theological questions. The prophetic text (from RV) appears at the top of the page, with corresponding comments beneath. Closes with an appendix (pp. 95–116), which presents the author's translation and a rearrangement of the text that he feels better represents the progression of thought.

Hammershaimb, Erling. *The Book of Amos: A Commentary*. Translated by J. Sturdy. New York: Schocken; Oxford: Basil Blackwell, 1970.
Brief, but helpful exegetical comments on the Hebrew text. No concern for attempting to reconstruct the text, and little interaction with or allusions to other scholarly positions except in occasional footnotes.

Hayes, John H. *Amos, the Eighth-Century Prophet: His Times & His Preaching*. Nashville: Abingdon, 1988.
Explains the text against a unique historical reconstruction of the context for the prophet. Believes that Amos's preaching could have been limited to a few days before the fall festival of 750–749, during a time of political and economic decline when Jeroboam II was facing a regional anti-Assyrian conspiracy led by Pekah. Helpful bibliographies precede the discussion of each pericope.

Honeycutt, Roy L. *Amos and His Message: An Expository Commentary*. Nashville: Broadman, 1963.
An expository commentary intended to probe the relevance of the prophetic text for today. Though designed for broad use, the exposition—through the discussion, footnotes, and bibliography—demonstrates an awareness of critical issues and other scholarly works.

Howard, J. K. *Amos among the Prophets*. Grand Rapids: Baker, 1968.

Begins with a general introduction to prophecy before turning to the book of Amos. An informed exposition written for the layperson.

Jeremias, Jörg. *The Book of Amos: A Commentary.* Translated by D. W. Stott. OTL. Louisville: Westminster John Knox, 1998.
A creative attempt to coordinate a form- and tradition-critical approach with an appreciation of the artistry of the final form. Posits that the entire book postdates the fall of Samaria and to a large degree that of Judah. Different redactional levels are identified by different font styles in the translation. Offers excursuses on the doxologies and the *marzēaḥ* feast. The reader is encouraged to consult Jeremias's *Hosea und Amos* (see below under "Monographs") for more detailed discussions on a number of issues. No interaction with social science or literary studies.

Kelley, Page H. *Amos: Prophet of Social Justice.* Grand Rapids: Baker, 1972.
Part of Baker's Contemporary Discussion Series. Each chapter closes with questions for reflection. The author states: "These discussion guides have been prepared out of a deep conviction that the Word of God has something vital to say to people in the twentieth century" (p. 6).

Loss, Nicolò M. *Amos e introduzione al profetismo biblico: versione, introduzione, note.* Nuovissima Versione Della Bibbia Dai Testi Originali 29. 2d ed. Rome: Paoline, 1984.
The introduction to prophetism occupies the first part of the book (pp. 7–66). The commentary on Amos itself is preceded by a lengthy introduction (pp. 69–107). Divides commentary into two large sections: the words (1:3–6:14) and the visions of Amos (7:1–9:10), with a closing section on the "Conclusion" (9:11–15). Cross-references in the margins; no interaction with other scholars.

Maag, Viktor. *Text, Wortschaft und Begriffswelt des Buches Amos.* Leiden: Brill, 1951.
The title of this work is a good reflection of its content. It is divided into four parts. The first offers a translation of each pericope with critical notes (pp. 1–62); the second is a listing in alphabetical order of the vocabulary of the book of Amos, with references to relevant scholarly sources (pp. 63–114); the third presents discussions of the difficult words from that list (pp. 115–207); and the last deals with twenty-five topics of the prophetic text by looking at the vocabulary, textual data, and scholarly perspectives concerning each issue (pp. 208–52).

Martin-Achard, Robert. *L'homme de Teqoa: Message et commentaire du livre d'Amos.* Aubonne, France: Moulin, 1990.
An attempt to relate the message of the prophet to a modern secularized society anesthetized to the word of God. The introduction locates the person and message of Amos in Israel of the eighth century B.C.E. and summarizes some critical positions for the reader (pp. 9–34). The commentary follows in a smaller type size. Discussions offer detailed observations on pericopes. No bibliography or indices.

Mays, James Luther. *Amos: A Commentary.* OTL. Philadelphia: Westminster, 1969.
A form-critical commentary written in a clear and concise style. The longest part of the introduction (pp. 1–14) deals with the theology of the book. Divides the text into thirty-three parts for discussion. A very select bibliography and judicious use of footnotes. Scholarly debates smoothly integrated into the exposition.

McFadyen, John Edgar. *A Cry for Justice: A Study in Amos*. Short Course Series. New
York: Charles Scribner's Sons, 1912.
> Not a commentary in the classical sense, but rather a series of nine studies
> designed as an orientation for ministers and laypersons. MacFadyen focuses par-
> ticularly on issues of social justice with occasional applications to his context
> (Britain at the beginning of the twentieth century). An appendix presents an
> annotated bibliography (pp. 139–47).

Mitchell, H. G. *Amos: An Essay in Exegesis*. Rev. ed. Boston: Houghton, Mifflin, 1900.
> An introductory section dealing with the person and date of the prophet and the
> structure is followed by observations on each phrase in every verse of the book
> (in the English version, with Hebrew relegated to the footnotes; pp. 36–175).
> The author's analysis is presented in a helpful chart form (pp. 33–35). Closes with
> three appendices: "Amos and the Hexateuch," "The Theology of Amos," and
> "Amos among the Prophets" (pp. 176–209).

Motyer, J. A. *The Day of the Lion: The Message of Amos*. Bible Speaks Today. Downers
Grove, Ill.: InterVarsity Press, 1974.
> Part of a series designed primarily to offer exposition that is pertinent to the life of
> the Christian and the church today. An acquaintance with Amos research and an
> interaction with technical issues are evidenced in the discussions and in the foot-
> notes. Highlights the prophet's moral indignation and the call to religious reform.

Neher, André. *Amos: Contribution à l'étude du prophétisme*. 2d ed. Paris: J. Vrin, 1950.
> This work is divided into three parts. The first offers comments on the text (pp.
> 3–152); the second analyzes the prophet's message (pp. 153–234); and the third,
> and briefest, is a more general discussion on prophets and prophetism (pp.
> 235–78). The comments on passages in the first part serve as starting points for
> broader theological reflections (e.g., on the "universalism" in Amos 1–3—which
> Neher links to a Noahic covenant concept—and the worship of Baal).

Paul, Shalom M. *Amos: A Commentary on the Book of Amos*. Hermeneia. Minneapolis:
Fortress, 1991.
> Although this is the second volume on Amos in this series, it is not billed as a
> replacement to the commentary by Wolff (1977). The strengths of this volume
> lie in the illuminating and ubiquitous use of materials from the ancient Near East
> and the careful observation of literary techniques at micro- and broader levels.
> Excursuses on a variety of important topics in Amos research are interspersed
> among the discussions of the pericopes. Very extensive bibliography, divided into
> sixteen different categories (pp. 299–367), followed by indices of passages,
> authors, and subjects (pp. 369–406).

Robinson, Theodore H. *The Book of Amos: Hebrew Text Edited with Critical and Grammatical Notes*. Texts for Students 30. London: SPCK, 1923, 1951.
> Each page is divided into two parts: the upper contains the Hebrew text, the bot-
> tom offers comments on grammatical, syntactical, and lexical issues in selected
> verses. Closes with a listing of the vocabulary of the book, with verse location
> and appropriate parsing.

Rösel, Hartmut N. *The Book of Amos* (Heb.). Haifa, Israel: University of Haifa Press, 1990.

A detailed, critical verse-by-verse commentary, which utilizes a wide range of sources—from rabbinic commentaries to modern works and archaeological data. Posits a preexilic Judaic composition of the book based upon the words of the eighth-century prophet.

Routtenberg, Hyman J. *Amos of Tekoa: A Study in Interpretation*. New York: Vantage, 1971.
Originally a dissertation completed at Boston University in 1943. Presents rabbinic views on the person of the prophet and on the entire book.

Ruíz González, Gregorio. *Comentarios hebreos medievales al libro de Amós*. Serie 1; Estudios, 31; Teología I, 20. Madrid: Universidad Pontificia Comillas, 1987.
The introduction serves to orient the reader to the nature of the method of some of the most famous medieval Jewish biblical commentators in Spain (pp. xi–xlix). Presents a translation of each verse of the Hebrew text with the corresponding notes of Rashi, de Beaugency, Ibn Ezra, Qimchi, and Ibn Caspi.

Smith, Gary V. *Amos: A Commentary*. Library of Biblical Interpretation. Grand Rapids: Zondervan, 1989.
The treatment of each section of the book is divided into four major parts: Introduction, Structure and Unity, Interpretation, and Theological Developments. The translation of the Hebrew text is flanked by an exegetical outline and followed by notes on text-critical issues. More technical items and other points of view are discussed in footnotes. Argues for the substantial unity and authenticity of the book.

Smith, Gary V. *Amos*. Mentor Commentary. Geanies House, Fearn, Ross-shire, U.K.: Christian Focus Publications, 1998.
A moderate revision of the 1989 volume (*Amos: A Commentary*), which incorporates new insights from the study of persuasion and the sociology of knowledge. Closes with an updated bibliography (pp. 385–98).

Snaith, Norman H. *The Book of Amos*, vol. 1: *Introduction*; vol. 2: *Translation and Notes*. London: Epworth, 1945–1946.
Volume 1 is a general introduction to the historical background, structure, and message of the book. Volume 2 provides a translation of the Hebrew with comments on selected issues in each pericope. Not overly technical, as originally designed to serve as "guidance of Methodist Probationer Ministers in their studies for the winter of 1945–6" (1:8).

Soggin, J. Alberto. *The Prophet Amos: A Translation and Commentary*. Translated by J. Bowden. London: SCM, 1987.
The discussion of each pericope is divided into three parts: a bibliography, technical notes on the translation, and the exposition. Generally follows Wolff's treatment of the book's literary genres, style, and composition. Treatment of the text is primarily focused on the pericope under analysis, along more traditional-critical lines, with little sense of broader literary features and connections.

Tatford, Frederick A. *Prophet of Social Justice: An Exposition of Amos*. Twentieth Century Series. Sussex, U.K.: Prophetic Witness Publishing House, 1974.

Basic exposition designed for a lay audience, with occasional, brief comments concerning lessons for Christians today. The introduction makes more of an effort to relate the prophetic message to modern issues. Identifies the closing verses (9:11–15) with the second coming of Christ and the millennial age.

Thorogood, Bernard. *A Guide to the Book of Amos, with Theme Discussions on Judgment, Social Justice, Priest and Prophet.* Theological Education Fund Study Guide 4. London: SPCK, 1971.
Part of a series prompted by Two-Thirds World teachers and students that focuses on application to the modern context. After a short introduction, Thorogood divides the book of Amos into five parts. Each discussion of shorter sections within the larger parts is followed by questions arising from the text and by suggestions for further reflection. The key to the former appears on pp. 111–16. Photographs of scenes from around the world contribute to give the exposition the sense of contemporary relevance.

Veldkamp, Herman. *The Farmer from Tekoa: On the Book of Amos.* Translated by T. Wever. St. Catherine's, Ontario: Paideia, 1977.
Exposition of text with an eye to modern applications to the Christian church. No bibliography or mention of scholarly sources, although it is acknowledged that the original Dutch edition is based on the exegetical work of C. van Gelderen's commentary on Amos.

Watts, John D. W. *Studying the Book of Amos.* Nashville: Broadman, 1966.
Based on material originally given as lectures to theological students in several countries. Designed to complement the study of Amos in the Southern Baptist Convention churches in 1967. Organizes the exposition of the book around the five visions, which are believed to reflect the sequential development of the ministry of the prophet.

Weiser, Artur. *Die Prophetie des Amos.* BZAW 53. Giessen: Töpelmann, 1929.
An extensive and detailed critical commentary, which is arranged topically into three primary parts: "The Words of Amos in Their Original Oral Structure" (pp. 9–248), "The Formation of the Book of Amos and Its Relationship to Prophecy" (pp. 249–90), and "The Religious Structure of the Prophecy of Amos" (pp. 290–321).

Weiss, Meir. *The Book of Amos* (Heb.). 2 vols. Perry Foundation for Biblical Research in the Hebrew University of Jerusalem. Jerusalem: Magnes, 1992.
This commentary was many years in the making. Vol. 1 is a detailed commentary on the text (301 pp.); vol. 2 contains the notes to the commentary (pp. 1–556), eight appendices on various disputed phrases and topics in Amos (pp. 557–69), and an extensive bibliography (pp. 570–630). The author follows a method he has labeled elsewhere as "total interpretation" (cf. idem, *The Bible from Within: The Method of Total Interpretation* [Jerusalem: Magnes, 1984]), which focuses more on the final form of the text than on possible textual reconstructions and redactions.

Werner, Herbert. *Amos.* Exempla Biblica 4. Göttingen: Vandenhoeck & Ruprecht, 1969.
Part of a series designed to provide a useful guide to the biblical text (and to critical scholarship on that text) in language understandable to the layperson. Deals

only with the superscription (1:1), the theological heading (1:2), the Oracles against the Nations (1:3–2:16), 5:21–24, the visions, and the confrontation with Amaziah (7:10–17). The closing chapter (pp. 166–201) is concerned with communicating this prophetic book in the teaching cycle of the German *Gymnasium*.

6. Monographs and Books, Both Scholarly and Popular

6.1. Studies on the Entire Book

Baker, Robert G. *Amos: Doing What Is Right. A Study Guide*. Macon, Ga.: Smyth & Helwys, 1995.
> Designed to communicate the prophet's call for justice and proper religion to the North American layperson; comments based on NRSV. Each of the four chapters (1:3–2:16; 3:1–6:14; 7:1–9:10; 9:11–15) is followed by a series of questions designed to stimulate discussion.

Barriocanal Gómez, José Luis. *La relectura de la tradición del Éxodo en el libro de Amós*. Tesi Gregoriana Teologia 58. Rome: Gregorian University Press, 2000.
> See under "Dissertations."

Barstad, Hans M. *The Religious Polemics of Amos: Studies in the Preaching of Amos 2,7B–8; 4,1–13; 5,1–27; 6,4–7; 8,14*. VTSup 34. Leiden: Brill, 1984.
> Argues that Amos was one of the Yahwistic prophets who struggled against the worship of other deities in Israel. The religious polemic was designed to demonstrate that Yahweh was the sole legitimate god and the true source of fertility. Appeals to archaeological evidence throughout to buttress the exegetical foundations of this perspective.

Carroll R., M. Daniel. *Contexts for Amos: Prophetic Poetics in Latin American Perspective*. JSOTSup 132. Sheffield: Sheffield Academic Press, 1992.
> See under "Dissertations."

Chávez, Moisés. *Modelo de oratoria. Obra basada en el análisis estilístico del texto hebreo del libro de Amós*. Miami: Editorial Caribe, 1979.
> After a general introduction to the prophet and his message (pp. 15–35) comes an extensive list and description of the many literary techniques and figures of speech utilized in the book. One appendix presents the author's own translation of the Hebrew text (pp. 115–29), and a second is his translation of the famous speech delivered by Martin Luther King in Washington in 1963 (pp. 133–39). Closes with an annotated bibliography (pp. 141–44).

Coote, Robert B. *Amos among the Prophets: Composition and Theology*. Philadelphia: Fortress, 1981.
> Develops the exposition on the basis of a three-stage theory of composition, each of which would reflect distinct theological and contextual concerns (A: the prophet and his disciples; B: seventh century; C: exilic and postexilic). A commitment to provide a more thorough social backdrop to the prophetic message is evident, for example, in a discussion of rent capitalism in stage A (pp. 24–42). Closes with an annotated listing of exegetical and sociological sources for further reading (pp. 135–38).

Cotton, Bill. *A Journey through the Old Testament with Amos as Your Guide*. Focus on the Bible. Fearn, Ross-shire, U.K.: Christian Focus, 1995.

"This book is not a commentary on Amos. Rather, Amos is used as a launching pad, a springboard, from which to move into a consideration of important aspects or disciplines which are essential for a comprehensive understanding of the Old Testament" (p. 10). Successive chapters place Amos within the frameworks of the history, geography, culture, theology, literature, social life, and prophecy of OT Israel. An appendix (pp. 179–82) discusses some relevant archaeological data for Amos.

Herntrich, Volkmar. *Amos, der Prophet Gottes*. Wege in die Bibel 4. Göttingen: Vandenhoeck & Ruprecht, 1941.

Sometimes rearranges verses for commentary. For example, under the heading "The Judgment on the 'Master Race,'" he presents as a continuous text and then discusses 6:1, 6b, 13, 2–7, 11, 14 (pp. 64–67). Old German script may make use difficult for some readers, especially with comments in different type sizes. No bibliography.

Jeremias, Jörg. *Hosea und Amos: Studien zu den Anfängen des Dodekapropheten*. FAT 13. Tübingen: Mohr, 1995.

Includes ten essays on Amos, two of which are previously unpublished. Though a variety of topics are considered, a consistent goal of the author is to try to reconstruct what he believes to be the redactional history of pericopes, sections, and the book of Amos as a whole. Creative understanding of work of tradents and the relationship between the two prophetic texts.

Kapelrud, Arvid S. *Central Ideas in Amos*. Oslo: Aschehoug (Nygaard), 1956.

A classic monograph in Amos research that deals with the perennial topics of debate: the call and background of the prophet, his relationship to the cult, the Oracles against the Nations, and the theology of the book (in particular the concept of God).

King, Philip J. *Amos, Hosea, Micah: An Archaeological Commentary*. Philadelphia: Westminster, 1988.

Discussion, diagrams, and pictures of archaeological data designed to illuminate and illustrate the biblical text. Topics include the historical and geographical setting, architecture, warfare, worship, and domestic life of eighth-century Judah and Israel.

Morgenstern, Julian. *Amos Studies: Parts I, II, and III*. 2 vols. Cincinnati: Hebrew Union College Press, 1941. (Reprinted from *HUCA* 11 [1936]: 19–140; 12/13 [1937–38]: 1–53; 15 [1940]: 59–305.)

Suggests that the prophet's ministry could have been limited to one single address (perhaps totaling just 30 minutes) delivered at Bethel during the New Year Festival in 751 B.C.E. The prophet spoke of the demands of Yahweh's special covenant relationship with Israel, as well as of a new message of the universal sovereignty of Yahweh. Offers lengthy and detailed analysis of the text, often suggesting conjectural emendations.

Park, Aaron Wonil. *The Book of Amos as Composed and Read in Antiquity*. Studies in Biblical Literature 37. New York: Peter Lang, 2001.
See under "Dissertations."

Pfeifer, Gerhard. *Die Theologie des Propheten Amos*. Frankfurt au Main: Peter Lang, 1995.
Focuses on what the author considers to be the particular thought forms and development of the ideas (*Denkformenanalyse*) of Amos the theologian. Accepts the authenticity of most of the prophetic book. Divided into two primary parts. The first provides a discussion of each pericope (pp. 21–88). The second deals with the names of God (pp. 89–96) and the relationship of the actions of God to Amos (pp. 96–109), Israel (pp. 110–34), other nations (pp. 135–40), and the created order (pp. 140–47).

Polley, Max E. *Amos and the Davidic Empire: A Socio-Historical Approach*. New York: Oxford University Press, 1989.
Interprets the book from the perspective that this prophet from Judah condemned the other nations and especially the Northern Kingdom primarily for rebellion against the Davidic monarchy. Israel's religious practice is seen as a betrayal of the only legitimate cult, which is in Jerusalem. The prophetic hope is then understood as a reuniting of the two kingdoms once again in the future under a Davidic king.

Reimer, Haroldo. *Richtet auf das Rechts! Studien zur Botschaft des Amos*. SBS 149. Stuttgart: Katholisches Bibelwerk, 1992.
See under "Dissertations."

Reventlow, H. Graf. *Das Amt des Propheten bei Amos*. FRLANT 80. Göttingen: Vandenhoeck & Ruprecht, 1962.
A classic monograph. Discusses in separate chapters 7:10–17, 3:3–8, the visions, 1:3–2:6, 4:6–11, and 9:13–15, all in relationship to the prophet's calling, vocation, and message within the context of the cult and covenant festivals.

Rosenbaum, Stanley N. *Amos of Israel: A New Interpretation*. Macon, Ga.: Mercer University Press, 1990.
The historical and philological research of the author has led him to believe that Amos was a relatively well-off mid-level bureaucrat of the northern monarchy, who was expelled from Israel for treason against the crown and its cult. The prophet's words would have been collected afterward in Judah.

Ruiz González, Gregorio. *Don Isaac Abrabanel y su comentario al libro de Amós. Texto hebreo del manuscrito de El Escorial, traducción y notas*. Estudios 30; Teología I/16. Madrid: Universidad Pontificia Comillas, 1984.
In an extensive introduction (pp. xi–clx) the author presents a biography of Abrabanel (1437–1508), a study of his exegetical method, a description of the manuscript that is the basis of this edition, and a bibliography of material by and on Abrabanel. The commentary itself has Abrabanel's unpointed Hebrew work and the author's Spanish translation and notes on opposite pages (pp. 2–247). Various indices round out the volume (pp. 249–71).

Schart, Aaron. *Die Entstehung des Zwölfprophetenbuchs: Neubearbeitungen von Amos im Rahmen schriftenübergreifender Redaktionsprozesse*. BZAW 260. Berlin: de Gruyter, 1998.
See under "Dissertations."

Schwantes, Milton. *Amós: Meditações e Estudos*. São Leopoldo: Sinodal; Petropolis: Vozes, 1987 (translated as *Das Land kann seine Worte nicht ertragen: Meditationen zu Amos*. Munich: Kaiser, 1991).

> The bulk of this work is based on studies given at the 7th Latin American Lutheran Congress held in Caracas, Venezuela, in April 1986. Two other essays, which were published first elsewhere, are added. Exposition and notes reflect acquaintance with European critical scholarship, but the book as a whole is designed to interact with and speak to Latin American sociopolitical realities.

Sutcliffe, Thomas Henry. *The Book of Amos*. Biblical Handbooks. London: SPCK, 1939.

> This lay-oriented commentary dedicates one chapter to each of the chapters of the prophetic book. A closing chapter (pp. 82–88) summarizes the teaching of the book under three headings: "Harshness and Severity," "Belief in One Supreme God," and "Justice, Including Right Living." Chapters commenting on Amos are sprinkled with helpful literary observations and with attempts to apply reflections based on the text to modern life.

Watts, John D. W. *Vision and Prophecy in Amos. 1955 Faculty Lectures, Baptist Theological Seminary, Rüschlikon-Zürich, Switzerland*. Leiden: Brill; Grand Rapids: Eerdmans, 1958.

> This material originally was presented as a series of lectures in 1955 at the Baptist Theological Seminary in Rüschlikon, Switzerland. The four chapters explore the nature of Amos's prophetic ministry, the visions, the hymnic fragments, and the eschatology of the book. Pays particular attention to textual-critical and theological issues.

Watts, John D. W. *Vision and Prophecy in Amos*. Expanded anniversary edition. Macon, Ga.: Mercer University Press, 1997.

> A reprint of the 1958 edition with the addition of four other chapters, three of which are articles previously published elsewhere; the fourth was a paper delivered at a national academic meeting. These chapters deal with the composition of the book, the person of the prophet, the author's account of his own involvement in Amos research, and the nature of the literary structure of the Book of the Twelve. The dates of this added material range from 1955 to 1990.

Wolff, Hans Walter. *Die Stunde des Amos: Prophetie und Protest*. Munich: Kaiser, 1979.

> An attempt to communicate the results of critical studies in the book of Amos to those not trained in that field. Divided into four principal parts: a general introduction to the person and message of the prophet, an explanation of critical exegesis of chapters 3 and 4 for the nonexpert, a series of sermons on the book, and the author's translation of the prophetic text.

Wood, Joyce Rilett. *Amos in Song and Culture*. JSOTSup 337. Sheffield: Sheffield Academic Press, 2002.

> See under "Dissertations."

Würthwein, Ernst. "Amos-Studien." *ZAW* 62, nos. 1–2 (1949–1950): 10–52. (Reprinted in E. Würthwein, *Wort und Existenz: Studien zum Alten Testament*, pp. 68–110. Göttingen: Vandenhoeck & Ruprecht, 1970.)

> Now a classic study within Amos research. Argues that Amos originally proclaimed salvation oracles of victory over Israel's enemies in the context of the

amphictyonic cult but who eventually became a prophet of judgment. This judg-ment was based on the violation of covenant. For a helpful summary, see J. J. M. Roberts, "Recent Trends in the Study of Amos." *ResQ* 13, no. 1 (1970): 1–16.

6.2. Studies on Particular Aspects

Balla, Emil. *Die Droh- und Scheltworte des Amos*. Leipzig: Edelmann, 1926.
    Marks an important stage in the scholarly debate concerning the relationship between the "threat" (*Drohrede*) and "reproach" (*Scheltwort*) in the prophetic lit-erature. Develops and extends the form-critical program initiated by Gunkel. For a summary and evaluation, see C. Westermann, *Basic Forms of Prophetic Speech*, 40–44. trans. H. C. White (reprint, Cambridge: Lutterworth; Louisville: Westminster John Knox, 1991).

Barton, John. *Amos's Oracles against the Nations: A Study of Amos 1:3–2:5*. SOTSMS 6. Cambridge: Cambridge University Press, 1980.
    A revised version of a chapter of the author's 1974 doctoral thesis. After review-ing discussions on the theological basis and the historical backgrounds of the oracles, the author argues that the prophetic message assumes the universal sov-ereignty of Yahweh as well as a broadly accepted customary law, especially as it pertains to conduct in warfare. Closes with an appendix of comparative material from elsewhere in the ancient Near East.

Baumann, Eberhard. *Der Aufbau der Amosreden*. BZAW 7. Giessen: Ricker (Töpel-mann), 1903.
    A brief monograph (69 pp.) that attempts to analyze the content, arrangement, and form of the speeches of Amos. The introduction (pp. 1–9) is followed by "literary-critical" (pp. 10–22) and "metric-text critical" (pp. 23–64) studies of the prophet's words. Interacts particularly with the approaches of Müller, Con-damin, Löhr, and Harper. Believes the book contains five speeches, which he reconstructs according to his criteria of authenticity and poetics.

Berg, Werner. *Die sogennanten Hymnenfragmente in Amosbuch*. Europäische Hochschul-schriften Reihe XXIII, Theologie 45. Bern: Herbert Lang; Frankfurt am Main: Peter Lang, 1974.
    A dissertation completed in 1974 at the Ludwig-Maximilians-Universität in Munich. Offers a survey of research up to that date and analyzes the "hymnic frag-ments" (4:13; 5:8; 9:5–6) from text-, form-, and redaction-critical points of view. Excursuses on Amos 5:9, the style of 4:13, the formula "Yahweh is his name," ancient Near Eastern parallels to that formula, and the relationship between 8:8 and 9:5.

Beyerlin, Walter. *Bleilot, Brecheisen oder Was sonst? Revision einer Amos-Vision*. OBO 81. Freiburg: Universitätsverlag; Göttingen: Vandenhoeck & Ruprecht, 1988.
    Argues that in Amos's third vision the disputed term *'ănāk* (7:7–8) should be translated as "tin," not "lead," as has been customary. Bases the linguistic argu-ment on the work of G. Brunet and W. L. Holladay and on an Akkadian cog-nate. Instead of using the image on behalf of Israel, God will use tin as a weapon against the nation.

Bjorndalen, Anders Jorgen. *Untersuchungen zur allegorischen Rede der Propheten Amos und Jesaja*. BZAW 165. Berlin: de Gruyter, 1986.

Basing the theoretical foundation especially on the work of A. J. Reichling, Bjorndalen argues that allegory arises with the juxtaposition of metaphors and that the concept can be appreciated in a broader way than it traditionally has. Metaphor and allegory have often been contrasted, and allegory has been seen as a rare or late phenomenon in biblical literature. Probes the use of language by the prophets in the communication of their messages. Applies method to several passages in Amos (2:9, pp. 135–56; 5:2, pp. 159–74).

Crenshaw, J. L. *Hymnic Affirmation of Divine Justice: The Doxologies of Amos and Related Texts in the Old Testament.* SBLDS 24. Missoula, Mont.: Scholars Press, 1975.
The bulk of this work is a reproduction of a 1964 doctoral thesis completed at Vanderbilt University under J. Philip Hyatt; a postscript is added to review research from that date until 1975 (pp. 147–58). Working from a form-critical perspective, Crenshaw's goal is to ascertain the role of the doxologies in their present context, their authenticity, and *Sitz im Leben.* The clause "Yahweh of Hosts is his name" is taken as the key for the analysis. Though understood as either exilic or postexilic, the doxologies are appropriate additions to the text and were designed to spur the community to penitence and faith.

Fey, Reinhard. *Amos und Jesaja. Abhängigkeit und Eigenständigkeit des Jesaja.* WMANT 12. Neukirchen-Vluyn: Neukirchener Verlag, 1963.
A dissertation completed in 1961 at the Theologischen Fakultät of the Georg-August-Universität in Göttingen. Explores the possibility of a dependence of Isaiah on the thinking of Amos (pp. 57–104), while also pointing out ideas unique to Isaiah (pp. 105–43). A concluding chapter (pp. 144–47) summarizes Fey's findings and also puts the results in chart form.

Fleischer, Günther. *Von Menschenverkäufern, Baschankühen und Rechtsverkehrern: Die Sozialkritik des Amosbuches in historisch-kritischer, sozialgeschictlicher und archäologischer Perspektive.* BBB 74. Frankfurt am Main: Athenäum, 1989.
See under "Dissertations."

Hunter, A. Vanlier. *Seek the Lord! A Study of the Meaning and Function of the Exhortation in Amos, Hosea, Isaiah, Micah, and Zephaniah.* Baltimore: St. Mary's Seminary and University, 1982.
A dissertation submitted to the University of Basel in 1981. The purpose of this work to investigate the function of the exhortation passages vis-à-vis the judgment announced by these five prophets. Analyzes 5:4–6, 14–15; 5:21–24; 4:12 and determines that these words in no way qualify or condition the imminent, comprehensive judgment prophesied by Amos (pp. 56–122).

Huré, Jacqueline Saveria. *L'homme de feu ou Amos, le prophète.* Paris: Cerf, 1993.
An imaginative reconstruction of the life of the prophet Amos in somewhat the form of a novelette. Begins with his life as a shepherd through to his call and ministry until his death in Judah after being expelled from Israel. Portrays the passing of the prophetic mantle to a younger Hosea.

Jaruzelska, Izabela. *Amos and the Officialdom in the Kingdom of Israel: The Socio-Economic Position of the Officials in the Light of the Biblical, the Epigraphic and Archaeological Evidence.* Seria Socjologia 25. Poznam: Wydawnictwo Naukowe Uniwersytetu im. Adam Mickiewicza, 1998.

Attempts to utilize a variety of sources (the biblical text, epigraphy, archaeology, and the socioeconomic theory of ownership) to clarify the social class status and institutional behavior of state officials in ancient Israel. The focus of the discussion of the prophetic text is 3:9–11,12b–15; 4:1–3; and 6:1–7. Influenced by Marxist theory concerning the social division of labor and ownership of the means of production. After bibliography and indices (pp. 201–34), offers summaries in French and Polish (pp. 235–40). Cf. idem, "Social Structure in the Kingdom of Israel in the Eighth Century B.C. as Reflected in the Book of Amos," *FO* 29 (1992–1993), pp. 91–117.

Koch, Klaus, et al. *Amos: Untersucht mit den Methoden einer Strukturalen Formgeschichte.* AOAT 30. 3 vols. Kevelaer: Butzon & Bercker; Neukirchen-Vluyn: Neukirchener Verlag, 1976.
An extremely detailed and thorough analysis of the prophetic text, with particular attention to what are deemed to be structural markers and patterns. Replete with charts. Prefers the notion of "composition" instead of redaction to better communicate the intricate interconnections of the text and the process of its compilation (which was substantially completed by the seventh century).

Markert, Ludwig. *Struktur und Bezeichnung des Scheltswort: Eine gattungskritische Studie anhand des Amosbuches.* BZAW 140. Berlin: de Gruyter, 1977.
Originally the author's dissertation completed in 1974 at the Friedrich-Alexander-Universität in Erlangen-Nürnberg. A detailed critical study of the judgment speeches, with Amos as his test case. Argues that scholarly use of the term and concept of the *Scheltwort* ("reproach") has been imprecise. He prefers to see the judgment oracles as made up of two parts (a reason and an announcement) and believes that they cannot be limited to the prophets. Includes a study on (pp. 232–77) as well as an appendix (pp. 297–321) of the Hebrew terms for the German semantic field of "reproach" ("das Wortfeld 'schelten'").

Nägele, Sabine. *Laubhütte Davids und Wolkensohn: Eine auslegungsgeschichtliche Studie zu Amos 9, 11 in der jüdischen und christlichen Exegese.* AGJU 24. Leiden: Brill, 1995.
See under "Dissertations."

Reimer, Haroldo. *Richtet auf des Rechts! Studien zur Botschaft des Amos.* SBS 149. Stuttgart: Katholisches Bibelwerk, 1992.
See under "Dissertations."

Rottzoll, Dirk U. *Studien zur Redaktion und Komposition des Amosbuches.* BZAW 243. Berlin: de Gruyter, 1996.
See under "Dissertations."

Seierstad, Ivar P. *Die Offenbarungserlebnisse der Propheten Amos, Jesaja und Jeremia: Eine Untersuchung der Erlebnisvorgänge unter besonderer Berücksichtung ihrer religiös-sittlichen Art und Auswirkung.* 2d ed. Oslo: Universitetsforlaget, 1965.
Examines the call and experiences of revelation of Amos, Jeremiah, and Isaiah. Sharply disagrees with those who propose the ecstatic view of prophecy and makes a marked distinction between the writing prophets and earlier prophets. Discussions particularly focused on the book of Amos appear on pp. 41–3, 52–9, 82–91, 156ff.

Vuilleumier, René. *La tradition cultuelle d'Israël dans la prophétie d'Amos et d'Osée.* Cahiers
théologiques 45. Neuchâtel: Delachaux & Niestlé, 1960.
> Believes that the study of a prophet's view of the cult should begin with a gen-
> eral study of the entire OT in order to place Amos's (and Hosea's) perception
> within that broader perspective. Focuses primarily (pp. 35–80) on the prophets'
> critique of the belief system, cultic practices and rituals, and "ministers" (fathers,
> priests, nazirites, king, etc.). Closes with an investigation of what could be rem-
> nants of liturgy, such as the Oracles against the Nations and the doxologies (pp.
> 81–90).

Willi-Plein, Ina. *Vorformen der Schriftexegese innerhalb des Alten Testaments: Untersuchungen zum literarischen Werden der auf Amos, Hosea und Micha zurückgehenden
Bücher im hebräischen Zwölfprophetenbuch.* BZAW 123. Berlin: de Gruyter, 1971.
> Originally a doctoral thesis completed at the University of Tübingen (1969).
> Attempts to isolate the authentic words of the prophet and then to suggest a
> hypothesis regarding the historical development of the book into its present
> form. Amos is divided into 151 units in order to identify the additions (pp.
> 15–69). Catalogs the glosses according to textual corruption, stylistic concerns,
> and other reasons such as tendencies later evident in rabbinic exegesis (pp.
> 254–68). Closes with an appendix presenting a reconstruction of the possible
> original prophetic message (pp. 269–72).

Witaszek, Gabriel. *Prorocy Amos i Micheasz wobec niesprawiedliwosci spolecznej* (Polish).
Tuchow: Mala Poligrafia Redemptorystow, 1992.
> See under "Dissertations."

6.3. Other Media

Bulkeley, Tim. "Amos." In *Postmodern Bible* (Multimedia Commentary online).
www.bible.gen.nz/amos
> Designed to exploit the possibilities of electronic multimedia so that the user can
> go in several different directions, depending on personal interests. Offers access
> to a glossary of terms, comments on highlighted terms in each verse, audio of
> the text in Hebrew and English, and historical and cultural background infor-
> mation and pictures. Goal is that this become part of a larger project of similar
> commentaries and studies by other like-minded scholars.

Frymer-Kensky, Tikva. "The Essence of Amos." (45 minute video.) Washington, D.C.:
Biblical Archaeology Society, 1999.
> An introductory lecture on the content of the final form of the book of Amos.
> Focuses on the socioeconomic message of the prophet. At the beginning says
> that the book has a ring structure with its center at 5:24, but does not develop
> the structural implications or insights in the exposition of the text. Posits that
> Amos is speaking of the Assyrian threat of invasion.

5

Specific Topics
and Significant Blocks of Text

Specific Topics

1. The Man and the Book within the Study of Prophetism

Alonso Díaz, José. "El nuevo tipo de profecía que inicia Amós." *CB* 23, no. 1 (1966): 36–42.

Auld, A. G. "Amos and Apocalyptic: Vision, Prophecy, Revelation." In *Storia e Tradizioni de Israele* (Festschrift J. A. Soggin). Edited by D. Garrone and F. Israel, 1–14. Brescia: Paideia, 1991.

Jeremias, Jörg. "Die Rolle des Propheten nach dem Amosbuch." In idem *Hosea und Amos: Studien zu den Anfängen des Dodekapropheten*, 272–84. FAT 13. Tübingen: Mohr, 1996.

Kelley, Page H. "Contemporary Study of Amos and Prophetism." *RevExp* 63, no. 4 (1966): 375–85.

Rothstein, Gustav. "Amos und seine Stellung innerhalb des israelitischen Prophetismus (Mit einem Exkurs über: Ort und Dauer der Wirksamkeit des Amos)." *TSK* 78, no. 3 (1905): 323–58.

2. Historical and Personal Background of the Prophet and the Book

2.1. Backgrounds to the Person of the Prophet (also see below "Theological Traditions" and the bibliography for 1:1 and 7:9, 10–17 and 7:14–15).

Bič, Milos. "Der Prophet Amos—ein Haepatoskopos." *VT* 1, no. 4 (1951): 293–96.

Budde, Karl. "Zur Geschichte des Buches Amos." In *Studien zur semitischen Philologie und Religionsgeschichte*. Edited by K. Budde, 63–77. BZAW 27. Giessen: Töpelmann, 1914.

Byargeon, Rick W. "Amos: The Man and His Times." *SwJT* 38, no. 1 (1995): 4–10.

Cohen, Simon. "Amos *Was* a Navi." *HUCA* 32 (1961): 175–78.

Danell, Gustaf Adolf. "Var Amos verkligen en nabie?" *SEÅ* 16 (1951): 7–20.

Davis, L. D. "The Herald of God's Justice." *TBT* 33, no. 5 (1995): 294–97.

Eichrodt, Walther. "Die Vollmacht des Amos: Zu einer schwierigen Stelle im Amosbuch." In *Beiträge zur alttestamentlichen Theologie* (Festschrift W. Zimmerli).

Edited by H. Donner, R. Hanhart, and R. Smend, 124–31. Göttingen: Vandenhoeck & Ruprecht, 1977.

Herntrich, Volkmar. "Das Berufungsbewußstein des Amos." *Christentum und Wissenschaft* 9 (1933): 161–76.

Hoffmann, Y. "Did Amos Regard Himself as a *Nabi*'?" *VT* 27, no. 2 (1977): 209–12.

Junker, Hubert. "Amos, der Mann, den Gott mit unwiderstehlicher Gewalt zum Propheten machte." *TTZ* 65, no. 6 (1956): 321–28.

Levey, Samson H. "Amos in the Rabbinic Tradition." In *Tradition as Openness to the Future* (Festschrift W. W. Fisher), ed. F. O. Francis and R. P. Wallace, 55–69. Lanham, Md.: University Press of America, 1984.

Levin, C. "Amos und Jeroboam I." *VT* 45, no. 3 (1995): 307–17.

Loretz, Oswald. "Die Enstehung des Amos-Buches im Licht der Prophetien aus Māri, Assur, Ishchali und der Ugarit-Texte." *UF* 24 (1992): 179–215.

Montgomery, James A. "Notes on Amos." *JBL* 223, no. 1 (1904): 94–96.

Morgenstern, Julian. "The Historical Antecedents of Amos." *HUCA* 15 (1940): 59–304 (= idem, *Amos Studies: Parts I, II, III*, 183–426, Cincinnati: Hebrew Union College, 1941).

Murtonen, A. E. "The Prophet Amos—a Hepatoscoper?" *VT* 2, no. 2 (1952): 170–71.

Overholt, Thomas W. "Commanding the Prophets: Amos and the Problem of Biblical Authority." *CBQ* 41, no. 4 (1979): 517–32.

Peifer, Claude J. "Amos the Prophet: The Man and His Book." *TBT* 19, no. 5 (1981): 295–300.

Reventlow, Henning Graf. *Das Amt des Propheten bei Amos*. FRLANT 80. Göttingen: Vandenhoeck & Ruprecht, 1962.

Rosenbaum, Stanley N. "Northern Amos Revisited: Two Philological Suggestions." *HS* 18 (1977): 132–48.

Rowley, H. H. "Was Amos a Nabi?" In *Festschrift Otto Eissfeldt zum 60. Geburtstag.* Edited by J. Fück, 209–12. Halle an der Saale: Max Niemeyer, 1947.

Schmidt, Hans. "Die Herkunft des Propheten Amos." In *Karl Budde zum siebzigsten Geburtstag.* Edited by K. Marti, 158–71. BZAW 34. Giessen: Töpelmann, 1920.

Schotroff, W. "Amos—das Porträt eines Propheten." *Stimme der Gemeinde* 24 (1972): 113–15, 145–56, 193–96, 225–27, 289–92.

Seierstad, Ivar P. "Erlebnis und Gehorsam beim Propheten Amos." *ZAW* 52, no. 1 (1934): 22–41.

Stamm, Johann Jakob. "Der Name des Propheten Amos und sein sprachlicher Hintergrund." In *Prophecy* (Festschrift G. Fohrer). Edited by J. A. Emerton, 137–42. BZAW 150. Berlin: de Gruyter, 1980.

Stoebe, Hans-Joachim. "Der Prophet Amos und sein bürgerlicher Beruf." *WuD* 5 (1957): 160–81.

Strijdom, P. D. F. "What Tekoa Did to Amos." *OTE* 9, no. 2 (1996): 273–93.

Stuhlmueller, Carroll. "Amos, Desert-Trained Prophet." *TBT* 1, no. 4 (1963): 224–30.

Wagner, Siegfried. "Überlegungen zur Frage nach den Beziehungen des Propheten Amos zum Südreich." *TLZ* 96, no. 9 (1971): 653–70.

Watts, John D. W. "What Kind of Prophet Was Amos?" In *Vision and Prophecy in Amos*, 1–26. Grand Rapids: Eerdmans; Leiden: Brill, 1958 (reprinted in *Vision and Prophecy in Amos*. Expanded anniversary edition, 29–58. Macon, Ga.: Mercer University Press, 1997).

Watts, John D. W. "Amos, the Man." *RevExp* 63, no. 4 (1966): 387–92.

Watts, John D. W. "Amos—the Man and his Message." *SwJT* 9, no. 1 (1966): 21–26 (reprinted in *Vision and Prophecy in Amos*. Expanded anniversary edition, 109–15. Macon, Ga.: Mercer University Press, 1997).

Zobel, Hans-Jürgen. "Prophet in Israel und Judah: Das Prophetenverständnis des Hosea und Amos." *ZTK* 82, no. 3 (1985): 281–99.

2.2. Backgrounds: Archaeological and Social Science Approaches

Barstad, Hans M. *The Religious Polemics of Amos: Studies in the Preaching of Amos 2,7B–8; 4,1–13; 5,1–27; 6,4–7; 8,14.* VTSup 34. Leiden: Brill, 1984.

Campbell, E. F. "Archaeological Reflections on Amos's Targets." In *Scripture and Other Artifacts* (Festschrift P. J. King). Edited by M. D. Coogan, J. C. Exum, and L. E. Stager, 32–52. Louisville: Westminster John Knox, 1994.

Carroll R., M. Daniel. *Contexts for Amos: Prophetic Poetics in Latin American Perspective,* 22–47. JSOTSup 132. Sheffield: Sheffield Academic Press, 1992.

Carroll R., M. Daniel. "Observaciones metodológicas para un estudio de la crítica profética a la economía." *Vox Scripturae* 7, no. 1 (1998): 3–20.

Carroll R., M. Daniel. "'For so you love to do': Probing Popular Religion in the Book of Amos." In *Rethinking Contexts, Rereading Texts: Contributions from the Social Sciences to Biblical Interpretation.* Edited by M. D. Carroll R., 168–89. JSOTSup 299. Sheffield: Sheffield Academic Press, 2000.

Casanova R., Humberto. "La época de Amós y la justicia social." *BolTeol* 50 (1993): 95–106.

Cohen, Simon. "The Political Background of the Words of Amos." *HUCA* 36 (1965): 153–60.

Dearman, John Andrew. *Property Rights in the Eighth-Century Prophets,* 18–34. SBLDS 106. Atlanta: Scholars Press, 1988.

de Geus, J. K. "Die Gesellschaftskritik der Propheten und die Archäologie." *ZDPV* 98 (1982): 50–57.

Deist, F. E. "Politics, Economics, Business, and Ethics: A Case Study from the Times of Ahab and Jeroboam II." *Theologia evangelica* 19 (1986): 36–46.

Freedman, David Noel, and A. Welch. "Amos's Earthquake and Israelite Prophecy." In *Scripture and Other Artifacts* (Festschrift P. J. King). Edited by M. D. Coogan, J. C. Exum, and L. E. Stager, 188–98. Louisville: Westminster John Knox, 1994.

Fritz, Volkmar. "Amosbuch, Amos-Schule und historischer Amos." In *Prophetenbuch* (Festschrift O. Kaiser). Edited by V. Fritz, 29–43. Berlin: de Gruyter, 1989.

Galil, Gershon. "The Boundaries of Aram-Damascus in the 9th–8th Centuries BCE." In *Studies in Historical Geography and Biblical Historiography.* Edited by G. Galil and M. Weinfeld, 35–41. VTSup 81. Leiden: Brill, 2000.

Giles, Terry. "An Introductory Investigation of Amos by Means of the Model of the Voluntary Social Movement." *Proceedings. Eastern Great Lakes and Midwest Biblical Societies* 8 (1988): 135–53.

Gordis, Robert. "Edom, Israel and Amos—an Unrecognized Source for Edomite History." In *Essays on the Occasion of the Seventieth Anniversary of the Dropsie University, 1909–1979.* Edited by A. I. Katsch and L. Nemoy, 109–32. Philadelphia: Dropsie University, 1979.

Gottwald, Norman K. "Amos." In *A Light to the Nations: An Introduction to the Old Testament,* 281–91. New York: Harper & Row, 1959.

Haran, Menahem. "Observations on the Historical Background of Amos 1:2–2:6." *IEJ* 18, no. 4 (1968): 201–12.

Haran, Menahem. "The Rise and Decline of the Empire of Jeroboam ben Joash." *VT* 17, no. 3 (1967): 266–97.

Jaruzelska, Izabela. "Social Structure in the Kingdom of Israel in the Eighth Century B.C. as Reflected in the Book of Amos." *FO* 29 (1992–1993): 91–117.

Jaruzelska, Izabela. "People Pronouncing Sentences in Court: Amos 5,7–12.16–17: An Attempt at Sociological Identification." *FO* 30 (1994): 77–94.

Jaruzelska, Izabela. *Amos and the Officialdom in the Kingdom of Israel: The Socio-Economic Position of the Officials in the Light of the Biblical, the Epigraphic and Archaeological Evidence.* Seria Socjologia 25. Poznam: Wydawnictwo Naukowe Uniwersytetu im. Adam Mickiewicza, 1998.

King, Philip J. *Amos, Hosea, Micah: An Archaeological Commentary.* Philadelphia: Westminster, 1988.

King, Philip J. "Using Archaeology to Interpret a Biblical Text: The *Marzēaḥ* Amos Denounces." *BAR* 14, no. 4 (1988): 34–44.

King, Philip J. "The *Marzēaḥ*: Textual and Archaeological Evidence" (in Hebrew). *EI* 20 (1989): 98–106.

Loretz, Oswald. "Ugaritisch-biblisch *mrzḥ* 'Kultmahl, Kultverein' in Jer 16, 5 und Am 6, 7." In *Künder des Wortes: Beiträge zur Theologie der Propheten* (Festschrift J. Schreiner). Edited by L. Ruppert et al., 87–93. Würzburg: Echter, 1982.

Loretz, Oswald. "*Marzi<u>h</u>u* im ugaritischen und biblischen Ahnenkult: Zu Ps 23; 133; Am 6,1–7 und Jer 16,5.8." In *Mesopotamia–Ugarit–Biblica* (Festschrift K. Bergerhof). Edited by M. Dietrich and O. Loretz, 93–144. AOAT 232. Neukirchen-Vluyn: Neukirchener Verlag, 1993.

Maier, Christl, and Ernst Michael Dörrfuß. "'Um mit ihnen zu sitzen, zu essen und zu trinken'. Am 6,7; Jer 16,5 und die Bedeutung von *marzēaḥ*." *ZAW* 111, no. 1 (1999): 45–57.

McLaughlin, John L. *The Marzēaḥ in the Prophetic Literature: References and Allusions in Light of the Extra-Biblical Evidence*, 80–128. VTSup 86. Leiden: Brill, 2001.

Muntingh, L. M. "Political and International Relations of Israel's Neighboring Peoples according to the Oracles of Amos." *OTWSA* 7–8 (1964–1965): 134–42.

Ogden, D. Kelly. "The Earthquake Motif in the Book of Amos." In *Goldene Apfel in silbernen Schalen: Collected Communications to the XIIIth Congress of the International Organization for the Study of the Old Testament.* Edited by K.-D. Schunk and M. Augustin, 69–80. BEATAJ 20. Frankfurt am Main: Lang, 1992.

Otzen, Benedikt. "Amos og afguderne." *NorTT* 84, no. 3 (1983): 167–85.

Pleins, J. David. *The Social Visions of the Hebrew Bible: A Theological Introduction*, 368–77. Louisville: Westminster John Knox, 2000.

Pope, Marvin H. "A Divine Banquet at Ugarit." In *The Use of the Old Testament in the New.* Edited by J. Efird, 170–203. Durham, N.C.: Duke University Press, 1972.

Pope, Marvin H. "Le *MRZH* à l'Ugarit et ailleurs." *Annales Archéologiques Arabes Syriennes* 28/30 (1978–1980): 141–43.

Pope, Marvin H. "The Cult of the Dead at Ugarit." In *Ugarit in Retrospect: Fifty Years of Ugarit and Ugaritic.* Edited by G. D. Young, 159–79. Winona Lake, Ind.: Eisenbrauns, 1981.

Ramírez, Guillermo. "The Social Location of Amos in Light of the Group/Grid Cultural Anthropology Model." In *Prophets and Paradigms* (Festschrift G. M. Tucker). Edited by S. B. Reid, 112–24. JSOTSup 229. Sheffield: Sheffield Academic Press, 1996.

Schottroff, Willy. "Der Prophet Amos: Versuch der Wurdigung seines Auftretens unter sozialgeschichtlichen Aspekt." In *Der Gott der kleinen Leute: Sozialgeschichtliche Bibelauslegungen.* Edited by W. Schotroff and W. Stegemann, 39–66. Munich: Kaiser, 1979 (translated by M. J. O'Connell, "The Prophet Amos: A Socio-Historical Assessment of His Ministry." In *God of the Lowly: Socio-Historical Interpretations of the Bible.* Edited by W. Schottroff and W. Stegemann, 27–46. Maryknoll, N.Y.: Orbis, 1984).

Smith, Gary V. "Amos: The End Has Come!" In *The Prophets as Preachers: An Intro-duction to the Hebrew Prophets*, 47–65. Nashville: Broadman & Holman, 1994.

Soggin, J. Alberto. "Das Erdbeben von Amos 1,1 und die Chronologie der Könige Ussia und Jotham von Juda." *ZAW* 82, no. 1 (1970): 117–21.

Soggin, J. Alberto. "Amos 6:13–14 und 1:3 auf dem Hintergrund der Beziehungen zwischen Israel und Damaskus in 9. und 8. Jahrhundert." In *Near Eastern Stud-ies in Honor of William Foxwell Albright*. Edited by H. Goedicke, 433–42. Balti-more: Johns Hopkins University Press, 1971.

Talmon, Shemaryahu. "Prophetic Rhetoric and Agricultural Metaphora." In *Storia e tradizioni di Israeli* (Festschrift J. A. Soggin). Edited by D. Garrone and F. Israel, 267–79. Brescia: Paideia, 1991.

van Selms, A. "Amos' Geographic Horizon." *OTWSA* 7–8 (1964–1965): 166–69.

Weippert, Helga. "Amos: Seine Bilder und ihr Milieu." In Helga Weippert, Klaus Seybold, and Manfred Weippert, *Beiträge zur prophetischen Bildsprache in Israel und Assyrien*, 1–29. OBO 64. Freiburg: Universitätsverlag, 1985.

Zeeb, Frank. "Alalakh VII und das Amosbuch." *UF* 27 (1995): 641–56.

2.3. Warfare in the Ancient Near East and in the Old Testament[1]

Bleibtreu, Erika. "Five Ways to Conquer a City." *BAR* 16, no. 3 (1990): 36–44.

Bleibtreu, Erika. "Grisly Assyrian Record of Torture and Death." *BAR* 17, no. 1 (1991): 52–61, 75.

Craigie, Peter C. *The Problem of War in the Old Testament*. Grand Rapids: Eerdmans, 1978.

Dalley, Stephanie. "Foreign Chariotry and Cavalry in the Armies of Tiglath-Pileser III and Sargon II." *Iraq* 47 (1985): 31–48.

Eph'al, Israel. "On Warfare and Military Control in the Ancient Near Eastern Empires: A Research Outline." In *History, Historiography and Interpretation: Studies in Bib-lical and Cuneiform Literatures*. Edited by H. Tadmor and M. Weinfeld, 88–106. Leiden: Brill; Jerusalem: Magnes, 1983.

Eph'al, Israel. "Ways and Means to Conquer a City, Based on Assyrian Queries to the Sungod." In *Assyria 1995: Proceedings of the 10th Anniversary Symposium of the Neo-Assyrian Text Corpus Project. Helsinki, September 7–11, 1995*. Edited by S. Parpola and R. M. Whiting, 49–53. Helsinki: Neo-Assyrian Text Corpus Proj-ect, 1997.

Hobbs, T. R. *A Time for War: A Study of Warfare in the Old Testament*. Old Testament Studies 3. Wilmington, Del.: Michael Glazier, 1989.

Niditch, Susan. *War in the Hebrew Bible: A Study in the Ethics of Violence*. New York: Oxford University Press, 1993.

Oded, Bustenay, *Mass Deportations and Deportees in the Neo-Assyrian Empire*. Weisbaden: Ludwig Reipert, 1979.

Pongratz-Leisten, Beate. "The Interplay of Military Strategy and Cultic Practice in Assyrian Politics." In *Assyria 1995: Proceedings of the 10th Anniversary Symposium of the Neo-Assyrian Text Corpus Project. Helsinki, September 7–11, 1995*. Edited by S. Parpola and R. M. Whiting, 245–52. Helsinki: Neo-Assyrian Text Corpus Project, 1997.

Postgate, J. N. "The Assyrian Army in Zamua." *Iraq* 62 (2000): 89–108.

Rad, Gerhard von. *Holy War in Ancient Israel*. Translated by M. J. Dawn. Grand Rapids: Eerdmans, 1991.

Reade, Julian. *Assyrian Sculpture*, 80–91. 2d ed. Cambridge: Harvard University Press, 1999.

Saggs, H. W. F. "Assyrian Warfare in the Sargonid Period." *Iraq* 25 (1963): 145–54.
Saggs, H. W. F. *The Might That Was Assyria*, 243–68. London: Sidgwick & Jackson, 1984.
Scurlock, JoAnn. "Neo-Assyrian Battle Tactics." In *Crossing Boundaries and Linking Horizons* (Festschrift M. C. Astour). Edited by G. D. Young, M. W. Chavalas, and R. E. Averbeck, 491–517. Bethesda, Md.: CDL Press, 1997.
Yadin, Yigael. *The Art of Warfare in Biblical Lands in the Light of Archaeological Study.* Translated by M. Pearlman. 2 vols. New York: McGraw-Hill, 1963.
Younger, K. Lawson, Jr. *Ancient Conquest Accounts: A Study in Ancient Near Eastern and Biblical History Writing.* JSOTSup 98. Sheffield: JSOT Press, 1990.
Younger, K. Lawson, Jr. "The Deportations of the Israelites." *JBL* 117, no. 2 (1998): 201–27.

2.4. Relationship of Amos to the Deuteronomistic History

Ackroyd, Peter R. "A Judgment Narrative Between Kings and Chronicles? An Approach to Amos 7:9–17." In *Canon and Authority: Essays in Old Testament Religion and Theology.* Edited by G. W. Coats and B. O. Long, 71–87. Philadelphia: Fortress, 1977.
Crüsemann, Frank. "Kritik an Amos im deuteronomistischen Geschichtwerk: Erwägungen zu Könige 14:27 2 ed." In *Probleme biblischer Theologie* (Festschrift G. von Rad). Edited by H. W. Wolff, 57–63. Munich: Kaiser, 1971.
Eissfeldt, Otto. "Amos und Jona in volkstümlicher Überlieferung." In *. . . und fragten nach Jesus* (Festschrift E. Barnikol). Edited by O. Eissfeldt, 9–13. Berlin: Evangelische Verlagsanstalt, 1964.
Fritz, Volkmar. "Die Fremdvölkersprüche des Amos," *VT* 37, no. 1 (1987): 26–38.
Gosse, Bernard. "Le recueil d'oracles contre les nations du livre d'Amos et l'Histoire Deuteronomique," *VT* 38, no. 1 (1988): 22–40.
Krause, Hans Helmut. "Die Gerichtsprophet Amos, ein Vorläufer des Deuteronomisten." *ZAW* 50, no. 4 (1932): 221–39.
Wittenberg, Günther H. "Amos and Hosea: A Contribution to the Problem of the Deuteronomistic History." *OTE* 6, no. 3 (1993): 295–311.
Wolff, Hans Walter. "Das Ende des Heiligtums in Bethel." In *Archäologie und Altes Testament* (Festschrift K. Galling). Edited by A. Kuschke and E. Kutsch, 287–98. Tübingen: Mohr, 1970.

3. Composition, Structure, and Literary Style

Balla, Emil. *Die Droh- und Scheltworte des Amos.* Leipzig: Edelman, 1926.
Baumann, Eberhard. *Der Aufbau der Amosreden.* BZAW 7. Giessen: Ricker, 1903.
Bjorndalen, Anders J. "Jahwe in den Zukunftsaussagendes Amos." In *Die Botschaft und die Boten* (Festschrift H.W. Wolff). Edited by J. Jeremias and L. Perlitt, 181–202. Neukirchen-Vluyn: Neukirchener Verlag, 1981.
Bjorndalen, Anders J. *Untersuchungen zur allegorischen Rede der Propheten Amos und Jesaja.* BZAW 165. Berlin: de Gruyter, 1986.
Botterweck, G. Johannes. "Zur Authentizität des Buches Amos." *BZ* 2 (1958): 176–89.
Bovati, Pietro, and Roland Meynet. *Le livre du prophète Amos.* Rhétorique biblique 3. Paris: Cerf, 1994.
Bramer, Stephen J. "The Literary Genre of the Book of Amos." *BSac* 156, no. 1 (1999): 42–60.
Bramer, Stephen J. "Analysis of the Structure of Amos." *BSac* 156, no. 2 (1999): 160–74.

Budde, Karl. "Zur Authentizität des Buches Amos." *BZ* 2 (1958): 176–89.

Carroll R., M. Daniel. "Reflecting on War and Utopia in the Book of Amos: The Relevance of a Literary Reading of the Prophetic Text for Central America." In *The Bible in Human Society* (Festschrift J. Rogerson). Edited by M. Daniel Carroll R., D. J. A. Clines, and P. R. Davies, 105–21. JSOTSup 200. Sheffield: Sheffield Academic Press, 1995.

Carroll R., M. Daniel. "God and His People in the Nations' History: A Contextualized Reading of Amos 1–2." *TynBul* 47, no. 1 (1996): 39–70.

Carroll R., M. Daniel. "The Prophetic Text and the Literature of Dissent in Latin America: Amos, García Márquez, and Cabrera Infante Dismantle Militarism." *BibInt* 4, no. 1 (1996): 76–100.

Carroll R., M. Daniel. "Living between the Lines: Reading Amos 9:11–15 in Post-War Guatemala." *R&T* 6, no. 1 (1999): 50–64.

Caspari, Wilhelm. "Wer hat die Aussprüche des Propheten Amos gesammelt?" *NKZ* 25, no. 9 (1914): 701–15.

Clements, R. E. "Amos and the Politics of Israel." In *Storia e tradizioni di Israeli* (Festschrift J. A. Soggin). Edited by D. Garrone and F. Israel, 49–64. Brescia: Paideia, 1991 (reprinted in R. E. Clements, *Old Testament Prophecy: From Oracles to Canon*, 23–34. Louisville: Westminster John Knox, 1996).

Coulot, Claude. "Propositions pour une structuration de livre d'Amos au niveau rédactionnel." *RevScRel* 51, no. 2–3 (1977): 169–86.

Day, Edward, and W. Chapin. "Is the Book of Amos Post-Exilic?" *AJSL* 18, no. 2 (1902): 65–93.

Del Barco, Francisco Javier. "La función sintáctica y poética de los acentos de la masora: ejemplos en el libro de Amós." *Sefarad* 60 (2000): 3–18.

Dell, K. J. "The Misuse of Forms in Amos." *VT* 45, no. 1 (1995): 45–61.

Dijkstra, M. "Gelijkenissen in Amos." *NedTTs* 48, no. 3 (1994): 177–90.

Dines, Jennifer. "Reading the Book of Amos." *ScrB* 16, no. 1 (1986): 26–32.

Dorsey, David A. "Literary Architecture and Aural Structuring Techniques in Amos." *Bib* 73, no. 3 (1992): 305–30.

Dorsey, David A. "Amos." In *The Literary Structure of the Old Testament: A Commentary on Genesis–Malachi*, 277–86. Grand Rapids: Baker, 1999.

Finley, Thomas J. "The *Waw*-Consecutive with 'Imperfect' in Biblical Hebrew: Theoretical Studies and its Use in Amos." In *Tradition and Testament* (Festschrift C. L. Feinberg). Edited by J. S. Feinberg and P. D. Feinberg, 241–62. Chicago: Moody, 1981.

Fishelov, David "The Prophet as Satirist." *Prooftexts* 9 (1989): 195–211.

Freedman, David N. "Confrontations in the Book of Amos." *PSB* 11, no. 3 (1990): 240–52.

Fuhs, Hans F. "Amos 1,1. Erwägungen zur Tradition und Redaction des Amosbuches." In *Bausteine biblischer Theologie* (Festschrift G. J. Botterweck). Edited by H. J. Fabry, 271–89. Bonn: Pater Hanstein, 1977.

Garrett, Duane A. "The Structure of Amos as a Testimony of Its Integrity." *JETS* 27, no. 3 (1984): 275–76.

Gese, Hartmut. "Kleine Beiträge zum Verständnis des Amosbuches." *VT* 12, no. 4 (1962): 415–38.

Gese, Hartmut. "Komposition bei Amos." In *Congress Volume, Vienna 1980*. Edited by J. A. Emerton, 75–95. VTSup 32. Leiden: Brill, 1981.

Gordis, Robert. "The Composition and Structure of Amos." *HTR* 33, no. 4 (1940): 239–51.

Harper, William Rainey. *The Structure of the Text of the Book of Amos*. Printed from First series, vol. 5, The Decennial Publications. Chicago: University of Chicago Press, 1904.

Hermanson, Eric A. "Biblical Hebrew: Conceptual Metaphor Categories in the Book of Amos." *OTE* 11, no. 3 (1998): 438–51.

Hunter, A. Vanlier. *Seek the Lord! A Study of the Meaning and Function of the Exhortation in Amos, Hosea, Isaiah, Micah, and Zephaniah*, 56–123. Baltimore: St. Mary's Seminary & University, 1982.

Jeremias, Jörg. "Amos 3–6: From the Oral Word to the Text." Translated by S. A. Irvine. In *Canon, Theology, and Old Testament Interpretation* (Festschrift B. S. Childs). Edited by G. M. Tucker, D. L. Petersen, and R. R. Wilson, 217–29. Philadelphia: Fortress, 1988.

Jeremias, Jörg. "Amos 3–6. Beobachtung zur Entstehungsgeschichte eines Prophetenbuches." *ZAW* 100 (1988 Supplement): 123–38 (reprinted in idem, *Hosea und Amos: Studien zu den Anfängen des Dodekapropheten*, 142–56. FAT 13. Tübingen: Mohr, 1996).

Jeremias, Jörg. "The Interrelationship between Amos and Hosea." In *Forming Prophetic Literature* (Festschrift J. D. W. Watts). Edited by J. D. W. Watts and P. R. House, 171–86. JSOTSup 235. Sheffield: Sheffield Academic Press, 1996 (= "Die Anfänge des Dodekapropheten: Hosea und Amos." In idem, *Hosea und Amos: Studien zu den Anfängen des Dodekapropheten*, 34–54. FAT 13. Tübingen: Mohr, 1996).

Jeremias, Jörg. "Rezeptionsprozesse in der prophetischen Überlieferung—am Beispiel der Visionsberichte des Amos." In *Rezeption und Auslegung im Alten Testament und in seinem Umfeld*. Edited by R. G. Kratz et al., 29–44. OBO 153. Fribourg: Universitätsverlag, 1997.

Jozaki, Susamu. "The Secondary Passages of the Book of Amos." *Kwansei University Annual Studies* 4 (1956): 25–100.

Koch, Klaus. "Die Rolle der hymnischen Abschnitte in der Komposition des Amos-Buches." *ZAW* 86, no. 4 (1974): 504–37.

Koch, Klaus. *Amos: Untersucht mit den Methoden einer Strukturalen Formgeschichte*. AOAT 30. 3 vols. Kevelaer: Butzon & Bercker; Neukirchen-Vluyn: Neukirchener Verlag, 1976.

Lescow, Theodor. "Das vorexilische Amosbuch: Erwägungen zu seiner Kompositionsgeschichte." *BN* 93 (1998): 23–55.

Limburg, James. "Sevenfold Structures in the Book of Amos." *JBL* 106, no. 2 (1987): 217–22.

Lindblom, Johannes. "Buch der Revelationen des Propheten Amos." In *Die literarische Gattung der prophetischen Literatur: Eine literargeschichtliche Untersuchung zum Alten Testament*, 66–97. Uppsala Universitets Årsskrift. Teologi 1. Uppsala: Lundequist, 1924.

Loretz, Oswald. "Die Entstehung des Amos-Buches im Licht der Propheten auf Māri, Assur, Ishchali und der Ugarit-Texte. Paradigmenwechsel in der Prophetenbuch Forschung." *UF* 24 (1992): 179–215.

McCullough, W. S. "Some Suggestions about Amos." *JBL* 72 (1953): 247–54.

Melugin, Roy F. "The Formation of Amos: An Analysis of Exegetical Method." In *SBLSP 1978*. Edited by P. J. Achtemeier, 1:369–92. Missoula, Mont.: Scholars Press, 1978.

Meynet, Roland. *Rhetorical Analysis: An Introduction to Biblical Rhetoric*, 286–308. JSOTSup 256. Sheffield: Sheffield Academic Press, 1998.

Möller, Karl. "'Hear This Word against You': A Fresh Look at the Arrangement and the Rhetorical Strategy of the Book of Amos." *VT* 50, no. 4 (2000): 499–518.

Moltz, Howard. "A Literary Interpretation of the Book of Amos." *Hor* 25, no. 1 (1998): 58–71.

Morganstern, Julian. "Amos Studies IV: The Address of Amos, Text and Commentary." *HUCA* 32 (1961): 295–350.

Newman, Louis I. "Parallelism in Amos." In L. I. Newman and W. Popper, *Studies in Biblical Parallelism*, part I: 1–209. Semicentennial Publications of the University of California. Berkeley: University of California Press, 1917.

Noble, P. R. "The Literary Structure of Amos: A Thematic Analysis." *JBL* 114, no. 2 (1995): 209–26.

O'Connell, Robert H. "Telescoping N+1 Patterns in the Book of Amos." *VT* 46, no. 1 (1996): 56–73.

Pfeifer, Gerhard. "Über den Unterschied zwischen Schriftstellern des zwangzisten Jahrhunderts nach und des ersten Jahrtausends vor Christus: Zur Entstehung des Amosbuches." *VT* 41, no. 1 (1991): 123–27.

Praetorius, Franz. *Die Gedichte des Amos: Metrische und textkritische Bemerkungen*. Halle: Niemeyer, 1924.

Rösel, Hartmut N. "Kleine Studien zur Entwicklung des Amosbuches." *VT* 43, no. 1 (1993): 88–101.

Rösel, Hartmut N. "Kleine Studien zur Auslegung des Amosbuches." *BZ* 42, no. 1 (1998): 2–18.

Rottzoll, Dirk U. *Studien zur Redaktion und Komposition des Amosbuches*. BZAW 243. Berlin: de Gruyter, 1996.

Rudolph, Wilhelm. "Schwierige Amosstellen." In *Wort und Geschichte* (Festschrift K. Elliger). Edited by H. Gese and H. P. Ruger, 157–62. AOAT 18. Neukirchen-Vluyn: Neukirchener Verlag, 1973.

Schmidt, Werner H. "Die deuteronomistische Redaktion des Amosbuches. Zu den theologischen Unterscheiden zwischen dem Prophetenwort und seiner Sammler." *ZAW* 77, no. 2 (1965): 168–93.

Smalley, W. A. "Recursion Patterns and the Sectioning of Amos." *BT* 30, no. 1 (1979): 118–27.

Spreafico, Ambrogio. "Amos: Struttura formale e spunti per una interpretazione." *RivB* 29, no. 2 (1981): 147–76.

Stephany, A. T. M. "Charakter und zeitliche Aufeinanderfolge der Drohsprüche in der Prophetie des Amos." *Christentum und Wissenschaft* 7 (1931): 281–89.

Stuart, Douglas K. "The Poetry of Amos." In *Studies in Early Hebrew Meter*, 197–213. HSM 13. Missoula, Mont.: Scholars Press, 1976.

Super, A. S. "Figures of Comparison in the Book of Amos." *Semitics* 3 (1973): 67–80.

Sweeney, Marvin A. "Formation and Form in Prophetic Literature." In *Old Testament Interpretation: Past, Present, and Future*. (Festschrift G. M. Tucker). Edited by J. L. Mays, D. L. Petersen, and K. H. Richards, 113–26. Nashville: Abingdon, 1995.

Terblanche, M. D. "Intertextuality in the Book of Amos." *OTE* 10, no. 2 (1997): 312–21.

van der Wal, Adri. "The Structure of Amos." *JSOT* 26 (1983): 107–13.

Vermeylen, J. "Les relectures deutéronomists des livres d'Amos et de Michée." In idem, *Du prophète Isaïe à l'apocalyptique. Isaïe, 1–35, miroir d'un demi-millénaire d'expérience religieuse en Israël*, 2:519–69. EBib. Paris: Gabalda, 1977–1978.

Walker, Larry L. "The Language of Amos." *SwJT* 9, no. 1 (1966): 37–48.

Warmuth, Georg. *Das Mahnwort: Seine Bedeutung für die Verkündigung der vorexilischen Propheten Amos, Hosea, Micha, Jesaja und Jeremia*, 25–36. BBET 1. Frankfort am Main: Lang, 1976.

Watts, John D. W. "The Origin of the Book of Amos." *ExpTim* 66, no. 4 (1955): 109–12 (reprinted in idem, *Vision and Prophecy in Amos*. Expanded anniversary edition, 1–7. Macon, Ga.: Mercer University Press, 1997).

Weimar, Peter. "Der Schluss des Amos-Buches. Ein Beitrag zur Redaktionsgeschichte des Amos-Buches." *BN* 16 (1981): 60–100.

Weisman, Zeev. "Stylistic Parallels in Amos and Jeremiah: Their Implications for the Composition of Amos." *Shnaton* 1 (1975): 129–49 (Heb.).

Wendland, Ernst R. "The 'Word of the Lord' and the Organization of Amos: A Dramatic Message of Conflict and Crisis in the Confrontation between the Prophet and People of Yahweh." *OPTT* 2, no. 4 (1988): 1–51.

Widbin, R. Bryan. "Center Structure in the Center Oracles of Amos." In *Go to the Lord and I Will Show You* (Festschrift D. W. Young). Edited by J. Coleson and V. Matthews, 177–92. Winona Lake, Ind.: Eisenbrauns, 1996.

Willi-Plein, Ina. *Vorformen der Schriftexegese innerhalb des Alten Testaments*. BZAW 123. Berlin: de Gruyter, 1971.

Wilson, Victor M. "The Book of Amos." In *Divine Symmetries: The Art of Biblical Rhetoric*, 157–80. Lanham, Md.: University Press of America, 1997.

Wood, Joyce Rilett. "Tragic and Comic Forms in Amos." *BibInt* 6, no. 1 (1996): 2–48.

4. Textual Criticism and Ancient Versions

Abegg, Martin, Jr., Peter Flint, and Eugene Ulrich, eds. *The Dead Sea Scrolls Bible*, 433–40. San Francisco: HarperSanFrancisco, 1999.

Archer, Gleason L., and Gregory Chirichigno. *Old Testament Quotations in the New Testament*, 150–55. Chicago: Moody, 1983.

Arieti, James A. "The Vocabulary of Septuagint Amos." *JBL* 93, no. 3 (1974): 338–47.

Barthélemy, Dominique. *Critique textuelle de l'Ancien Testament*, 3:642–96. OBO 50/3. Fribourg: Éditions Universitaires; Göttingen: Vandenhoeck & Ruprecht, 1992.

Bruce, F. F. "Prophetic Interpretation in the Septuagint." *BIOSCS* 12 (1979): 15–26.

Carbone, Sandro P., and Giovanni Rizzi. *Il libro di Amos, lettura ebraica, greca e aramaica*. Bologna: Dehoniane, 1993.

de Waard, Jan. "A Greek Translation-Technical Treatment of Amos 1:15." In *On Language, Culture, and Religion* (Festschrift E. A. Nida). Edited by M. Black and W. A. Smalley, 111–18. Approaches to Semiotics 56. The Hague: Mouton, 1974.

de Waard, Jan. "Translation Techniques Used by the Greek Translators of Amos." *Bib* 59, no. 3 (1978): 339–50.

Diez Macho, A., and J. A. G. Larraya. "El Ms. 4083f.9 de la Biblioteca Nacional y Universitaria de Estrasburgo. (Fragmento de Amos 1:3–3:7, en hebreo y targum babilónicos)." *EstBib* 19, no. 1 (1960): 91–95.

Dines, Jenifer. "Jerome and the Hexapla: The Witness of the Commentary on Amos." In *Origen's Hexapla and Fragments: Papers Presented at the Rich Seminar on the Hexapla, Oxford Centre for Hebrew and Jewish Studies, 25th–3rd August 1994*. Edited by A. Salvesen, 421–36. TSAJ 58. Tübingen: Mohr/Siebeck, 1998.

Fischer, J. "In welcher Schrift lag das Buch Amos den LXX vor?" *TQ* 106, no. 2 (1925): 308–35.

Hirscht, Arthur. "Textkritische Untersuchungen über das Buch Amos." *ZWT* 44, no. 1 (1903): 11–73.

Howard, G. "Some Notes on the Septuagint of Amos." *VT* 20, no. 1 (1970): 108–12.

Howard, G. "Revision toward the Hebrew in the Septuagint of Amos." *EI* 16 (1982): 125–33.

Jones, Barry Alan. *The Formation of the Book of the Twelve: A Study in Text and Canon.* SBLDS 149. Atlanta: Scholars Press, 1995.

Lohman, Paul. "Einige Textkonjekturen zu Amos." *ZAW* 32, no. 2 (1912): 274–77.

Muraokao, Takamitsu. "Is the Septuagint Amos 8,12–9,10 a Separate Unit?" *VT* 20, no. 4 (1970): 496–500.

Oesterley, W. O. E. *Studies in the Greek and Latin Versions of the Book of Amos.* Cambridge: Cambridge University Press, 1902.

Orlinsky, Harry M., and Milton Weinberg, "Notes on Some *Masora Parva* of Amos." *Sefarad* 46, nos. 1–2 (1986): 381–90.

Sawyer, John F. A. "'Those Priests in Damascus': A Possible Example of Anti-Sectarian Polemic in the Septuagint Version of Amos 3:12." *ASTI* 8 (1970–1971): 123–30.

Szabó, A. "Textual Problems in Amos and Hosea." *VT* 25, no. 4 (1975): 500–525.

Thompson, J. David. *A Critical Concordance to the Septuagint Amos.* Computer Bible 80. Lewiston: Edwin Mellen, 2000.

Turner, P. "Two Septuagintalisms with *stērízein.*" *VT* 28, no. 4 (1978): 481–82.

Wainwright, G. A. "The Septuagint's *Kappadokía* for Caphtor." *JJS* 7, nos. 1–2 (1956): 91–92.

5. Amos and the Book of the Twelve

Bosshard, E. "Beobachtungen zum Zwölfprophetenbuch." *BN* 40, no. 1 (1987): 30–62.

Budde, Karl. "Eine folgenschwere Redaktion des Zwolfprophetenbuchs." *ZAW* 39, no. 2 (1921): 218–29.

Collins, Terence. "The Scroll of the Twelve." In *The Mantle of Elijah: The Redaction Criticism of the Prophetical Books*, 59–87. Biblical Seminar 20. Sheffield: JSOT Press, 1993.

Fuller, Russell. "The Form and Formation of the Book of the Twelve: The Evidence from the Judean Desert." In *Forming Prophetic Literature* (Festschrift J. D. W. Watts). Edited by J. D. W. Watts and P. R. House, 86–101. JSOTSup 235. Sheffield: Sheffield Academic Press, 1996.

House, Paul R. *The Unity of the Twelve.* JSOTSup 77. Sheffield: Sheffield Academic Press, 1990.

House, Paul R. *Old Testament Theology*, 346–401. Downers Grove, Ill.: InterVarsity Press, 1998.

House, Paul R. "The Character of God in the Book of the Twelve." In *Reading and Hearing the Book of the Twelve*. Edited by J. D. Nogalski and M. A. Sweeney, 125–45. Semeia Studies, 15. Atlanta: Society of Biblical Literature, 2000.

Jeremias, Jörg. "Die Anfänge des Dodekapropheten: Hosea und Amos." In *Congress Volume, Paris 1992*. Edited by J. A. Emerton, 87–106. VTSup 61. Leiden: Brill, 1995 (reprinted in idem, *Hosea und Amos: Studien zu den Anfängen des Dodekapropheten*, 34–54. FAT 13. Tübingen: Mohr, 1996).

Jeremias, Jörg. "The Interrelationship between Amos and Hosea." In *Forming Prophetic Literature* (Festschrift J. D. W. Watts). Edited by J. W. Watts and P. R. House, 171–86. JSOTSup 235. Sheffield: Sheffield Academic Press, 1996.

Jones, Barry Alan. *The Formation of the Book of the Twelve: A Study in Text and Canon.* SBLDS 149. Atlanta: Scholars Press, 1995.

Nogalski, James. *Literary Precursors to the Book of the Twelve*, 74–122. BZAW 217. Berlin: de Gruyter, 1993.

Nogalski, James. *Redactional Processes in the Book of the Twelve.* BZAW 218. Berlin: de Gruyter, 1993.

Pfeifer, Gerhard. "Das nachgestellte erläuternde Partizip—eine Stileigentümlichkeit des Amosbuches." *ZAH* 6 (1993): 235–38.

Schart, Aaron. *Die Entstehung des Zwölfprophetenbuchs: Neubearbeitungen von Amos im Rahmen schriftenübergreifender Redaktionsprozesse.* BZAW 260. Berlin: de Gruyter, 1998.

Steck, Odil Hannes. *Der Abschluß der Prophetie im Alten Testament: Ein Versuch zur Frage der Vorgeschichte des Kanons.* Biblisch-theologische Studien 17. Neukirchen-Vluyn: Neukirchener Verlag, 1991.

Van Leeuwen, Raymond C. "Scribal Wisdom and Theodicy in the Book of the Twelve." In *In Search of Wisdom* (Festschrift J. G. Gammie). Edited by L. G. Perdue et al., 31–49. Louisville: Westminster John Knox, 1993.

Watts, John D. W. "Prophetic Genre in the Book of the Twelve." In *Vision and Prophecy in Amos.* Expanded anniversary edition, 123–33. Macon, Ga.: Mercer University Press, 1997.

Wolfe, Rolland Emerson. "The Editing of the Book of the Twelve." *ZAW* 53, no. 1 (1935): 90–129.

6. Use at Qumran and in Rabbinic Literature

Blechmann, Malke. *Das Buch Amos im Talmud und Midrasch.* Leipzig: Oswald Schmidt, 1937.

Brooke, George L. "The Amos–Numbers Midrash (CD 7:13b–8:1a) and Messianic Expectation." *ZAW* 92, no. 3 (1980): 397–404.

Brooke, George J. *Exegesis at Qumran: 4QFlorilegium in Its Jewish Context.* JSOTSup 29. Sheffield: JSOT Press, 1985.

Fuller, Russell E. "The Twelve." In E. Ulrich et al., *Qumran Cave 4,* vol. 10: *The Prophets,* 246–49, 294–309. DJD 15. Oxford: Clarendon, 1997.

Iwry, Samuel. "Was There a Migration to Damascus? The Problem of *šby yśr'l.*" In *W. F. Albright Volume.* Edited by A. Malamat, 80–88. *EI,* 9. Jerusalem: Israel Exploration Society, 1969.

Knibb, Michael A. "The Interpretation of Damascus Document VII,9b–VIII,2a and XIX,5b–14." *RevQ* 15, nos. 1–2 (1991): 242–51.

Levey, Samson H. "Amos in the Rabbinic Tradition." In *Tradition as Openness to the Future* (Festschrift W. W. Fisher). Edited by F. O. Francis and R. P Wallace, 55–69. Lanham, Md.: University Press of America, 1984.

Murphy-O'Connor, Jerome. "A Literary Analyis of Damascus Document VI,2–VIII,3." *RB* 78, no. 2 (1971): 210–32.

Murphy-O'Connor, Jerome. "The Original Text of CE 7:9–8:2 = 19:5–14." *HTR* 64 (1971): 379–86.

Murphy-O'Connor, Jerome. "The Damascus Document Revisited." *RB* 92, no. 3 (1985): 210–32.

Nägele, Sabine. *Laubhütte Davids und Wolkensohn: Eine auslegungsgeschichlichte Studie zu Amos 9, 11 in der jüdischen und christlichen Exegese.* AGJU 24. Leiden: Brill, 1995.

Routtenberg, Hyman J. *Amos of Tekoa: A Study in Interpretation.* New York: Vantage, 1971.

7. Use in the New Testament

Aldrich, Willard M. "The Interpretation of Acts 15:13–18." *BSac* 111, no. 4 (1954): 317–23.

Braun, Michael A. "James' Use of Amos at the Jerusalem Council: Steps Toward a Solution of the Textual and Theological Problems (Acts 15)." *JETS* 20, no. 2 (1977): 113–21.

Catchpole, David R. "Paul, James and the Apostolic Decree." *NTS* 23, no. 4 (1977): 428–44.

DuPont, Jaques. "Un peuple d'entre les nations (Actes 15:14)." *NTS* 31, no. 3 (1985): 321–35.

Kaiser, W. C., Jr. "The Davidic Promise and the Inclusion of the Gentiles (Amos 9:9–15 and Acts 15:13–18): A Test Passage for Theological Systems." *JETS* 20, no. 2 (1977): 97–111 (reprinted in idem, *The Uses of the Old Testament in the New*, 177–94. Chicago: Moody, 1985).

King, David M. "The Use of Amos 9:11–12 in Acts 15:16–18." *Ashland Theological Journal* 21, no. 1 (1989): 8–13.

Mauro, Philip. "Building Again the Tabernacle of David." *Evangelical Quarterly* 9, no. 4 (1937): 398–417.

Nägele, Sabine. *Laubhütte Davids und Wolkensohn: Eine auslegungsgeschichtliche Studie zu Amos 9, 11 in der jüdischen und christlichen Exegese*. AGJU 24. Leiden: Brill, 1995.

Paulo, Pierre-Antoine. *Le problème ecclésiaste des Actes à la lumière des deux prophéties d'Amos*. Montreal: Editions Bellarmin; Paris: Cerf, 1985.

Richard, Earle. "The Creative Use of Amos by the Author of Acts." *NovT* 24, no. 1 (1982): 37–55.

Riesner, Rainer. "James's Speech (Acts 15:13–21) (Luke 2:29–32), Simeon's Hymn, and Luke's Sources." In *Jesus of Nazareth: Lord and Christ: Essays on the Historical Jesus and New Testament Christology*. Edited by J. B. Green and M. Turner, 263–78. Grand Rapids: Eerdmans, 1994.

Zimmerman, Charles. "To This Agree the Words of the Prophets." *Grace Journal* 4, no. 1 (1963): 28–40.

8. General Theology and Message

Allen, Leslie C. "Amos, Prophet of Solidarity." *Vox Evangelica* 6, no. 1 (1969): 42–53.

Amsler, Samuel. "Amos, prophète de la onzième heure." *TZ* 21, no. 4 (1965): 318–28.

Andrew, M. E. "Places, Times and Identities in the Book of Amos." *Asian Journal of Theology* 14, no. 2 (2000): 328–44.

Asen, B. A. "No, Yes, and Perhaps in Amos and the Yahwist." *VT* 43, no. 4 (1993): 433–41.

Auld, A. G. "Amos and Apocalyptic: Vision, Prophecy and Revelation." In *Storia e tradizioni di Israeli* (Festschrift J. A. Soggin). Edited by D. Garrone and F. Israel, 1–14. Brescia: Paideia, 1991.

Auneau, Joseph. "De la justice d'Amos à la justice de Paul." *VSp* 146 (1992): 307–22.

Bach, Robert. "Gottesrecht und weltliches Recht in der Verkündigung des Propheten Amos." In *Festschrift für Günther Dehn*. Edited by W. Schneemelcher, 23–34. Neukirchen-Vluyn: Neukirchener Verlag, 1957.

Bailey, D. Waylon. "Theological Themes in the Prophecy of Amos." *TTE* 52, no. 1 (1995): 79–85.

Barton, John. "History and Rhetoric in the Prophets." In *The Bible as Rhetoric: Studies in Biblical Persuasion and Credibility*. Edited by M. Warner, 51–64. Warwick Studies in Philosophy and Literature. London: Routledge, 1990.

Bell, Robert D. "The Theology of Amos." *BV* 27, no. 2 (1993): 47–54.

Benson, A. "'From the Mouth of the Lion': The Messianism of Amos." *CBQ* 19, no. 2 (1957): 199–212.

Berridge, John M. "Jeremia und die Prophetie des Amos." *TZ* 35 (1979): 321–41.

Bruston, Edouard. "Messages prophétiques: I. Le message d'Amos." *ETR* 7 (1932): 158–72.

Caspari, Wilhelm. "Wer hat die Aussprüche des Propheten Amos gessamelt?" *NKZ* 25, no. 9 (1914): 701–15.

Caspari, Wilhelm. "Erwarten Amos und Hosea den Messias?" *NKZ* 41, no. 12 (1930): 812–24.

Cramer, Karl. *Amos. Versuch einer theologischen Interpretation*. BWANT 51. Stuttgart: Kohlhammer, 1930.

Crook, Margaret B. "Did Amos and Micah Know Isaiah 9:2–7 and 11:1–9?" *JBL* 73, no. 3 (1954): 144–51.

Davies, G. Henton. "Amos—the Prophet of Reunion." *ExpTim* 92, no. 7 (1981): 196–99.

Deissler, Alfons. "Die Propheten Amos und Hosea als 'Wegweiser' für das Gottesvolk." In *Die alttestamentliche Botschaft als Wegweisung*. Edited by J. Zmijewski, 43–57. Stuttgart: Katholisches Bibelwerk, 1990.

Dempster, Stephen. "The Lord Is His Name: A Study of the Distribution of the Names and Titles of God in the Book of Amos." *RB* 98, no. 2 (1991): 170–89.

Dijkema, F. "Le fond des prophéties d'Amos." *OTS* 2 (1943): 18–34.

Eissfeldt, Otto. "Amos und Jona in volkstümlicher Überlieferung." In *Kleine Schriften*, 4:137–42. Tübingen: Mohr, 1960.

Feuillet, André. "L'universalisme et l'alliance dans la religion d'Amos." *BVC* 17 (1957): 17–29.

Frades G., Eduardo. "El rostro de Dios según Amós." *Iter* 20 (1999): 139–66.

García de la Fuente, O. "La búsqueda de Dios según el profeta Amós." *Augustinianum* 12, no. 2 (1972): 257–76.

Giles, T. "The Dual Occurrences of *qwm* in the Book of Amos." *IBS* 12 (1990): 106–16.

Gillingham, Sue. "'Who Makes the Morning Darkness': God and Creation in the Book of Amos." *SwJT* 45, no. 2 (1992): 165–84.

Gottlieb, Hans. "Amos und Jerusalem." *VT* 17, no. 4 (1967): 430–63.

Hasel, Gerhard F. *The Remnant: The History and Theology of the Remnant Idea from Genesis to Isaiah*. Andrews University Monographs 5. Berrien Springs, Mi.: Andrews University Press, 1972.

Hasel, Gerhard F. "'Remnant' as a Meaning of '*bryt*." In *The Archaeology of Jordan and Other Studies*. Edited by L. Geraty and L. G. Herr, 511–24. Berrien Springs, Mi.: Andrews University Press, 1986.

Hasel, Gerhard F. "The Alleged 'No' of Amos and Amos' Eschatology." *AUSS* 29, no. 1 (1991): 3–18.

Helberg, J. L. "Divine Accountability and Human Accountability in the Book of Amos" (Afrikaans). *In die Skriflig* 31, no. 4 (1997): 403–19.

Helberg, J. L. "Amos: A Theology of Threat?" (Afrikaans). *In die Skriflig* 32, no. 3 (1998): 349–64.

Hoffmann, Yair. "A North Israelite Typological Myth and a Judean Historical Tradition: The Exodus in Hosea and Amos," *VT* 39, no. 2 (1989): 169–82.

Hunter, A. Vanlier. *Seek the Lord! A Study of the Meaning and Function of the Exhortation in Amos, Hosea, Isaiah, Micah, and Zephaniah*, 56–123. Baltimore: St. Mary's Seminary & University, 1982.

Irwin, W. A. "The Thinking of Amos." *AJSL* 49, no. 2 (1932): 102–14.

Jeremias, Jörg. "Jakob im Amosbuch." In *Die Väter Israels: Beiträge zur Theologie der Patriarchenüberlieferungen im Alten Testament* (Festschrift J. Scharbert), ed. M. Görg, 139–54. Stuttgart: Katholisches Bibelwerk, 1989 (reprinted in idem, *Hosea und Amos: Studien zu den Anfängen des Dodekapropheten*, 257–71. FAT, 13. Tübingen: Mohr, 1996).

Johnson, Rick. "Prepare to Meet the Lion: The Message of Amos." *SwJT* 38, no. 1 (1995): 20–28.

Kapelrud, Arvid S. "God as Destroyer in the Preaching of Amos and in the Ancient Near East." *JBL* 71, no. 1 (1952): 33–38.

Kapelrud, Arvid S. "His Idea of God." In *Central Ideas in Amos*, 33–59. Oslo: Aschehoug, (Nygaard), 1956.

Kapelrud, Arvid S. "New Ideas in Amos." In *Volume du Congrès, Genève 1965*. Edited by G. W. Anderson et al., 193–206. VTSup 15. Leiden: Brill, 1966.

Keel, Othmar. "Rechttun oder Annahme des drohenden Gerichts? Erwägungen zu Amos, dem früheren Jesaia und Micha." *BZ* 21 (1977): 200–218.

Koch, Klaus. *The Prophets*, vol. 2: *The Assyrian Period*, 36–76. Translated by M. Kohl. Philadelphia: Fortress, 1983.

Kroeker, Jacob. *Amos und Hosea. Künder der Gerichtigkeit und Liebe*, 67–126. Das lebendige Wort 4. 2d ed. Giessen and Basel: Brunnen, 1960.

Labuschagne, C. J. "Amos' Conception of God and the Popular Theology of His Time." *OTWSA* 7–8 (1964–1965): 122–33.

Leahy, Michael. "The Popular Idea of God in Amos." *ITQ* 22, no. 1 (1955): 68–73.

Loretz, Oswald. "Exodus, Dekalog, und Ausschliesslichkeit im Amos- und Hosea-Buch in der Perspektive ugaritischer Poesie." *UF* 24 (1992): 217–48.

Mamie, Pierre. "Le livre d'Amos: Les châtiments et le 'reste d'Israël.'" *Nova et Vera* 37, no. 3 (1962): 217–23.

Meynet, Roland. "'Le lion a rugi. Qui ne craindrait?' La peur dans le livre d'Amos." *LVitae* 49, no. 2 (1994): 157–65.

Morgenstern, Julian. "The Universalism in Amos." In *Essays Presented to Leo Baeck on the Occasion of His Eightieth Birthday*, 106–26. London: East & West Library, 1954.

Mousset, Pazifique. "La pédagogie d'un prophète: Amos." *Catéchistes* 27 (1956): 267–73.

Müller, Hans-Peter. "Ein Paradigma zur Theologie der alttestamentlichen Wissenschaft: Amos, seine Epigonen und Interpreten." *NZSTR* 33, no. 2 (1991): 112–38.

Ogden, D. Kelly. "The Earthquake Motif in the Book of Amos." In *Goldene Äpfel in silbernen Schalen: Collected Communications to the XIIIth Congress of the International Organization for the Study of the Old Testament, Leuven*. Edited by K.-D. Schunck and M. Augustin, 69–80. BEATAJ 20. Frankfurt am Main: Lang, 1992.

Pfeifer, Gerhard. "Das Ja des Amos." *VT* 39, no. 4 (1989): 497–503.

Pfeifer, Gerhard. "Amos und Deuterojesaia denkformenanalytisch verglichen." *ZAW* 93, no. 3 (1981): 439–43.

Pfeifer, Gerhard. "Jahwe als Schöpfer der Welt und Herr ihrer Mächte in der Verkündigung des Propheten Amos." *VT* 41, no. 4 (1991): 475–81.

Pfeifer, Gerhard. *Die Theologie des Propheten Amos*. Frankfurt au Main: Peter Lang, 1995.

Reimer, Haroldo. *Richtet auf das Rechts! Studien zur Botschaft des Amos*. SBS 149. Stuttgart: Katholisches Bibelwerk, 1992.

Rudolph, Wilhelm. "Gott und Mensch bei Amos." In *Imago Dei* (Festschrift G. Krüger). Edited by H. Bornkamm, 19–31. Giessen: Töpelmann, 1932.

Savarie-Hure, Jacqueline. *L'homme de feu ou Amos, le prophète*. Paris: Cerf, 1993.

Schmidt, J. M. "Ausgangspunkt und Ziel prophetischer Verkündigung im 8. Jahrhundert." *VF* 22, no. 1 (1977): 65–82.

Schmitt, John J. "The Virgin of Israel: Referent and Use of the Phrase in Amos and Jeremiah." *CBQ* 53, no. 3 (1991): 365–87.

Schmitt, John J. "Samaria in the Books of the Prophets of the Eighth Century BCE." In *Proceedings of the Eleventh World Congress of Jewish Studies. Jerusalem, June 22–29, 1993*. Edited by D. Assaf, 115–21. Jerusalem: World Union of Jewish Studies, 1994.

Smend, Rudolf. "Das Nein des Amos." *EvT* 23, no. 8 (1963): 404–23.

Smend, Rudolf. "'Das Ende ist gekommen.' Ein Amoswort in der Priesterschrift." In *Die Botschaft und die Boten* (Festschrift H. W. Wolff), ed. J. Jeremias and L. Perlitt, 67–72. Neukirchen-Vluyn: Neukirchener Verlag, 1981 (reprinted in *Die Mitte des Alten Testament*. Edited by E. Jüngel and R. Smend, 154–59. BEvT 99. Munich: Kaiser, 1986).

Staples, W. E. "Epic Motifs in Amos." *JNES* 25, no. 2 (1966): 106–12.

Stephoulis, Johannes. "Der 'Tag des Herrn' und der Prophet Amos." *Greg* 76 (1993): 307–21.

Talshir, Z. "The Representation of the Divine Epithet *sb'wt* in the Septuagint and the Accepted Divisions of the Books of the Kingdoms." *JQR* 78, no. 1 (1987): 57–75.

Thompson, Michael E.W. "Amos—a Prophet of Hope?" *ExpTim* 104, no. 3 (1992–1993): 71–76.

Urbrock, William J. "The Book of Amos: The Sounds and the Silences." *CurTM* 23, no. 4 (1996): 245–53.

van der Merwe, B. J. "A Few Remarks on the Religious Terminology in Amos and Hosea." *OTWSA* 7–8 (1964–1965): 143–52.

van Selms, A. "Isaac in Amos." *OTWSA* 7–8 (1964–1965): 157–65.

Vermaak, Petrus S. "The Meaning of *pesha* in the Book of Amos." In *Proceedings of the Eleventh World Congress of Jewish Studies. Jerusalem, June 22–29, 1993*, ed. D. Assaf, 107–14. Jerusalem: World Union of Jewish Studies, 1994.

Watts, John D. W. "Amos's Eschatology." In *Vision and Prophecy in Amos*, 68–84. Grand Rapids: Eerdmans; Leiden: Brill, 1958 (reprinted in *Vision and Prophecy in Amos*. Expanded anniversary edition, 91–108. Macon, Ga.: Mercer University Press, 1997).

Williams, Donald L. "The Theology of Amos." *RevExp* 63, no. 4 (1966): 393–403.

Wolff, Hans Walter. *Die Stunde des Amos. Prophetie und Protest*. Munich: Chr. Kaiser, 1969.

Wolff, Hans Walter. "The Irresistible Word (Amos)." *CurTM* 10, no. 1 (1983): 4–13 (reprinted in *Confrontations with Prophets: Discovering the Old Testament's New and Contemporary Significance*, 9–21. Philadelphia: Fortress, 1983).

Zenger, Erich. "Die eigentliche Botschaft des Amos: Von der Relevanz der Politischen Theologie in einer exegetischen Kontroverse." In *Mystik und Politik: Theologie im Ringen um Geschichte und Gesellschaft* (Festschrift J. B. Metz). Edited by E. Schille-beeckz, 394–406. Mainz: Grünewald, 1988.

Zimmerli, Walter. "Das Gottesrecht bei den Propheten Amos, Hosea und Jesaja." In *Werden und Wirken des Alten Testaments* (Festschrift C. Westermann). Edited by R. Albertz, H.-P. Müller, and H. W. Wolff, 216–35. Göttingen: Vandenhoeck & Ruprecht; Neukirchen-Vluyn: Neukirchener Verlag, 1980.

9. Theological Traditions

9.1. General

Jeremias, Jörg. "Jakob im Amosbuch." In *Die Väter Israels. Beiträge zur Theologie der Patriarchenüberlieferungen im Alten Testament* (Festschrift J. Scharbert). Edited by M. Görg, 139–54. Stuttgart: Katholisches Bibelwerk, 1989.

Schmid, Hans Heinrich. "Amos: Zur Frage nach der 'geistigen Heimat' des Propheten." In *Altorientalische Welt in der alttestamentlichen Theologie*, 121–44. Zurich: Theologische Verlag, 1974.

Smith, Gary V. "Continuity and Discontinuity in Amos' Use of Tradition." *JETS* 34, no. 1 (1991): 33–42.

9.2. Historical Traditions

Barriocanal Gómez, José Luis. "La ubicación de la tradición del Éxodo en el libro de Amós." *Burgense* 41 (2000): 327–44.

Barriocanal Gómez, José Luis. *La relectura de la tradición del Éxodo en el libro de Amós*. Tesi Gregoriana Teologia 58. Rome: Gregorian University Press, 2000.

Collins, John J. "History and Tradition in the Prophet Amos." *ITQ* 41, no. 2 (1974): 120–33 (reprinted in *The Bible in Its Literary Milieu: Contemporary Essays*. Edited by J. R. Maier and V. L. Tollers, 121–33. Grand Rapids: Eerdmans, 1979).

Hoffmann, Y. "A North Israelite Typological Myth and a Judean Historical Tradition: The Exodus in Hosea and Amos." *VT* 39, no. 2 (1989): 169–82.

Loretz, Oswald. "Exodus, Dekalog und Ausschließlichkeit Jahwes im Amos- und Hosea-Buch in der Perspektive ugaritischer Poesie." *UF* 24 (1993): 217–48.

Proksch, Otto. *Die Geschichtsbetrachtung bei Amos, Hosea und Jeremia*. Königsberg: Hartung, 1901.

Vollmer, Jochen. *Geschichtliche Rückblicke und Motive in der Prophetie des Amos, Hosea und Jesaja*. BZAW 119. Berlin: de Gruyter, 1971.

9.3. Cult (also note the references under 1:1; 5:21–27; 7:14–15)

Bach, Robert. "Gottesrecht und weltliches Recht in der Verkündigung des Propheten Amos." In *Festschrift für Günther Dehn*. Edited by W. Schneemelcher, 23–34. Neukirchen-Vluyn: Neukirchener Verlag, 1957.

Bentzen, A. "The Ritual Background of Amos I,2–II,16." *OTS* 8 (1950): 85–99.

Brueggemann, Walter. "Amos IV 4–13 and Israel's Covenant Worship." *VT* 15, no. 1 (1965): 1–15.

Crenshaw, James L. "Amos and the Theophanic Tradition." *ZAW* 80, no. 2 (1968): 203–15.

Farr, Georges. "The Language of Amos, Popular or Cultic?" *VT* 16, no. 3 (1966): 312–24.

Gant, C. "Religious Worship in the Book of Amos." *Melita Theologica* 3 (1950): 75–93; 4 (1951): 34–48.

Kapelrud, Arvid S. "Cult and Prophetic Words." *ST* 4, no. 1 (1951): 5–12.

Kapelrud, Arvid S. *Central Ideas in Amos*. Oslo: Aschehoug (Nygaard), 1956.

Maigret, Jacques. "Amos et le sanctuaire de Bethel." *BTS* 47 (1962): 5–6.

Neubauer, Karl Wilhelm. "Erwägungen zu Amos 5:14–15." *ZAW* 78, no. 3 (1966): 292–316.

Reventlow, H. Graf. *Das Amt des Propheten bei Amos*. FRLANT 80. Göttingen: Vandenhoeck & Ruprecht, 1962.

Smend, Rudolf. "Das Nein des Amos." *EvT* 23, no. 8 (1963): 404–23.

Story, Cullen I. K. "Amos–Prophet of Praise." *VT* 30, no. 1 (1980): 67–80.

Vuilleumier, René. *La tradition culturelle d'Israël dans la prophétie d'Amos et d'Osée*. Cahiers théologiques 45. Neuchâtel: Delachaux & Niestlé, 1960.

Weiss, Meir. "Concerning Amos' Repudiation of the Cult." In *Pomegranates and Golden Bells* (Festschrift J. Milgrom). Edited by D. P. Wright et al., 199–214. Winona Lake, Ind.: Eisenbrauns, 1995.

Würthwein, Ernst. "Amos-Studien." *ZAW* 62, nos. 1–2 (1949–1950): 10–52 (reprinted in *Wort und Existenz: Studien zum Alten Testament*, 68–110. Göttingen: Vandenhoeck & Ruprecht, 1970).

Würthwein, Ernst. "Kultpolemik oder Kultbescheid?" In *Tradition und Situation* (Festschrift A. Weiser). Edited by O. Kaiser and E. Würthwein, 115–31. Göttingen: Vandenhoeck & Ruprecht, 1963 (reprinted in E. Würthwein, *Wort und Existenz: Studien zum Alten Testament*, 144–60. Göttingen: Vandenhoeck & Ruprecht, 1970).

9.4. Covenant and Law

Bach, Robert. "Gottesrecht und weltliches Recht in der Verkündigung des Propheten Amos." In *Festschrift für Günther Dehn*. Edited by W. Schneemelcher, 23–34. Neukirchen-Vluyn: Neukirchener Verlag, 1957.

Brueggemann, Walter. "Amos IV 4–13 and Israel's Covenant Worship." *VT* 15, no. 1 (1965): 1–15.

Boyle, Marjorie O'Rourke. "The Covenant Lawsuit of the Prophet Amos: III 1–IV 13." *VT* 21, no. 3 (1971): 338–62.

Dion, Paul E. "Le message moral du prophète Amos s'inspirait-il du 'droit de l'alliance'?" *ScEs* 27, no. 1 (1975): 5–34.

Dürr, Lorenz. "Altorientalisches Recht bei Propheten Amos und Hosea." *BZ* 23, no. 1 (1935): 150–57.

Fensham, F. Charles. "Curses of Protection in Hittite Vassal-Treaties and the Old Testament." *VT* 13, no. 2 (1963): 133–43.

Fensham, F. Charles. "Common Trends in Curses of the Near Eastern Treaties and *Kudurru*-Inscriptions Compared with the Maledictions of Amos and Isaiah." *ZAW* 75, no. 2 (1963): 155–75.

Feuillet, André. "L'universalisme et l'alliance dans la religion d'Amos." *BVC* 17 (1957): 17–29.

Reventlow, H. Graf. *Das Amt des Propheten bei Amos*. FRLANT 80. Göttingen: Vandenhoeck & Ruprecht, 1962.

Robscheit, Helmuth. "Die Thora bei Amos und Hosea." *EvT* 10, no. 1 (1950): 26–38.

Seilhamer, Frank H. "The Role of the Covenant in the Mission and Message of Amos." In *A Light unto My Path* (Festschrift J. M. Myers). Edited by H. N. Bream, R. D. Heim, and C. A. Moore, 435–51. Philadelphia: Temple University Press, 1974.

Sinclair, L. A. "The Courtroom Motif in the Book of Amos." *JBL* 85, no. 3 (1966): 351–53.

Snyder, George. "The Law and Covenant in Amos." *ResQ* 25, no. 3 (1982): 158–66.

Vogels, Walter. "Invitation à revenir à l'alliance et universalisme en Amos IX 7." *VT* 32 (1972): 223–39.

Würthwein, Ernst. "Amos-Studien." *ZAW* 62, nos. 1–2 (1949–1950): 10–52.

9.5. Wisdom

Crenshaw, J. L. "The Influence of the Wise on Amos: The 'Doxologies of Amos' and Job 5,9–16; 9:5–10." *ZAW* 79, no. 1 (1967): 42–52.

Crenshaw, J.L. "Amos and the Theophanic Tradition." *ZAW* 80, no. 2 (1968): 203–15.

Fey, Reinhard. *Amos und Jesaja. Abhändigigkeit und Eigenständigkeit des Jesaja*. WMANT 12. Neukirchen-Vluyn: Neukirchener Verlag, 1963.

Schmid, H. H. "Amos. Zur Frage nach der 'geistige Heimat' des Propheten." *WuD* 10 (1969): 85–103.

Soggin, J. Alberto. "Amos and Wisdom." In *Wisdom in Ancient Israel* (Festschrift J. A. Emerton). Edited by J. Day et al., 119–23. Cambridge: Cambridge University Press, 1995.

Stoebe, Hans-Joachim. "Überlegungen zu den geistlichen Voraussetzungen der Prophetie des Amos." In *Wort–Gebot–Glaube* (Festschrift W. Eichrodt). Edited by H.-J. Stoebe et al., 209–15. ATANT 59. Zurich: Zwingli, 1970.

Terrien, S. "Amos and Wisdom." In *Israel's Prophetic Heritage* (Festschrift J. Muilenburg), ed. B. W. Anderson and W. Harrelson, 108–15. New York: Harper, 1962.

Whybray, R. N. *The Intellectual Tradition in the Old Testament*. BZAW 135. Berlin: de Gruyter, 1974.

Whybray, R. N. "Prophecy and Wisdom." In *Israel's Prophetic Tradition* (Festschrift P. R. Ackroyd). Edited by R. Coggins, A. Phillips, and M. Knibb, 181–99. Cambridge: Cambridge University Press, 1982.

Wittenberg, Günther H. "A Fresh Look at Amos and Wisdom." *OTE* 4, no. 1 (1991): 7–18.

Wolff, Hans Walter. *Amos the Prophet: The Man and His Background*. Translated by F. R. McCurley. Philadelphia: Fortress, 1973.

10. Specific Topics of Theology

10.1. The Day of the Lord

Hoffmann, Y. "The Day of the Lord as a Concept and a Term in the Prophetic Literature." *ZAW* 93, no. 1 (1981): 37–50.

McCullough, W. S. "Israel's Eschatology from Amos to Daniel." In *Studies on the Ancient Palestinian World* (Festschrift F. V. Winnett). Edited by J. W. Wevers and D. B. Redford, 86–101. Toronto Semitic Texts and Studies 2. Toronto: University of Toronto Press, 1972.

Rad, Gerhard von. "The Origin of the Concept of the Day of Yahweh." Translated by H. H. Rowley and P. R. Weiss. *JSS* 4 (1959): 97–108.

Stuart, D. "The Sovereign Day of Conquest: A Possible Ancient Near Eastern Reflex of the Israelite 'Day of the Lord.'" *BASOR* 221 (1976): 159–64.

van Leeuwen, C. "The Prophecy of the *yōm YHWH* in Amos 5:18–20." In *Language and Meaning: Studies in Hebrew Language and Biblical Exegesis*. Edited by A. S. van der Woude, 113–34. *OTS* 19. Leiden: Brill, 1974.

Weiss, Meir. "The Origin of the 'Day of the Lord' Reconsidered." *HUCA* 37 (1966): 29–60.

10.2. Justice: Socioeconomic, Political, Gender (also note below, 11. "Contemporary Relevance and Pastoral Use")

Alger, B. "The Theology and Social Ethic of Amos." *Scripture* 17 (1965): 109–16.

Amsler, Samuel. "Amos et les droits de l'homme (Étude d'Am 1 et 2)." In *De la Tôrah au Messie* (Festschrift H. Cazelles). Edited by M. Carrez, J. Doré, and P. Grelot, 181–87. Paris: Desclée, 1981.

Andrews, Mary E. "Hesiod and Amos." *JR* 23, no. 3 (1943): 194–205.

Atger, Jacques and Françoise. "Le message d'Amos." *Christianisme Social* 74 (1966): 303–12.

Bailey, Joseph G. "Amos: Preacher of Social Reform." *TBT* 19, no. 5 (1981): 306–13.

Berquist, Jon L. "Dangerous Waters of Justice and Righteousness: Amos 5:18–27." *BTB* 23, no. 2 (1993): 54–63.

Bird, Phyllis A. "Poor Man or Poor Woman? Gendering the Poor in Prophetic Texts." In *On Reading Prophetic Texts: Gender-Specific and Related Studies in Memory of F. van Dijk-Hemmes*. Edited by B. Becking and M. Dijkstra, 37–51. Leiden: Brill, 1993 (reprinted in *Missing Persons and Mistaken Identities: Women and Gender in Ancient Israel*, 67–78. OBT. Minneapolis: Fortress, 1997).

Bohlen, Reinhold. "Zur Sozialkritik des Propheten Amos." *TTZ* 95 (1986): 282–301.

Botterweck, G. Johannes. "'Sie verkaufen den Unschuldigen um Geld.' Zur sozialen Kritik des Propheten Amos." *BibLeb* 12, no. 4 (1971): 215–31.

Carroll R., M. Daniel. "The Prophetic Text and the Literature of Dissent in Latin America: Amos, García Márquez, and Cabrera Infante Dismantle Militarism." *BibInt* 4, no. 1 (1996): 76–100.

Casanova R., Humberto. "La época de Amós y la justicia social." *BolTeol* 50 (1993): 95–106.

Clines, David J. A. "Metacommentating Amos." In *Of Prophets' Visions and the Wisdom of Sages* (Festschrift R. N. Whybray). Edited by H. A. McKay and D. J. A. Clines, 142–60. JSOTSup 162. Sheffield: Sheffield Academic Press, 1993.

Deist, F. E. "Politics, Economics, Business, and Ethics: A Case Study from the Times of Ahab and Jeroboam II." *Theologia Evangelia* 19 (1986): 36–46.

del Valle, J. L. "Amós: justicia 'versus' poder." *BibFe* 20 (1994): 28–42.

Dempsey, Carol J. *The Prophets: A Liberation-Critical Reading*, 7–21. Minneapolis: AugsburgFortress, 2000.

Escobar, Donoso S. "Social Justice in the Book of Amos." *RevExp* 92, no. 2 (1995): 169–74.

Fendler, Marlene. "Zur Sozialkritik des Amos: Versuch einer wirtschafts- und sozialgeschichtlichen Interpretation alttestamentlicher Texte." *EvT* 33, no. 1 (1973): 32–53.

Finley, Thomas John. "An Evangelical Response to the Preaching of Amos." *JETS* 28, no. 4 (1985): 411–20.

Fleischer, Günther. *Von Menschenverkäufern, Baschankühen und Rechtsverkehrern: Die Sozialkritik des Amosbuches in historisch-kritischer, sozialgeschichtlicher und archäologischer Perspektive*. BBB 74. Frankfurt am Main: Athenäum, 1989.

Giles, T. "*dl* and *'bywn*: The Poor and the Needy in the Book of Amos." *BRT* 1 (1991): 12–20.

Gossai, Hemchand. *Justice, Righteousness, and the Social Critique of the Eighth-Century Prophets*. American University Studies, Series VII: Theology and Religion 141. New York: Peter Lang, 1993.

Grimsrud, Ted. "Healing Justice: The Prophet Amos and a 'New' Theology of Justice." In *Peace and Justice Shall Embrace: Power and Theopolitics in the Bible*. Edited by T. Grimsrud and L. L. Johns, 64–85. Telford, Pa.: Pandora; Scottdale, Pa.: Herald, 1999.

Howington, Nolan P. "Toward an Ethical Understanding of Amos." *RevExp* 63, no. 4 (1966): 405–12.

Huey, F. B., Jr. "The Ethical Teaching of Amos: Its Content and Relevance." *SwJT* 9, no. 1 (1966): 59–67.

Huffmon, Herbert B. "The Social Role of Amos' Message." In *The Quest for the Kingdom of God* (Festschrift G. E. Mendenhall). Edited by H. B. Huffmon, F. A. Spina, and A. R. Green, 109–16. Winona Lake, Ind.: Eisenbrauns, 1983.

Jaramillo Rivas, Pedro. *La injusticia social y la opresión en el lenguaje figurado de los profetas*, 181–234. Navarra, Spain: Verbo Divino, 1992.

Jaruzelska, Izabela. "Social Structure in the Kingdom of Israel in the Eighth Century B.C. as Reflected in the Book of Amos." *FO* 29 (1992–1993): 91–117.

Jaruzelska, Izabela. "People Pronouncing Sentences in Court: Amos 5,7–12.16–17: An Attempt at Sociological Identification." *FO* 30 (1994): 77–94.

Jaruzelska, Izabela. *Amos and the Officialdom in the Kingdom of Israel: The Socio-Economic Position of the Officials in the Light of the Biblical, the Epigraphic and Archaeological Evidence*. Seria Socjologia 25. Poznam: Wydawnictwo Naukowe Uniwersytetu im. Adam Mickiewicza, 1998.

Lattes, Dante. "Amos, prophète de la justice." *Madregoth* 1 (1940): 23–31.

Levin, Christoph. "Das Amosbuch der Anawim." *ZTK* 94, no. 4 (1997): 407–36.

McFadyen, John Edgar. *A Cry for Justice: A Study in Amos*. Short Course Series. New York: Charles Scribner's Sons, 1912.

Owan, Kris. "Championing the Cause of the Less Privileged: Human Promotion in Nigeria in the Light of Prophet Amos." *Revue Africaine de Théologie* 17, no. 2 (1993): 37–57.

Randellini, Lino. "Ricchi e poveri nel libro del Profeta Amos." *Studium Biblicum Franciscanum Liber Annuus* 2 (1951–52): 5–86.

Randellini, Lino. "Il profeta Amos, defensor del poveri." *Bolletino del l'Amicizia Ebraico-Cristiana di Firenze* 6 (1971): 35–43.

Reimer, Haroldo. *Richtet auf des Rechts! Studien zur Botschaft des Amos*. SBS 149. Stuttgart: Katholisches Bibelwerk, 1992.

Reimer, Haroldo. "Agentes y mecanismos de opresión y explotación en Amós." *RIBLA* 12 (1992): 69–81.

Sanderson, J. E. "Amos." In *The Women's Bible Commentary*. Edited by C. A. Newsome and S. H. Ringe, 205–9. Louisville: Westminster John Knox, 1992.

Sicre, José Luis. *Los dioses olvidados. Poder y riqueza en los profetas de Israel*. Estudios de Antiguo Testamento 1. Madrid: Cristiandad, 1979.

Sicre, José Luis. *'Con los pobres de la tierra.' La justicia social en los profetas de Israel*. Madrid: Cristiandad, 1984.

Spiegel, Shalom. "Amos vs. Amaziah." In *The Jewish Expression*. Edited by J. Goldin, 38–65. New Haven: Yale University Press, 1976.

Strydom, J. G. "Sosiale geregtigheid by die profeet Amos: Die landsbelofte as vertrekpunt." *HervTS* 52, nos. 2–3 (1996): 431–48.

Vesco, J.-L. "Amos de Teqoa, défenseur de l'homme." *RB* 87, no. 4 (1980): 481–543.

Wacker, Marie-Therese. "Das Buche Amos: Die Wahrheit ist konkret." In *Kompendium feministische Bibelauslegung*. Edited by L. Schotroff and M.-T. Wacker, 320–26. Gütersloh: Gütersloher Verlagshaus, 1998.

Witaszek, Gabriel. *Prorocy Amos i Micheasz wobec niesprawiedliwosci spolecznej*. Tuchow: Mala Poligrafia Redemptorystow, 1992.

Zenger, Erich. "Die eigentliche Botschaft des Amos: Von der Relevanz der politischen Theologie in einer exegetischen Kontroverse." In *Mystik und Politik: Theologie im Ringen um Geschichte und Gesellschaft* (Festschrift J. B. Metz). Edited by E. Schillebeeckz, 394–406. Mainz: Grünewald, 1988.

11. Contemporary Relevance and Pastoral Use

Achtemeier, Elizabeth. *Preaching from the Minor Prophets*, 36–49. Grand Rapids: Eerdmans, 1998.

Aerathedathu, Thomas. "The Challenge of the Indian Situation and the Relevance of Amos' Teaching for India." *Indian Journal of Spirituality* 4 (1991): 279–98.

Barackman, Paul F. "Preaching from Amos." *Int* 13, no. 3 (1959): 296–315.

Baumann, Franz. *Amos. Eine Botschaft aus alter Zeit für uns moderne Menschen*. Zurich: Gotthelf, 1962.

Beyer, Douglas. "Preaching from Amos." *SwJT* 38, no. 1 (1995): 36–43.

Camroux, Martin. "Let Justice Roll (Amos 7:10–15)." *ExpTim* 105, no. 8 (1994): 244–45.

Casalils, Georges. "Du texte au sermon: Amos 8." *ETR* 46, no. 2 (1971): 113–24.

Deist, F. E. "Politics, Economics, Business, and Ethics: A Case Study from the Times of Ahab and Jeroboam II." *Theologia Evangelia* 19 (1986): 36–46.

Drinkard, Joel F. "Thus Says the Lord." *RevExp* 92, no. 2 (1995): 219–33.

Fabian, Norbert. *Protest gegen Ausbeter: Amos' sozialkritische Ansätze in der alttestamentlichen Prophetie. Ein Werkbuch für Religionsunterricht, Gemeinschaftskunde und Gemeindearbeit*. Pfeiffer Werkbücher 118. Munich: Pfeiffer, 1973.

Francisco, Clyde T. "Teaching Amos in the Churches." *RevExp* 63, no. 4 (1966): 413–25.

Francisco, Clyde T. "Expository Outline of the Book of Amos." *RevExp* 63, no. 4 (1966): 427–28.

Haag, Ernst. "Das Schweigen Gottes. Ein Wort des Propheten Amos (Am 8,11–12)." *BibLeb* 10 (1969): 157–64.

Honeycutt, Roy L. "Amos and Contemporary Issues." *RevExp* 63, no. 4 (1966): 441–57.

Howie, Carl G. "Expressly for Our Time: The Theology of Amos." *Int* 13, no. 3 (1959): 273–85.

Jobling, David and Nathan Loewen, "Sketches for Earth Readings of the Book of Amos." In *Readings from the Perspective of the Earth*. Edited by N. C. Habel, 72–85. Earth Bible 1. Sheffield: Sheffield Academic Press, 2000.

Keller, Carl A. "Notes bibliques de prédication sur les textes du prophète Amos." *VCaro* 15, no. 4 (1961): 390–98.

Loscalzo, Craig A. "Preaching Themes from Amos." *RevExp* 92, no. 2 (1995): 195–206.

Lüthi, Walter. *Dies ist's, was der Prophet Amos gesehen hat*. 10th ed. Basel: Reinhart, 1946 (translated as *In the Time of Earthquake: An Exposition of the Book of the Prophet Amos in Relation to Our Own Times*. Translated by J. L. M. Haire and I. Henderson. London: Hodder and Stoughton, 1940).

Martin-Achard, Robert. "Le prédication d'Amos. Remarques exégétiques et homilétiques." *ETR* 41, no. 1 (1966): 13–19.

Martin-Achard, Robert. *Amos. L'homme, le message, l'influence*, 161–271. Geneva: Labor et Fides, 1984.

Nogalski, James D. "A Teaching Outline for Amos." *RevExp* 92, no. 2 (1995): 147–51.

Richardson, Paul A. "Worship Resources for Amos." *RevExp* 92, no. 2 (1995): 207–17.

Schmitt, Armin. *Eines offenes Wort. Das Prophetenbuch Amos für unsere Zeit erschlossen*. Regensberg: F. Pustet, 1985.

Schultes, J. L. "Gott redet auch durch sein Schweigen. Bibel Meditation zu Amos 8:4–7, 11–12." *BL* 48 (1975): 256–59.

Strange, John O. "Preaching from Amos." *SwJT* 9, no. 1 (1966): 69–79.

Vischer, Wilhelm. "'Perhaps the Lord Will Be Gracious' (A Sermon)," (trans. D. C. Miller). *Int* 13, no. 3 (1959): 286–95.

Ward, James, and Christine Ward. *Preaching from the Prophets*, 114–20. Nashville: Abingdon, 1995.

Warwick, Frederick S. "Amos and Hosea—Action and Reaction." *ExpTim* 105, no. 1 (1993): 13–14.

Westermann, Claus. *A Thousand Years and a Day: Our Time in the Old Testament*, 200–212. Translated by S. Rudman. Philadelphia: Muhlenberg; London: SCM, 1962.

Wolff, Hans Walter. "Predigt über Amos 5,1–5." *EvT* 28, no. 1 (1968): 1–8.

Wolff, Hans Walter. "Hunger nach Gerechtigkeit—ungestillt." In *Zuwendung und Gerechtigkeit: Heidelberger Predigten III* (Festschrift C. Westermann). Edited by P. Philippi, 29–35. Göttingen: Vandenhoeck & Ruprecht, 1969.

Wolff, Hans Walter. "The Irresistible Word (Amos)." *CurTM* 10, no. 1 (1983): 4–13. (reprinted in *Confrontations with Prophets: Discovering the Old Testament's New and Contemporary Significance*, 9–21. Philadelphia: Fortress, 1983).

Zenger, Erich. "Die eigentliche Botschaft des Amos: Von der Relevanz der politischen Theologie in einer exegetischen Kontroverse." In *Mystik und Politik: Theologie im Ringen um Geschichte und Gesellschaft* (Festschrift J. B. Metz). Edited by E. Schillebeeckx, 394–406. Mainz: Grünewald, 1988.

Significant Blocks of Text

1. Studies on the Book as a Whole

Gese, Hartmut. "Kleine Beiträge zum Verständnis des Amosbuches." *VT* 12, no. 4 (1962): 417–38.

Gordis, Robert. "Studies in the Book of Amos." *Proceedings of the American Academy for Jewish Research* 46–47 (1979–1980): 201–64.

Lehming, Sigo. "Erwägungen zu Amos." *ZTK* 55, no. 2 (1958): 145–69.

McCullough, W. Stewart. "Some Suggestions about Amos." *JBL* 72, no. 4 (1953): 247–54.

Owens, John Joseph. "Exegetical Studies in the Book of Amos." *RevExp* 63, no. 4 (1966): 429–40.

Pratorius, Franz. "Zum Texte des Amos." *ZAW* 34, no. 1 (1914): 42–44.

Pratorius, Franz. "Bemerkungen zu Amos." *ZAW* 35, no. 1 (1915): 12–25.

Speier, Salomon. "Bemerkungen zu Amos." *VT* 3, no. 3 (1955): 305–10.

van Hoonacker, Albin. "Notes d'exégèse sur quelques passages difficiles d'Amos." *RB* 14, no. 2 (1905): 163–87.

Winter, Alexander. "Analyse des Buches Amos." *TSK* 83 (1910): 323–74.

2. Oracles against the Nations (1:3–2:16)

Amsler, Samuel. "Amos et les droits de l'homme (Étude d'Am 1 et 2)." In *De la Tôrah au Messie* (Festschrift H. Cazelles). Edited by M. Carrez, J. Doré, and P. Grelot, 181–87. Paris: Desclée, 1981.

Barré, Michael. "The Meaning of *l' šybnw* in Amos 1:3–2:6." *JBL* 105, no. 4 (1986): 611–31.

Barton, John. *Amos's Oracles against the Nations. A Study of Amos 1:3–2:5.* SOTSMS 6. Cambridge: Cambridge University Press, 1980.

Beaucamp, E. "Amos 1–2. Le pèshá' d'Israel et celui des nations." *ScEs* 21 (1969): 435–41.

Bentzen, A. "The Ritual Background of Amos 1:2–2:6." *OTS* 8 (1950): 85–99.

Carlson, Agge. "Profeten Amos och Davidsriket." *Religion och Bibel* 25 (1966): 57–78.

Carroll R., M. D. "God and His People Within the Nations' History: A Contextualized Reading of Amos 1–2." *TynBul* 47, no. 1 (1996): 49–70.

Ceresko, Anthony R. "Janus Parallelism in Amos's 'Oracles against the Nations' (Amos 1:3–2:16)." *JBL* 113, no. 4 (1994): 485–93.

Chisolm Jr., Robert B. "'For Three Sins . . . Even for Four': The Numerical Sayings in Amos." *BSac* 147, no. 2 (1990): 188–97.

Christensen, Duane L. "The Prosodic Structure of Amos 1–2." *HTR* 67, no. 4 (1974): 427–36.

Christensen, Duane L. *Transformations of the War Oracle in Old Testament Prophecy: Studies in the Oracles against the Nations.* HDR 3. Missoula, Mont.: Scholars Press, 1975.

Condamin, A. "Amos 1,2–3,8. Authenticité et structure poétique." *RSR* 20 (1930): 298–311.

Dietrich, W. "JHWH, Israel und die Völker beim Propheten Amos." *TZ* 48, nos. 3–4 (1992): 315–28.

Diez Macho, A., and J. A. G. Larraya. "El Ms. 4083f.9 de la Biblioteca Nacional y Universitaria de Estrasburgo. (Fragmento de Amos 1:3–3:7, en hebreo y targum babilónicos)." *EstBib* 19, no. 1 (1960): 91–95.

Freedman, D. N. "Counting Formulae in the Akkadian Epics." *JANESCU* 3 (1971): 65–81.

Fritz, Volkmar. "Die Fremdvölkersprüche des Amos." *VT* 37, no. 1 (1987): 26–38.

Gevirtz, Stanley. "On Canaanite Rhetoric: The Evidence of the Amarna Letters from Tyre." *Or* 42 (1973): 162–77.

Geyer, J. B. "Mythology and Culture in the Oracles against the Nations." *VT* 36, no. 2 (1986): 129–45.

Ginat, L. "Toward the Sequence of Amos's Prophecies against the Nations" (Heb.). *BMik* 34, no. 3 (1989): 250–54.

Gosse, Bernard. "Le recueil d'oracles contre les nations du livre d'Amos et l'histoire deutéronomique." *VT* 38, no. 1 (1988): 22–40.

Hall, Kevin. "Listen Up! The Lion Has Roared: A Study of Amos 1–2." *SwJT* 38, no. 1 (1995): 11–19.

Haran, Menahem. "Some Problems of the Historical Background of 'Prophecies of the Nations' in the Book of Amos" (Heb.). *Yediot* 30 (1966): 56–69.

Haran, Menahem. "Observations on the Historical Background of Amos 1:2–2:6." *IEJ* 18, no. 4 (1968): 201–12.

Haran, Menahem. "Biblical Studies: The Literary Applications of the Numerical Sequence X/X+1 and Their Connections with the Patterns of Parallelism." (Heb.). *Tarbiz* 39 (1969–1970): 109–36. = Haran, Menahem. "The Graded Numerical Sequence and the Phenomenon of 'Automatism' in Biblical Poetry." In *Congress Volume, Uppsala 1971*, 238–67. VTSup 22. Leiden: Brill, 1972.

Hayes, John H. "The Usage of Oracles against the Nations in Ancient Israel." *JBL* 87, no. 1 (1968): 81–92.

Hayes, John H. "Amos's Oracles against the Nations (1:2–2:16)." *RevExp* 92, no. 2 (1995): 153–67.

Hoffmann, Yair. "From Oracle to Prophecy: The Growth, Crystallization and Disintegration of a Biblical Gattung." *JNSL* 10 (1982): 75–81.

Jeremias, Jörg. "Völkersprüche und Visionsberichte im Amosbuche." In *Prophet und Prophetenbuch* (Festschrift O. Kaiser). Edited by V. Fritz, K.-F. Pohlmann, and H. C. Schmitt, 82–97. BZAW 185. Berlin: de Gruyter, 1989 (reprinted in *Hosea und Amos: Studien zu den Anfängen des Dodekapropheten*, 157–71. FAT 13. Tübingen: Mohr, 1996).

Jeremias, Jörg. "Zur Entstehung der Völkersprüche im Amosbuch." In idem, *Hosea und Amos: Studien zu den Anfängen des Dodekapropheten*, 172–82. FAT 13. Tübingen: Mohr, 1996.

Kapelrud, Arvid S. "Execrations of Foreign Nations and of Israel." In *Central Idea in Amos*, 17–33. Oslo: Aschehoug (Nygaard), 1956.

Knierim, Rolf P. "'I Will Not Cause It to Return' in Amos 1 and 2." In *Canon and Authority: Essays in Old Testament Religion and Theology*. Edited by G. W. Coats and B. O. Long, 163–75. Philadelphia: Fortress, 1977.

Köchert, M. "Das Gesetz und die Propheten in Amos 1–2." In *Alttestamentliche Glaube und biblischer Theologie* (Festschrift H. D. Preuss). Edited by J. Hausmann and H.-J. Zobel, 145–54. Stuttgart: Kohlhammer, 1992.

Lempp, W. "Nations in Amos." *South East Asia Journal of Theology* 1, no. 3 (1960): 20–33.

Linville, James R. "What Does 'It' Mean? Interpretation at the Point of No Return in Amos 1–2." *BibInt* 8, no. 4 (2000): 400–424.

Loewenstamm, S. E. "The Climax of Seven Days in Ugaritic Epic Literature." *IEJ* 15 (1965): 121–33.

Loewenstamm, S. E. "The Phrase 'X (or) X Plus One' in Biblical and Old Oriental Laws." *Bib* 53, no. 4 (1972): 543.

Luria, B. Z. "The Prophecies unto the Nations in the Book of Amos from the Point of View of History" (Heb., Eng. summary). *BMik* 54, no. 3 (1973): 285–301, 421–22.

Marti, Karl. "Zur Komposition von Amos 1,3–2,5." In *Abhandlungen zur semitischen Religionsgeschichte und Sprachwissenschaft* (Festschrift W. W. G. Baudissin). Edited by W. Frankenberg and F. Küchler, 323–30. BZAW 33. Giessen: Töpelmann, 1918.

Mosley, Harold R. "The Oracles against the Nations." *TTE* 52 (1995): 37–45.

Müller, Hans-Peter. "Phönizien und Juda in exilisch-nachexilischer Zeit." *WO* 6, no. 2 (1971): 189–204.

Muntingh, L. M. "Political and International Relations of Israel's Neighboring Peoples according to the Oracles of the Book of Amos." *OTWSA* 7–8 (1964–1965): 134–42.

Nielsen, Eduard. "Om formkritik som hjaelpemmiddel i historisk-genetisk forskning, belyst ved eksemplar fra Amos 1–2 og Mika 1." *DTT* 52, no. 4 (1989): 243–50.

Niemann, H. M. "Theologie in geographischen Gewand. Zum Wachstumsprozess der Völkerspruchsammlung Amos 1–2." In *Nachdenken über Israel: Bibel und Theologie* (Festschrift K.-D. Schunk). Edited by H. M. Niemann et al., 177–96. BEATAJ 37. Bern: Peter Lang, 1994.

Noble, Paul R. "Israel among the Nations." *HBT* 15, no. 1 (1993): 56–82.

Noble, Paul R. "'I Will Not Bring "It" Back' (Amos 1:3): A Deliberately Ambiguous Oracle?" *ExpTim* 106, no. 4 (1995): 105–9.

Paul, Shalom M. "Amos 1:3–2:3: A Concatenous Literary Pattern." *JBL* 90, no. 4 (1971): 397–403.

Paul, Shalom M. "A Literary Reinvestigation of the Authenticity of the Oracles against the Nations." In *De la Torah au Messie* (Festschrift H. Cazelles). Edited by M. Carrez, J. Doré, and P. Grelot, 189–204. Paris: Desclée, 1981.

Pfeifer, Gerhard. "Denkformenanalyse als exegetische Methode, erläutert an Amos 1:2–2:16." *ZAW* 88, no. 1 (1976): 56–71.

Pfeifer, Gerhard. "Die Fremdvölkersprüche des Amos—spätere *vaticinia ex eventu*?" *VT* 38, no. 2 (1988): 230–33.

Roth, W. W. M. "The Numerical Sequence X/X+1 in the Old Testament." *VT* 12, no. 3 (1962): 300–311.

Roth, W. W. M. *Numerical Sayings in the Old Testament*. VTSup 13. Leiden: Brill, 1965.

Rudolph, Wilhelm. "Die angefochtenen Völkerspruche in Amos 1 und 2." In *Schalom. Studien zu Glaube und Geschichte Israels* (Festschrift A. Jepsen). Edited by K.-H. Bernhardt, 45–49. AzTh 1/46, Stuttgart: Calwer, 1971.

Schoville, K. N. "A Note on the Oracles of Amos against Gaza, Tyre, and Edom." In *Studies in Prophecy*. Edited by D. Lys, 55–63. VTSup 26. Leiden: Brill, 1974.

Schoville, K. N. "The Sins of Aram in Amos 1." In *Proceedings of the Sixth World Congress of Jewish Studies*, ed. A. Shinan, 1:363–75. 3 vols. Jerusalem: World Union of Jewish Studies, 1977.

Segert, Stanislav. "A Controlling Device for Copying Stereotype Passages (Amos I 3–II 8; VI 1–6)." *VT* 34, no. 4 (1984): 481–82.

Soper, B. Kingston. "For Three Transgressions and for Four: A New Interpretation of Amos 1,3 etc." *ExpTim* 71, no. 3 (1959): 86–87.

Steinman, A. E. "The Order of Amos's Oracles Against the Nations: 1:3–2:16." *JBL* 111, no. 4 (1992): 683–89.

Strus, A. "Interprétation des noms propres dans les oracles contre les nations." In *Congress Volume, Salamanca 1973*. Edited by J. A. Emerton, 272–85. VTSup 36. Leiden: Brill, 1985.

Ulrichsen, J. H. "Oraklene i Amos 1,3ff." *NorTT* 85, no. 1 (1984): 39–54.

Vieweger, Dieter. "Zur Herkunft der Völkerworte im Amosbuch unter besonderer Berücksichtigung des Aramäerspruchs (Am 1:3–5)." In *Altes Testament, Forschung und Wirkung* (Festschrift H. G. Reventlow). Edited by P. Mommer and W. Thiel, 103–19. Bern: Peter Lang, 1994.

Virgulin, Stefano. "Gli oracoli contro le nazioni (Am 1,3–2,15)." *PSV* 27 (1993): 37–48.

Watson, W. G. E. *Classical Hebrew Poetry: A Guide to Its Techniques*. JSOTSup 26. Sheffield: JSOT Press, 1984.

Weiss, Meir. "The Pattern of Numerical Sequence in Amos 1–2: A Re-examination." *JBL* 86, no. 4 (1967): 416–23.

3. Doxologies (or Hymns) (4:13; 5:8–9; 9:5–6)

Berg, Werner. *Die sogennanten Hymnenfragmente in Amosbuch*. Europäische Hochschulschriften, Reihe XXII, Theologie 45. Bern: Herbert Lang; Frankfurt am Main: Peter Lang, 1974.

Byargeon, Rick W. "The Doxologies of Amos: A Study of Their Structure and Theology." *TTE* 52, no. 1 (1995): 47–56.

Carny, P. "Doxologies: A Scientific Myth." *HS* 18 (1977): 149–59.

Crenshaw, J. L. "The Influence of the Wise on Amos: The 'Doxologies of Amos' and Job 5,9–16; 9,5–10." *ZAW* 79, no. 1 (1967): 42–52.

Crenshaw, J. L. "*YHWH Ṣᵉbā'ôt Šᵉmô*: A Form-Critical Analysis." *ZAW* 81, no. 2 (1969): 156–75.

Crenshaw, J. L. "*wdrk 'l bmty 'rs*." *CBQ* 34, no. 1 (1972): 39–53.

Crenshaw, J. L. *Hymnic Affirmation of Divine Justice: The Doxologies of Amos and Related Texts in the Old Testament*. SBLDS 24, Missoula, Mont.: Scholars Press, 1975.

Crüsemann, Frank. *Studien zur Formgeschichte von Hymnus und Danklied in Israel*, 97–106. WMANT 32. Neukirchen-Vluyn: Neukirchener Verlag, 1969.

de Waard, J., and C. Dieterle. "Le dieu créateur dans l'hymne du livre d'Amos." *Foi et Vie* 83, no. 5 (1984): 35–44.

Foresti, Fabrizio. "Funzione semantica dei brani participali de Amos: 4,13; 5,8s.; 9,5s." *Bib* 62, no. 2 (1981): 169–84.

Gaster, T. H. "An Ancient Hymn in the Prophecies of Amos." *JMEOS* 19 (1935): 23–26.

Gillingham, Sue. "'Who Makes the Morning Darkness': God and Creation in the Book of Amos." *SJT* 45, no. 2 (1992): 165–84.

Habel, Norman C. "He Who Stretches Out the Heavens." *CBQ* 34, no. 4 (1972): 417–30.

Horst, Friedrich. "Die Doxologien im Amosbuch." *ZAW* 47, no. 1 (1929): 45–54 (reprinted in *Gottes Recht: Gesammelte Studien zum Recht im Alten Testament. Aus Anlass der Vollendung seines 65. Lebensjahres.* Edited by H. W. Wolff, 155–66. TB 12. Munich: Kaiser, 1961.

Kapelrud, Arvid S. "God as Destroyer in the Preaching of Amos and in the Ancient Near East." *JBL* 71, no. 1 (1952): 33–38.

Koch, Klaus. "Die Rolle der hymnischen Abschnitte in der Komposition des Amos-Buches." *ZAW* 86, no. 4 (1974): 504–37.

McComiskey, T. E. "The Hymnic Elements of the Prophecy of Amos: A Study of Form-Critical Methodology." In *A Tribute to Gleason Archer*, ed. W. C. Kaiser Jr. and R. Youngblood, 105–28. Chicago: Moody, 1986 (reprinted in *JETS* 30, no. 2 [1987]: 139–57).

Paas, S. "De Here als schepper en koning: de hymnen in Amos." *NedTTs* 49 (1995): 124–39.

Pfeifer, Gerhard. "Jahwe als Schöpfer der Welt und Herr ihrer Mächte in der Verkündigung des Propheten Amos." VT 41, no. 4 (1991): 475–81.

Story, Cullen I. K. "Amos—a Prophet of Praise." *VT* 30, no. 1 (1980): 67–80.

Thompson, J. A. "The 'Response' in Biblical and Non-Biblical Literature with Particular Reference to the Hebrew Prophets." In *Perspectives on Language and Text* (Festschrift F. I. Andersen). Edited by E. W. Conrad and E. G. Newing, 255–68. Winona Lake, Ind.: Eisenbrauns, 1987.

Watts, John D. W. "An Old Hymn Preserved in the Book of Amos." *JNES* 16, no. 1 (1956): 33–40 (reprinted in *Vision and Prophecy in Amos*, 51–67. Grand Rapids: Eerdmans; Leiden: Brill, 1958; and *Vision and Prophecy in Amos:* Expanded anniversary edition, 9–27. Macon, Ga.: Mercer University Press, 1997).

Zalcman, Lawrence. "Astronomical Illusions in Amos." *JBL* 100, no. 1 (1981): 53–58.

4. Woe Oracles (5:18; 6:1; cf. 2:7; 5:7; 6:13)

Clements, R. E. "The Form and Character of Prophetic Woe Oracles." *Semitics* 8 (1982): 17–29.

Clifford, R. J. "The Use of *Hôy* in the Prophets." *CBQ* 28, no. 4 (1966): 458–64.

Gerstenberger, Erhard. "The Woe–Oracles of the Prophets." *JBL* 81, no. 3 (1962): 249–63.

Herrmann, Siegfried. *Die prophetischen Heilserwartungen im Alten Testament.* BWANT 85. Stuttgart: Kohlhammer, 1965.

Hillers, Delbert R. "*Hôy* and *Hôy*-Oracles: A Neglected Syntactic Aspect." In *The Word of the Lord Shall Go Forth* (Festschrift D. N. Freedman). Edited by C. L. Meyers and M. O'Connor, 185–88. Winona Lake, Ind.: Eisenbrauns, 1983.

Janzen, W. *Mourning Cry and Woe Oracles.* BZAW 125. New York: de Gruyter, 1972.

Wanke, Gunther. "*'wy* und *hwy.*" *ZAW* 78, no. 2 (1966): 215–18.

Westermann, Claus. *Basic Forms of Prophetic Speech,* 190–98. Translated by H. C. White. Reprint, Cambridge: Lutterworth; Louisville: Westminster John Knox, 1991.

Williams, J. G. "The Alas-Oracles of the Eighth-Century Prophets." *HUCA* 38 (1967): 75–91.

5. Visions (7:1–9; 8:1–3; 9:1–4)

Auld, A. G. "Amos and Apocalyptic: Vision, Prophecy, Revelation." In *Storia e Tradizioni de Israele. Scritti in onore di J. Alberto Soggin.* Edited by D. Garrone and F. Israel, 1–14. Brescia: Paideia, 1991.

Bartczek, Günter. *Prophetie und Vermittlung: Zur literarischen Analyse und theologischen Interpretation der Visionsberichte des Amos.* Europäische Hochschulschriften, Series 23, vol. 120. Frankfort am Main: Lang, 1980.

Becker, Uwe. "Der Prophet als Fürbitter: Zum literarhistorischen Ort der Amos-Visionen." *VT* 51, no. 2 (2001): 141–65.

Bergler, Siegfried. "'Auf der Mauer—auf dem Altar.' Noch einmal die Visionen des Amos." *VT* 50, no. 4 (2000): 445–71.

Beyerlin, Walter. *Reflexe der Amosvisionen im Jeremiabuch.* OBO 93. Freiburg: Universitätverlag; Göttingen: Vandenhoeck & Ruprecht, 1989.

Brin, Gershon. "The Visions of the Book of Amos (7:1–8:3): Studies in Structure and Ideas" (Heb.). In *Isaac Leo Seeligmann Volume: Essays on the Bible and the Ancient World.* Edited by A. Rofé and Y. Zakovitch, 2:275–90. 3 vols. Jerusalem: Rubinstein, 1982–1985.

Brueggemann, Walter. "Amos' Intercessory Formula." *VT* 19, no. 4 (1969): 386–99.

Cole, R. Dennis. "The Visions of Amos 7–9." *TTE* 52, no. 1 (1995): 57–68.

Eslinger, Lyle. "The Education of Amos." *HAR* 11 (1987): 35–57.

Heynes, Dalene. "Teologie in beeld. Oor die visioene van Amos." *NGTT* 36 (1995): 139–51.

Jeremias, Jörg. "Völkersprüche und Visionsberichte im Amosbuche." In *Prophet und Prophetenbuch* (Festschrift O. Kaiser). Edited by V. Fritz, K.-F. Pohlmann, and H. C. Schmitt, 82–97. BZAW 185. Berlin: de Gruyter, 1989 (reprinted in idem, *Hosea und Amos: Studien zu den Anfängen des Dodekapropheten,* 157–71. FAT 13. Tübingen: Mohr, 1996).

Jeremias, Jörg. "Rezeptionsprozesse in der prophetischen Überlieferung—am Beispiel der Visionsberichte des Amos." In *Rezeption und Auslegung im Alten Testament und in seinem Umfeld* (Festschrift O. H. Steck). Edited by R. G. Kratz and T. Krüger, 29–44. OBO 153. Freiburg: Universitätverlag; Göttingen: Vandenhoeck & Ruprecht, 1997.

Landy, Francis. "Vision and Poetic Speech in Amos." *HAR* 11 (1987): 223–46.

Linville, J. R. "Visions and Voices: Amos 7–9." *Bib* 80, no. 1 (1999): 22–42.

Niditch, Susan. *The Symbolic Vision in Biblical Tradition,* 21–41. HSM. Chico, Calif.: Scholars Press, 1980.

Schwantes, M. "Jacob el pequeño: Visiones en Amós 7–9." *RIBLA* 1 (1988): 87–99.

Talmon, Shemaryahu. "The Gezer Calendar and the Seasonal Cycle of Ancient Canaan." *JAOS* 83 (1963): 234–40.

van Leeuwen, Cornelius. "Quelques problèmes de traduction dans les visions d'Amos chapitre 7." In *Übersetzung und Deutung. Studien zu dem Alten Testament und seiner Umwelt* (Festschrift A. R. Hulst). Edited by H. A. Brongers et al., 103–12. Nijkerk: Callenbach, 1977.

Watts, John D. W. "Vision and Oracle in Amos." In *Vision and Prophecy in Amos,* 27–50. Grand Rapids: Eerdmans; Leiden: Brill, 1958 (reprinted in *Vision and Prophecy in Amos.* Expanded anniversary edition, 59–89. Macon, Ga.: Mercer University Press, 1997).

Weisman, Zeev. "Patterns and Structure in the Visions of Amos" (Heb.). *BMik* 14, no. 4 (1969): 40–57.

Werner, Herbert. "Der Visionsstrophenzyklus (7,1–9; 8,1–3; 9,1–4)." In *Amos,* 129–45. Göttingen: Vandenhoeck & Ruprecht, 1969.

Zenger, Erich. "Die eigentliche Botschaft des Amos. Von der Relevanz der politischen Theologie in einer exegetischen Kontroverse." In *Mystik und Politik: Theologie im Ringen um Geschichte und Gesellschaft* (Festschrift J. B. Metz). Edited by E. Schillebeeckz, 394–406. Mainz: Grünewald, 1988.

6

Chapters and Verses

1:1

Bič, Milos. "Der Prophet Amos—ein Haepatoskopos." *VT* 1, no. 4 (1951): 293–96.

Bič, Milos. "*Maštîn B^{e}qîr*," *VT* 4, no. 4 (1954): 411–16.

Craigie, Peter C. "Amos the *nōqēd* in the Light of Ugaritic." *SR* 11, no. 1 (1982): 29–33.

Diebner, Bernard Jörg. "Berufe und Berufung des Amos (Am 1,1 und 7,14f.)." *DBAT* 23 (1986): 97–120.

Dietrich, Manfried, and Oswald Loretz. "Die ugaritische Berufsgruppe der *nqdm* und das Amt des *rb nqdm*." *UF* 9 (1977): 336–37.

Freedman, David Noel, and A. Welch. "Amos's Earthquake and Israelite Prophecy." In *Scripture and Other Artifacts* (Festschrift P. J. King). Edited by M. D. Coogan, J. C. Exum, and L. E. Stager, 188–98. Louisville: Westminster John Knox, 1994.

Fuhs, Hans F. "Amos 1,1: Erwägungen zur Tradition und Redaction des Amosbuches." In *Bausteine biblischer Theologie* (Festschrift G. J. Botterweck). Edited by H. J. Fabry, 271–89. BBB 50. Bonn: Pater Hanstein, 1977.

Gilead, C. "Amos—from the Herdsman in Tekoa" (Heb.). *BMik* 18, no. 3 (1972): 375–81.

Isbell, Charles D. "A Note on Amos 1:1." *JNES* 36 (1977): 213–14.

Jeremias, Jörg. "'Zwei Jahre vor dem Erdbeben' (Amos 1,1)." In *Altes Testament, Forschung und Wirkung* (Festschrift H. G. Reventlow). Edited by P. Mommer and W. Thiel, 15–31. Bern: Peter Lang, 1994 (reprinted in idem, *Hosea und Amos: Studien zu den Anfängen des Dodekapropheten*, 183–97. FAT 13. Tübingen: Mohr, 1996).

Luria, Ben Zion. "Teqoa—the City of Amos" (Heb.). In *Sepher E. Auerbach*. Edited by A. Biram, 104–15. Jerusalem: Kiryat Sepher, 1956.

Meek, T. J. "The Accusative of Time in Amos 1:1." *JAOS* 61, no. 1 (1941): 63–64.

Meek, T. J. "Again the Accusative of Time in Amos 1:1." *JAOS* 61, no. 2 (1941): 190–91.

Murtonen, A. E. "The Prophet Amos—a Hepatoscoper?" *VT* 2, no. 2 (1952): 170–71.

Ogden, D. Kelly. "The Earthquake Motif in the Book of Amos." In *Goldene Äpfel in silbernen Schalen: Collected Communications to the XIIIth Congress of the International Organization for the Study of the Old Testament, Leuven 1989*. Edited by

K.-D. Schunk and M. Augustin, 69–80. BEATAJ 20. Frankfurt am Main: Peter Lang, 1992.

Peiser, Felix Ernst. "*šᵉnātayim lipnê hārāʿaš:* Eine philologische Studie." *ZAW* 36 (1916): 218–24.

Pfeifer, Gerhard. "Amos 1,1: Worte des Amos?" In *Dort ziehen Schiffe dahin* . . . . Edited by M. Augustin et al., 165–68. Bern: Peter Lang, 1996.

Segert, Stanislav. "Zur Bedeutung des Wortes *nōqēd.*" In *Hebräische Wortforschung* (Festschrift W. Baumgartner). Edited by B. Hartmann et al., 279–83. VTSup 16. Leiden: Brill, 1967.

Soggin, J. Alberto. "Das Erdbeben von Amos 1,1 und die Chronologie der Könige Ussia und Jotham von Juda." *ZAW* 82, no. 1 (1970): 117–21.

Stamm, Johann Jakob. "Der Name des Propheten Amos und sein sprachlicher Hintergrund." In *Prophecy* (Festschrift G. Fohrer). Edited by J. A. Emerton, 137–42. BZAW 150. Berlin: de Gruyter, 1980.

Stoebe, Hans-Joachim. "Der Prophet Amos und sein bürgerlicher Beruf." *WuD* 5 (1957): 160–81.

Tucker, Gene M. "Prophetic Inscriptions and the Growth of the Canon." In *Canon and Authority: Essays in Old Testament Religion and Theology.* Edited by G. W. Coats and B. O. Long, 56–70. Philadelphia: Fortress, 1977.

Waitz, Y. "Amos: Sheep Breeder, Cattle Breeder, and Sycamore Fig Slitter?" (Heb.). *BMik* 13, no. 2 (1968): 141–44.

Wright, J. "Did Amos Inspect Livers?" *AusBR* 23, no. 1 (1975): 3–11.

Yadin, Yigael. et al. *Hazor II: An Account of the Second Season of Excavations, 1956.* Jerusalem: Magnes, 1960.

Yamashita, Tadanori. "Professions, no. 28: *nqd.*" In *Ras Shamra Parallels: The Texts from the Hebrew Bible and Ugarit.* Edited by L. R. Fisher, 2:63–64. AnOr 50. Rome: Pontifical Biblical Institute, 1975.

1:2

Budde, Karl. "Amos 1:2." *ZAW* 30, no. 1 (1910): 37–41.

Loewenstamm, S. E. "Some Remarks on Biblical Passages in the Light of Their Akkadian Parallels" (Heb.). In *Bible Studies* (Festschrift J. M. Grintz). Edited by B. Uffenheimer, 187–96. Tel Aviv: Tel Aviv University Press, 1982.

van Leeuwen, Cornelius. "Amos 1:2—Epigraphe du livre entier ou introduction aux oracles des chapitres 1–2?" In *Verkenningen in een Stroogebied. Proeven van oudtestamentisch onderzoek* (Festschrift M. A. Beek). Edited by M. Boertien, 93–101. Amsterdam: University of Amsterdam Press, 1974.

Weiss, Meir. "In the Footsteps of One Biblical Metaphor" (Heb. with Eng. summary). *Tarbiz* 34, no. 2 (1965): 107–28; no. 3 (1965): 211–23; no. 4 (1965): 303–18.

Weiss, Meir. "Methodologisches über die Behandlung der Metaphor dargelegt an Am. 1,2." *TZ* 23, no. 1 (1967): 1–25.

Weiss, Meir. "Images: Amos 1:2." In *The Bible from Within: The Method of Total Interpretation,* 194–221. Jerusalem: Magnes, 1984.

1:3–5

Galil, Gershon. "The Boundaries of Aram-Damascus in the 9th–8th Centuries BCE." In *Studies in Historical Geography and Biblical Historiography.* Edited by G. Galil and M. Weinfeld, 35–41. VTSup 81. Leiden: Brill, 2000.

Vieweger, D. "Zur Herkunft der Völkerworte im Amosbuch unter besonder Berücksichtigung des Aramäerspruchs (Am 1.3–5)." In *Altes Testament, Forschung und*

Wirkung (Festschrift H. G. Reventlow). Edited by P. Mommer and W. Thiel, 103–19. Bern: Peter Lang, 1994.

1:3

Grether, H. G. "Some Problems of Equivalence in Amos 1:3." *BT* 22, no. 3 (1971): 116–17.

Noble, Paul R. "'I Will Not Bring "It" Back' (Amos 1:3): A Deliberately Ambiguous Oracle?" *ExpTim* 106, no. 4 (1995): 105–9.

Soggin, J. Alberto. "Amos 6:13–14 und 1:3 auf dem Hintergrund der Beziehungen zwischen Israel und Damascus im 9. und 8. Jahrhundert." In *Near Eastern Studies in Honor of William Foxwell Albright*. Edited by H. Goedicke, 433–42. Baltimore: Johns Hopkins University Press, 1971.

Soper, B. K. "For Three Transgressions and for Four: A New Interpretation of Amos 1:3." *ExpTim* 71, no. 3 (1959): 86–87.

Zorell, F. "Auf Amos 1:3,6. usw." *Bib* 6, no. 2 (1925): 171–73.

1:4

Höffken, Peter. "Eine Bemerkung zum 'Haus Hasaels' in Amos 1:4." *ZAW* 94, no. 3 (1982): 413–15.

1:5

Eitan, Israel. "Biblical Studies II: Stray Notes to Minor Prophets." *HUCA* 14 (1939): 5–6.

Malamat, Abraham. "Amos 1:5 in the Light of the Til Barsip Inscriptions." *BASOR* 129 (1953): 25–26.

Millard, Allan. "Eden, Bit Adani and Beth Eden." *EI* 24 (1993): 173–77.

Tsumura, David T. "'Inserted Bicolon,' the AXYB Pattern in Amos i 5 and Psalm ix 7." *VT* 38, no. 2 (1988): 234–36.

1:6

Grintz, Josef M. "Because They Exiled a Whole Exile to Deliver to Edom" (Heb.). *BMik* 13, no. 1 (1967): 24–26.

Haupt, Paul. "Heb. *galût šôlēmâ*, a Peaceful Colony." *JBL* 35, nos. 3–4 (1916): 288–92.

Zorell, F. "Auf Amos 1:3,6. usw." *Bib* 6, no. 2 (1925): 171–73.

1:8

Eitan, Israel. "Biblical Studies II: Stray Notes to Minor Prophets." *HUCA* 14 (1939): 5–6.

1:9–10

Cazelles, H. "L'arrièrre-plan historique d'Amos 1,9–10." *Proceedings of the Sixth World Congress of Jewish Studies*, 1:71–76. 3 vols. Jerusalem: World Union of Jewish Studies, 1977.

Müller, Hans Peter. "Phönizien und Juda in exilisch-nachexilischer Zeit." *WO* 6, no. 2 (1971): 189–204.

1:9

Bartlett, J. R. "The Brotherhood of Edom." *JSOT* 2 (1977): 2–27.

Priest, J. "The Covenant of Brothers." *JBL* 84, no. 4 (1965): 400–406.

1:11

Barré, Michael. "Amos 1:11 Reconsidered." *CBQ* 47, no. 3 (1985): 420–27.
Bartlett, J. R. "The Brotherhood of Edom." *JSOT* 2 (1977): 2–27.
Coote, Robert B. "Amos 1:11: *Rḥmyw*." *JBL* 90, no. 2 (1971): 206–8.
Fishbane, Michael. "The Treaty Background of Amos 1:11 and Related Matters." *JBL* 89, no. 3 (1970): 313–18.
Fishbane, Michael. "Additional Remarks on *Rḥmyw* (Amos 1:11)." *JBL* 91, no. 3 (1972): 391–93.
Matthews, Claire R. *Defending Zion: Edom's Desolation and Jacob's Restoration (Isaiah 34–35) in Context*, 103–7. BZAW 236. Berlin: de Gruyter, 1995.
Sperber, D. "Varia Midrahica IV. 1: Esau and His Mother's Womb—a Note on Amos 1:11." *REJ* 137, nos. 1–2 (1978): 149–53.

1:13

Cogan, M. "'Ripping Open Pregnant Women' in Light of an Assyrian Analogue." *JAOS* 103 (1983): 755–57.
Reider, Joseph. "Etymological Studies in Biblical Hebrew." *VT* 4, no. 3 (1954): 276–95.

1:15

Puech, Emile. "Milkom, le dieu ammonite, en Amos 1:15." *VT* 27, no. 1 (1977): 117–25.
de Waard, J. "A Greek Translation-Technical Treatment of Amos 1:15." In *On Language, Culture and Religion* (Festschrift E. A. Nida). Edited by M. Black and W. Smalley, 111–18. The Hague: Mouton, 1974.

2:1

Braslavi, J. "*dwd ḥ'sym, 'smwt lsyd, mrspwt syd*" (Heb.). *BMik* 13, no. 1 (1962): 34–36.

2:2

Praetorius, F. "Zum Texte des Amos." *ZAW* 34, no. 1 (1942): 42.

2:4–5

Bons, Eberhard. "Das Denotat von *kzbyhm* 'ihre Lügen' in Judaspruch Am 2,4–5." *ZAW* 108, no. 2 (1996): 201–13.

2:6

Albert, Edwin. "Einige Bemerkungen zu Amos." *ZAW* 33, no. 3 (1913): 265–71.
Lang, Bernhard. "Sklaven und Unfreie im Buch Amos (ii 6, viii 6)." *VT* 31, no. 4 (1981): 482–88.
Oesterley, W. O. E. "The Symbolism of the 'Pair of Shoes' in Amos 2:6." *Society of Biblical Archaeology, Proceedings* 23 (1901): 36–38.

2:6–8

Beek, M. A. "The Religious Background of Amos 2:6–8." *OTS* 5 (1948): 132–41.
Jeremias, Jörg. "Amos 8,4–7—ein Kommentar zu 2,6f." In *Text, Methode und Grammatik* (Festschrift W. Richter). Edited by W. Gross et al., 205–20. St. Ottilien: EOS, 1991. (reprinted in idem, *Hosea und Amos: Studien zu den Anfängen des Dodekapropheten*, 231–43. FAT 13. Tübingen: Mohr, 1996).

Orel, Vladimir. "Textological Notes." *ZAW* 109, no. 3 (1997): 408–13.
Thiel, Winfried. "Amos 2,6–8 und der Einfluss Hoseas auf die Amos-Traditionen." In *Verbindungslininen* (Festschrift W. H. Schmidt). Edited by A. Graupner, H. Delkurt, and A. B. Ernst, 385–97. Neukirchen-Vluyn: Neukirchener Verlag, 2000.

2:6–16

Bohlen, Reinhold. "Zur Sozialkritik des Propheten Amos." *TTZ* 95 (1986): 282–301.
Happel, O. "Am 2:6–16 in der Urgestalt." *BZ* 3 (1905): 355–67.
Schwantes, M. "Profecia e Organização: Anotações à luz de um texto (Am 2,6–16)." *EstBíb* 5 (1985): 26–39.

2:7

Arango, José Roberto. "Opresión y profanación del santo nombre de Dios: Estudio del vocabulario de Amos 2,7b." *RIBLA* 11 (1992): 49–63.
Arango, José Roberto. "La mujer y la familia, víctimas de la injusticia en Amós, 2:7b." *ThX* 45 (1995): 341–56.
Barstad, Hans M. *The Religious Polemics of Amos: Studies in the Preaching of Am 2:7B–8; 4:1–13; 5:1–27; 6:4–7; 8:14*, 11–36. VT Sup 34. Leiden: Brill, 1984.
Bewer, Julius A. "Critical Notes on Amos 2:7 and 8:4." *AJSL* 19, no. 2 (1903): 116–17.
Bewer, Julius A. "Note on Amos 2:7a." *JBL* 28, no. 2 (1909): 200–202.
Bronznick, N. "More on *ḥlk 'l*." *VT* 35, no. 1 (1985): 98–99.
McLaughlin, John L. *The Marzēaḥ in the Prophetic Literature: References and Allusions in Light of the Extra-Biblical Evidence*, 120–27. VT Sup 86. Leiden: Brill, 2001.
Orlinsky, H. M., and M. Weinberg. "The Masorah on *'ănāwîm* in Amos 2.7." In *Estudios Masoréticos* (Festschrift H. M. Orlinsky). Edited by E. Fernández Tejero, 25–35. Textos y Estudios "Cardenal Cisneros" 33. Madrid: Instituto "Arias Montano" C.S.I.C., 1983.
Paul, Shalom M. "Two Cognate Semitic Terms for Mating and Copulation." *VT* 32, no. 4 (1982): 492–94.
Reider, Joseph. "Contributions to the Scriptural Text." *HUCA* 24 (1952–1953): 94–96.
Torczyner, H. "Dunkle Bibelstellen. Am. 2:7." In *Vom Alten Testament* (Festschrift K. Marti). Edited by K. Budde, 278–79. BZAW 41. Giessen: Töpelmann, 1925.
Zolli, I. "Note Esegetiche (Amos 2:7a)." *RSO* 16, no. 2 (1936): 178–83.

2:8

Dahood, Mitchell J. "To Pawn One's Cloak." *Bib* 42, no. 3 (1961): 359–66.
Hillers, Delbert R. "Palmyrene Aramaic Inscriptions and Old Testament, especially Amos 2,8." *ZAH* 8, no. 1 (1995): 55–62.
Oesterley, W. O. E. "Amos 2:8: 'Pledged Clothes.'" *ExpTim* 13, no. 1 (1901–1902): 40–41.

2:9

Albert, Edwin. "Einige Bemerkungen zu Amos." *ZAW* 33, no. 3 (1913): 265–71.
Bjorndalen, Anders Jorgen. *Untersuchungen zur allegorischen Rede der Propheten Amos und Jesaja*, 135–56. BZAW 165. Berlin: de Gruyter, 1986.
Ginsberg, H. L. "'Roots Below and Fruit Above' and Related Matters." In *Hebrew and Semitic Studies Presented to G. R. Driver*. Edited by D. Winton Thomas and W. D. Hardy, 72–76. Oxford: Clarendon, 1963.

Noth, Martin. "Der Gebrauch von *'mry* im Alten Testament." *ZAW* 58, no. 2 (1940–1941): 182–89.

2:10

Albert, Edwin. "Einige Bemerkungen zu Amos." *ZAW* 33, no. 3 (1913): 265–71.
Hobbs, T. R. "Amos 3,1b and 2,10." *ZAW* 81, no. 3 (1969): 384–87.

2:11

Weiss, Meir. "'And I Raised up Prophets from among Your Sons'—a Note about the History and Character of Israelite Prophecy" (Heb.). In *Isac Leo Seeligmann Volume: Essays in the Bible and the Ancient World*. Edited by A. Rofé and Y. Zakovitch, 1:257–74. 3 vols. Jerusalem: E. Rubinstein, 1982–1985.

2:13

Müller, Hans-Peter. "Die Wurzeln *'yq, y'q,* und *'wq.*" *VT* 21, no. 4 (1971): 556–64.
Wilbers, H. "Étude sur trois textes relatifs à l'agriculture: Isa 28:27–28; Amos 2:13; 9:9." *MUSJ* 5, no. 1 (1911): 269–82.

2:13–16

Rendtorff, Rolf. "Zu Amos 2,14–16." *ZAW* 85, no. 2 (1973): 226–27.
Richardson, H. Neil. "Amos 2:13–16: Its Structure and Function within the Book." In *SBLSP 1978*. Edited by P. J. Achtemeier, 361–68. Missoula, Mont.: Scholars Press, 1978.
Schmidt, Daniel. "Critical Note: Another Word-Play in Amos?" *GTJ* 8, no. 1 (1987): 141–42.

3:1

Hobbs, T. R. "Amos 3,1b and 2,10." *ZAW* 81, no. 3 (1969): 384–87.

3:1–2

van der Wal, A. J. O. "Background and Function of Amos 3:1–2." *ACEBT* 6 (1985): 83–90.

3:1–15

Boyle, Marjorie O'Rourke. "The Covenant Lawsuit of the Prophet Amos: III 1–IV 13." *VT* 21, no. 3 (1971): 338–62.
Bulkeley, Tim. "Cohesion, Rhetorical Purpose and the Poetics of Coherence in Amos 3." *AusBR* 47 (1999): 16–28.
Dempster, Stephen G. "Amos 3: Apologia of a Prophet." *BRT* 5 (1995): 35–51.
Gitay, Yehoshua. "A Study of Amos's Art of Speech: A Rhetorical Analysis of Amos 3:1–15." *CBQ* 42, no. 3 (1980): 293–309.

3:2

Huffmon, H. "The Treaty Background of Hebrew *Yāda'.*" *BASOR* 181, no. 1 (1966): 31–37.
Vriezen, Theodorus C. "Erwägungen zu Amos 3,2." In *Archäologie und Altes Testament* (Festschrift K. Galling). Edited by A. Kuschke and E. Kutsch, 255–58. Tübingen: Mohr/Siebeck, 1970.

3:3

Thomas, D. Winton. "Note on *nôʿādû* in Amos 3:3." *JTS* 7, no. 1 (1956): 69–70.

3:3–8

Baumgartner, Walter. "Amos 3:3–8." *ZAW* 33, no. 1 (1913): 78–80.

Daiches, Samuel. "Amos III:3–8." *ExpTim* 26, no. 5 (1915): 237.

Eichrodt, Walther. "Die Vollmacht des Amos: Zu einer schwierigen Stelle im Amos-buch." In *Beiträge zur alttestamentlichen Theologie* (Festschrift W. Zimmerli). Edited by H. Donner et al., 124–31. Göttingen: Vandenhoeck & Ruprecht, 1977.

Holwerda, Benne. "Da exegese van Amos 3,3–8." In *Begonnen hebbende van Mozes*, 31–47. Terneuzen: D. H. Littooij, 1953.

Junker, Hubert. "*Leo rugiet, quis non timebit? Deus locutus est, quis non prophetabit?* Eine textkritische und exegetische Untersuchung über Amos 3:3–8." *TTZ* 59 (1950): 4–13.

Lindström, F. *God and the Origin of Evil: A Contextual Analysis of Alleged Monistic Evidence in the Old Testament*, 199–214. Translated by F. H. Cryer. ConBOT 21. Lund: Gleerup, 1983.

Linville, James R. "Amos among the 'Dead Prophets Society': Re-Reading the Lion's Roar." *JSOT* 90 (2000): 55–77.

Melamed, E. Z. "Breakup of Stereotype Phrases as an Artistic Device in Biblical Poetry." *ScrHier* 8 (1961): 115–53.

Mittmann, Siegfried. "Gesetalt und Gehalt einer prophetischen Selbstrechtfertigung (Am 3,3–8)." *TQ* 151, no. 2 (1971): 134–45.

Overholt, T. W. "Commanding the Prophets: Amos and the Problem of Prophetic Authority." *CBQ* 41, no. 4 (1979): 517–32.

Paul, Shalom M. "Amos 3:3–8: The Irresistible Sequence of Cause and Effect." *HAR* 7 (1983): 203–20.

Pfeifer, Gerhard. "Unausweichliche Konsequenzen: Denkformenanalyse von Amos iii 3–8." *VT* 33, no. 3 (1983): 341–47.

Renaud, Bernard. "Genèse et Théologie d'Amos 3,3–8." In *Mélanges bibliques et orientaux* (Festschrift H. Cazelles). Edited by A. Caquot et al., 353–72. AOAT 212. Neukirchen-Vluyn: Neukirchener Verlag, 1981.

Schenker, Adrian. "Steht der Prophet unter dem Zwang zu weissagen, oder steht Israel vor der Evidenz der Weisung Gottes in der Weissagung des Propheten? Zur Interpretation von Amos 3,3–8." *BZ* 30, no. 2 (1986): 250–56.

Shapiro, D. S. "The Seven Questions of Amos." *Tradition* 20, no. 4 (1982): 327–31.

Werner, Wolfgang. *Studien zur alttestamentlichen Vorstellung vom Plan Jahwes*, 167–81. BZAW 173. Berlin: de Gruyter, 1988.

3:4

Ashbel, D. "Notes on the Prophecy of Amos: 'Does a Lion Raise His Voice from His Lair Unless He Has Caught Something?'" (Heb.). *BMik* 11, nos. 1–2 (1965): 103–7.

Braslavi, J. "Does a Lion Roar in the Forest When He Has No Prey?" (Heb.). *BMik* 12, no. 2 (1967): 12–16.

Hope, Edward R. "Problems of Interpretation in Amos 3,4." *BT* 42, no. 2 (1991): 201–5.

3:5

Ashbel, D. "Notes on the Prophecy of Amos: 'Does a Bird Fall into a Trap . . .?'" (Heb.). *BMik* 11, nos. 1–2 (1966): 103–7.

Gehman, H. S. "Notes on *mwqš*." *JBL* 58, no. 3 (1939): 277–81.

3:6

Akao, J. O. "Yahweh the Author of All Evils? Understanding Amos 3:6 in Israelite Tradition and among People of Primal World View." *BTF* 32 (2000): 15–23.

Mulder, Martin Jan. "Ein Vorschlag zur Übersetzung von Amos iii 6b." *VT* 34, no. 1 (1984): 106–8.

3:7

Auld, A. Graeme. "Amos and Apocalyptic: Vision, Prophecy, Revelation." In *Storia e Tradizione de Israele* (Festschrift J. A. Soggin). Edited by D. Garrone and F. Israel, 1–13. Brescia: Paideia, 1991.

3:8

Meynet, Roland. "'Le lion a rugi; qui ne craindrait?' La peur dans le livre d'Amos." *LVitae* 49 (1994): 157–65.

3:9

Joüon, P. "Notes de lexicographie hébraïque. 12. *mhwmh* pour *m'wmh** dans Ez. 22:5; Am. 3:9; Prov. 15:16." *MUSJ* 10 (1925): 16–17.

Snyman, S. D. "A Note on Ashdod and Egypt in Amos iii 9," *VT* 44, no. 4 (1994): 559–62.

3:9–11

Jaramillo Rivas, Pedro. *La injusticia social y la opresión en el lenguaje figurado de los profetas*, 181–92. Navarra, Spain: Verbo Divino, 1992.

Pfeifer, Gerhard. "Die Denkform des Propheten Amos (III 9–11)." *VT* 34, no. 4 (1984): 476–81.

Snyman, S. D. "Amos 6:1–7 as an Intensification of 3:9–11." (Afrikaans) *In die Skriflig* 28, no. 2 (1994): 213–22.

3:10

Snyman, S. D. "'Violence' in Amos 3,10 and 6,3." *ETL* 71, no. 1 (1995): 30–47.

3:11

Pelser, H. "Amos 3:11—a Communication." In *Studies on the Book of Amos: Papers Read at the 8th Meeting of Die Ou-Testamentiese Werkgemeenskap in Suid-Afrika at Pretoria University 1965*. Edited by A. H. van Zyl, 153–56. *OTWSA* 7–8 (1964–65). Potchefstroom: Pro Rege–Pers Beperk, 1965.

Rinaldi, G. "Due note ad Amos." *RSO* 28 (1953): 149–52.

3:12

Guillaume, A. "Hebrew Notes: Amos 3,12." *PEQ* 79, no. 1 (1947): 42–44.

Loretz, Oswald. "Vergleich und Kommentar in Amos 3,12." *BZ* 20, no. 1 (1976): 122–25.

Mittmann, Siegfried. "Amos 3,12–15 und das Bett der Samarier." *ZDPV* 92 (1976): 149–67.

Moeller, Henry R. "Ambiguity at Amos 3:12." *BT* 15, no. 1 (1964): 31–34.

Pfeifer, Gerhard. "'Rettung' als Beweis der Vernichtung (Amos 3,12)." *ZAW* 100, no. 2 (1988): 269–77.

Rabinowitz, I. "The Crux at Amos III,12." *VT* 11, no. 2 (1961): 228–31.

Reider, J. "*dmšq* in Amos 3:12." *JBL* 67, no. 3 (1948): 245–48.

Sawyer, John F. A. "'Those Priests in Damascus': A Possible Example of Anti-Sectarian Polemic in the Septuagint Version of Amos 3:12." *ASTI* 8 (1970–71): 123–30.

3:12–15

Mittmann, S. "Amos 3:12–15 und das Bett der Samarier." *ZDPV* 92, no. 2 (1976): 149–76.

3:15

Glanzman, G. S. "Two Notes: Amos 3,15 and Os. 11,8–9." *CBQ* 23, no. 2 (1961): 227–33.

Paul, Shalom M. "Amos iii 15: Winter and Summer Mansions." *VT* 28, no. 3 (1978): 358–59.

4:1

Barstad, Hans M. "Die Basankühe in Amos 4:1." *VT* 25, no. 2 (1975): 286–97.

Jacobs, Paul F. "'Cows of Bashan': A Note on the Interpretation of Amos 4:1." *JBL* 104 (1985): 109–10.

McLaughlin, John L. *The Marzēaḥ in the Prophetic Literature: References and Allusions in Light of the Extra-Biblical Evidence*, 109–19. VT Sup 36. Leiden: Brill, 2001.

4:1–3

Barstad, Hans M. *The Religious Polemics of Amos: Studies in the Preaching of Am 2: 7B–8; 4:1–13; 5:1–27; 6:4–7; 8:14*, 37–75. VT Sup 34. Leiden: Brill, 1984.

Jaramillo Rivas, Pedro. *La injusticia social y la opresión en el lenguaje figurado de los profetas*, 193–208. Navarra, Spain: Verbo Divino, 1992.

Kleven, Terence. "The Cows of Bashan: A Single Metaphor at Amos 4:1–3." *CBQ* 58, no. 2 (1996): 215–27.

Mishael, Yosef. "'Seht, Tage kommen über euch' (Amos 4:1–3)" (Heb.). *BMik* 36, no. 2 (1991): 160–65.

Watts, John D. W. "A Critical Analysis of Amos 4:1ff." In *SBL Proceedings 1972*. Edited by L. C. McGaughy, 2:489–500. 2 vols. Missoula, Mont.: Scholars Press, 1972.

Williams, J. G. "A Further Suggestion about Amos IV 1–3." *VT* 29, no. 2 (1979): 206–11.

4:2

Luria, B. Z. "Amos 4:2b" (Heb.). *BMik* 12, no. 2 (1967): 6–11.

Paul, S. M. "Fishing Imagery in Amos 4:2." *JBL* 97, no. 2 (1978): 183–90.

Schwantes, S. J. "Note on Amos 4,2b." *ZAW* 79, no. 1 (1967): 82–83.

Zolli, E. "Amos 4:2b." *Antonianum* 30, no. 2 (1955): 188–89.

4:3

Freedman, D. N., and Francis I. Andersen. "Harmon in Amos 4:3." *BASOR* 198 (1970): 41.

Glück, J. J. "The Verb *prṣ* in the Bible and in the Qumran Literature." *RevQ* 5 (1964–1965): 123–27.

4:4–5

Nishizu, T. J. "Amos 4:4–5: A Post-Exilic Redaction" (Jap.). *Nanzan Shingaku* 6 (1983): 1–21.

4:4–13

Brueggemann, Walter. "Amos IV 4–13 and Israel's Covenant Worship." *VT* 15, no. 1 (1965): 1–15.

Crenshaw, J. L. "A Liturgy of Wasted Opportunity (Am. 4,6–12; Isa. 9,7–10,4; 5,25–29." *Semitics* 1 (1970): 27–37.

Fensham, F. C. "Common Trends in Curses of the Near Eastern Treaties and *Kudurru*-Inscriptions Compared with Maledictions of Amos and Isaiah." *ZAW* 75, no. 2 (1963): 155–75.

Grätz, Sebastian. "Amos 4:4–13." In *Der strafende Wettergott: Erwägungen zur Traditionsgeschichte des Adad-Fluchs im Alten Orient und im Alten Testament*, 228–53. BBB 114. Bodenheim: Philo, 1998.

Jeremias, Jörg. "Die Mitte des Amosbuches (Am 4,4–13; 5,1–17)." In idem, *Hosea und Amos: Studien zu den Anfängen des Dodekapropheten*, 198–213. FAT 13. Tübingen: Mohr, 1996.

Rudolph, Wilhelm. "Amos 4,6–13." In *Wort–, Gebot–, Glaube: Beiträge zur Theologie des Alten Testaments* (Festschrift W. Eichrodt). Edited by H.-J. Stoebe, 27–38. ATANT 59. Zurich: Zwingli, 1970.

Weiser, Artur. "Zu Amos 4:6–13." *ZAW* 5, no. 1 (1928): 49–59.

4:7

Ulrichsen, J. H. "Der Einschub Amos 4,7b–8. Sprachliche Erwägungen zu einem umstrittenen Text." *Orientalia Suecana* 41–42 (1992–1993): 284–98.

4:10

Speier, S. "Did Rashi Have a Different Vorlage in Amos 4:10 Than Is Found in the Usual Edition?" (Heb.). *Leš* 33 (1969): 15–17.

4:12

Ramsey, G. W. "Amos 4:12—a New Perspective." *JBL* 89, no. 2 (1970): 187–91.

Youngblood, Ronald. "*lqr't* in Amos 4:12." *JBL* 90, no. 1 (1971): 98.

4:13   (see chap. 4, "Specific Topics and Significant Blocks of Text: Doxologies")

Carny, P. "Doxologies: A Scientific Myth." *HS* 18 (1977): 149–59.

Devescovi, Urbano. "'Camminare sulle alture.'" *RivB* 9 (1969): 235–42.

Dijkstra, Meindert. "Textual Remarks on the Hymn-Fragment Amos 4:13." In *"Lasset uns Brücken bauen. . . ."* Edited by K.-D. Schunk et al., 245–53. BEATAJ 42. Frankfurt am Main: Peter Lang, 1998.

Foresti, F. "Funzioni semantica dei brani participiali di Amos: 4,13; 5,8s; 9,5." *Bib* 6, no. 2 (1981): 169–84.

Mowinckel, Sigmund. "The Verb *śîaḥ* and the Nouns *śîḥ, 'śîḥâ.*" *ST* 15 (1961): 1–10.

Smythe, H. R. "Interpretation of Amos 4:13 in St. Athanasius and Didymus." *JTS* 1, no. 2 (1950): 158–68.

5:1–3

Bjorndalen, Anders Jorgen. *Untersuchungen zur allegorischen Rede der Propheten Amos und Jesaja*, 159–74. BZAW 165. Berlin: de Gruyter, 1986.

5:1-17

de Waard, Jan. "The Chiastic Structure of Amos 5:1–17." *VT* 27, no. 2 (1977): 170–77.

Hesse, Franz. "Amos 5,4–6. 14f." *ZAW* 68, no. 1 (1956): 1–17.

Jaruzelska, Izaabel. "People Pronouncing Sentence in Court: Amos 5,7–12. 16–17: An Attempt at Sociological Identification." *FO* 30 (1994): 77–94.

Jeremias, Jörg. "Die Mitte des Amosbuches (Am 4,4–13; 5,1–17)." In idem, *Hosea und Amos: Studien zu den Anfängen des Dodekapropheten*, 198–213. FAT 13. Tübingen: Mohr, 1996.

Jeremias, Jörg. "Tod und Leben in Am 5,1–17." In *Der Weg zum Menschen* (Festschrift A. Deissler). Edited by R. Mosis and L. Ruppert, 134–52. Freiburg: Herder, 1989 (reprinted in idem, *Hosea und Amos: Studien zu den Anfängen des Dodekapropheten*, 214–30. FAT 13. Tübingen: Mohr, 1996).

Lust, J. "Remarks on the Redaction of Amos V 4–6, 14–15." In *Remembering All the Way*. Edited by B. Albrektson, 129–54. OTS 21. Leiden: Brill, 1981.

Neubauer, K. W. "Erwägungen zu Amos 5,4–15." *ZAW* 78, no. 3 (1966): 292–316.

Tromp, N. "Amos 5:1–17. Towards a Stylistic and Rhetorical Analysis." In *Prophets, Worship and Theodicy: Studies in Prophetism, Biblical Theology and Structural and Rhetorical Analysis and on the Place of Music in Worship*. Edited by A. S. van der Woude, 56–84. OTS 23. Leiden: Brill, 1984.

Westermann, Claus. "Amos 5,4–6.14.15: Ihr werdet leben!" In *Erträge der Forschung am Alten Testament. Gesammelte Studien III*. Edited by R. Albertz, 107–18. TB, 73. Munich: Kaiser, 1984.

Wicke, Donald W. "Two Perspectives (Amos 5:1–17)." *CurTM* 13 (1986): 89–96.

5:1–27

Berridge, John M. "Zur Intention der Botschaft des Amos: Exegetische Überlungen zu Am. 5." *TZ* 32, no. 6 (1976): 321–40.

Rector, Larry J. "Israel's Rejected Worship: An Exegesis of Amos 5." *ResQ* 21, no. 3 (1978): 161–75.

5:4–6

Hesse, Franz. "Amos 5,4–6. 14f." *ZAW* 68, no. 1 (1956): 1–17.

Lust, J. "Remarks on the Redaction of Amos V 4–6, 14–15." In *Remembering All the Way*, ed. B. Albrektson, 129–54. OTS 21. Leiden: Brill, 1981.

Reider, Joseph. "Contributions to the Scriptural Text." *HUCA* 24 (1952–1953): 94–96.

Schmidt, Werner H. "'Suchet den Herrn, so werdet ihr Leben': Exegetische Notizen zum Thema 'Gott suchen' in der Prophetie." In *Ex Orbe Religionem I* (Festschrift G. Widengren). Edited by C. J. Bleeker, 127–40. SHR 21. Leiden: Brill, 1972.

5:6

Tawil, Hayim. "Hebrew ṣlḥ/ḥṣlḥ, Akkadian ešēru/šūšuru: A Lexicographical Note." *JBL* 95, no. 3 (1976): 405–13.

5:7

Jaramillo Rivas, Pedro. *La injusticia social y la opresión en el lenguaje figurado de los profetas*, 209–22. Navarra, Spain: Verbo Divino, 1992.
Watts, John D. W. "Note on the Text of Amos 5:7." *VT* 4, no. 2 (1954): 215–16.

5:8

Luria, B. Z. "'Who Calls the Waters of the Sea and Spills Them on the Face of the Earth' (Amos 5:8; 9:6)" (Heb.). *BMik* 30, no. 2 (1985): 259–62.

5:8–9   [see Chap. 4 Specific Topics and Significant Blocks of Text Doxologies"]

Foresti, F. "Funzioni semantica dei brani participiali di Amos: 4,13; 5,8s; 9,5." *Bib* 62, no. 2 (1981): 169–84.
Glück, J. J. "Three Notes on the Book of Amos." *OTWSA* 7–8 (1964–1965): 115–21.

5:9

Driver, G. R. "Two Astronomical Passages in the Old Testament." *JTS* 4, no. 2 (1953): 208–12.
Montgomery, James A. "Notes on the Old Testament. 6. *mblyg*, Amos 5:9." *JBL* 31, no. 3 (1912): 143.
Zalcman, Lawrence. "Astronomical Illusions in Amos." *JBL* 100, no. 1 (1981): 53–58.

5:11

Dietrich, M., and O. Loretz. "Ug. *'BŠ, TBŠ, hebr. *ŠBS (Am. 5,11) sowie ug. TŠY und ŠBŠ." *UF* 10 (1978): 434–35.
Fenton, Terry L. "Ugaritica-Biblica." *UF* 1 (1969): 65–70.

5:13

Jackson, Jared J. "Amos 5,13 Contextually Understood." *ZAW* 98, no. 3 (1986): 434–35.
Maag, Viktor. "Zur Übersetzung von Maskil in Amos 5:13, Ps. 47:8, und in den Überschriften einiger Psalmen." *Schweizerische theologische Umschau* 12, no. 5 (1943): 108–15.
Ruiz González, G. "Amos 5:13: ¿prudencia en la denuncia profética?" *CB* 25, no. 253 (1973): 347–52.
Sellin, Ernst. "Drei umstrittene Stellen des Amosbuches." *ZDPV* 52 (1929): 141–48.
Smith, Gary V. "Amos 5:13—the Deadly Silence of the Prosperous." *JBL* 107, no. 2 (1988): 288–90.
van der Wal, A. "Amos 5.13—een omstreder texst." *NorTT* 41 (1987): 89–98.

5:14

Burais, T. "Amos 5:14." *ST* 19 (1967): 492–503.

5:14–15

Hesse, Franz. "Amos 5,4–6. 14f." *ZAW* 68, no. 1 (1956): 1–17.
Lust, J. "Remarks on the Redaction of Amos V 4–6, 14–15." In *Remembering All the Way*. Edited by B. Albrektson, 129–54. *OTS* 21. Leiden: Brill, 1981.

Neubauer, Karl Wilhelm. "Erwägungen zu Amos 5:14–15." *ZAW* 78, no. 3 (1966): 292–316.

5:16

Glück, J. J. "Three Notes on the Book of Amos." *OTWSA* 7–8 (1964–1965): 115–21.

5:16–17

Joüon, P. "Notes de critique textuelle—Amos 5:16–17." *MUSJ* 4 (1910): 30.

5:17

Haun, Michael James. "The Background and Meaning of Amos 5:17b." *HTR* 79 (1986): 337–48.

5:18–20

Barstad, Hans M. *The Religious Polemics of Amos: Studies in the Preaching of Am 2:7B–8; 4:1–13; 5:1–27; 6:4–7; 8:14,* 89–110. VT Sup 34. Leiden: Brill, 1984.

Berquist, Jon L. "Dangerous Waters of Justice and Righteousness: Amos 5:18–27." *BTB* 23, no. 2 (1993): 54–63.

Smelik, K. A. D. "The Meaning of Amos V 18–20." *VT* 36, no. 2 (1986): 246–48.

van Leeuwen, Cornelius. "The Prophecy of the *yôm Yhwh* in Amos 5:18–20." In *Language and Meaning: Studies in Hebrew Language and Biblical Exegesis.* Edited by A. S. van der Woude, 113–34. *OTS* 19. Leiden: Brill, 1974.

5:21

Kutsch, Ernst. "Die Wurzel *ʿṣr* im Hebräischen." *VT* 2, no. 1 (1952): 57–69.

5:21–27

Barstad, Hans M. *The Religious Polemics of Amos: Studies in the Preaching of Am 2:7B–8; 4:1–13; 5:1–27; 6:4–7; 8:14,* 111–18. VT Sup 34. Leiden: Brill, 1984.

Berquist, Jon L. "Dangerous Waters of Justice and Righteousness: Amos 5:18–27." *BTB* 23, no. 2 (1993): 54–63.

Krech, Volkhard. "Prophetische Kritik am Beispiel von Amos 5,21–27." *DBAT* 23 (1986): 121–35.

Sacon, K. K. "Amos 5: 21–27—an Exegetical Study" (Jap.). In *The Bible, Its Thoughts, History, and Language* (Festschrift M. Sekeine). Edited by S. Arai, 278–99. Tokyo: Yamamoto Shoten, 1972.

Weiss, Meir. "Concerning Amos' Repudiation of the Cult." In *Pomegranates and Golden Bells* (Festschrift J. Milgrom). Edited by D. P. Wright, D. N. Freedman, and A. Hurvitz, 199–214. Winona Lake, Ind.: Eisenbrauns, 1995.

Würthwein, Ernst. "Amos 5:21–27." *TLZ* 72 (1947): 143–52 (reprinted in *Wort und Existenz: Studien zum Alten Testament,* 55–67. Göttingen: Vandenhoeck & Ruprecht, 1970).

5:22

Loretz, Oswald. "*Šlm* in Am. 5,22 und das *šlmjm* Opfer." *UF* 13 (1981): 127–31.

5:23–24

Hyatt, J. Philip. "The Translation and Meaning of Amos 5,23.24." *ZAW* 68, no. 1 (1956): 17–24.

5:24

Jaramillo Rivas, Pedro. *La injusticia social y la opresión en el lenguaje figurado de los profetas*, 223–34. Navarra, Spain: Verbo Divino, 1992.

5:25

Albert, Edwin. "Einige Bemerkungen zu Amos." *ZAW* 33, no. 3 (1913): 265–71.
Dobbie, Robert. "Amos 5:25." *Transactions of the Glasgow University Oriental Society* 17 (1957–1958): 62–64.

5:25–27

Erlandsson, Seth. "Amos 5:25–27 et crux interpretum." *SEÅ* 33 (1968): 76–82.
Junker, Hubert. "Amos und die 'opferlose Mosezeit.' Ein Beitrag zur Eklärung von Amos 5:25–26." *TGl* 27 (1935): 686–95.
Osten-Sacken, P. von der. "Die Bücher der Tora als Hütte der Gemeinde: Amos 5:26f in der Damaskusschrift." *ZAW* 91, no. 3 (1979): 423–35.
van der Woude, A. S. "Bemerkungen zu einigen umstrittenen Stellen im Zwölfprophetenbuch: Amos 5:25–26." In *Mélanges bibliques et orientaux* (Festschrift H. Cazelles). Edited by A. Caquot and M. Delcor, 485–90. AOAT 212. Neukirchen-Vluyn: Neukirchener Verlag, 1981.

5:26

Barstad, Hans M. *The Religious Polemics of Amos: Studies in the Preaching of Am 2:7B–8; 4:1–13; 5:1–27; 6:4–7; 8:14*, 118–26. VT Sup 34. Leiden: Brill, 1984.
Borger, R. "Amos 5,26, Apostelgeschichte 7,43 und Šurpu II, 180." *ZAW* 100, no. 1 (1988): 70–81.
Brown, Walter E. "Amos 5:26: A Challenge to Reading and Interpretation." *TTE* 52 (1995): 69–78.
Burrows, E. "Cuneiform and the Old Testament: Three Notes (I. *Sakkût* in Amos)." *JTS* 28 (1926–1927): 184–85.
Gevirtz, Stanley. "A New Look at an Old Crux: Amos 5:26." *JBL* 87, no. 3 (1968): 267–76.
Isbell, Charles D. "Another Look at Amos 5:26." *JBL* 97, no. 1 (1978): 97–99.
Loretz, Oswald. "Die babylonischen Gottesnamen *Sukkut* und *Kajjamānu* in Amos 5,26. Ein Beitrag zur jüdischen Astrologie." *ZAW* 101, no. 2 (1989): 286–89.
Speiser, E. A. "Note on Amos 5:26." *BASOR* 108 (1947): 5–6.

6:1

Holladay, W. L. "Amos VI 1bβ: A Suggested Solution." *VT* 22, no. 1 (1972): 107–10.

6:1–7

Barstad, Hans M. *The Religious Polemics of Amos: Studies in the Preaching of Am 2:7B–8; 4:1–13; 5:1–27; 6:4–7; 8:14*, 127–42. VT Sup 34. Leiden: Brill, 1984.

Blum, Erhard. "'Amos' in Jerusalem: Beobachtungen zu Am 6, 1–7." *Hen* 16, no. 1 (1994): 23–47.

Eissfeldt, Otto. "*marzēaḥ* und *marzăḥā*': 'Kultmahlgenossenschaft' im spätjüdischen Schrifttum." In *Kleine Schriften zum Alten Testament*. Edited by P. Sellheim and F. Maass, 5:136–42. Tübingen: Mohr, 1962–1979.

Greenfield, J. C. "The *Marzēaḥ* as a Social Institution." In *Wirtschaft und Gesellschaft im Alten Vorderasien*. Edited by J. Harmatta and G. Komoróczy, 451–55. Budapest: Akadémiai Kiadó, 1976.

King, Philip J. "Using Archaeology to Interpret a Biblical Text: The *Marzēaḥ* Amos Denounces." *BAR* 14, no. 4 (1988): 34–44.

King, Philip J. *Amos, Hosea, Micah: An Archaeological Commentary*, 137–61. Philadelphia: Westminster, 1988.

King, Philip J. "The *Marzēaḥ*: Textual and Archaeological Evidence" (Heb.). *EI* 20 (1989): 98–106.

Loretz, Oswald. "Ugaritisch-biblisch *mrzḥ* 'Kultmahl, Kultverein' in Jer 16,5 und Am 6,7." In *Künder des Wortes: Beiträge zur Theologie der Propheten* (Festschrift J. Schreiner). Edited by L. Ruppert et al., 87–93. Würzburg: Echter, 1982.

Loretz, Oswald. "*Marziḥu* im ugaritischen und biblischen Ahnenkult: Zu Ps 23; 133; Am 6,1–7 und Jer 16,5.8." In *Mesopotamia, Ugaritica, Biblica* (Festschrift K. Bergerhof). Edited by M. Dietrich and O. Loretz, 93–144. AOAT 232. Neukirchen-Vluyn: Neukirchener Verlag, 1993.

McLaughlin, John L. *The Marzēaḥ in the Prophetic Literature: References and Allusions in Light of the Extra-Biblical Evidence*, 80–109. VT Sup 86. Leiden: Brill, 2001.

Pope, Marvin H. "A Divine Banquet at Ugarit." In *The Use of the Old Testament in the New*. Edited by J. Efird, 170–203. Durham, N.C.: Duke University Press, 1972.

Pope, Marvin H. "Le *MRZḤ* à l'Ugarit et ailleurs." *Annales Archéologiques Arabes Syriennes* 29–30 (1979–1980): 141–43.

Pope, Marvin H. "The Cult of the Dead at Ugarit." In *Ugarit in Retrospect: Fifty Years of Ugarit and Ugaritic*. Edited by G. D. Young, 159–79. Winona Lake, Ind.: Eisenbrauns, 1981.

Roberts, J. J. M. "Amos 6.1–7." In *Understanding the Word* (Festschrift B. W. Anderson). Edited by J. T. Butler et al., 155–66. JSOTSup 37. Sheffield: JSOT Press, 1985.

Schmidt, Brian B. *Israel's Beneficent Dead: Ancestor Cult and Necromancy in Ancient Israelite Religion and Tradition*, 144–47 (Winona Lake, Ind.: Eisenbrauns, 1996).

Segert, Stanislav. "A Controlling Device for Copying Stereotype Passages (Amos I 3–II 8; VI 1–6)." *VT* 34, no. 4 (1984): 481–82.

Snyman, S. D. "Amos 6:1–7 as an Intensification of 3:9–11." (Afrikaans) *In die Skriflig* 28, no. 2 (1994): 213–22.

Snyman, S. D. "Towards a Theological Interpretation of HMS in Amos 6:1–7." In *Dort ziehen Schiffe dahin. . . .* Edited by M. Augustin et al., 201–9. BEATAJ 28. Bern: Peter Lang, 1996.

von Soden, Wolfram. "Zu einigen Ortsbenennungen bei Amos und Micha." *ZAH* 3, no. 2 (1990): 214–20.

Wittenberg, G. "Amos 6:1–7: 'They dismiss the day of disaster but you bring near the rule of violence." *JTSA* 58 (1987): 57–69.

6:1–14

Schotroff, Willy. "'Auferestanden aus Ruinen . . .': Bibelarbeit über Amos 6,1–14." In

Die kostbare Liebe zum Leben. Edited by L. Schotroff et al., 107–24. Biblische Inspirationen. Munich: Kaiser, 1991.

6:2

Daiches, Samuel. "Amos VI:2." *ExpTim* 26, no. 12 (1915): 562–63.
Sellin, Ernst. "Drei umstrittene Stellen des Amosbuches." *ZDPV* 52 (1929): 141–48.

6:3

Snyman, S. D. "'Violence' in Amos 3,10 and 6,3." *ETL* 71, no. 1 (1995): 30–47.

6:5

Daiches, Samuel. "Amos VI:5." *ExpTim* 26, no. 11 (1915): 521–22.
Elhorst, Hendrick J. "Amos 6:5." *ZAW* 35, no. 1 (1915): 62–63.
Freedman, D. N., and Francis I. Andersen. "But Did David Invent Musical Instruments?" *BR* 1, no. 2 (1985): 49–51.
Lohman, Paul. "Einige Textkonjekturen zu Amos." *ZAW* 32, no. 2 (1912): 274–77.
Montgomery, J. A. "Notes from the Samaritan: The Root *prt*—Amos 6:5." *JBL* 25, no. 1 (1906): 51–52.

6:6

Dahmen, Ulrich. "Zur Text- und Literarkritik von Am 6,6a." *BN* 32 (1986): 7–10.

6:7

Braslavi, J. "Jeremiah 16:5 and Amos 6:7" (Heb.). *BMik* 17, no. 1 (1971): 5–16.
Maier, Christl, and Ernst Michael Dörrfuß. "'Um mit ihnen zu sitzen, zu essen und zu trinken'. Am 6,7; Jer 16,5 und die Bedeutung von *marzēᵃḥ*." *ZAW* 111, no. 1 (1999): 45–57.

6:8

Dahood, Mitchell. "Amos 6,8 *mᵉtā'ēb*." *Bib* 59, no. 2 (1978): 265–66.

6:10

Ahlström, G. W. "King Josiah and the *dwd* of Amos 6:10." *JSS* 26, no. 1 (1981): 7–9.
Driver, G. R. "A Hebrew Burial Custom." *ZAW* 66, no. 3 (1954): 314–15.
Kutscher, Y. "Lexicographical Problems of Rabbinic Hebrew: 'He Who Anoints the Dead with Resin'" (Heb.). *Leš* 21 (1957): 251–55 (reprinted in *Hebrew and Aramaic Studies*. Edited by Z. Ben-Hayyim, A. Dotan, and G. Sarfatti, 338–40. Jerusalem: Magnes, 1977).
Lohman, Paul. "Einige Textkonjekturen zu Amos." *ZAW* 32, no. 2 (1912): 274–77.
Noble, Paul R. "A Note on *ûnᵉśā'ô dôdô ûmᵉsarᵉpô* (Amos 6,10)." *ZAW* 111, no. 3 (1999): 419–22.
Smelik, Willem F. "The Use of *hzkyr bšm* in Classical Hebrew: Josh 23:7; Isa 48:1; Amos 6:10; Ps 20:8; 4Q504 iii 4; 1QS 6:27." *JBL* 118, no. 2 (1999): 321–32.

6:12

Cooper, Alan. "The Absurdity of Amos 6:12a." *JBL* 107, no. 4 (1988): 725–27.

Dahood, Mitchell. "Can One Plough without Oxen? (Amos 6:12): A Study of *ba-* and *'al*." In *The Bible World* (Festschrift C. H. Gordon). Edited by G. Rendsburg et al., 13–23. New York: Ktav, 1980.

Jaramillo Rivas, Pedro. *La injusticia social y la opresión en el lenguaje figurado de los profetas*, 209–22. Navarra, Spain: Verbo Divino, 1992.

Loretz, Oswald. "Amos VI 12." *VT* 39, no. 2 (1989): 240–42.

6:13

Metzger, M. "Lodebar und der *tell el-mghannije*." *ZDPV* 76, no. 1 (1960): 97–102.

6:13–14

Soggin, J. Alberto. "Amos VI,13–14 und I,3 auf dem Hintergrund der Beziehungen zwischen Israel und Damaskus im 9. und 8. Jahrhundert." In *Near Eastern Studies in Honor of W. F. Albright*. Edited by H. Goedicke, 433–41. Baltimore: Johns Hopkins University Press, 1971.

6:14

Eissfeldt, Otto. "Der Zugang zu Hamath." *OrAnt* 10 (1971): 269–76.

Mazar, Benjamin. "Lebo-Hamath and the Northern Border of Canaan" (Heb.). *Bulletin of the Jewish Palestine Exploration* 12 (1946): 91–102 (reprinted in *Cities and Districts in Eretz-Israel*, 167–81. Jerusalem: Bialik, 1975).

7:1

Power, E. "A Note to Amos 7:1." *Bib* 8, no. 1 (1927): 87–92.

7:1–6

Brueggemann, Walter. "Amos' Intercessory Formula." *VT* 19, no. 4 (1969): 386–99.

Manakatt, Mathew. "The Intercessary Prayer of Amos in Amos 7:1–6." *LW* 100 (1994): 182–91.

Rossier, François. "Les intercessions d'Amos: Am 7,1–6." In *L'intercession entre les hommes dans la Bible hébraïque: L'intercession entre les hommes aux origines de l'intercession auprès de Dieu*, 305–38. OBO 152. Freiburg: Editions Universitaires; Göttingen: Vandenhoeck & Ruprecht, 1996.

7:1–17 (see Specific Topics and Significant Blocks of Text: Visions)

7:2

Mitchell, H. G. "*whyh* of the Past." *JBL* 33, no. 1 (1914): 48–55.

Montgomery, J. A. "Notes on Amos." *JBL* 23, no. 1 (1904): 94–96.

Seidl, T. "Heuschreckenschwarm und Prophetenintervention. Textkritische und syntaktische Erwägungen zu Am 7,2." *BN* 37 (1987): 129–38.

7:4

Hillers, Delbert R. "Amos 7,4 and Ancient Parallels." *CBQ* 26, no. 2 (1964): 221–25.

Limburg, James. "Amos 7:4: A Judgment with Fire?" *CBQ* 35, no. 3 (1973): 346–49.

Mittmann, S. "Der Rufende im Feuer (Amos 7:4)." *JNSL* 20, no. 1 (1994): 165–70.

Montgomery, J. A. "Notes on Amos." *JBL* 23, no. 1 (1904): 94–96.

Rinaldi, Giovanni. "Due note ad Amos." *RSO* 28 (1953): 149–52.
Talmon, S. "The Ugaritic Background of Amos 7:4" (Heb.). *Tarbiz* 35 (1965–1966): 301–3.

7:7–9

Baltzer, Klaus. "Bild und Wort: Erwägungen zu der Vision Amos in Am 7:7–9." In *Text, Methode und Grammatik* (Festschrift W. Richter). Edited by W. Gross et al., 11–16. St. Ottilien: EOS, 1991.
Beyerlin, Walter. *Bleilot, Brecheisen oder was sonst? Revision einer Amos-Vision.* OBO 81. Freiburg: Universitätsverlag; Göttingen: Vandenhoeck & Ruprecht, 1988.
Brunet, G. "La vision de l'étain: Réinterprétation d'Amos, VII, 7–9." *VT* 16, no. 4 (1966): 387–95.
Condamin, Albert. "Le prétendu 'fil à plom' de la vision d'Amos." *RB* 9, no. 4 (1900): 586–94.
Cooper, Alan. "The Meaning of Amos's Third Vision (Amos 7:7–9)." In *Tehillah le-Moshe* (Festschrift M. Greenberg). Edited by M. Cogan, B. L. Eichler, and J. H. Tigay, 13–21. Winona Lake, Ind.: Eisenbrauns, 1997.
Cornet, P. B. "Une 'crux' Amos VII, 7–9: *'nk* = bélier." *Études Franciscaines* 2, no. 4 (1951): 61–83.
Hoffmeier, James K. "Once Again the 'Plumb Line' Vision of Amos 7.7–9: An Interpretive Clue from Egypt?" In *Boundaries of the Ancient Near Eastern World* (Festschrift C. H. Gordon). Edited by M. Lubetski, C. Gottlieb, and S. Keller, 304–19. JSOTSup 273. Sheffield: Sheffield Academic Press, 1998.
Holladay, W. L. "Once More, *'ᵃnak* = 'tin,' Amos VII 7–8." *VT* 20, no. 4 (1970): 492–94.
Junker, Hubert. "Text und Bedeutung der Vision Amos 7:7–9." *Bib* 17, no. 3 (1936): 359–64.
Landsberger, Benno. "Tin and Lead: The Adventure of Two Vocables." *JNES* 24, no. 3 (1965): 185–96.
Mackenzie, H. S. "The Plumb-Line (Amos 7:8)." *ExpTim* 60, no. 6 (1949): 159.
Madden, R., T. S. Wheeler, and J. D. Muhly. "Tin in the Ancient Near East: Old Questions and New Finds." *Expedition* 19 (1977): 42–47.
Muhly, J. D. "Sources of Tin and the Beginnings of Bronze Metallurgy." *AJA* (1985): 275–91.
Ouellette, J. "Le mur d'étain dans Amos, VII, 7–9." *RB* 80, no. 3 (1973): 321–31.
Rinaldi, Giovanni. "De III et IV Visione Libri Amos." *VD* 17, no. 3 (1937): 82–87; no. 4 (1937): 114–16.
Rinaldi, Giovanni. "*'ᵃnāk* (Amos 7,7s)." *BeO* 4 (1962): 83–84.
Uehlinger, C. "Der Herr auf der Zinnmauer. Zur Dritten Amos-Vision (Amos vii 7–8)." *BN* 48 (1989): 89–104.
Weigl, Michael. "Eine 'unendliche Geschichte': *'nk* (Am 7,7–8)." *Bib* 76, no. 3 (1995): 343–87.
Williamson, H. G. M. "The Prophet and the Plumbline: A Redaction-Critical Study of Amos vii." In *In Quest of the Past: Studies on Israelite Religion, Literature and Prophetism.* Edited by A. S. van der Woude, 101–21. OTS 26. Leiden: Brill, 1990 (reprinted in *This Place Is Too Small for Us: The Israelite Prophets in Recent Scholarship.* Edited by R. P. Gordon, 453–77. SBTS 5. Winona Lake, Ind.: Eisenbrauns, 1995).

7:9, 10–17

Ackroyd, Peter R. "A Judgment Narrative Between Kings and Chronicles? An Approach to Amos 7:9–17." In *Canon and Authority: Essays in Old Testament Reli-*

gion and Theology. Edited by G. W. Coats and B. O. Long, 71–87. Philadelphia: Fortress, 1977 (reprinted in *Studies in the Religious Tradition of the Old Testament,* 195–208. London: SCM, 1987).

Bjorndalen, A. J. "Erwägungen zur Zukunft des Amazja und Israels nach der Überlieferung Amos 7:10–17." In *Werden und Wirken des Alten Testaments* (Festschrift C. Westermann). Edited by R. Albertz et al., 181–202. Neukirchen-Vluyn: Neukirchener Verlag, 1980.

Breytenbach, A. P. B. "Die herfsfees en die koningsrite by Bet-El as interteks van Amos 7:10–8:14 en Hosea 9:1–9." *HervTS* 53, no. 3 (1997): 513–28.

Clements, R. E. "Amos and the Politics of Israel." In *Storia e tradizioni di Israeli* (Festschrift J. A. Soggin). Edited by D. Garrone and F. Israel, 49–64. Brescia: Paideia, 1991 (reprinted in idem, *Old Testament Prophecy: From Oracles to Canon,* 23–34. Louisville: Westminster John Knox, 1996).

Freedman, David Noel. "Confrontations in the Book of Amos." *PSB* 11, no. 3 (1990): 240–52.

García-Treto, F. O. "A Reader-Response Approach to Prophetic Conflict: The Case of Amos 7.10–17." In *The New Literary Criticism and the Hebrew Bible.* Edited by J. C. Exum and D. J. A. Clines, 114–24. JSOTSup 143. Sheffield: Sheffield Academic Press, 1993.

Gilbert, Pierre. "A New Look at Amos's Prophetic Status (Amos 7:10–17)." *EgT* 28, no. 3 (1997): 291–300.

Hardmeier, Christof. "Alttestamentliche Exegese und linguistische Erzählforschung: Grundfragen der Erzählinterpretation am Beispiel von Amos 7,10–17." *WuD* 18 (1985): 49–71.

Hauret, C. "La vocation d'un prophète. Am 7:12–15." *Assemblées du Seigneurs* 46 (1974): 30–35.

Herntrich, V. "Das Berufungsbewusstsein des Amos." *Christentum und Wissenschaft* 9 (1933): 161–76.

Jaruzelska, Izabela. "'Amasyah—prêtre de Béthel—fonctionnaire royal (essai socio-économique préliminaire)." *FO* 31 (1995): 53–69.

Mallau, Hans Harald. "Las reacciones frente a los mensajes proféticos y el problema de la distinción entre profetas verdaderos y falsos. A propósito de Amós 7:10–17." *RivB* 1 (1972): 33–39.

Miller, Patrick D. "The Prophetic Critique of Kings." *Ex Auditu* 2 (1986): 82–95 (reprinted in *Israelite Religion and Biblical Theology.* Edited by idem, 527–47. JSOTSup 267. Sheffield: Sheffield Academic Press, 2000).

Mowinckel, Sigmund. "Die Offenbarungserlebnisse der Propheten Amos, Jesaya und Jeremia." *NorTT* 49 (1948): 120–28.

Overholt, Thomas W. "Commanding the Prophets: Amos and the Problem of Prophetic Authority." *CBQ* 41, no. 4 (1979): 517–32.

Pfeifer, Gerhard. "Die Ausweisung eines lästigen Ausländers Amos 7,10–17." *ZAW* 96, no. 1 (1984): 112–18.

Rost, Leonhard. "Zu Amos 7:10–17." In *Festgabe für Theodor Zahn,* 229–36. Leipzig: Deichert, 1928.

Schmidt, Daniel. "Critical Note: Another Word-Play in Amos?" *GTJ* 8, no. 1 (1987): 141–42.

Seierstad, Ivar P. "Erlebnis und Gehorsam beim Propheten Amos." *ZAW* 52, 11, no. 1 (1934): 22–41.

Seierstad, Ivar P. *Die Offenbarungserlebnisse der Propheten Amos, Jesaja und Jeremia: Eine Untersuchung der Erlebnisvorgänge unter besonderer Berücksichtung ihrer religiös-sittlichen Art und Auswirkung.* 2d ed. Oslo: Universitetsforlaget, 1965.

Spiegel, Shalom. "Amos vs. Amaziah." In *The Jewish Expression*. Edited by J. Goldin, 38–65. New Haven: Yale University Press, 1976.

Stoebe, H. J. "Noch einmal zu Amos vii 10–17." *VT* 39, no. 3 (1989): 341–54.

Tucker, Gene M. "Prophetic Authenticity: A Form-Critical Study of Amos 7:10–17." *Int* 27, no. 4 (1973): 423–34.

Utzschneider, H. "Die Amazjaerzählung (Am 7,10–17) zwischen Literatur und Historie." *BN* 41 (1988): 76–101.

Vincent, Jean Marcel. "'Visionnaire, va-t'en!': Interprétation d'Amos 7:10–17 dans son contexte." *ETR* 75, no. 2 (2000): 229–50.

Weiser, Artur A. "Die Berufung des Amos." *TBl* 7, no. 7 (1928): 177–82.

Werlitz, Jürgen. "Amos und sein Biograph. Zur Entstehung und Intention der Prophetenerzählung. Am 7,10–17." *BZ* 44, no. 2 (2000): 233–51.

Williamson, H. G. M. "The Prophet and the Plumbline: A Redaction-Critical Study of Amos vii." In *In Quest of the Past: Studies on Israelite Religion, Literature and Prophetism*. Edited by A. S. van der Woude, 101–21. *OTS* 26. Leiden: Brill, 1990 (reprinted in *This Place Is Too Small for Us: The Israelite Prophets in Recent Scholarship*. Edited by R. P. Gordon, 453–77. SBTS 5. Winona Lake, Ind.: Eisenbrauns, 1995).

Zevit, Ziony. "A Misunderstanding at Bethel, Amos VII 12–17." *VT* 25, no. 4 (1975): 783–90.

7:11

Bjorndalen, Anders Jorgen. "Zu den Zeitstufen der Zitatformel *kh 'mr* im Botenverkehr." *ZAW* 86, no. 4 (1974): 393–404.

7:12

Bechar, Schlomo. "'Seer, go, flee.'" (Heb.). *BMik* 114, no. 2 (1988): 392–96.

7:14–15

Abbott, Walter M., and S. Abramski. "I am not a prophet nor a son of a prophet." In *Studies in the Bible Dedicated to the Memory of Umberto Cassuto on the 100th Anniversary of His Birth*. Edited by S. E. Loewenstamm, 64–68. Jerusalem: Magnes, 1987.

Ackroyd, Peter R. "Amos 7:14." *ExpTim* 68, no. 3 (1956): 94.

Bach, Robert. "Erwägungen zu Amos 7,14." In *Die Botschaft und die Boten* (Festschrift H. W. Wolff). Edited by J. Jeremias and L. Perlitt, 203–16. Neukirchen-Vluyn: Neukirchener Verlag, 1981.

Bartina, Sebastián. "Hiendo los higos de los sicomoros (Amós 7:14)." *EstBíb* 25, nos. 3–4 (1966): 349–54.

Baumann, Eberhard. "Eine Einzelheit." *ZAW* 64, no. 1 (1952): 62.

Bič, Milos. "Der Prophet Amos—ein Haepatoskopos." *VT* 1, no. 4 (1951): 293–96.

Braslavi, J. "Amos—*Nōqēd, Bôqēr*, and *Bôlēs Šikmîm*" (Heb.). *BMik* 12, no. 3 (1967): 87–101.

Cohen, Simon. "Amos *Was* a Navi." *HUCA* 32 (1961): 175–78.

Danell, Gustaf Adolf. "Var Amos verkligen en nabi?" *SEÅ* 16 (1951): 7–20.

Diebner, Bernd Jörg. "Berufe und Berufung des Amos (Am 1,1 und 7,14f.)." *DBAT* 23 (1986): 97–120.

Driver, G. R. "Amos 7:14." *ExpTim* 67, no. 3 (1955): 91–92.

Driver, G. R. "*Waw* Explicative in Amos 7:14." *ExpTim* 68, no. 10 (1957): 302.

Driver, G. R. "Affirmation by Exclamatory Negation." *JANESCU* 5 (1973): 107–8.

Galil, J. "An Ancient Technique for Ripening Sycamore Fruit in East-Mediterranean Countries." *Economic Botany* 22 (1968): 178–90.

Galil, J., and D. Eisikowitch. "Flowery Cycles and Fruit Types of *Ficus Sycamorus*." *New Phytologist* 67 (1968): 752–55.

Giles, Terry. "A Note on the Vocation of Amos 7:14." *JBL* 111, no. 4 (1992): 690–92.

Glück, J. J. "Three Notes on the Book of Amos." *OTWSA* 7–8 (1964–1965): 115–21.

Gunneweg, A. H. J. "Erwägungen zu Amos 7,14." *ZTK* 57, no. 1 (1960): 1–16.

Haupt, P. "Was Amos a Sheepman?" *JBL* 35, nos. 3–4 (1916): 280–87.

Hoffmann, Yair. "Did Amos Regard Himself as a *nābî*?" *VT* 27, no. 2 (1977): 209–12.

Keimer, Ludwig. "Eine Bemerkung zu Amos 7:14." *Bib* 8, no. 4 (1927): 441–44.

Loretz, Oswald. "Die Berufung des Propheten Amos (7:14–15)." *UF* 6 (1974): 487–88.

MacCormack, J. "Amos 7:14a, 'I Was (Am) No Prophet, Neither Was (Am) I a Prophet's Son.'" *ExpTim* 67, no. 10 (1956): 318.

Richardson, H. Neil. "A Critical Note on Amos 7:14." *JBL* 85, no. 1 (1966): 89.

Roberts, J. J. M. "Exegesis: A Note on Amos 7:14 and Its Context." *ResQ* 8, no. 3 (1965): 175–78.

Rottzoll, Dirk U. "II Sam 14,5—eine Parallele zu Am 7,14f." *ZAW* 100, no. 3 (1988): 413–15.

Rowley, H. H. "Was Amos a Nabi?" In *Festschrift Otto Eissfeldt zum 60. Geburtstag.* Edited by J. Fück, 209–12. Halle an der Saale: Max Niemeyer, 1947.

Schmid, Herbert. "'Nicht Prophet bin ich, noch bin ich Prophetensohn.' Zur Erklärung von Amos 7,14a." *Jud* 23, no. 2 (1967): 68–74.

Schult, Hermann. "Amos 7:15a und die Legitimation des Aussenseiters." In *Probleme biblischer Theologie* (Festschrift G. von Rad). Edited by H. W. Wolff, 462–78. Munich: Kaiser, 1971.

Segert, Stanislav. "Zur Bedeutung des Wortes *nōqēd*." In *Hebräische Wortforschung* (Festschrift W. Baumgartner). Edited by B. Hartmann et al., 279–83. VTSup 16. Leiden: Brill, 1967.

Spiegel, Shalom. "Amos vs. Amaziah." In *The Jewish Expression*. Edited by J. Goldin, 38–65. New Haven: Yale University Press, 1976.

Stoebe, H. J. "Der Prophet Amos und sein bürgerlicher Beruf." *WuD* 5 (1957): 160–81.

Treu, Ursula. "Amos 7:14, Schenute und Physiologus." *NT* 10, nos. 2–3 (1968): 234–40.

Tsevat, Matitiahu. "Amos 7:14—Present or Preterite." In *The Tablet and the Scroll* (Festschrift W. W. Hallo). Edited by M. E. Cohen et al., 256–58. Bethesda, Md.: CDL, 1993.

van Hoonacker, Albin. "Le sens de la protestation d'Amos 7:14–15." *ETL* 18 (1941): 65–67.

Vogt, Ernst. "*Waw* Explicative in Amos VII,14." *ExpTim* 68, no. 10 (1957): 301–2.

Waitz, Yosef. "Amos— *Nōqēd, Bôqer*, and *Bôles Sikmîm*" (Heb.). *BMik* 13, no. 2 (1968): 141–44.

Weiss, Meir. *The Bible from Within: The Method of Total Translation*, 102–6, 417–21. Jerusalem: Magnes, 1984.

Weiser, Artur. "Die Berufung des Amos." *TBl* 7, no. 7 (1928): 177–82.

Wolff, Hans Walter. "The Irresistible Word (Amos)." *CurTM* 10, no. 1 (1983): 4–13 (reprinted in H. W. Wolff, *Confrontations with Prophets: Discovering the Old Testament's New and Contemporary Significance*, 9–21. Philadelphia: Fortress, 1983).

Wright, Samuel Lee. "O homem de Deus e o homem do rei." *RevT* 2, no. 3 (1986): 37–42.

Wright, T. J. "Amos and the 'Sycamore Fig.'" *VT* 26, no. 3 (1976): 362–68.
Zalcman, Lawrence. "Piercing the Darkness at *bôqēr* (Amos VII 14)." *VT* 30, no. 2 (1980): 252–55.
Zevit, Ziony. "Expressing Denial in Biblical Hebrew and Mishnaic Hebrew." *VT* 29, no. 4 (1979): 505–9.
Ziv, Judah. "Amos 7:14" (Heb.). *BMik* 28, no. 1 (1982–1983): 49–53.

7:15

Schult, H. "Amos 7:15a und die Legitimation des Aussenseiters." In *Probleme biblischer Theologie* (Festschrift G. von Rad). Edited by H. W. Wolff, 462–78. Munich: Kaiser, 1971.

8:1–3

Loewenstamm, S. E. "*klwb qys* (A Remark on the Typology of the Prophetic Vision [Amos 8:1–3])" (Heb.). *Tarbiz* 34 (1965): 319–22.
Rahtjen, Bruce D. "A Critical Note on Amos 8:1–2." *JBL* 83, no. 4 (1964): 416–17.
Rinaldi, Giovanni. "De III et IV Visione Libri Amos." *VD* 17, no. 3 (1937): 82–87; no. 4 (1937): 114–16.
Wolters, Al. "Wordplay and Dialect in Amos 8:1–2." *JETS* 31, no. 4 (1988): 407–10.

8:4

Bewer, J. A. "Critical Notes on Amos 2:7 and 8:4." *AJSL* 19, no. 2 (1903): 116–17.

8:4–8

Bohlen, Reinhold. "Zur Sozialkritik des Propheten Amos." *TTZ* 95 (1986): 282–301.
Desrousseaux, L. "Acheter le malheureux pour un peu d'argent." *Asemblées du Seigneur* 56 (1974): 56–61.
Gese, Hartmut. "Amos 8:4–8: Der kosmische Frevel händlerischer Habgier." In *Prophet und Prophetenbuch* (Festschrift O. Kaiser), ed. V. Fritz et al., 59–72. Berlin: de Gruyter, 1989.
Jeremias, Jörg. "Amos 8,4–7—ein Kommentar zu 2,6f." In *Text, Methode und Grammatik* (Festschrift W. Richter). Edited by W. Gross et al., 205–20. St. Ottilien: EOS, 1991 (reprinted in idem, *Hosea und Amos: Studien zu den Anfängen des Dodekapropheten* 231–43. FAT 13. Tübingen: Mohr, 1996).
Kessler, R. "Die angeblicher Kornhändler von Amos VIII 4–7." *VT* 39, no. 1 (1989): 13–22.
Schultes, J. L. "Gott redet auch durch sein Schweigen: Bibel Meditation zu Amos 8:4–7, 11–12." *BL* 48 (1975): 256–59.

8:5

Givati, Meir. "The *Šabbat* of the Prophet Amos" (Heb.). *BMik* 22, no. 2 (1977): 194–98, 278–79.
Halevi, Benjamin. "When Will the New Moon Be Gone?" (Heb.). *BMik* 21, no. 3 (1976): 333–46, 493.
Lohman, Paul. "Einige Textkonjekturen zu Amos." *ZAW* 32, no. 2 (1912): 274–77.

8:6

Lang, Bernhard. "Sklaven und Unfreie im Buch Amos (ii 6, viii 6)." *VT* 31, no. 4 (1981): 482–88.

8:11–13

Albert, Edwin. "Einige Bemerkungen zu Amos." *ZAW* 33, no. 3 (1913): 265–71.

Haag, Ernst. "Das Schweigen Gottes: Ein Wort des Propheten Amos (Am 8,11s)." *BibLeb* 10 (1969): 157–64.

Muraokao, Taakamitsu. "Is the Septuagint Amos 8,12–9,10 a Separate Unit?" *VT* 20, no. 4 (1970): 496–500.

Rusche, Helga. "Wenn Gott sein Wort entzieht: Meditation zu Amos 8:11–12." *BibLeb* 10 (1969): 219–21.

Schultes, J. L. "Gott redet auch durch sein Schweigen: Bibel Meditation zu Amos 8:4–7, 11–12." *BL* 48 (1975): 256–59.

Szwarc, Urzula. "Glód Slowa Bozego Analiza Egzegetycno-Teologiczna Tekstu Am 8,11–12" (Eng. summary). *Roczniki Teologiczno-Kanoniczne: Annales de Théologie et du Droit Canon* 27, no. 1 (1980): 43–51.

8:14

Ackroyd, Peter. "The Meaning of Hebrew *dôr* Considered." *JSS* 13, no. 1 (1968): 4–10.

Barstad, Hans M. *The Religious Polemics of Amos: Studies in the Preaching of Am 2: 7B–8; 4:1–13; 5:1–27; 6:4–7; 8:14*, 143–201. VT Sup 34. Leiden: Brill, 1984.

Bartina, Sebastián. "'Vivit Potentia Beer-seba!' (Amos 8,14)." *VD* 34 (1956): 202–10.

Hadley, Judith M. *The Cult of Asherah in Ancient Israel and Judah: Evidence for a Hebrew Goddess*, 77. Cambridge: Cambridge University Press, 2000.

Mulzer, Martin. "Amos 8,14 in der LXX: Ein Einwurf in die Tel Dan–Text Debatte." *BN* 84 (1996): 54–58.

Neuberg, Frank J. "An Unrecognized Meaning of Hebrew *dôr*." *JNES* 9, no. 4 (1950): 215–17.

Olyan, Saul M. "The Oath in Amos 8:14." In *Priesthood and Cult in Ancient Israel*. Edited by G. A. Anderson and S. M. Olyan, 121–49. JSOTSup 125. Sheffield: Sheffield Academic Press, 1991.

9:1

Cathcart, Kevin J. "*rōʾš*, 'Poison,' in Amos ix 1." *VT* 44, no. 3 (1994): 393–96.

9:1–4

Jeremias, Jörg. "Das unzugängliche Heiligtum: Zur letzen Vision des Amos." In *Konsequente Traditionsgeschichte* (Festschrift K. Baltzer). Edited by R. Barthelmus et al., 155–67. OBO 126. Göttingen: Vandenhoeck & Ruprecht, 1993 (reprinted in idem, *Hosea und Amos: Studien zu den Anfängen des Dodekapropheten*, 244–56. FAT 13. Tübingen: Mohr, 1996).

Mathias, Dietmar. "Beobachtungen zur fünften Vision des Amos (9, 1–4)." In *Gedenkt an das Wort*. Edited by Ch. Kähler et al., 150–74. Leipzig: Evangelische Verlagsanstalt, 1999.

Waschke, Ernst-Joachim. "Die fünfte Vision des Amosbuches (9,1–4)—eine Nachinterpretation." *ZAW* 106, no. 3 (1994): 434–45.

Oulette, Jean. "The Shaking of the Threshholds in Amos 9:1." *HUCA* 43 (1972): 23–27.

Sellin, Ernst. "Drei umstrittene Stellen des Amosbuches." *ZDPV* 52 (1929): 141–48.

9:1–15

Weimar, Peter. "Der Schluss des Amos-Buches. Ein Beitrag zur Redaktionsgeschichte des Amos-Buches." *BN* 16 (1981): 60–100.

9:4

Turner, P. "Two Septuagintalisms with stērízein." *VT* 28, no. 4 (1978): 481–82.

9:5–6 (see chap. 4, "Specific Topics and Significant Blocks of Text: Doxologies")

Foresti, F. "Funzioni semantica dei brani participiali di Amos: 4,13; 5,8s; 9,5." *Bib* 62, no. 2 (1981): 169–84.

9:6

Lang, Martin. "Gott erbaut sein himmlisches Heiligtum: Zur Bedeutung von '*gddtw* in Am 9,6." *Bib* 82, no. 1 (2001): 93–98.

Luria, B. Z. "'Who Calls the Waters of the Sea and Spills Them on the Face of the Earth' (Amos 5:8; 9:6)." (Heb.). *BMik* 30, no. 2 (1985): 259–62.

Paas, Stefan. "'He Who Builds His Stairs into Heaven . . .' (Amos 9:6a)." *UF* 25 (1993): 319–25.

Rinaldi, Giovanni. "Sull'uso de '*gdh* ('*aguddâ*) nell'AT." BeO 24 (1985): 202–4.

9:7–8

Adamo, D. T. "Amos 9.7–8 in an African Perspective." *Orita* 24, nos. 1–2 (1992): 76–84.

Brueggemann, Walter. "Exodus in the Plural (Amos 9:7)." In *Many Voices, One God: Being Faithful in a Pluralistic World*. Edited by W. Brueggemann and G. W. Stroup, 15–34. Louisville: Westminster John Knox, 1998 (reprinted in *Texts that Linger, Words that Explode: Listening to Prophetic Voices*. Edited by P. D. Miller, 89–103. Minneapolis: Fortress, 2000).

Delcor, M. "Les Kerethim et les Cretois." *VT* 28, no. 4 (1978): 409–22.

Fang, C. "Universalism and the Prophet Amos." *Collectanea Theologica Universitatis Fujen* 5, no. 20 (1974): 165–71.

Feuillet, A. "L'universalisme et l'alliance dans le religion d'Amos." *BVC* 17 (1957): 17–29.

Gese, Hartmut. "Das Problem von Amos 9,7." In *Textgemass: Aufsätze und Beiträge zur Hermeneutik des Alten Testaments* (Festschrift E. Würthwein). Edited by A. H. J. Gunneweg and O. Kaiser, 33–38. Göttingen: Vandenhoeck & Ruprecht, 1979 (reprinted in *Alttestamentliche Studien*, 116–21. Tübingen: Mohr, 1991).

Holter, Knut. "Is Israel Worth More to God than Cush? An Interpretation of Amos 9:7." In *Yahweh in Africa: Essays on Africa and the Old Testament*, 115–25. Bible and Theology in Africa 1. New York: Peter Lang, 2000.

Nagah, Rivka. "Are You Not Like the Ethiopians to Me (Amos 9:7)?" (Heb.). *BMik* 27, nos. 2–3 (1981–1982): 174–82.

Prignaud, J. "Caftorim et Kerétim." *RB* 71, no. 2 (1962): 215–29.

Rice, G. "Was Amos a Racist?" *JRT* 35, no. 1 (1978): 35–44.

Smith, Regina. "A New Perspective on Amos 9:7a: 'To Me, O Israel, you are just like the Kushites.'" *JITC* 22 (1994): 36–47.

Strange, James. *Caphtor/Keftiu. A New Investigation*. Acta theologica danica 14. Leiden: Brill, 1980.

van Wyk, W. C. "Die Kusiete in Amos 9:7." *HervTS* 22, no. 4 (1967): 38–45.

Vogels, Walter. "Invitation à revenir à l'alliance et universalisme en Amos IX 7." *VT* 32, no. 2 (1972): 223–39.
Wainwright, G. A. "Caphtor-Cappadocia." *VT* 6, no. 2 (1956): 199–210.
Wainwright, G. A. "The Septuagint's *Kappadokía* for Caphtor." *JJS* 7, nos. 1–2 (1956): 91–92.

9:7–15

Bramer, Stephen. "The Structure of Amos 9:7–15." *BSac* 156, no. 3 (1999): 272–81.
Florival, Ephrem. "Le jour du jugement (Amos 9:7–15)." *BVC* 8 (1954–1955): 61–75.
Kaiser, W. C., Jr. "The Davidic Promise and the Inclusion of the Gentiles (Amos 9:9–15 and Acts 15:13–18): A Test Passage for Theological Systems." *JETS* 20 (1977): 97–111 (reprinted in idem, *The Uses of the Old Testament in the New*, 177–94. Chicago: Moody, 1985).
McCullough, W. S. "Some Suggestions about Amos." *JBL* 72, no. 4 (1953): 247–54.
Schullerus, Konrad. "Überlegungen zur Redaktionsgeschichte des Amosbuches anhand von Am 9,7–10." *BN* 85 (1996): 56–69.

9:9

Volz, Paul. "Zu Am 9:9." *ZAW* 38, no. 1 (1919): 105–11.
Wilbers, H. "Étude sur trois textes relatifs à l'agriculture: Isa 28:27–28; Amos 2:13; 9:9." *MUSJ* 5, no. 1 (1911): 269–82.

9:9–10

Hoffmann, Hans Werner. "Zur Echtheitsfrage von Amos 9,9f." *ZAW* 82, no. 1 (1970): 121–22.
Reider, Joseph. "Contributions to the Scriptural Text." *HUCA* 24 (1952–1953): 85–106 (94–96).

9:11

Davies, Philip R. "*Bytdwd* and *Swkt Dwyd*: A Comparison." *JSOT* 64 (1994): 23–24.
Homan, Michael M. "Booths or Succoth? A Response to Yigael Yadin." *JBL* 118, no. 4 (1999): 691–97.
Nägele, Sabine. *Laubhütte Davids und Wolkensohn: Eine auslegungsgeschichtliche Studie zu Amos 9,11 in der judischen und christlichen Exegese*. AGJU 24. Leiden: Brill, 1995.
Nogalski, James D. "The Problematic Suffixes of Amos IX 11." *VT* 43, no. 3 (1993): 411–18.
Richardson, H. Neil. "*Skt* (Amos 9:11). 'Booth' or 'Succoth'?" *JBL* 92, no. 3 (1973): 375–81.
Turner, P. "'*Anoikodomein* and Intra-Septugintal Borrowing." *VT* 27, no. 4 (1977): 492–93.

9:11–15

Firth, D. G. "Promise as Polemic: Levels of Meaning in Amos 9:11–15." *OTE* 9, no. 3 (1996): 372–82.
Kellermann, Ulrich. "Der Amosschluss als Stimme deuteronomistischer Heilshoffnung." *EvT* 29, no. 4 (1969): 169–83.
Nel, W. A. G. "Amos 9:11–15: An Unconditional Prophecy of Salvation during the Period of the Exile." *OTE* 2, no. 1 (1984): 81–97.

Pomykala, Kenneth E. *The Davidic Dynasty Tradition in Early Judaism: Its History and Significance for Messianism*, 61–63. SBLEJL 7. Atlanta: Scholars Press, 1995.

Terblanche, M. D. "'Rosen und Lavendel nach Blut und Eisen': Intertextuality in the Book of Amos." *OTE* 10, no. 2 (1997): 312–21.

Weimar, Peter. "Der Schluss des Amos-Buches. Ein Beitrag zur Redaktionsgeschichte des Amos-Buches." *BN* 16 (1981): 60–100.

9:12

Braun, Michael A. "James' Use of Amos at the Jerusalem Council: Steps Toward a Solution of the Textual and Theological Problems." *JETS* 20, no. 2 (1977): 113–21.

Haller, M. "Edom im Urteil der Propheten." In *Vom Alten Testament* (Festschrift K. Marti). Edited by K. Budde, 109–17. BZAW 41. Berlin: de Gruyter, 1925.

Jones, Barry Alan. *The Formation of the Book of the Twelve: A Study in Text and Canon*, 175–91. SBLDS 149. Atlanta: Scholars Press, 1995.

Lohfink, N. "Die Bedeutung von Heb. *yrš* Qal und Hif." *BZ* 27 (1983): 14–33.

Matthews, Claire R. *Defending Zion: Edom's Desolation and Jacob's Restoration (Isaiah 34–35) in Context*, 107–8. BZAW 236. Berlin: de Gruyter, 1995.

9:13

Weiss, Meir. "These Days and the Days to Come according to Amos 9:13" (Heb.). *EI* 14 (1978): 69–73, 125.

9:14

Baumann, E. "*šwb šbwt*: Eine exegetische Untersuchung." *ZAW* 47, no. 1 (1929): 17–44.

Holladay, W. L. *The Root Šûbh in the Old Testament*. Leiden: Brill, 1958.

7

Doctoral Dissertations, 1985–2000

INTRODUCTION

Only those dissertations contributing to the Ph.D. or Th.D. degree have been considered for summary.[1] The first group of dissertations deals exclusively with matters pertaining to the book of Amos. The second group comprises dissertations that handle portions or the entirety of the book of Amos as they relate to other concerns. This latter group is labeled "selected," because an exhaustive listing would have been impossible. Those chosen to appear in this listing represent a variety of topics that might be of interest to potential researchers of this prophetic text. If a dissertation has been published, then cited page numbers refer to those of that publication. In the case of unpublished works this list specifies which are available through UMI (University Microfilms Inc., now called Bell & Howell Information and Learning Company). A list of D.Min. dissertations appears at the end of this chapter.

DISSERTATIONS DEDICATED SOLELY TO AMOS

Barriocanal Gómez, José Luis. "La relectura de la tradición del Éxodo en el libro de Amós." Ph.D. thesis, Gregorian University (Rome), 1999. Published as a monograph with the same title. Tesi Gregoriana Teologia 58. Rome: Gregorian Pontifical University Press, 2000. 327 pp.
  [This work attempts to compare and contrast the different ways in which the exodus tradition is used in the book of Amos. In the first part the author examines the tradition in Deuteronomy 4 and Ezekiel 20. The second part is devoted to analyzing the tradition in Amos. The results are of two kinds: Early in his ministry the prophet appealed to the exodus to elicit a positive response from the people; later, after the prophet sees no escape from judgment, the tradition is utilized to provide a theological rationale for the divine punishment.]

Booy, Casper Hendrick. "An Exegetical Study of Amos 9:11–15." Unpublished Ph.D. thesis, University of Pretoria (Republic of South Africa), 1999. (Afrikaans)
[Attempts to push scholarly discussion on this passage beyond an inordinate focus on questions of authenticity and authorship. Although Booy does hold that these verses are exilic, he argues that they contribute in an important way to the message of the final form of the book of Amos. This closing pericope is an unconditional salvation oracle, which underscored to the exilic community that Yahweh is the faithful God of the covenant and that the judgment oracles of the rest of the book are not his final word.]

Bramer, Stephen John. "The Contribution of Literary Structure to the Argument of Amos." Unpublished Ph.D. thesis, Dallas Theological Seminary, 1997. 305 pp. Available through UMI.
After surveying critical approaches and analyses of the macrostructure of Amos, Bramer applies rhetorical criticism to the final form of the text to demonstrate that it coheres and sequentially advances its argument (which he defines as "the synchronic development of the message of the book"). Proposes a prologue + four section structure and suggests that the genre of the book is a "covenant enforcement document." Minimal use of non-English sources. This thesis is synthesized and reproduced in a three-part series entitled "Studies in the Structure of the Book of Amos," *BSac* 156 (1999): 42–60, 160–74, 272–81.

Carroll R., M. Daniel. "Prophecy in Context: From Old Testament Text to Liberating Faith." Ph.D. thesis, University of Sheffield (Great Britain), 1990. Published as *Contexts for Amos: Prophetic Poetics in Latin American Perspective*. JSOTSup 132. Sheffield: Sheffield Academic Press, 1992. 362 pp.
The primary goal is to try to develop a multidisciplinary methodology to contextualize the prophetic text, particularly into Latin America. Toward that end the author coordinates the sociology of knowledge, cultural anthropology, narrative ethics, and literary theory (pp. 48–175). After a detailed poetic reading of chapters 3–6 (pp. 176–277), Carroll R. interacts with some of the recent theological trends on that continent. Offers two appendices: "Tradition and History in Amos" and "Textual Method in Latin American Liberation Theology" (pp. 307–19).

Dines, Jennifer Mary. "The Septuagint of Amos: A Study of Interpretation." Unpublished Ph.D. thesis, University of London, 1992.
[An attempt to identify the translation techniques, theological perspective, and cultural context of the translator(s) of Amos. Does not discount the possibility of a different Hebrew *Vorlage* in certain passages. Traces the subsequent interpretation of Septuagint Amos to the mid-fifth century C.E. with an analysis of the commentaries of Theodore of Mopsuestia, Theodoret of Cyrrhus, Cyril of Alexandria, and Jerome. Suggests an Egyptian Jewish setting for the translation in the decades following the Maccabean revolt.]

Ebo, D. J. I. O. "'O that Jacob would survive': A Study of Hope in the Book of Amos." Unpublished Ph.D. thesis, University of Nigeria, 1985.
[Argues against the critical position that takes the hope passages in the book of Amos to be later additions. Proposes that the remnant motif, the selective judgment reflected in the visions, the prophetic exhortations, and the closing oracle

(9:11–15) all work together to point to the reality of an element of hope within the original message of Amos.]

Fleischer, Günther. "Von Menschenverkäufern, Baschankühen und Rechtsverkehrern: Die Sozialkritik des Amosbuches in historisch-kritischer, sozialgeschictlicher und archäologischer Perspektive." Ph.D. thesis, Rheinische Friedrich-Wilhelms-Universität Bonn, 1988. Published as a monograph with the same title. BBB 74. Frankfurt am Main: Athenäum, 1989. xiv + 486 pp.

Surveys the various tradition critical and sociohistorical hypotheses that have been postulated to explain the social critique of Amos. Basing his view on a careful, but critical, study of the relevant biblical texts and on studies by the French historian F. LeRoy Languedoc, the author proposes that the prophet's message reflects a society affected by population growth, inheritance problems, and changes brought about by the development of the monarchy.

Giles, Terry. "Amos and the Law." Unpublished Ph.D. thesis, Michigan State University, 1989. 247 pp. Available through UMI.

An attempt to apply Habermas's notion of the interrelationship between tradition, social labor, and domination to the book of Amos. Provides a description of the development from a rural to an urban society (following Frick) and distributional economy (Borowski). Offers breakdown of Amos passages as parallel to or not parallel to covenant stipulations. Types of indictments and changes in their wording can be explained by the confluence of socioeconomic factors. Closes with tables of findings. Extensive bibliography (pp. 200–247), yet discussion uses few sources (especially the textual discussion). Habermas's theory is stated, but neither developed nor nuanced.

Habberstad, Rakotondrazaka. "Le fin d'Israël selon la prophétie d'Amos: Nature et fonction des récits de vision." Unpublished Th.D. thesis, Université de Sciences Humaines de Strasbourg (France), 1999. ix + 299 pp.

[Analyzes whether the prophetic mission of Amos is to announce the final judgment upon Israel or to call the nation to conversion. Two points are emphasized: (1) the visions function as a background for the structure of the prophetic discourse; (2) two literary levels are developed: a core, which goes back to the prophet himself, and a peripheral level, which most likely reflects a postexilic interpretation of the prophet's words. The conclusion is that the prophet, because of what he has seen, calls Israel to conversion. Israel refuses to listen and therefore will suffer irremediable ruin.]

Heyns, M. "Amos—Advocate for Freedom and Justice: A Socio-Historical Investigation" (Afrikaans). Unpublished Ph.D. thesis, UNISA (Republic of South Africa), 1992.

[An attempt to reconstruct the social context for the message and ministry of the prophet. Takes the text of the prophetic book seriously as a primary source, but adds information from archaeology and other OT passages. Highlights the agricultural circumstances in eighth-century Judah to interpret the words of Amos.]

Hockenhull, Brenda Rae. "The Use of Series in the Book of Amos." Unpublished Th.D. thesis, New Orleans Baptist Theological Seminary, 1987. 226 pp. Available through UMI.

Attempts to apply elements of form and rhetorical criticism to the five series in the book of Amos (these can be continuous or separated): the Oracles against the Nations, the exhortations to "Hear this word," the woes, the doxologies, and the visions. A chapter dedicated to each series offers a very basic exegesis and discussion of the genre, possible social contexts for the genre (usually taken as a festival at a sanctuary), theological motifs, and the contribution of each to the overall message of the book. No use of non-English sources.

Mahaffey, Edward Lamar. "An Investigation of Social Justice as It Relates to the Message of Amos." Unpublished Ph.D thesis, New Orleans Baptist Seminary, 1993. 172 pp. Available through UMI.
  Very basic exegesis of pertinent texts in Amos with the aim of ascertaining the basis for the prophetic condemnation of social injustice by other nations and within Israel. Argues that the universal sovereignty of Yahweh was the foundation for judging the nations, while the covenant was the basis for castigating Israel. No use of non-English sources.

Manakatt, Mathew. "A Judgment Narrative and Two Pairs of Visions (Amos 7,1–8,3)." Unpublished Th.D. thesis, Gregorian Pontifical University (Rome), 1992. Available through UMI.
  [Explores the significance and interrelationships between the two pairs of visions and the narrative that appears between those of the second pair—that is, between visions three and four (7:10–17). The visions reveal progressively the judgment upon Israel, while the narrative reveals that the most serious sin of all is silencing the Word of God (cf. 2:12).]

Mbele, Philemon. "La justice sociale ou l'ultimate possibilité de salut pour Israel selon le prophète Amos." Unpublished Ph.D. thesis, Faculté de théologie protestante de Montpellier (France), 1988. 189 pp.
  [Analyzes the book of Amos from the perspective of social justice as set over against final salvation for the nation of Israel. It is argued that (1) faith in Yahweh must reflect obedience to his commandments for a just society; (2) violation of those commandments is not suspended by rituals; and (3) Israel must establish a just society to avoid total destruction.]

Möller, Karl. "Presenting a Prophet in Debate: An Investigation of the Literary Structure and the Rhetoric of Persuasion in the Book of Amos." Ph.D. thesis, Cheltenham and Gloucester College of Higher Education (Great Britain), 1999. 232 pp.
  An investigation into the rhetorical strategy of the compilers of the present form of the book of Amos. Argues that the goal was to convince a preexilic Judean audience not to repeat the obstinance of the Northern Kingdom of Israel and thus avoid the judgment of Yahweh. Presents the theoretical basis for such a rhetorical approach and applies the methodology to Amos 1–4.

Moore, Dana Charles. "Amos' Apologia: A Defense of His Prophetic Ministry." Unpublished Ph.D. thesis, Southwestern Baptist Theological Seminary, 1994. 196 pp. Available through UMI.
  Has as its goal to demonstrate the importance of an apologia for the prophet within the final form of the book of Amos. As an initial component of the apologia, this study presents the various means by which the prophet's message and

ministry are presented and defended (the call, the reception of visions, continuity with prophetic tradition, and the writing down of Amos's message) against the criticisms that would have been generated by his words. The second component is a basic exegesis of two key passages: 3:3–8 and 7:10–17. The conclusion extends the findings to comparisons with other prophets, especially Jeremiah. No use of non-English sources.

Nägele, Sabine. "Laubhütte Davids und Wolkensohn: Eine auslegungsgeschichltiche Studie zu Amos 9,11 in der jüdischen und christlichen Exegese." Ph.D. thesis, Eberhard Karls Universität (Tübingen), 1993. Published as a monograph with the same title. AGJU 24. Leiden: Brill, 1995.

> Reviews tendencies over several centuries within Jewish interpretations (Qumran, Targum, Talmud, and midrashim; the NT is also placed here.) and Christian exegesis (church fathers, Reformers, and the Enlightenment). Presents an exegesis of 9:11 and argues, on the basis of parallels in other languages and relevant biblical data, that "booth" is a reference to Jerusalem within the theological context of the Feast of Booths. Detailed English summary, pp. 223–38.

Oliver, Anthony. "Creation and Redemption in Amos: A Multi-faceted Approach with Emphasis on the Hymns." Unpublished Ph.D. thesis, Trinity Evangelical Divinity School, 1998. 276 pp. Available through UMI.

> Disputes the view that creation motifs are late and secondary to the book of Amos. Proposes that creation theology is pervasive and foundational to the message of the prophet. The judgment and subsequent restoration of the people is to be understood as divine intervention to both preserve and reestablish the moral order of the universe. The author bases his textual study on a "multi-faceted methodology" that incorporates insights from rhetorical criticism and text linguistics into the analysis of the final form of the text.

Park, Aaron Wonil. "Composition and Transmission of the Book of Amos: With Special Attention to Amos 5:25–27 and 9:11–15." Ph.D. thesis, Claremont Graduate University, 1999. Published as *The Book of Amos as Composed and Read in Antiquity*. Studies in Biblical Literature 37. New York: Peter Lang, 2001. xix + 256 pp.

> Has two goals: to demonstrate that 9:11–15 is a seventh-century B.C.E. redaction designed to reverse the theology of 5:25–27 and to trace the use and interpretation of these two passages from within the Bible through the early Christian church and Rabbinic literature. Posits a three-stage redaction process. Defines his method as grounded in form criticism and carefully distinguishes between text formation, composition, redaction, and transmission. Detailed discussion of appropriation of Amos by later tradents accompanied with helpful charts.

Park, Sang Hoon. "Eschatology in the Book of Amos: A Text-Linguistic Analysis." Unpublished Ph.D. thesis, Trinity Evangelical Divinity School, 1996. x + 292 pp. Available through UMI.

> After reviewing the history of prophet and Amos research (pp. 15–64), Park proposes the use of text linguistics to analyze the eschatological passages in the final form of the book (pp. 65–76). The fourth chapter supports the broad definition of the term "eschatology" as "a future in which the circumstances of history are changed to such an extent that one can speak of a new, entirely different, state of things without, in doing so, necessarily leaving the framework of history" (E. Jenni).

There is, in other words, both discontinuity and continuity between the past and the future (pp. 97–101). The material in Amos is separated into three categories: the judgment motif (5:18–20), the remnant motif (5:14–15), and the restoration motif (9:11–15). These are each dealt with in turn in the succeeding chapters.

Pungumbu Shaondo, Lody. "L'intervention sociale d'Amos—une contribution à l'étude de la mission prophétique en Afrique aujourd'hui." Unpublished Ph.D. thesis, Faculté Universitaire de Théologie Protestante (Belgium), 1992. 301 pp.
[Analyzes the social message of the book of Amos and argues that this constitutes a plea in favor of the oppressed lower classes. The situation in Africa today is similar to that of Israel in the time of the prophet, as the lower class suffers. In light of this reality, the church is called to fulfill a prophetic role of finding ways to help Africa be a place where people can live in peace.]

Ramírez, Guillermo. "The Social Location of the Prophet Amos in Light of a Cultural Anthropological Model." Unpublished Ph.D. thesis, Emory University, 1993. ii + 358 pp. Available through UMI.
An attempt to present a more complex and realistic approach to the social setting of the prophet by utilizing the group/grid model, as developed by M. Douglas and B. Malina, in order to supplement form critical studies. A discussion of the theoretical nature of the model is followed by its application to fifteen passages in Amos. Places the prophet within the strong group/high grid quadrant. No extensive interaction with Amos research in exegetical section. For a distillation of this work see "The Social Location of Amos in Light of the Group/Grid Cultural Anthropology Model," in *Prophets and Paradigms* (Festschrift G. M. Tucker), ed. S. B. Reid, 112–24 (JSOTSup 22; Sheffield: Sheffield Academic Press, 1996).

Reimer, Haroldo. "Ein 'totales Ends'? Studien zum Inhalt der Anklagen und zur sozialen Identität der vom Unheil Bedrohten in der radikalen Prophetie des Amos anhand der 'frühesten Kompositionen' im Amosbuch." Ph.D. thesis, Kirchlichen Hochschule Bethel-Bielefeld (Germany), 1990. A revised version was published as *Richtet auf das Rechts! Studien zur Botschaft des Amos.* SBS 149. Stuttgart: Katholisches Bibelwerk, 1992. 256 pp.
Contrasts Western (especially German) scholarly work on the book of Amos with insights and methodologies of Latin American liberation theology. Utilizes redaction-critical and sociohistorical analysis to work back to what he feels is the original message of the prophet: denunciation of oppressive political and economic structures and of individuals that exploit the poor. The earliest redaction level foresees a future without these unjust structures. A synthesis of some of his conclusions appears in "Agentes y mecanismos de opresión y explotación en Amos," *RIBLA* 12 (1992): 69–81.

Rottzoll, Dirk U. "Studien zur Redaktion und Komposition des Amosbuches." Ph.D. thesis, Philipps-Universität (Marburg), 1996. Published under the same title as a monograph. BZAW 243. Berlin: de Gruyter, 1996. 319 pp.
A redactional-critical commentary that argues for a concentric pattern for the entire book of Amos with its center at the hymn in 5:8–9. Contends that there may have been twelve stages in the composition of the prophetic text. These are helpfully summarized in succinct fashion in the closing chapter (pp. 285–90). Offers six excursuses on a variety of topics. Reflects the interest of his adviser

(Jörg Jeremias) to propose a redactional history of the development of the careful literary structures of the final form.

Schart, Aaron. "Die Entstehung des Zwölfprophetenbuchs: Neubearbeitungen von Amos im Rahmen schriftenübergreifender Redaktionsprozesse." Ph.D. thesis, Phillips-Universität (Marburg), 1996. Published as a monograph with the same title. BZAW 260. Berlin: de Gruyter, 1998.

> Connecting his work to the critical reconstructions of the book of Amos by Wolff and Jeremias, Schart proposes that the Book of the Twelve developed in six stages, the first of which began with an early collection of the oracles in Amos 3–6. The successive stages grew as intentionally interconnected pieces (linked lexically and thematically) of an ever-expanding body, a process sparked by different sociohistorical and religious contexts. The results of this study are presented in a helpful and very readable graphic form in two concluding appendices (pp. 315–17).

Shelly, Patricia Joyce. "Amos and Irony: The Use of Irony in Amos's Prophetic Discourse." Unpublished Ph.D. thesis, Iliff School of Theology and University of Denver, 1992. 184 pp. Available through UMI.

> After surveying Amos research (chap. 1) and scholarly discussion on irony—both outside and within biblical research (chap. 2)—Shelly discusses the use of irony in this prophetic book. The focus is on "a particular kind of irony which is rhetorical, intentional, covert and involves an element of negation" (p. 52). Investigates the rhetorical effect of irony in the various conventional prophetic speech forms, in the reversal of expectations in the citation of theological traditions, and in various other genres (chaps. 3–5).

Siquera, Reinaldo W. "The Presence of the Covenant Motif in Amos 1:2–2:16." Unpublished Ph.D. thesis, Andrews University, Berrien Springs, Michigan, 1996. 355 pp. Available through UMI.

> Provides a thorough survey of scholarly views in the twentieth century regarding the presence of the covenant(s) in the prophets in general, more particularly in the book of Amos and most specifically in the OAN (Oracles against the Nations). On the basis of terminology, themes, and structure (especially the covenant lawsuit) the author argues for the interrelated use of four covenants in the OAN: Noahic, Abrahamic, Mosaic, and Davidic. Extensive bibliographic references in the footnotes.

Thomas, Puthenvilayil Pappy. "Social Conditions during the Reign of Jeroboam II: A Social-Scientific Study Based on the Biblical Materials and Archaeological Discoveries." Unpublished Ph.D. thesis, Lutheran School of Theology (Chicago), 2000. 286 pp. Available through UMI.

> [Attempts to fill in the lack of information in the biblical text concerning Jeroboam II (both in 2 Kgs. 14 and in the book of Amos) with evidence drawn primarily from archaeological data of that period. Posits that Israel's monarchy at that time was characterized by military power, social violence and victimization, latifundialization, and debt slavery.]

Vanhorn, William Wayne. "An Investigation of 'Yom Yahweh' as It Relates to the Message of Amos." Unpublished Th.D. thesis, New Orleans Baptist Theological Seminary, 1987. 207 pp. Available through UMI.

 Begins with a very short survey of scholarly research on the "Day of the Lord" (pp. 10–19). Exegesis of texts designed to demonstrate that passages concerning the "day" are interrelated and grounded in covenant. All underscore covenant violation and inescapable judgment—except 9:11–15, which allows for restoration according to covenant promise. No correlation with the Book of the Covenant or other pertinent passages concerning specific covenant stipulations, little acknowledgment of critical issues, and almost no mention of non-English sources.

Wood, Joyce Rilett. "Amos: Prophecy as a Performing Art and Its Transformation in Book Culture." Ph.D. thesis, University of St. Michael's College (Toronto), 1993. Published as *Amos in Song and Culture*. JSOTSup 337. Sheffield: Sheffield Academic Press, 2002. 283 pp.

 Proposes that Amos was originally an itinerant poet, who composed and performed a coherent seven-poem drama that can be classified as a "tragedy" (follows N. Frye). Amos's reviser, a creative author and theologian in his own right, added material and comments to the original work. The resulting book now fits into the category of a "comedy" and was no longer designed for live performance. Presents extensive comparisons with eighth- and seventh-century B.C.E. Greek poetry and dramatic works. The thrust of this work was also presented in "Tragic and Comic Forms in Amos," *BibInt* 6, no. 1 (1998): 20–48.

SELECTED DISSERTATIONS THAT DEAL WITH AMOS IN THE CONTEXT OF BROADER DISCUSSIONS

Alvarez Barredo, Miguel. "Relecturas deuteronomísticas de Amós, Miqueas y Jeremías." Ph.D. thesis, Pontificia Universidà Urbaniana (Spain), 1992. Published as a monograph with the same title. Instituto Teológico Franciscano, Serie Mayor, 10. Murcía, Spain: Espigas, 1993. 228 pp. Available through UMI.

 Surveys terminology and theological concepts from the book of Deuteronomy that are the identifying characteristics of the Deuteronomistic redaction of Amos, Micah, and Jeremiah (pp. 27–51). Attention is primarily directed at Jeremiah. In regard to Amos, the author recognizes that research has been pioneered by W. H. Schmidt, H. W. Wolff, and J. Vermeylen. Points out the Deuteronomistic additions in the book, along with brief explicatory comments (pp. 53–82, 186–87).

Beach, Eleanor Ferris. "Image and Word: Iconology in the Interpretation of Hebrew Scriptures." Unpublished Ph.D. thesis, Claremont Graduate School, 1991. xvii + 372 pp. Available through UMI.

 Biblical literature drew upon powerful cultural symbols in dynamic and complex ways. Utilizes the contributions of various disciplines to establish a more comprehensive theoretical framework for relating the visual (artifacts as symbols) to texts. From this perspective Beach focuses on the Samarian ivories, as they are embedded in banquet furniture and paired with a specific cluster of religious symbols, in order to reinterpret several passages, for example, Amos's mourning imagery and allusions to the *marzēaḥ* feast ironically reverse a misplaced complacent ideology within an unjust society (pp. 268–73, 311–18, passim). Provides an appendix of illustrations (pp. 319–35).

Block, Michael David. "Samuel Terrien's 'The Elusive Presence' as Reflected in the Day of the Lord in Amos, Joel, and Zephaniah." Unpublished Ph.D. thesis, Southwestern Baptist Theological Seminary, 1990. 225 pp. Available through UMI.

Offers a general description of Terrien's theology within the context of a history of OT theologies before moving on specifically to that theologian's conceptualization of the day of the Lord. Block believes that Amos endeavors to correct the popular understanding of the presence of Yahweh in the past, present, and future. He suggests that it is helpful to consider Terrien's idea of the divine "elusive presence" as the underlying theme behind the day of the Lord in these preexilic prophets. No use of non-English sources.

Diop, Ganoune. "The Name 'Israel' and Related Expressions in the Books of Amos and Hosea." Unpublished Ph.D. thesis, Andrews University (Berrien Springs, Michigan), 1995. 451 pp. Available through UMI.

A study of the occurrences of "Israel" and related terms ("Judah," "Jacob," "Joseph," "Isaac," "David," and "Ephraim"), along with their combinations in Amos and Hosea in order to ascertain their referents and theological purpose. The survey of research and the exegesis of the relevant texts yields the result that no simple categorization can adequately explain all the uses. The variety of connotations—whether tribal, sociopolitical, or cultic—must be determined by the context. Arguing from the view that all of Amos is authentic, Diop suggests that the prophet attempted to emphasize the covenant obligations of the entire people of God (i.e., their concerns extended beyond the Northern Kingdom) and to present the eschatological hope of a continuity of this entity into the future through the preservation of a faithful remnant beyond the judgment (pp. 53–232).

Gilbert, Pierre. "Le motif imprécatoire chez les prophètes bibliques du 8e siècle A.C. à la lumière du Proche-Orient ancien." Unpublished Ph.D. thesis, Université de Montréal, Faculté des études supérieures, 1994. 515 pp. Available through UMI.

Argues that the eighth-century prophets utilized a judgment speech genre that was common in the ancient Near East. Although the form, vocabulary, and function of these passages find many links in comparative literature, two distinctions emerge. On the one hand, a pedagogical intent to motivate Israel to respond to Yahweh appears in addition to the usual conditional and unconditional frameworks of the curses. On the other hand, behind these judgment speeches lies a theology of the special covenant Yahweh had made with Israel at Sinai. Exegesis of Amos 4:4–12 (pp. 175–93), 2:6–16 (pp. 247–77), and 3:9–12 (pp. 278–93) in the section explaining spheres of existence affected by judgment.

Grätz, Sebastian. "Der strafende Wettergott: Erwägungen zur Traditionsgeschichte des Adad-Fluchs im Alten Orient und im Alten Testament." Ph.D. thesis, Christian-Albrechts-Universität (Kiel), 1997. Published as a monograph with same title. BBB 114. Bodenheim: Philo, 1998. 328 pp.

An investigation into the adoption of ancient Near Eastern notions of the weather god into the OT picture of Yahweh. Deals with Amos 4:4–13 (pp. 228–53), which he deems late, and connects it with the catalog of curses in Deut.

28 (and Lev. 26). The Deuteronomy passage is considered evidence for the survival of this early and ubiquitous weather god idea into the exilic and postexilic
eras.

Green, Timothy Mark. "Class Differentiation and Power(lessness) in Eighth-Century
BCE Israel and Judah." Unpublished Ph.D. thesis, Vanderbilt University, 1997. In
two volumes, ix + 663 pp. Available through UMI.
From a macrosociological perspective, Green utilizes political and economic
anthropology to explore the class differentiation and the complex realities of
sociopolitical and economic power within the agrarian states of Israel and Judah
in the eighth century B.C.E. Distinguishes between the central ruling sphere, secondary elites within the states' political-economic apparatus, and the ruled stratum. The prophetic indictments would have been aimed primarily at the second
group. Presents a detailed exegetical treatment of Amos 2:6–8; 4:1–3; 5:7, 10–11;
and 8:4–6 (pp. 403–63). A significant piece of research that surveys the field,
posits new insights, and suggests avenues for future study.

Hobbs, A. G. W. "The Communication of the Prophetic Message in Pre-Exilic Israel."
Unpublished Ph.D. thesis, University of Kent (Great Britain), 1990. 421 pp. Available through UMI.
Utilizes role theory and transactional analysis to analyze the prophets' reception
of the divine message, their communication of that message to their audience,
and the reception of that word by the audience. The theoretical discussion is
indebted particularly to D. L. Petersen and R. R. Wilson. This construct is
applied to Amos 7:10–17 in order to explain the confrontation between Amaziah
and Amos as one of role conflict and reversal (pp. 151–85).

Israel, Richard D. "Prophecies of Judgment: A Study of the Protasis-Apodosis Text
Structures in Hosea, Amos and Micah." Unpublished Ph.D. thesis, Claremont
Graduate University, 1989. 429 pp. Available through UMI.
Investigates the prophetic speech pattern of judgment, which has a protasis (the
condemned action) and an apodosis (the future consequence of that action). The
extensive survey and interaction with the history of research yields the conclusion that both elements are constitutive of the pattern and that it is difficult to
limit the possible origin of the pattern to one social setting. The exegesis of the
relevant prophetic texts demonstrates the adaptation of a wide diversity of genres in the pattern, which points away from an institutional setting to a consistent
prophetic perception of the correlation between act and consequence. This connection, whether due to a legal framework or the ontology of a certain dynamism
between the two, is ultimately grounded in the sovereignty of Yahweh R.

Jaramillo Rivas, Pedro. "La injusticia y la opresión en el lenguaje profético de los profetas." Ph.D. thesis, Pontifical Università Gregoriana (Rome), 1986. Published as a
monograph with the same title. Institución San Jerónimo 26. Navarra, Spain: Verbo
Divino, 1992. xvii + 328 pp.
Attempts to explore the meaning, significance, and impact of the metaphors used by
the prophets to describe and denounce injustice in ancient Israel. The introduction
discusses the nature of metaphor in general and in biblical studies (pp. 1–19). Separate chapters deal with Amos 3:9–11; 4:1–3; 5:7; 6:12; and 5:24 (pp. 181–233). Each
chapter is divided into three parts: situation-context, images, conclusions. The final

chapter classifies images into three broad categories: figurative language to describe oppressive actions, figurative language to describe the situation and fruit of oppression, and figurative language to evaluate the anti-neighbor actions (pp. 283–99).

Jones, Barry Alan. "The Formation of the Book of the Twelve: A Study in Text and Canon." Ph.D. thesis, Duke University, 1994. Published as a monograph with the same title. SBLDS 149. Atlanta: Scholars Press, 1995. xii + 266 pp.
  Utilizes textual evidence from the MT, the LXX, and 4QXII[a] to offer a hypothesis regarding the development of the collection of the Minor Prophets into its present shape. Jones believes that Amos 9:12 in the LXX reflects an earlier and different *Vorlage*, which was later changed by scribal editors of the MT to serve as a connecting link with Obadiah as they worked toward establishing the canonical order of the Book of the Twelve. Obadiah occupies a different location in the LXX and was subsequently moved to its present place (pp. 170–220).

Lowery, Jenny Manasco. "The Form and Function of Symbolic Vision Reports in the Hebrew Bible." Unpublished Ph.D. thesis, Southern Baptist Theological Seminary, 1999. x + 218 pp. Available through UMI.
  Sets an analysis of dream accounts and symbolic vision reports against the background of dream interpretation in the ancient Near East. Begins the study of symbolic visions (pp. 61–171) with a discussion of visions three and four of Amos (7:7–9; 8:1–3, pp. 64–79). These are classified with the material in Jeremiah (pp. 79–99, 164) and contrasted with the more dreamlike material in Daniel and Zechariah. The concluding chapter summarizes findings, and an appendix presents a number of ancient Near Eastern texts of dreams (pp. 183–200).

McLaughlin, John L. "The *Marzēaḥ* in the Prophetic Literature: An Examination of the References and Possible Allusions in Light of the Extra-Biblical Evidence." Ph.D. thesis, University of St. Michael's College (Toronto), 1998. Published as *The Marzēaḥ in the Prophetic Literature: References and Allusions in Light of the Extra-Biblical Evidence*. VTSup 86. Leiden: Brill, 2001. xviii + 264 pp.
  Based upon a "minimalist" approach to the extrabiblical data concerning the *marzēaḥ* feast, the author postulates three consistent features: "(1) drinking, (2) by members of the upper class, (3) in a religious context" (although religious, the feast was noncultic). These criteria are then applied to both the specific references to the feast in Amos 6:1–7 and Jer. 16:5–9 and to the possible allusions in ten other prophetic passages. Of the latter, only four are claimed to be clear: Amos 4:1; Hos. 4:16–19; Isa. 28:7–8(22); and Ezek. 39:17–20. A funerary setting for the religious element is evident only in a few cases. Offers detailed exegesis and study of Amos 6:1–7; 4:1; and 2:7c–8 against the background of the findings from the wider data (pp. 80–128).

Moulton, Brian Keith. "The Use of the Davidic Covenant in Acts 15." Unpublished Th.D. thesis, Dallas Theological Seminary, 1999. 290 pp. Available through UMI.
  An attempt from a classical dispensational framework to refute newer trends in "progressive dispensationalism." Argues that Amos 9 envisages the future reuniting of Israel and Judah and the establishment of a universal kingdom under a Davidic monarch. This original meaning is not changed in Acts 15, where the prophetic passage is used as an analogy to what the early Christian church was witnessing: Gentiles are included now in the salvific plans of God just as they will

be in the millennial kingdom. Acts 15:16–17 points to a chronological schema according to this theological stance. Little use of non-English sources.

Newell, James O. "The Means of Maintaining a Right Relationship with Yahweh: An Investigation of Selected Passages from the Hebrew Prophets of the Eighth Century B.C." Unpublished Th.D. thesis, New Orleans Baptist Theological Seminary, 1988. v + 186 pp. Available through UMI.

The thesis is divided into three chapters. After an opening chapter that investigates the eighth-century context, the remaining two survey, respectively, the unacceptable and the essential ways of establishing a proper relationship with Yahweh. Negative categories relevant to the book of Amos are: rejection of *tôrâ* (2:4–5), social injustice (2:6–8; 5:7, 10–12; 8:4–6), and vain worship (4:4–5; 5:21–23). The positive recommendations of Amos are found in 5:4–6, 14–15, 24. No use of non-English sources.

Nogalski, James. "Redactional Layers and Intentions: Uniting the Writings of the Book of the Twelve." Th.D. thesis, Universität Zurich, 1991. Published in two volumes: *Literary Precursors to the Book of the Twelve*, BZAW 217. ix + 301 pp.; *Redactional Processes to the Book of the Twelve*, BZAW 218. ix + 300 pp. Berlin: de Gruyter, 1993.

Nogalski's hypothesis concerns the intentional use of catchwords to connect prophetic books in order to explain the redactional history of the individual prophetic books and of the Book of the Twelve as a whole. Argues that Amos was part of an original Deuteronomistic corpus (Hosea, Amos, Micah, Zephaniah). Suggests a series of postexilic redactional developments in 9:11–15, which would have been designed to link Amos with both Joel and Obadiah at a later phase of the development of the Book of the Twelve (*Literary Precursors*, 74–122).

Olyan, Saul Mitchell. "Problems in the History of the Cult and Priesthood in Ancient Israel." Unpublished Ph.D. thesis, Harvard University, 1985. 225 pp. Available through UMI.

The first chapter ("Your Kinsman Lives, Beersheba," pp. 1–50) is an analysis of Amos 8:14. The general thesis is that Amos decries pilgrimage when religion is not accompanied by social justice. The more particular focus, however, is a defense of the emendation *dôd* ("kinsman") as an epithet for Yahweh. Includes an excursus on *paḥad yiṣḥāq*, which he (with Albright) believes is a divine epithet in Beersheba. A revised version of this chapter (without the excursus) appears as "The Oath in Amos 8:14," in *Priesthood and Cult in Ancient Israel*, ed. G. A. Anderson and S. M. Olyan, 121–49 (JSOTSup 125; Sheffield: Sheffield Academic Press, 1991).

Pleins, J. David. "Biblical Ethics and the Poor: The Language and Structures of Poverty in the Writings of the Hebrew Prophets." Unpublished Ph.D. thesis, University of Michigan, 1986. 336 pp. Available through UMI.

Surveys various approaches to the social criticism of the prophets and investigates the terminology for poverty in the prophetic literature. This research is the foundation for the exegesis of the relevant texts in order to probe the theological basis of the prophetic critique. Pleins compares these findings with the legal and wisdom traditions. Proposes that the prophets underscored the contrasts between the urban and peasant communities, defended the cause of the poor before the monarchy and the ruling elite, and envisioned that the basic issue was a conflict of value systems. Two helpful appendices catalog the lexical data.

Rossier, François. "L'intercession entre les hommes dans la Bible hébraïque. L'intercession entre les hommes aux origines de l'intercession auprès de Dieu." Ph.D. thesis, Universität Friburg (Germany), 1995. Published as a monograph with the same title. OBO 152. Friburg: Editions Universitaires; Göttingen: Vandenhoeck & Ruprecht, 1996.

Argues that intercession with the Deity finds its origins in intercession between humans and that it is a verbal act on behalf of another before a superior person (thereby eliminating from consideration other nonverbal actions as intercession). The detailed analysis of Amos 7:1–6 (pp. 305–38) probes a number of theological and ethical issues concerning the fate of the people, the character of Yahweh, and the relationship between the intercession of the prophet in the first two visions and his subsequent ceasing of that effort in the following visions.

Saíd, Dalton H. "A Study on the Cry and Hope of the Poor in the Old Testament." Unpublished Ph.D. thesis, University of Edinburgh, 1987. 421 pp. Available through UMI.

A theological and exegetical study whose aim is to demonstrate God's commitment to the poor and the oppressed. The writer works from the concerns generated by the harsh social realities of Latin America. Chapter 6 deals with the eighth-century prophets, of which the major part is dedicated to passages in the book of Amos (pp. 315–25). Provides a summary exegesis of 2:6–8; 3:9–11; 5:7, 10–12, 21–24; 6:1–7; 8:4–6. In the prophetic literature hope for the marginalized can be based on the prophetic denunciation of injustice and the expectation of a different future. These texts continue to engender hope when read today.

Sánchez, Edesio. "God and Gods: Issues in Biblical Theology from a Latin American Perspective." Unpublished Ph.D. thesis, Union Theological Seminary, Virginia, 1987. 212 pp. Available through UMI.

Written from a declared confessional (Presbyterian) and contextual (Latin America) point of view. The argument follows three tracks in selected OT books: the inseparability of faithfulness and social justice; their relationship with the exodus; and the role of the covenant. The contribution of Amos to each point appears on pp. 11–19, 90–95, and 126–29, respectively. The proper understanding of each theme defines the uniqueness of Israel's God and the kind of faith he demands. In the last chapter the author interacts with authors from the North Atlantic (W. H. Schmidt, McBride, Sicre) and Latin America (Croatto, Miranda) on their consideration of these themes (pp. 162–95).

Sparks, Kenton L. "Ethnicity and Identity in Ancient Israel: Prolegomena to the Study of Ethnic Sentiments and Their Expression in the Hebrew Bible." Ph.D. thesis, University of North Carolina (Chapel Hill), 1996. Revised version published as a monograph with the same title. Winona Lake, Ind.: Eisenbrauns, 1998.

An investigation of the conceptions of ethnicity in ancient Israel. The discussion of Amos is based on the Oracles against the Nations, 6:1–7, 7:10–17, and 9:7–10 (pp. 168–94). The author argues that the prophet includes the notions of migration and kinship under the universal sovereignty of Yahweh as the defining characteristics of ethnicity of both Israel and its neighbors. As for Israel itself, identity is linked more to socioeconomic concerns and religious belief than to ethnicity and is also connected to Judah. The exposition of the material in Amos is part of a broader presentation of a reconstruction of the development of sentiments about ethnicity in the Hebrew Bible.

Witaszek, Gabriel. "I profeti Amos e Micha nella lotta per lagiustizia sociale nell'VIII secola a.C." Ph.D. thesis, Gregorian Pontifical University (Rome), 1986. Published in an abbreviated form as *Prorocy Amos i Micheasz wobec niesprawiedliwosci spolecznej*. Tuchow, Poland: Mala Poligrafia Redemptorystow, 1992.
[The work is divided into three parts. The first investigates the sociopolitical and religious social context of the prophet. The second looks at the basis and essence of the prophetic message in Amos and Micah. Basic to Amos's message are the themes of election, covenant, and wisdom. Part three compares and contrasts the messages of these two prophets. Closes with an attempt to probe the relevance of the prophets' words for today.]

Woo, Taek Joo. "The *Marzēaḥ* Institution and Rites for the Dead: A Comparative and Systemic Study with Special Attention to the Eighth-Century Prophets." Unpublished Ph.D. thesis, Graduate Theological Union, 1998. xii + 310 pp. Available through UMI.
The goal of the author is to try to coordinate the scholarly discussion of the possible cultic dimensions of the *marzēaḥ* feast with the sociopolitical and economic realities of eighth-century Israel and Judah. Compares the biblical data with the Mesopotamian *kispu(m)* ritual, West African mortuary customs, cults of the dead in modern rural Palestine, and Korean ancestor worship and then situates the institution within a social science approach to ancient Israel. Argues that the *marzēaḥ* feasts often, though not always, were the locus for rites for venerating ancestors of the ruling elites and also had implications for continuity of inheritance and status. Amos 6:1–7 is considered to be a prophetic diatribe against a *marzēaḥ* that ironically prefigures the death of the elite, who exploit the poor in their desire to perpetuate their position and power (pp. 174–95).

A LISTING OF D.MIN. DISSERTATIONS

Coppick, Glendon C. "Justice: The Redistribution of Wealth and Power in Amos, Rawls, and City Hall." San Francisco Theological Seminary, 1986.

Doorly, William John. "Preaching from the Book of Amos to Address Problems of Economic Justice." Lancaster Theological Seminary, 1987.

Heininger, Edward Cline. "Evangelism, Reluctance and Faith Development." School of Theology at Claremont, 1985.

Montgomery, Jimmy Jonathan. "Analyzing a Local Church Ministry in Terms of Justice as Reflected in the Book of Amos for the Enhancement of Mission and Liberation Using Systems Theory." Emory University, 1987.

Morris, Stanley L. "Using Computers to Teach the Bible in Local Congregations." Hartford Seminary, 1994.

Powers, Leo. "The Use of Feedback and Small Discussion Groups in Improving the Effectiveness of Preaching the Book of Amos." Harding Graduate School of Religion, 1994.

Taylor, Joel Damon. "Biblical Preaching that Establishes the Norm for Social Activism (St. Paul Missionary Baptist Church, Chicago, Illinois)." United Theological Seminary (Canton, Ohio), 1998.

Tsai, Rei-Yi. "Equipping the Chinese Lay People to Use the Historical Method in Interpreting the Book of Amos." Southwestern Baptist Theological Seminary, 1986.

Notes

Chapter 1: A History of Amos Research

1. James L. Mays, "Words about the Words of Amos: Recent Study of the Book of Amos," *Int* 13, no. 3 (1959): 259–72. This quotation is from p. 259.
2. David L. Petersen, "The Book of the Twelve/The Minor Prophets," in *The Hebrew Bible Today: An Introduction to Critical Issues*, ed. S. L. McKenzie and M. P. Graham, (Louisville: Westminster John Knox, 1998), 107.
3. Ludwig Köhler, "Amos-Forschungen von 1917 bis 1932," *TRu* 4, no. 4 (1932): 195–213; J. Philip Hyatt, "The Book of Amos," *Int* 3, no. 3 (1949): 338–48; Mays, "Words about the Words of Amos"; Page H. Kelley, "Contemporary Study of Amos and Prophetism," *RevExp* 63, no. 4 (1966): 375–85; J. J. M. Roberts, "Recent Trends in the Study of Amos," *ResQ* 13, no. 1 (1970) 1–16; John F. Craghan, "The Prophet Amos in Recent Literature," *BTB* 2, no. 3 (1972): 242–61; L. Monloubou, "Amos," *DBSup* 8 (1972), 706–24.
4. Adri van der Wal, *Amos: A Classified Bibliography* (3d ed.; Applicatio 3; Amsterdam: Free University Press, 1986).
5. Robert Martin-Achard, *Amos: L'homme, le message, l'influence* (Publications de la Faculté de Théologie de l'Université de Genève 7; Geneva: Labor et Fides, 1984); A. G. Auld, *Amos* (OTG; Sheffield: JSOT Press, 1986). To these can be added the bibliographies that appear in some of the commentaries—e.g., Hans Walter Wolff, *Joel and Amos*, trans. W. Janzen, S. D. McBride Jr., and C. A. Muenchow (Hermeneia; Philadelphia: Fortress, 1977), 358–71; John H. Hayes, *Amos, the Eighth-Century Prophet: His Times & His Preaching* (Nashville: Abingdon, 1988), 28–39. For well-documented and judicious surveys of scholarly research on the prophets in general during the period covered in this essay, see Otto Eissfeldt, "The Prophetic Literature," in *The Old Testament and Modern Study: A Generation of Discovery and Research*, ed. H. H. Rowley (Oxford: Clarendon, 1951), 115–61; H. H. Rowley, "The Nature of Old Testament Prophecy in the Light of Recent Study," in idem, *The Servant of the Lord and Other Essays on the Old Testament* (London: Lutterworth, 1952), 91–129; idem, "Ritual and the Hebrew Prophets," *JSS* 1, no. 4 (1956): 338–60; Georg Fohrer, "Remarks on Modern Interpretation of the Prophets," *JBL* 80, no. 3 (1961): 307–19; Ronald E. Clements, *One Hundred Years of Old Testament Interpretation* (Philadelphia: Westminster, 1976), 51–75.
6. Wellhausen was not the first scholar to present the idea of the prophets predating the law and the concept of their ethical idealism, but all recognize that it was his *articulation* of these views (with the subsequent translation into English and dissemination by other scholars) that led to the widespread acceptance of this

perspective. Note especially John W. Rogerson, *Old Testament Criticism in the Nineteenth Century: England and Germany* (London: SPCK, 1984; Philadelphia: Fortress, 1985), 28–78, 257–89; idem, *The Bible and Criticism in Victorian England: Profiles of F. D. Maurice and William Robertson Smith* (JSOTSup 201; Sheffield: Sheffield Academic Press, 1995), 94–103; cf. Walther Zimmerli, *The Law and the Prophets: A Study of the Meaning of the Old Testament*, trans. R. E. Clements (New York: Harper & Row, 1965), 17–30.

7. For Wellhausen, this degeneration would eventually lead to the Judaism of Jesus' day. For a discussion of a possible nascent anti-Semitism in Wellhausen, see Lou H. Silberman, "Wellhausen and Judaism," *Semeia* 25 (1982): 75–82; John Barton, "Wellhausen's *Prolegomena to the History of Israel*: Influences and Effects," in *Text & Experience: Towards a Cultural Exegesis of the Bible*, ed. D. L. Smith-Christopher (Biblical Seminar 35, Sheffield: Sheffield Academic Press 1995), 316–29; cf. Julius Wellhausen, *Prolegomena to the History of Ancient Israel* (reprint, Atlanta: Scholars Press, 1994), xv, n. 23.

8. Cf. Wellhausen, *Prolegomena*, 417–25.

9. Ibid., 472.

10. Ibid., 470.

11. Julius Wellhausen, *Die kleinen Propheten übersetzt und erklärt* (1898 ed.; reprint, Berlin: de Gruyter, 1963), 78–79. Emphasis added.

12. "Die alte Antithese: kein Cultus, sondern Justiz!" (ibid., 83).

13. "Rosen und Lavendel statt Blut und Eisen" (ibid., 96 [on Amos 9:13–15]).

14. For example, George Adam Smith, "Amos," in *The Book of the Twelve Prophets*, vol. 1: *Amos, Hosea, Micah* (rev. ed.; London: Hodder and Stoughton; New York: Harper & Brothers, 1928), 94–103, 157–87; Theodore H. Robinson, *Prophecy and the Prophets in Ancient Israel* (2d ed.; London: Duckworth, 1953), 60–71; Charles Francis Whitley, *The Prophetic Achievement* (London: Mowbray, 1963), 52–54, 73–77.

15. E.g., Karl Marti, *Das Dodekapropheten eklärt* (KAT 13. Tübingen: Mohr [Siebeck], 1904), 180, 194; Artur Weiser, *Die Prophetie des Amos* (BZAW 53; Giessen: Töpelmann, 1929), 318–19.

16. Though agreeing with the notion of a marked dissonance between the cult and the ethical demands of God, not all would necessarily agree with Wellhausen's particular reconstruction of the history of Israel or his stated reasons for Amos's rejection of the cult.

17. E.g., Rolland Wolfe, *Meet Amos and Hosea: the Prophets of Israel* (New York: Harper & Brothers, 1945), 62–69; Robert H. Pfeiffer, *Introduction to the Old Testament* (New York: Harper & Brothers, 1951), 580–82; Richard S. Cripps, *A Commentary on the Book of Amos* (2d ed.; Limited Classical Reprint Library; Minneapolis: Klock & Klock, 1981), xxviii–xxxiii, 338–40.

18. Cf. William Rainey Harper, *A Critical and Exegetical Commentary on Amos and Hosea* (ICC 18; Edinburgh: T. & T. Clark, 1905), cxxi–cxxiv.

19. G. Hölscher, *Die Propheten: Untersuchungen zur Religionsgeschichte Israels* (Leipzig: Hinrich, 1914).

20. Note, e.g., Georg H. A. von Ewald, *Commentary on the Prophets of the Old Testament*, trans. J. F. Smith (5 vols.; London: Williams and Norgate, 1875–81), 1:15–17, 38–42; A. B. Davidson, *Old Testament Prophecy* (Edinburgh: T. & T. Clark, 1903), 115–43; Hermann Gunkel, "The Israelite Prophecy from the Time of Amos," in *Twentieth Century Theology in the Making*, vol. 1: *Themes of Biblical Theology*, ed. J. Pelikan, trans. R. A. Wilson (New York: Harper & Row,

1969), 48–55 (= "Propheten IIB. Propheten Israels seit Amos," in *Die Religion in Geschichte und Gegenwart* [2d ed.; Tübingen: Mohr (Siebeck), 1930], 1538–54).

21. Items that came under consideration included the prophetic call, visions, the reception of oracles, the circle of disciples, and especially those passages which describe apparently abnormal behavior (note the references in the following paragraph).

22. Note, e.g., Abraham J. Heschel, *The Prophets* (New York: Harper & Row, 1962), 324–426; Whitley, *Prophetic Achievement*, 1–23; Ivar P. Seierstad, *Die Offen-barungserlebnisse der Propheten Amos, Jesaja und Jeremia: Eine Untersuchung der Erlebnisvorgänge unter besonderer Berücksichtung ihrer religiös-sittlichen Art und Auswirkung* (Oslo: Universitetsforlaget, 1964); cf. Walther Eichrodt, *Theology of the Old Testament*, trans. J. A. Baker (2 vols.; OTL; Philadelphia: Westmin-ster, 1961–1965), 1:309–44.

23. J. Lindblom, *Prophecy in Ancient Israel* (Philadelphia: Fortress, 1962).

24. For example, Harold Knight, *The Hebrew Prophetic Consciousness* (London: Lut-terworth, 1947), 33–105; Robinson, *Prophecy and Prophets in Ancient Israel*, 39–49.

25. Robinson, *Prophecy and Prophets in Ancient Israel*, 42. Note the similar descrip-tion in Knight, *Hebrew Prophetic Consciousness*, 55–57.

26. Lindblom, *Prophecy in Ancient Israel*, 107.

27. Cripps, *Amos*, 18–19.

28. Ibid., 18–19, n. 4. This is Cripps's translation from Hölscher, *Propheten*, 197. For Hölscher's treatment of Amos, see Hölscher, *Propheten*, 189–204. For Cripps's fuller discussion of ecstasy, see *Amos*, 18–22, 87–97.

29. Gunkel, "Israelite Prophecy," 61.

30. Ibid., 66.

31. Robinson, *Prophecy and Prophets*, 52.

32. Gunkel, "Israelite Prophecy," 61–75; Robinson, *Prophecy and Prophets*, 50–59. Gunkel does believe that Amos may have written some of his words down after his expulsion form Bethel (7:10–17), although the original delivery was none-theless strictly oral.

33. Harper, *Amos and Hosea*, viii.

34. Ibid., cxxx–cxl, clxiv–clxix.

35. Wolfe, *Meet Hosea and Amos*, xx–xxi.

36. Hölscher, *Propheten*, 143.

37. Sigmund Mowinckel, *Psalmenstudien* (1921–1924). For his developed views, see idem, *The Psalms in Israel's Worship*, trans. D. R. Ap-Thomas (2 vols. in 1; Nashville: Abingdon, 1962).

38. Mowinckel held that with the "reforming prophets" of the eighth century the concept of Yahweh's call and empowerment had changed (here he is concerned with the debate over ecstasy). Amos, he believes, for this reason disavows any connection with the *nĕbî'îm* (7:14–15), even though the prophet sensed some sort of continuity with the earlier *nĕbî'îm* (2:11) ("The Spirit and the Word in the Preexilic Prophets," *JBL*, 52, no. 3 [1934] 199–227). It also is interesting to observe Mowinckel's pastoral concern for the modern church vis-à-vis the topic of ecstasy ("A Postscript to the Paper 'The Spirit and the Word in the Preex-ilic Prophets,' in *JBL*, LII, 199ff.," *JBL* 56, no. 3 [1937]: 261–65).

39. Mowinckel, *Psalms in Israel's Worship*, 1:106–92; 2:53–73. The so-called Uppsala or Scandinavian School with which the name of Mowinckel is associated had much in common with the British Myth and Ritual School in terms of certain

convictions on issues like the annual New Year Festival of the enthronement of Yahweh, the role of the king in this rite, and the existence of cult prophets. A discussion of sacral kingship and related issues within these "schools" lies beyond the purview of this essay, but at the very least one must recognize that a more comprehensive understanding of the scholarly view of prophetism at that time would need to consider this larger scholarly theological and historical framework. In terms of the scholars cited in the discussion here, this observation is relevant for Mowinckel, Engnell, Haldar, and Johnson.

40. Mowinckel, *Psalms in Israel's Worship*, 1:154.
41. Alfred Haldar, *Associations of Cult Prophets among the Ancient Semites*, trans. H. S. Harvey (Uppsala: Almquist & Wiksell, 1945).
42. Note, e.g., that the juxtaposition of priest and prophet in Jer. 5:30–31; 6:13; 23:11; 26:7, 16 (observe the temple setting); 35:4.
43. Aubrey R. Johnson, *The Cultic Prophet in Ancient Israel* (2d ed.; Cardiff: University of Wales Press, 1962). In some areas Johnson followed and built upon the work of Mowinckel. Examples of this connection would include the notion that the cult prophets, after their loss of prestige with the fall of Jerusalem, eventually developed into the singers of the Second Temple. He also pursued in more detail the issue of the relationship between the prophets and the Psalms in idem, *The Cultic Prophet and Israel's Psalmody* (Cardiff: University of Wales Press, 1979).
44. Haldar, *Associations*, 112. As support for his comment on *nōqēd* Haldar refers to Engnell (112 n. 4; cf. Ivan Engnell, *Studies in Divine Kingship in the Ancient Near East* [Oxford: Basil Blackwell, 1967], 87). In light of our wider discussion, it is worth mentioning that Haldar's allusion to Amos is found in the section on the *nĕbî'îm*, in which he stresses the ecstatic nature of the office (*Associations*, 108–26). He also cites Amos 2:12 and 3:7–8 to say that the prophet saw himself as one in the line of these ecstatics (p. 120).
45. Johnson, *Cultic Prophet*, 57. He also mentions Amos 7:12, 14 in the context of a discussion on terminology distinctions between *r'h* and *ḥzh* and their importance for reconstructing the history of prophetism (*Cultic Prophet*, 9–29, especially pp. 11, 14, 17).
46. Milos Bič, "Der Prophet Amos—ein Haepatoskopos," *VT* 1, no. 4 (1951): 293–96.
47. A. S. Kapelrud, *Central Ideas in Amos* (Oslo: Aschehoug [Nygaard], 1956), 5–6, 68–78; cf. idem, "Cult and Prophetic Words." *ST* 4, no. 1 (1951): 5–12; idem, "New Ideas in Amos," in *Volume du Congrès, Genève 1965*, ed. G. W. Anderson et al. (VTSup 15; Leiden: Brill, 1966), 193–206.
48. Lindblom, *Prophecy in Ancient Israel*, 182–84, 209.
49. John D. W. Watts, *Vision and Prophecy in Amos: 1955 Faculty Lectures, Baptist Theological Seminary, Rüschlikon-Zürich, Switzerland* (Leiden: Brill; Grand Rapids: Eerdmans, 1958), 1–22, 74–76.
50. Besides the commentaries, note J. Wright, "Did Amos Inspect Livers?" *AusBR* 23, no. 1 (1975): 3–11; Peter C. Craigie, "Amos the *nōqēd* in the Light of Ugaritic," *SR* 11, no. 1 (1982): 29–33.
51. Allan Rosengren Petersen, *The Royal God: Enthronement Festivals in Ancient Israel and Ugarit?* (JSOTSup 259; Copenhagen International Seminar 5. Sheffield: Sheffield Academic Press, 1998).
52. Both form and tradition criticism trace their roots back to Gunkel. For good introductions to form-critical work in the prophets, see John H. Hayes, "The

History of the Form-Critical Study of Prophecy," in *SBLSP* 1973, vol. 1: 60–99 (Cambridge, Mass.: Society of Biblical Literature, 1973); W. Eugene Marsh, "Prophecy," in *Old Testament Form Criticism*, ed. John H. Hayes (San Antonio: Trinity University Press, 1974), 141–77; and Claus Westermann, *Basic Forms of Prophetic Speech*, trans. H. C. White (reprint, Cambridge: Lutterworth; Louisville: Westminster John Knox, 1991). Gene M. Tucker's *Form Criticism of the Old Testament* (Guides to Biblical Scholarship; Philadelphia: Fortress, 1971) actually uses the book of Amos (1:1–2; 3:1–2) to illustrate the basic principles of that discipline (pp. 71–74). For tradition criticism see Douglas A. Knight, *Rediscovering the Traditions of Israel: The Development of the Traditio-Historical Research of the Old Testament, with Special Consideration of Scandinavian Contributions* (rev. ed.; SBLDS 9; Missoula, Mont.: Scholars Press, 1975); and Ronald E. Clements, *Prophecy and Tradition* (Growing Points in Theology; Atlanta: John Knox, 1975). It bears mentioning that form and tradition critics have different evaluations of the value of source-criticism. Note, e.g., Mowinckel's account of the rise of these disciplines as due to the perceived limitations of source-critical theory and practice (*Prophecy and Tradition: The Prophetic Books in the Light of the Study of the Growth and History of the Tradition* [Oslo: Dybwad, 1946] 5–36).

53. There was much debate, however, concerning the relationship between the oral and written stages—i.e., at what point the traditions might have been written down and the reliability of oral transmission. See, e.g., the survey and point of view of Mowinckel (*Prophecy and Tradition*, 15–19, 60–66) and the discussion in Knight, *Rediscovering the Traditions of Israel*, 385–92, passim.

54. Different scholars would trace the covenant idea back to various starting points, such as the person of Abraham, an early amphictyonic league, or the figure of Moses. The concept of an amphictyony, or tribal confederation, of premonarchic Israel bound together by covenant was forcefully argued by Noth. For an explanation of the rise of scholarly support for the covenant idea, see Ernest W. Nicholson, *God and His People: Covenant and Theology in the Old Testament* (Oxford: Clarendon, 1986), 3–82.

55. See, e.g., for the prophets, Eichrodt, *Theology of the Old Testament*, 51–52, 338–91. For Amos, note especially Karl Cramer, *Amos. Versuch einer theologischen Interpretation* (BWANT 51; Stuttgart: Kohlhammer, 1930); and André Neher, *Amos: Contribution à l'étude du prophétisme* (Paris: Vrin, 1950). Cf. Gerhard von Rad's tradition-critical discussion of Amos, which appears in his *Old Testament Theology*, trans. D. M. G. Stalker (2 vols.; New York: Harper & Row, 1962–1965), 2:129–38.

56. For a survey, see Westermann, *Basic Forms of Prophetic Speech*, 13–89.

57. Emil Balla, *Die Droh- und Scheltworte des Amos* (Leipzig: Edelmann, 1926). Cf. Ludwig Markert, *Struktur und Bezeichnung des Scheltsworts: Eine gattungskritische Studie anhand des Amosbuches* (BZAW 140; Berlin: de Gruyter, 1977), 5–45.

58. Ernst Würthwein, "Amos-Studien," *ZAW* 62, nos. 1–2 (1949–1950): 10–52; cf. idem, "Der Ursprung der prophetischen Gerichtsrede," *ZTK* 49 (1952): 1–16. Note the summaries and evaluations in Westermann, *Basic Forms of Prophetic Speech*, 70–80; Roberts, "Recent Trends."

59. The significance of the verbless clauses of Amos's response in 7:14 continues to be the subject of scholarly debate. Würthwein interacts with the exegesis of Rowley, who had put the interpretation of the meaning as in the past tense on firmer ground (H. H. Rowley, "Was Amos a Nabi?" in *Festschrift für Otto Eissfeldt zum*

60. Geburtstag, ed. J. Fück; [Halle: Niemeyer, 1947], 191–98). At least two items
in this verse require attention: Is Amos saying that he had not previously been a
professional prophet but now was, or that he was not presently a professional
prophet and was just fulfilling a call to prophesy? Is there any distinction to be
made between "to prophesy," "prophet," and "son of a prophet"? These questions obviously have implications for Würthwein's argument, and he does address
them. My goal here, however, is to provide just the main contours of his position.

60. Note also Würthwein, "Amos 5:21–27," *TLZ* 72, no. 3 (1947): 143–52; idem,
"Kultpolemik oder Kultbeschied? Beobachtungen zu dem Thema 'Prophetie
und Kult,'" in *Tradition und Situation: Studien zur alttestamentlichen Prophetie*
(Festschrift A. Weiser), ed. O. Kaiser and E. Würthwein (Göttingen: Vandenhoeck & Ruprecht, 1963), 115–31.

61. At the time scholars were discussing whether the norms to which the prophets
appealed should be limited to the apodictic laws or should include as well the
casuistic laws. Cf. R. Bach, "Gottesrecht und weltliches Recht in der Verkündigung des Propheten Amos," in *Festschrift für Günther Dehn*, ed. W. Schneemelcher (Neukirchen-Vluyn: Neukirchener Verlag, 1957), 23–34.

62. H. Graf Reventlow, *Das Amt des Propheten bei Amos* (FRLANT 80; Göttingen:
Vandenhoeck & Ruprecht, 1962); cf. A. H. J. Gunneweg, "Erwägungen zu
Amos 7:14," *ZTK* 57, no. 1 (1960): 1–16; Rudolf Smend, "Das Nein des Amos,"
EvT 23, no. 8 (1963): 404–23. These other scholars, of course, would not agree
with all of Reventlow's argumentation. For example, Smend says that the message of the prophet contained absolutely no words of hope; any such lines represented a later addition.

63. Here Reventlow follows Bentzen. The latter proposed that Amos 1 and 2 were
patterned after the Egyptian execration texts and that the prophet's message was
part of a purgatory rite performed at the annual ascension ceremony of the New
Year Festival (A. Bentzen, "The Ritual Background of Amos i 2–ii 16," *OTS* 8,
ed. P. A. H. Boer [Leiden: Brill, 1950], 85–99; cf. Kapelrud, *Central Ideas in
Amos*, 19–20).

64. Walter Brueggemann, "Amos iv 4–13 and Israel's Covenant Worship," *VT* 15,
no. 1 (1965): 1–15.

65. J. L. Crenshaw, "'A Liturgy of Wasted Opportunity' (Am. 4:6–12; Isa. 9:7–10:4,
5:25–29)." *Semitics* 1 (1970): 27–37. At the time, there were also scholars who
avoided the issues of form and setting and limited their support for a covenantal theology in Amos on the basis of the book's vocabulary and theological ideas
(e.g., Paul E. Dion, "Le message moral du prophète Amos s'inspirait-il du 'droit
de l'alliance'?" *ScEs* 27, no. 1 [1975]: 5–34).

66. F. Charles Fensham, "Curses of Protection in Hittite Vassal-Treaties and the
Old Testament," *VT* 13, no. 2 (1963): 133–43; idem, "Common Trends in
Curses of the Near-Eastern Treaties and *Kudurru*-Inscriptions Compared with
Maledictions of Amos and Isaiah." *ZAW* 75, no. 2 (1963): 155–75; Delbert R.
Hillers, *Treaty-Curses and the Old Testament Prophets* (BibOr 16; Rome: Pontifical Bible Institute, 1964); Julien Harvey, "Le 'Rîb-Pattern,' réquisitoire prophétique sur la rupture de l'alliance," *RB* 43, no. 2 (1962): 172–96; idem, *Le
plaidoyer prophétique contre Israël après la rupture de l'alliance: Étude d'une formule
littéraire de l'Ancien Testament* (Studia: Travaux de recherche, 22; Paris: Desclée
de Brouwer; Montreal: Bellarmin, 1967). Within scholarly debate it is important to distinguish the background of the treaty form as such from the possible
Sitz im Leben of its utilization within Israel. Sometimes this distinction is not

clearly articulated. One could hold, e.g., that the form came from international law, while at the same time suggesting that in Israel it would have been used in a cult ceremony expressing the covenant relationship between Yahweh and the nation. Scholars have differed on both dimensions of the discussion.

67. Hillers, *Treaty-Curses*, 29, 58, 71, 76; James Luther Mays, *Amos* (OTL; Philadelphia: Westminster, 1969), 7–8, 79–81; Marjorie O'Rourke Boyle, "The Covenant Lawsuit of the Prophet Amos: III 1–IV 13." *VT* 21, no. 3 (1971): 338–62; Frank H. Seilhamer, "The Role of the Covenant in the Mission and Message of Amos," in *A Light unto My Path* (Festschrift J. M. Myers), ed. H. M. Bream, R. D. Heim, and C. A. Moore (Philadelphia: Temple University Press, 1974), 435–51. Cf. Ronald E. Clements, *Prophecy and Covenant* (SBT 1/43; Naperville, Ill.: Allenson, 1965); John Bright, *Covenant and Promise: The Prophetic Understanding of the Future in Pre-Exilic Israel* (Philadelphia: Westminster, 1976).

68. Note, e.g., Werner H. Schmidt, "Die deuteronomische Redaktion des Amos-buches: Zu den theologischen Unterschieden zwischen dem Prophetenwort und seinem Sammler," *ZAW* 77, no. 2 (1965): 168–93; Ulrich Kellermann, "Der Amosschluss als Stimme deuteronomischer Heilshoffnung," *EvT* 29 (1969): 169–83.

69. Georges Farr, "The Language of Amos, Popular or Cultic?" *VT* 16, no. 3 (1966): 312–24. This quotation is from p. 324.

70. Dennis J. McCarthy, *Old Testament Covenant: A Survey of Current Opinions* (Atlanta: John Knox, 1972); Clements, *Prophecy and Tradition*; Nicholson, *God and His People*.

71. Note especially Douglas Stuart, *Hosea–Jonah* (WBC 31; Waco: Word, 1987), xxxi–xlii; Jeffrey Niehaus, "Amos," in *The Minor Prophets: An Expositional and Expository Commentary*, ed. T. E. McComiskey (3 vols.; Grand Rapids: Baker, 1992–1998), 1:315–27.

72. E.g., George Snyder, "The Law and Covenant in Amos," *ResQ* 25, no. 3 (1982): 158–66; Francis I. Andersen and David Noel Freedman, *Amos: A New Translation with Introduction and Commentary* (AB 24A; New York: Doubleday, 1989).

73. In actuality there was more than one alternative to the position of a cultic provenance of the judgment speeches. Westermann, for instance, traces the prophetic address back to what he calls the "messenger speech" and holds the more natural setting of the prophetic accusations to be not in the cult but instead in the legal environment of a juridical procedure (Westermann, *Basic Forms of Prophetic Speech*, 90–189). Nevertheless, I limit this discussion to the two principal alternatives in Amos research: the cult and wisdom circles.

74. Within Amos studies note, e.g., Harper's view of how the prophet might have had an impact on wisdom thought, as—like many of that day—he believed wisdom to be a relatively late phenomenon (Harper, *Amos and Hosea*, cxxxvii).

75. Some scholars posited a heated conflict between the classical prophets and the professional wise men and counselors of the king (cf. Johannes Fichtner, "Isaiah among the Wise" (trans. B. W. Kovacs), in *Studies in Ancient Israelite Wisdom*, ed. J. L. Crenshaw [Library of Biblical Studies; New York: Ktav, 1949), 429–38; William McKane, *Prophets and Wise Men* [SBT 1/44; London: SCM, 1965]). Fichtner denied any wisdom influence on Amos but did hold that Isaiah had come from the "guild of the wise in Jerusalem."

76. S. Terrien, "Amos and Wisdom," in *Israel's Prophetic Heritage* (Festschrift J. Muilenburg), ed. B. W. Anderson and W. Harrelson (New York: Harper, 1962), 108–15; cf. Lindblom, *Prophecy in Ancient Israel*, 201–3.

77. Hans Walter Wolff, *Amos the Prophet: The Man and His Background*, trans. F. R. McCurley (Philadelphia: Fortress, 1973); idem, *Joel and Amos*, passim. Wolff did disagree with Terrien, however, on the latter's citation of *sôd* in 3:7, as he considered the verse to be a secondary addition.

78. The appeal to the woe cries and the notion of clan wisdom are based on Erhard Gerstenberger, "The Woe-Oracles of the Prophets," *JBL* 81, no. 2 (1962): 249–63. The distinction between court and clan wisdom is expressed in Wolff's discussion of Isaiah's dependence on Amos (*Amos the Prophet*, 80–85).

79. J. L. Crenshaw, "The Influence of the Wise upon Amos: The 'Doxologies of Amos' and Job 5:9–16; 9:5–10," *ZAW* 79, no. 1 (1967): 45–52; idem, "Amos and the Theophanic Tradition," *ZAW* 80, no. 2 (1968): 203–15; Hans Heinrich Schmid, "Amos: Zur Frage nach der 'geistigen Heimat' des Propheten," *WuD* 10 (1969): 85–103; Hans-Joachim Stoebe, "Überlegungen zu den geistlichen Voraussetzungen der Prophetie des Amos," in *Wort–Gebot–Glaube* (Festschrift W. Eichrodt), ed. H.-J. Stoebe et al. (ATANT 59; Zurich: Zwingli, 1970), 209–15; R. N. Whybray, *The Intellectual Tradition in the Old Testament* (BZAW 135; Berlin: de Gruyter, 1974), 140–42; idem, "Prophecy and Wisdom," in *Israel's Prophetic Tradition* (Festschrift P. R. Ackroyd), ed. R. Coggins, A. Phillips, and M. Knibb (Cambridge: Cambridge University Press, 1982), 181–99; J. Alberto Soggin, "Amos and Wisdom," in *Wisdom in Ancient Israel* (Festschrift J. A. Emerton), ed. J. Day et al. (Cambridge: Cambridge University Press, 1995), 119–23.

80. See, e.g., Martin-Achard, *Amos*, 82, 95–97; José Luis Sicre, *'Con los pobre de la tierra.' La justicia social en los profetas de Israel* (Madrid: Cristiandad, 1984), 165–66.

81. The historical approaches highlighted later in this section deal with recent archaeological finds. Studies not discussed include those arguing for new perspectives on the historical setting for the prophet. For instance, John H. Hayes places Amos's ministry about 750 B.C.E. within the turmoil caused by Pekah (*Amos, the Eighth-Century Prophet*, 38–39, 45–47); Stanley N. Rosenbaum believes Amos was not from Judah, but rather a mid-ranking official in Israel (*Amos of Israel: A New Interpretation* [Macon, Ga.: Mercer University Press, 1990]). Interestingly, during a time when interest in a variety of sociohistorical reconstructions has been (and continues to be) high, some believe that such efforts might be misdirected. Robert P. Carroll calls the descriptions of Israel's society in prophetic texts ideological and "imaginative creations of their writers." One should be more suspicious, he says, of their value for reconstructing with confidence actual historical settings and events ("Prophecy and Society," in *The World of Ancient Israel: Sociological, Anthropological and Political Perspectives*, ed. R. E. Clements [Cambridge: Cambridge University Press, 1989], 203–25). A. G. Auld argues that much of the terminology for these spokespersons of God is postexilic and a reading back of later views into their lives; therefore, it is harder than most realize to get back to what these individuals actually might have thought of themselves and their task ("Prophets through the Looking Glass: Between Writings and Moses," *JSOT* 27 [1983]: 3–23; for an application to Amos, see idem, *Amos*, 16–40).

82. Wolff, *Joel and Amos*, 91–100, passim.

83. Ibid., 106–13; W. H. Schmidt, "Die deuteronomische Redaktion des Amosbuches."

84. Wolff, *Joel and Amos*, 107.

85. Ibid., 113.

86. Those following Wolff include, e.g., Robert B. Coote, *Amos among the Prophets: Composition and Theology* (Philadelphia: Fortress, 1981), although Coote simplifies Wolff's six stages to three; J. Alberto Soggin, *The Prophet Amos: A Translation and Commentary*, trans. J. Bowden (London: SCM, 1987), 12–28; J. Vermeylen, *Du prophète Isaïe à l'Apocalyptique: Isaïe, I–XXXV, miroir d'un demi-millénaire d'expérience religieuse en Israël* (2 vols.; EBib; Paris: Gabalda, 1977–1998), 2:519–69. Of course, other prominent scholars were not taken by Wolff's proposal. Note especially Wilhelm Rudolph, *Joel, Amos, Obadja, Jona* (KAT XIII/2; Gütersloh: Mohn, 1971), 93–292. Rudolph's is a substantial, moderately critical commentary, which has not received the attention it deserves in English-speaking circles. Unlike Wolff (and more recently Jeremias), his work has not been translated.

87. Ina Willi-Plein, *Vorformen der Schriftexegese innerhalb des Alten Testaments: Untersuchungen zum literarischen Werden der auf Amos, Hosea und Micha zurückgehenden Bücher im hebräischen Zwölfprophetenbuch* (BZAW 123; Berlin: de Gruyter, 1971); Roy F. Melugin, "The Formation of Amos: An Analysis of Exegetical Method," in *SBLSP 1978*, ed. P. J. Achtemeier (Missoula, Mont.: Scholars Press, 1978), 369–91; Coote, *Amos among the Prophets*; cf. Clements, *One Hundred Years*, 71–74.

88. Coote, *Amos among the Prophets*, 3–4.

89. Klaus Koch et al., *Amos: Untersucht mit den Methoden einer strukturalen Formgeschichte* (AOAT 30; Neukirchen-Vluyn: Neukirchener Verlag, 1976). For summaries and critiques of this work, see Melugin, "Formation of Amos"; Auld, *Amos*, 55–58.

90. Volkmar Fritz, "Die Fremdvölkersprüche des Amos," *VT* 37, no. 1 (1987): 26–38; Bernard Gosse, "Le recueil d'oracles contre les nations du livre d'Amos et l'Histoire Deutéronomique,'" *VT* 38, no. 1 (1988): 22–40.

91. The best popular presentation of the archaeological material for the book of Amos is Philip J. King, *Amos, Hosea, Micah: An Archaeological Commentary* (Philadelphia: Westminster, 1988).

92. Note the helpful summaries of these finds in J. S. Holladay Jr., "Religion in Israel and Judah under the Monarchy: An Explicitly Archaeological Approach," in *Ancient Israelite Religion* (Festschrift F. M. Cross), ed. P. D. Miller Jr., P. D. Hanson, and S. D. McBride (Philadelphia: Fortress, 1987), 249–99; Mark S. Smith, *The Early History of God: Yahweh and Other Deities in Ancient Israel* (San Francisco: Harper & Row, 1990). Post–1990 studies will be mentioned in the next chapter.

93. The number of published studies concerning these two finds has been immense. Note the summaries and evaluations of the different theories about the meaning of the data and the bibliographies in Richard S. Hess, "Yahweh and His Asherah? Epigraphic Evidence for Religious Pluralism in Old Testament Times," in *One God, One Lord in a World of Religious Pluralism*, ed. A. D. Clarke and B. W. Winter (Cambridge: Tyndale House, 1991), 5–33; Othmar Keel and Christoph Uehlinger, *Gods, Goddesses, and Images of God in Ancient Israel*, trans. T. H. Trapp (Minneapolis: Fortress, 1998), 210–48; Judith M. Hadley, *The Cult of Asherah in Ancient Israel and Judah* (University of Cambridge Oriental Publications 57; Cambridge: Cambridge University Press, 2000).

94. Opinions have differed, however, over what the term "popular" means. See J. Berlinerblau, "The 'Popular Religion' Paradigm in Old Testament Research: A Sociological Critique," *JSOT* 60 (1993): 3–26; M. Daniel Carroll R.,

"Re-examining 'Popular Religion': Issues of Definition and Sources: Insights from Interpretive Anthropology," in *Rethinking Contexts, Rereading Texts: Contributions from the Social Sciences to Biblical Interpretation*, ed. M. Daniel Carroll R. (JSOTSup 299; Sheffield: Sheffield Academic Press, 2000), 146–67.

95. King, *Amos, Hosea, Micah*, 137–61. Hans M. Barstad, *The Religious Polemics of Amos: Studies in the Preaching of Am. 2, 7B–8; 4, 1–13; 5, 1–27; 6, 4–7; 8, 14* (VTSup 34; Leiden: Brill, 1984), 128–38; T. J. Lewis, *Cults of the Dead in Ancient Israel and Ugarit* (HSM 39; Atlanta: Scholars Press, 1989), 80–94.

96. Barstad, *Religious Polemics of Amos*, 33–44, 138–42.

97. Note, e.g., Andersen and Freedman, *Amos*, 566–68, passim.

98. Coote, *Amos among the Prophets*, 36–39; Wolff, *Joel and Amos*; Soggin, *Amos*; Hayes, *Amos, the Eighth-Century Prophet*, all ad loc.

99. Wolff, *Joel and Amos*, 265–66, 332–34; O. Loretz, "Die babylonischen Gottesnamen *Sukkut* und *Kajjāmanu* in Amos 5,26: Ein Beitrag zur jüdischen Astrologie," *ZAW* 101, no. 2 (1989): 286–89.

100. J. W. McKay, *Religion in Judah under the Assyrians 732–609 BC* (SBT 2/26; Naperville, Ill.: Allenson, 1973), 45–59, 67–73; M. Cogan, *Imperialism and Religion: Assyria, Judah, and Israel in the Eighth and Seventh Centuries B.C.E.* (SBLMS 19; Missoula, Mont.: Scholars Press, 1974), 103–4; Barstad, *Religious Polemics of Amos*, 118–26, 143–201; Andersen and Freedman, *Amos*, 533–37.

101. Andersen and Freedman, *Amos*, 828–29.

102. For "Ashima" see Barstad, *Religious Polemics of Amos*, 157–81. For "A/asherah" see J. H. Tigay, *You Shall Have No Other Gods: Israelite Religion in the Light of Hebrew Inscriptions* (HSS 31; Atlanta: Scholars Press, 1986), 26 n. 31; cf. *BHS*.

103. Whereas form criticism had long been interested in the social background of genres, its reconstructions were often based on textual observations and not on detailed sociological studies or social theory. At this juncture mention can be made of Max Polley's monograph, which claims to be a "socio-historical approach." Apparently by this he means that his study looks at the ministry of Amos ideologically as a critique of the Northern monarchy and its supporting religious system and as championing the Davidic line and Jerusalem cult as the only legitimate government and religion. His work does not utilize social theory as such (*Amos and the Davidic Empire: A Socio-Historical Approach* [New York: Oxford University Press, 1989]).

104. Max Weber, *Ancient Judaism*, trans. H. H. Gerth and D. Martindale (Glencoe, N.Y.: Free Press, 1952), 90–117, 267–335. For a summary and evaluation of Weber's work, see M. Daniel Carroll R., *Contexts for Amos: Prophetic Poetics in Latin American Perspective* (JSOTSup 132; Sheffield: Sheffield Academic Press, 1992), 26–36. Another early attempt at a sociological reconstruction of the rise and role of the prophets is represented by Louis Wallis, *Sociological Study of the Bible* (Chicago: University of Chicago Press, 1912); idem, *God and the Social Process: A Study in Hebrew History* (Chicago: University of Chicago Press, 1935).

105. Robert R. Wilson, *Prophecy and Society in Ancient Israel* (Philadelphia: Fortress, 1980).

106. Ibid., 21–88.

107. Ibid., 266–70. Also note David L. Petersen, *The Roles of Israel's Prophets* (JSOTSup 17; Sheffield: JSOT Press, 1981). The theoretical basis of Petersen is role theory. He classifies the various titles given to prophets according to their provenance (Judah or Israel) and their social location. In Petersen's view, Amaziah's use of terms from two different roots in Amos 7:12 can be explained

by understanding *ḥōzeh* ("seer") and *nābîʾ* ("prophet") as referring to Judahite and Israelite central morality prophets, respectively. The high priest, therefore, is demanding that Amos return to his proper prophetic role in the south (*Roles*, 56–63; for a critique see Carroll R., *Contexts for Amos*, 34–36).

108. Thomas W. Overholt, "Commanding the Prophets: Amos and the Problem of Prophetic Authority," *CBQ* 41, no. 4 (1979): 517–32; idem, "Seeing Is Believing: The Social Setting of Prophetic Acts of Power," *JSOT* 23 (1982): 3–31; idem, *Channels of Prophecy: The Social Dynamics of Prophetic Activity* (Minneapolis: Fortress, 1989).

109. Norman K. Gottwald, "A Hypothesis about Social Class in Monarchic Israel in the Light of Contemporary Studies of Social Class and Social Stratification," in idem, *The Hebrew Bible in Its Social World and in Ours* (Semeia Studies; Atlanta: Scholars Press, 1993), 139–64. This phraseology marks a change in Gottwald's vocabulary, who in earlier works had used the terms "egalitarian" (instead of "communitarian") and "Asiatic Mode of Production" (instead of "tributary"). Note his comment, ibid., 139.

110. Marvin L. Chaney, "Systemic Study of the Israelite Monarchy," *Semeia* 37 (1986): 53–76; idem, "Bitter Bounty: The Dynamics of Political Economy Critiqued by the Eighth-Century Prophets," in *Reformed Faith and Economics*, ed. R. L. Stivers (Lanham, Md.: University Press of America, 1989), 15–30; D. N. Premnath, "Latifundialization and Isaiah 5.8–10," *JSOT* 40 (1988): 49–60.

111. For critical surveys, see Sicre, *'Con los pobre de la tierra,'* 76–83, 141–68; Günther Fleischer, *Von Menschenverkäufern, Baschankühen und Rechtsverkehrern: Die Sozialkritik des Amosbuches in historisch-kritischer, sozialkritischer und archäologischer Perspektive* (BBB 74; Frankfurt am Main: Athenäum, 1989).

112. Coote, *Amos among the Prophets*, 24–32; Bernhard Lang, "Sklaven und Unfreie im Buch Amos (II 6, VIII 6)," *VT* 31, no. 4 (1981): 482–88; idem, "The Social Organization of Peasant Poverty in Biblical Israel," in *Monotheism and the Prophetic Minority: An Essay in Biblical History and Sociology* (SWBA 1; Sheffield: Almond Press, 1983), 114–27; cf. O. Loretz, "Die prophetische Kritik des Rentcapitalismus: Grundlagen-Probleme der Prophetenforschung." *UF* 7 (1975): 271–78.

113. John Andrew Dearman, *Property Rights in the Eighth-Century Prophets: The Conflict and Its Background* (SBLDS 106; Atlanta: Scholars Press, 1988), 15, 133–35. It should be noted that Dearman's critique is grounded more in textual evidence and comparisons with Neo-Assyrian practices than in social theory.

114. Fleischer, *Von Menschenverkäufern*, 359–62, 365–90. Another scholar who sees the economic decline in eighth-century Israel as part of a longer process, although within a different theoretical framework, is J. K. de Geus ("Die Gesellschaftskritik der Propheten und die Archäologie," *ZDPV* 98, no. 1 [1982]: 50–57). Also note the work by Marlene Fendler, who tries to avoid a simple two-class economic system in ancient Israel ("Zur Sozialkritik des Amos: Versuch einer wirschaft- und sozialgeschichtlichen Interpretation alttestmentlicher Texte," *EvT* 33, no. 1 [1973]: 32–53). At this juncture mention should be made of M. Silver, an economist, who holds that the message and efforts of the prophets proved to be too critical of an emerging economy and helped lead to the nation's demise (*Prophets and Markets: The Political Economy of Ancient Israel* [Boston: Kluwer-Nijhoff, 1983]). Apparently, they should have been more capitalistic!

115. See, e.g., Hayes, *Amos, the Eighth-Century Prophet*; Rosenbaum, *Amos of Israel*. These two authors offer an occasional literary observation in their comments

on passages, but this is not a major concern of their work. Nevertheless, the commitment to the received text and the awareness of at least some literary features merit their mention in this section. I should also point out that each of these scholars offers a very different historical reconstruction of Amos's context and ministry.

116. Andersen and Freedman, *Amos*, 73–88. Earlier scholars who also argued for a biographical reconstruction of the stages of the book's composition include Robert Gordis, "The Composition and Structure of Amos," *HTR* 33, no. 4 (1940): 239–51; John D. W. Watts, "The Origin of the Book of Amos," *ExpTim* 66, no. 4 (1955): 109–12.

117. Andersen and Freedman, *Amos*, 143–44.

118. Brevard S. Childs, *Introduction to the Old Testament as Scripture* (Philadelphia: Fortress, 1979), 399.

119. Ibid., 400.

120. Ibid., 408–9.

121. Examples would be Robert Alter, *The Art of Biblical Poetry* (New York: Basic Books, 1985); Harold Fisch, *Poetry with a Purpose: Biblical Poetics and Interpretation* (Indiana Studies in Biblical Literature; Bloomington, Ind.: Indiana University Press, 1988).

122. Some of the studies cited in this paragraph do wed a literary approach with critical convictions about the passages authentic to Amos. For example, Gese argues that the Oracles against the Nations exhibit the book's characteristic technique of presenting a series of five items, once the oracles against Tyre, Edom, and Judah are removed as secondary (Hartmut Gese, "Komposition bei Amos," in *Congress Volume, Vienna 1980*, ed. J. A. Emerton [VTSup 32; Leiden: Brill, 1981], 86–94). Others with critical presuppositions include Claude Coulot, "Propositions pour une structuration du livre d'Amos au niveau rédactionnel," *RevScRel* 51, nos. 2–3 (1977): 169–86; J. Lust, "Remarks on the Redaction of Amos V 4–6, 14–15," in *Remembering All the Way*, ed. B. Albrektson (*OTS* 21; Leiden: Brill, 1981), 129–54; N. J. Tromp, "Amos V 1–17: Towards a Stylistic and Rhetorical Analysis," in J. Barton et al., *Prophets, Worship and Theodicy: Studies in Prophetism, Biblical Theology and Structural and Rhetorical Analysis and on the Place of Music in Worship* (*OTS* 23; Leiden: Brill, 1984), 56–84.

123. Moisés Chávez, *Modelo de oratoria. Obra basada en el análisis estilístico del texto hebreo del libro de Amós* (Miami: Caribe, 1979).

124. Gese, "Komposition bei Amos," 74–95; J. Limburg, "Sevenfold Structures in the Book of Amos," *JBL* 106, no. 2 (1987): 217–22.

125. Y. Gitay, "A Study of Amos's Art of Speech: A Rhetorical Analysis of Amos 3.1–15," *CBQ* 42, no. 3 (1980): 293–309.

126. Francis Landy, "Vision and Poetic Speech in Amos," *HAR* 11 (1987): 223–46.

127. Jan de Waard, "Chiastic Structure of Amos V 1–17," *VT* 27, no. 2 (1977): 170–77; Coulot, "Propositions," 179–80; Lust, "Remarks"; Tromp, "Amos V 1–17."

128. Jan de Waard and William A. Smalley, *A Translator's Handbook on the Book of Amos* (Helps for Translators; New York: United Bible Societies, 1979), 189–214.

129. Ernst R. Wendland, "The 'Word of the Lord' and the Organization of the Book of Amos," *OPTT* 2, no. 4 (1988): 1–51.

130. Leland Ryken, *Words of Delight: A Literary Introduction to the Bible* (Grand Rapids: Baker, 1987), 334; cf. idem, "Amos," in *A Complete Literary Guide to the*

Bible, ed. idem and T. Longman III (Grand Rapids: Zondervan, 1993), 337–47. For another author who appeals to Frye and includes Amos in his discussion of satire, see Thomas Jemielty, *Satire and the Hebrew Prophets* (Literary Currents in Biblical Interpretation; Louisville: Westminster John Knox, 1992), 84–116.

131. Ryken, "Amos," 342.

132. Paul R. House, *The Unity of the Twelve* (Bible and Literature Series 27; Sheffield: Almond Press, 1990).

133. Feminist concerns, of course, echo these convictions, but no feminist studies focused exclusively on Amos during the time frame under study. The same can be said of African American theology (although see allusions to Amos in African American sources in Chapter 3). Interestingly, Chávez quotes Martin Luther King's famous "I Have a Dream" speech (Washington, D.C.; 28 August 1963) in its entirety as an example of a modern Amos-like prophetic pronouncement (Chávez, *Modelo de oratoria*, 133–39). King quotes Amos 5:24.

134. Martin-Achard, *Amos*, 201–71.

135. H. R. Weber, "Prophecy in the Ecumenical Movement: Ambiguities and Questions," in *Prophetic Vocation in the New Testament and Today*, ed. J. Panagopoulos (Supplement to Novum Testamentum 45; Leiden: Brill, 1977), 218–28.

136. See, e.g., F. B. Huey Jr., "The Ethical Teaching of Amos, Its Content and Relevance." *SwJT* 9, no. 1 (1966) 57–67; Thomas J. Finley, "An Evangelical Response to the Preaching of Amos." *JETS* 28, no. 4 (1985): 411–20; Sicre, *'Con los pobres de la tierra'*.

137. For a presentation and evaluation of several Latin American liberationist studies on the text of Amos until 1988, see Carroll R., *Contexts for Amos*, 312–19. For an introduction and survey of the hermeneutics of this approach, see ibid., 109–20; and idem, "Liberation Theology: Latin America," in *The Oxford Illustrated History of the Bible*, ed. J. W. Rogerson (Oxford: Oxford University Press, 2001), 316–29.

138. Elsa Tamez, *Bible of the Oppressed*, trans. M. J. O'Connell (Maryknoll, N.Y.: Orbis, 1982).

139. José Porfirio Miranda, *Marx and the Bible: A Critique of the Philosophy of Oppression*, trans. J. Eagleson (Maryknoll, N.Y.: Orbis, 1974), 55–56.

140. Ibid., 35–76.

141. Ibid., 166–68.

142. Ibid., 137–69.

143. José Severino Croatto, *Biblical Hermeneutics: Toward a Theory of Reading as the Production of Meaning*, trans. R. R. Barr (Maryknoll, N.Y.: Orbis, 1987).

144. Ibid., 56–57.

145. Croatto, "Del juicio a la reconciliación: Una lectura de textos proféticos." *Cuad-Teol* 8 (1987): 7–16.

146. Pablo Rubén Andriñach, "Amós: memoria y profecía. Análisis estructural y hermeneútica," *RevistB* 43 (1983): 209–301.

147. Milton Schwantes, *Amós: Meditações e Estudos* (São Leopoldo: Sinodal; Petrópolis: Voces, 1987).

148. Ibid., 10.

149. Ibid., 79–92.

150. For discussions on relevant evangelical views and sources, see M. Daniel Carroll R. with Guillermo Méndez, "Another Voice from Latin America: Concerned Evangelicals and the Challenge of a Continent in Crisis. An Introductory and Bibliographic Essay," *The Modern Churchman* 30, no. 4 (1989): 42–46;

and Carroll R., "Context, Bible and Ethics: A Latin American Perspective," *Themelios* 19, no. 3 (1994): 9–15; idem, "Desíos de coyuntura: pensamientos acerca del futuro de la religión en América Latina," *Kairós* 21 (1997): 71–82. The concern for the context by the institutional Roman Catholic Church in Latin America is evident in the documents of the continent-wide Bishops Conferences held in Medellín (1968), Puebla (1979), and Santo Domingo (1992). Of course, these documents also reflect the results of (sometimes fierce) internal debates concerning contextual issues, as the church interacted with liberation theology at the level of theology (with such prominent figures as Juan Luis Segundo and Gustavo Gutiérrez) and ecclesiastical structure (especially in Nicaragua during the Sandinista regime, 1979–1990; also note the conflict with Leonardo Boff). For the most recent statement by Pope John Paul II, see *Ecclesia in America* (San Salvador: Ricaldone, 1999).

151. Washington Padilla, *Amós–Abdías* (Comentario Bíblico Hispanoamericano; Miami: Editorial Caribe, 1989), 147.

152. Ibid., 17.

Chapter 2: The State of Amos Research

1. Gerhard F. Hasel, *Understanding the Book of Amos: Basic Issues in Current Interpretations* (Grand Rapids: Baker, 1991).

2. For example, *RevEx* 92, no. 2 (1995); *SwJT* 38, no. 1 (1995). More popular level journal issues include *BV* 27, no. 2 (1993); *TTE* 52 (1995); and *DosB* 59 (1995).

3. Roy F. Melugin, "Amos in Recent Research," *CR:BS* 6 (1998): 65–101.

4. Henry O. Thompson, *The Book of Amos: An Annotated Bibliography* (ATLA Bibliographies 42; Lanham, Md.: Scarecrow Press, 1997). Extensive bibliographies have also appeared in some of the commentaries. Note especially Shalom M. Paul, *Amos: A Commentary on the Book of Amos* (Hermeneia; Minneapolis: Fortress, 1991), xix–xxvi, 299–367.

5. For helpful surveys of these critical approaches, see in addition to the commentaries Hartmut N. Rösel, "Kleine Studien zur Entwicklung des Amosbuches," *VT* 43, no. 1 (1993): 88–101; idem, "Kleine Studien zur Auslegung des Amosbuches," *BZ* 42, no. 1 (1998): 2–18; and Melugin, "Amos in Recent Research," 78–87. Other studies not covered in these surveys or below in my discussion include, e.g., Konrad Schullerus, "Überlegungen zur Redaktionsgeschichte des Amosbuches anhand von Am 9,7–10," *BN* 85 (1996): 56–69; Theodor Lescow, "Das vorexilische Amosbuch: Erwägungen zu seiner Kompositionsgeschichte," *BN* 93 (1998): 23–55.

6. An enthusiastic advocate of this persuasion is Odil Hannes Steck, *The Prophetic Books and Their Theological Witness*, trans. J. D. Nogalski (St. Louis, Mo.: Chalice, 2000). Not all who believe in redactional prehistories behind the prophetic texts, however, agree on how the process is conceptualized. Note Brevard S. Childs's reservations from his canon criticism perspective: "Retrospective Reading of the Old Testament Prophets," *ZAW* 108, no. 2 (1996): 362–77.

7. The collection is entitled *Hosea und Amos: Studien zu den Anfängen des Dodekapropheten* (FAT 13; Tübingen: Mohr, 1996). The essays include "Amos 3–6: Beobachtungen zur Entstehungsgeschichte eines Prophetenbuches," *ZAW* 100 (1988 Supplement): 123–38 (reprinted in idem, *Hosea und Amos*, 142–56); "Amos 3–6: From Oral Word to the Text," in *Canon, Theology, and Old Testament Interpretation* (Festschrift B. S. Childs), ed. G. M. Tucker, D. L. Petersen, and R. R. Wilson (Philadelphia: Fortress, 1988), 217–29; "Völker-

sprüche und Visionsberichte im Amosbuch," in *Prophet und Prophetenbuch* (Festschrift O. Kaiser), ed. V. Fritz, K.-F. Pohlmann, and H.-C. Schmitt (BZAW 185. Berlin: de Gruyter, 1989), 82–97 (reprinted in idem, *Hosea und Amos*, 157–71); "Tod und Leben in Am 5,1–17," in *Der Weg zum Menschen* (Festschrift A. Deissler), ed. R. Mosis and L. Ruppert (Freiburg: Herder, 1989), 134–52 (reprinted in idem, *Hosea und Amos*, 214–30); "Am 8,4–7: Ein Kommentar zu 2,6f," in *Text, Methode und Grammatik* (Festschrift W. Richter), ed. W. Gross, H. Irsigler, and T. Seidl (St. Ottilien: EOS, 1991), 205–20 (reprinted in idem, *Hosea und Amos*, 231–43); "Rezeptionsprozesse in der prophetischen Überlieferung—am Beispiel der Visionsberichte des Amos," in *Rezeption und Auslegung im Alten Testament und in seinem Umfeld*, ed. R. G. Kratz et al. (OBO 153; Freibourg: Universitätsverlag, 1997), 29–44.

8. Jeremias, *The Book of Amos: A Commentary*, trans. D. W. Stott (OTL; Louisville: Westminster John Knox, 1998).

9. Ibid., 5.

10. Jeremias, "Amos 3–6: From Oral Word to the Text," 217–29; idem, *Amos*, 5–9.

11. Jeremias, "Tod und Leben in Am 5,1–17"; idem, *Amos*, 81–97.

12. Jeremias, "Völkersprüche und Visionsberichte im Amosbuch"; idem, "Am 8,4–7." Of course, several scholars who have focused on the literariness of the text also have pointed out how different parts of the book consciously build off of other sections. Note, e.g., M. D. Terblanche, "'Rosen und Lavendel nach Blut und Eisen': Intertextuality in the Book of Amos," *OTE* 10, no. 2 (1997): 312–21. What makes Jeremias's presentation especially distinctive is how these textual observations are incorporated into a redaction history scheme for the book.

13. Jeremias, "Die Anfänge des Dodekapropheten: Hosea und Amos," in *Congress Volume*, ed. J. A. Emerton (VTSup 61; Leiden: Brill, 1995), 87–106 (reprinted in idem, *Hosea und Amos*, 34–54); idem, "The Interrelationship between Amos and Hosea," in *Forming Prophetic Literature* (Festschrift J. D. W. Watts), ed. J. D. W. Watts and P. R. House (JSOTSup 235. Sheffield: Sheffield Academic Press, 1996), 171–86.

14. Dirk U. Rottzoll, *Studien zur Redaktion und Komposition des Amosbuches* (BZAW 243; Berlin: de Gruyter, 1996). This is a revision of a doctoral thesis supervised by Jeremias.

15. Oswald Loretz, "Die Enstehung des Amos-Buches im Licht der Prophetien aus Märi, Assur, Ishchali und der Ugarit-Texte," *UF* 24 (1992): 179–215.

16. Loretz is aware that his position is a return to something akin to that of Wellhausen and others, who argued that the prophets predated the Law. However, he is adding new reasoning to substantiate that claim.

17. Brian Peckham, *History and Prophecy: The Development of Late Judean Literary Traditions* (Anchor Bible Reference Library; New York: Doubleday, 1993), 158–85.

18. Ibid., 158.

19. Joyce Rilett Wood, whose doctoral thesis was supervised by Peckham, has given this approach a bit of a twist by applying Northrop Frye's categories of tragedy and comedy to the two editions of Amos. See *Amos in Song and Culture* (JSOT-Sup 337; Sheffield: Sheffield Academic Press, 2002); cf. idem, "Tragic and Comic Forms in Amos," *BibInt* 6, no. 1 (1998): 20–48. She believes that Amos was a shepherd turned poet, who wrote and performed a tragedy (of seven poems) as a dramatic monologue in the temple of Jerusalem during the reign

of Manasseh. She compares him to the Greek dramatists of that general time period. A later editor (probably about fifty years after the fall of Jerusalem) changed this drama designed for live performance into a book to be read with a different and comic ending. Peckham mentions Wood in *History and Prophecy*, 222, n. 108.

20. H. G. M. Williamson, "The Prophet and the Plumb-Line: A Redaction-Critical Study of Amos vii," in *In Quest of the Past: Studies on Israelite Religion, Literature and Prophetism*, ed. A. van der Woude (*OTS* 26; Leiden: Brill, 1990), 101–20; Ronald E. Clements, "Amos and the Politics of Israel," in *Storia e Tradizioni di Israele* (Festschrift J. A. Soggin), ed. D. Garrone and F. Israel (Brescia: Paideia, 1991), 49–64 (reprinted in *Old Testament Prophecy: From Oracles to Canon* (Louisville: Westminster John Knox, 1996, 23–34). Recent studies on the visions themselves include E.-J. Waschke ("Die fünfte Vision des Amosbuches (9.1–4)—Nachinterpretation," *ZAW* 106, no. 3 [1994]: 434–45) and Siegfried Bergler ("'Auf der Mauer—auf dem Alter': Noch einmal die Visionen des Amos," *VT* 50, no. 4 [2000]: 445–71).

21. Williamson also lists additional connections between the book of Amos and the Deuteronomistic History, such as the similarities between 7:9–17 and 1 Kgs. 13 and the possible links between some of the opening oracles and several passages in 2 Kings ("Prophet and Plumb-Line," 119–21).

22. Clements understands the difficult term *'ănāk* ("tin") to refer to some sort of weapon, the tin as alloyed with copper to produce bronze (note the mention of the sword in 7:9). For Williamson, Amos himself is the "plumb line," the representation of the divine standard. Observe how the interpretations given by Williamson and Clements to *'ănāk* fit with their particular reconstruction of the purpose of the redactional addition(s) to the third vision. See further discussion below.

23. Hermann Michael Niemann, "Theologie in geographischen Gewand. Zum Wachstumsprozeß der Völkerspruchsammlung Amos 1–2," in *Nachdenken über Israel, Bibel und Theologie* (Festschrift K.-D. Schunk), ed. M. Augustin and W. H. Schmidt (BEATAJ 37; Frankfurt am Main: Peter Lang, 1994), 177–96. Other recent publications on the Oracles against the Nations include Matthias Köchert, "Das Gesetz und die Propheten in Amos 1–2," in *Alttestamentliche Glaube und biblische Theologie* (Festschrift H. D. Preuss), ed. J. Hausmann and H.-J. Zobel (Stuttgart: Kohlhammer, 1992), 145–54; Dieter Vieweger, "Zur Herkunft der Völkerworte im Amosbuch unter besonder Berücksichtigung des Aramäerspruchs (Am 1.3–5)," in *Altes Testament, Forschung und Wirkung* (Festschrift H. G. Reventlow), ed. P. Mommer and W. Thiel (Bern: Peter Lang, 1994), 103–19.

24. Niemann draws on Jeremias, "Völkersprüche und Visionsberichte im Amosbuch."

25. For surveys of research, see James Nogalski, *Literary Precursors to the Book of the Twelve* (BZAW 217; Berlin: de Gruyter, 1993), 3–12; Barry Allan Jones, *The Formation of the Book of the Twelve: A Study in Text and Canon* (SBLDS 149; Atlanta: Scholars Press, 1995), 13–40; Aaron Schart, *Die Entstehung des Zwölfprophetenbuchs: Neubearbeitungen von Amos im Rahmen schriftenübergreifender Redaktionsprozesse* (BZAW 260; Berlin: de Gruyter, 1998), 12–21; idem, "Reconstructing the Redaction History of the Twelve Prophets: Problems and Methods," in *Reading and Hearing the Book of the Twelve*, ed. J. D. Nogalski and M. A. Sweeney (SBLSymS 15; Atlanta: Society of Biblical Literature, 2000), 38–45.

Of course, there are those who see some of these efforts as misplaced and based on faulty reasoning. Note Ehud Ben Zvi, "Twelve Prophetic Books or 'The Twelve': A Few Preliminary Considerations," in *Forming Prophetic Literature*, ed. Watts and House, 125–56.

26. See Jeremias, *Amos*, passim; Richard James Coggins, *Joel and Amos* (New Century Bible Commentary; Sheffield: Sheffield Academic Press, 2000), 1–6; Marvin A. Sweeney, *The Twelve Prophets* (Berit Olam; Collegeville, Minn.: Liturgical Press, 2000), xv–xxxix.

27. Jeremias, "Anfänge des Dodekapropheten"; idem, "Interrelationship between Amos and Hosea."

28. Schart, *Entstehung des Zwölfprophetenbuchs*; idem, "Reconstructing the Redaction History."

29. Nogalski, *Literary Precursors*, 12–57; idem, "Intertextuality in the Twelve," in *Forming Prophetic Literature*, ed. Watts and House, 102–24; idem, "Joel as 'Literary Anchor' for the Book of the Twelve," in *Reading and Hearing*, ed. Nogalski and Sweeney, 91–109. By the "catchword" principle he means that the end of one prophetic book contains significant words that reappear in opening sections of the following one.

30. Nogalski, "Intertextuality in the Twelve," 112.

31. Nogalski, *Literary Precursors*, 74–122; *Redactional Processes in the Book of the Twelve* (BZAW 218; Berlin: de Gruyter, 1993), 42–48, 61–74.

32. Jones, *Formation*, 175–91. One of Jones's criticisms of Nogalski is that he bases much of his hypothesis only on the MT.

33. It is interesting to note that these scholars have commented on and critiqued one another's models. For example, see Jones on Nogalski (Jones, *Formation*, 32–40), Nogalski on Schart (Nogalski, review of Schart in *TLZ* 124, no. 5 [1999]: 503–5), and Schart on Nogalski and Jones (Schart, *Entstehung des Zwölfprophetenbuchs*, 14–16 and 18–20, respectively).

34. Others who have combined a diachronic analysis with a synchronic reading are Herbert Marks, "The Twelve Prophets," in *The Literary Guide to the Bible*, ed. R. Alter and F. Kermode (Cambridge: Harvard University Press, 1987), 207–33; Terrence Collins, "The Scroll of the Twelve," in idem, *The Mantle of Elijah: The Redactional Criticism of the Prophetical Books* (Biblical Seminar 20; Sheffield: JSOT Press, 1993), 59–87.

35. Raymond C. Van Leeuwen, "Scribal Wisdom and Theodicy in the Book of the Twelve," in *In Search of Wisdom* (Festschrift J. G. Gammie), ed. L. G. Perdue, B. B. Scott, and W. J. Wiseman, 31–49 (Louisville: Westminster John Knox 1993). This quotation is from p. 32.

36. Sweeney, *Twelve Prophets*; cf. idem, "Formation and Form in Prophetic Literature," in *Old Testament Interpretation Past, Present, and Future* (Festschrift G. M. Tucker), ed. J. L. Mays, D. L. Petersen, and K. H. Richards (Nashville: Abingdon, 1995), 113–26. Jones also gives readings based on the MT and the LXX (*Formation*, 234–42).

37. Sweeney, *Twelve Prophets*, xxxii.

38. Sweeney, "Formation and Form in Prophetic Literature," 122–26; idem, *Twelve Prophets*, 191–95. Even though the fact that Joel is located after Micah in the LXX suggests less of a focus on Zion, Sweeney does not take this purpose to be substantially different in the Greek version. He adds, "The LXX version of the Twelve appears to present an initial concern with the punishment and restoration of the northern kingdom of Israel, which then provides a model for

understanding the experience of Jerusalem/Judah and the nations" (Sweeney, *Twelve Prophets*, xxix).

39. Even though this last perspective does not truly fit into the context of this discussion of the redaction of Amos, it is included at this juncture to complete the presentation of studies on the Book of the Twelve.

40. Paul R. House, *The Unity of the Twelve* (JSOTSup 97; Bible and Literature Series 27; Sheffield: Almond Press, 1990), 172–85; idem, *Old Testament Theology* (Downers Grove, Ill.: InterVarsity Press, 1998), 346–401; idem, "The Character of God in the Book of the Twelve," in *Reading and Hearing*, ed. Nogalski and Sweeney, 125–45. *The Unity of the Twelve* provides the foundation for his more recent work. For the character of God in Amos, see his *Old Testament Theology*, 357–63; idem, "Character of God," 133–34.

41. Paul, *Amos*, 194–98, 210–12, 268–72, respectively.

42. Ibid., xxvii.

43. Philip J. King, *Amos, Hosea, Micah: An Archaeological Commentary* (Philadelphia: Westminster, 1988).

44. Edward F. Campbell, "Archaeological Reflections on Amos's Targets," in *Scripture and Other Artifacts* (Festschrift P. J. King), ed. M. D. Coogan, J. C. Exum, and L. E. Stager (Louisville: Westminster John Knox, 1994), 32–52.

45. David Noel Freedman and Andrew Welch, "Amos's Earthquake and Israelite Prophecy," in *Scripture and Other Artifacts*, 188–98.

46. Brian B. Schmidt, *Israel's Beneficent Dead: Ancestor Cult and Necromancy in Ancient Israelite Religion and Tradition* (Winona Lake, Ind.: Eisenbrauns, 1996), 144–47; cf. Christl Maier and Michael Dörrfuß, "'Um mit ihnen zu sitzen, zu essen und zu trinken': Am 6,7; Jer 16,5 und die Bedeutung von *marzēaḥ*," *ZAW* 111, no. 1 (1999): 45–57. John L. McLaughlin believes that there is some religious component to the feast but is circumspect, like Schmidt, about connecting it to some sort of funerary cult; the prophet's text focuses its attention on the injustices associated with the feast; cf. idem, *The "Marzēaḥ" in the Prophetic Literature: References and Allusions in Light of the Extra-Biblical Evidence* (VTSup 86; Leiden: Brill, 2001), 80–217.

47. Elizabeth Bloch-Smith, *Judahite Burial Practices and Beliefs about the Dead* (JSOTSup 123; JSOT/ASOR Monograph Series 7; Sheffield: Sheffield Academic Press, 1992), 109–32; Karel van der Toorn, *Family Religion in Babylonia, Syria, and Israel* (Leiden: Brill, 1996), 206–35. Of the commentaries see Gary V. Smith, *Amos: A Commentary* (Grand Rapids: Zondervan, 1989), 192–94; Paul, *Amos*, 210–12; Jeremias, *Amos*, 110–12. In addition to the published sources cited in this and the preceding note, mention can also be made of two recent dissertations that deal with *marzēaḥ* in Amos: J. L. McLaughlin, *The Marzēaḥ in the Prophetic Literature* and Taek Joo Woo, "The *Marzēaḥ* Institution and Rites for the Dead: A Comparative and Systemic Study with Special Attention to the Eighth-Century Prophets" (Graduate Theological Union, 1998). See summaries in chapter 7 below.

48. See the discussions by S. M. Olyan, "The Oaths of Amos 8.14," in *Priesthood and Cult in Ancient Israel*, ed. G. A. Anderson and S. M. Olyan (JSOTSup 125; Sheffield: Sheffield Academic Press, 1991), 121–49; Paul, *Amos*, 268–70; Judith M. Hadley, *The Cult of Asherah in Ancient Israel and Judah: Evidence for a Hebrew Goddess* (Cambridge: Cambridge University Press, 2000), 77. Other studies that touch on religious issues related to Amos include Grätz's consideration of a storm god theology behind texts such as Amos 4:4–13 (Sebastian Grätz, *Der*

strafende Wettergott: Erwägungen zur Traditionsgeschichte des Adad-Fluchs im Alten Orient und im Alten Testament [BBB 114; Bodenheim: Philo, 1998], 228–53) and Paas's comparison of 9:6 with Egyptian images of royal and divine thrones (Stefan Paas, "'He Who Builds His Stairs into Heaven . . .' [Amos 9:6a]," *UF* 25 [1993]: 319–25).

49. Significant works since 1990 include Rainer Albertz, *A History of Israelite Religion in the Old Testament Period*, vol. 1: *From the Beginnings to the End of the Monarchy*, trans. J. Bowden (OTL; Louisville: Westminster John Knox, 1994), 156–95; Othmar Keel and Christoph Uehlinger, *Gods, Goddesses, and Images of God in Ancient Israel*, trans. T. H. Trapp (Minneapolis: Fortress, 1998), 228–32; Patrick D. Miller, *The Religion of Ancient Israel* (LAI; Louisville: Westminster John Knox, 2000), 29–40, 51–56; cf. W. G. Dever, "'Will the Real Israel Please Stand Up?' Part II: Archaeology and the Religions of Ancient Israel," *BASOR* 298 (1995): 37–58; Karel van der Toorn, "Currents in the Study of Israelite Religion," *CR:BS* 6 (1998): 9–30.

50. For a lengthy survey of research, see Michael Weigl, "Eine 'unendliche Geschichte': *'nk* (Am 7,7–8)," *Bib* 76, no. 3 (1995): 343–87. A monograph on the term was published in 1988 (Walter Beyerlin, *Bleilot, Brecheisen oder was sonst? Revision einer Amos-Vision* [OBO 81; Freiburg: Universitätverlag; Göttingen: Vandenhoeck & Ruprecht, 1988]), but the more pronounced recent interest in this discussion precluded including that work in our survey of pre–1990 research.

51. Williamson, "Prophet and Plumb-Line," 105–21. His comments on *'ănāk* are part of a larger discussion concerning the redaction of 7:10–17, which was discussed earlier in this essay. It is interesting to note in passing that within a broader discussion of certain linguistic data that in his mind substantiates that Amos was from Israel and not Judah, Stanley N. Rosenbaum considers this loanword to be evidence of the fact that Amos was not a poor peasant but a well-educated government official (*Amos of Israel: A New Interpretation* [Macon, Ga.: Mercer University Press, 1990], 91).

52. James K. Hoffmeier, "Once Again the 'Plumb Line' Vision of Amos 7.7–9: An Interpretive Clue from Egypt?" in *Boundaries of the Ancient Near Eastern World* (Festschrift C. H. Gordon), ed. M. Lubetski, C. Gottlieb, and S. Keller (JSOTSup 273; Sheffield: Sheffield Academic Press, 1998), 304–19.

53. Several of the most recent studies that survey the field include Paula McNutt, *Reconstructing the Society of Ancient Israel* (LAI; London: SPCK; Louisville: Westminster John Knox, 1999), 1–31; Norman K. Gottwald, *The Politics of Ancient Israel* (LAI; Louisville: Westminster John Knox, 2001), 1–31; M. Daniel Carroll R., "Introduction: Issues of 'Context' within Social Science Approaches to Biblical Studies," in *Rethinking Contexts, Rereading Texts: Contributions from the Social Sciences to Biblical Interpretation*, ed. M. Daniel Carroll R. (JSOTSup 299; Sheffield: Sheffield Academic Press, 2000), 13–21.

54. M. Daniel Carroll R., *Contexts for Amos: Prophetic Poetics in Latin American Perspective* (JSOTSup 132; Sheffield: Sheffield Academic Press, 1992), 31–47; idem, "Observaciones metodológicas para un estudio de la crítica profética a la economía," *Vox Scripturae* 7, no. 1 (1998): 3–20.

55. W. G. Runciman, *A Treatise on Social Theory*, vol. 1: *The Methodology of Social Theory* (Cambridge: Cambridge University Press, 1983); cf. John W. Rogerson, "The Use of Sociology in Old Testament Studies," VTSup 36 (in *Congress Volume, Salamanca 1983*, ed. J. A. Emerton; Leiden: Brill, 1985), 245–56. Carroll R.

utilizes Runciman's points to evaluate the hypothesis of "rent capitalism" (discussed in the previous essay), in particular Bernhard Lang's "The Social Organization of Peasant Poverty in Biblical Israel," in *Monotheism and the Prophetic Minority: An Essay in Biblical History and Sociology* (SWBA 1; Sheffield: Almond Press, 1983), 114–27.

56. In anthropology this distinction is labeled etics and emics, respectively. See T. N. Headland, K. L. Pike, and M. Harris, *Emics and Etics: The Insider/Outsider Debate* (Frontiers of Anthropology 7; Newbury Park: Sage, 1990); cf. Carroll R., *Contexts for Amos*, 54–63.

57. Carroll R., *Contexts for Amos*, 49–63; idem, "Re-examining 'Popular Religion': Issues of Definition and Sources. Insights from Interpretive Anthropology"; and idem, "'For so you love to do': Probing Popular Religion in the Book of Amos," in *Rethinking Contexts, Rereading Texts*, 146–67 and 168–89, respectively. Carroll R.'s perspective on popular religion is utilized by Thomas W. Overholt, "Elijah and Elisha in the Context of Israelite Religion," in *Prophets and Paradigms* (Festschrift G. M. Tucker), ed. S. B. Reid (JSOTSup 229; Sheffield: Sheffield Academic Press, 1996), 94–111. Three other anthropological studies on Amos are Gary V. Smith, *The Hebrew Prophets as Preachers: An Introduction to the Hebrew Prophets* (Nashville: Broadman & Holman, 1994), 47–65; Guillermo Ramírez, "The Social Location of the Prophet Amos in Light of the Group/Grid Cultural Anthropology Model," in *Prophets and Paradigms*, ed. Reid, 112–24; and Kenton L. Sparks, *Ethnicity and Identity in Ancient Israel: Prolegomena to the Study of Ethnic Sentiments and Their Expression in the Hebrew Bible* (Winona Lake, Ind.: Eisenbrauns, 1998), 168–94. Smith utilizes communication theory and the sociology of knowledge to analyze how the prophet transmits his message of doom. Ramírez uses the group/grid model, associated with the anthropologist Mary Douglas, to examine Amos 7:10–17 and the prophet's self-understanding. Sparks investigates the Oracles against the Nations, 6:1–7, and 7:10–17 to ascertain Amos's perception and valorization of ethnicity.

58. Izabela Jaruzelska, "Social Structure in the Kingdom of Israel in the Eighth Century B.C. as Reflected in the Book of Amos," *FO* 29 (1992–1993): 91–117; idem, "People Pronouncing Sentences in Court: Amos 5, 7–12, 16–17: An Attempt at Sociological Identification," *FO* 30 (1994): 77–94; idem, *Amos and the Officialdom in the Kingdom of Israel: The Socio-Economic Position of Officials in the Light of the Biblical, the Epigraphic and Archaeological Evidence* (Seria Socjologia 25; Poznán, Poland: Poznánska Drukarnia Naukowa, 1998).

59. For helpful surveys of how "ideology" has been understood and applied to biblical studies, see Jonathan E. Dyck, "A Map of Ideology for Biblical Critics," in *Rethinking Contexts, Rereading Texts*, ed. Carroll R., 108–28; James Barr, *History and Ideology in the Old Testament: Biblical Studies at the End of a Millennium* (Oxford: Oxford University Press, 2000), 102–40; Norman K. Gottwald, *Politics of Ancient Israel*, 1–31. An earlier work is Gottwald, *The Hebrew Bible: A Socio-Literary Introduction* (Philadelphia: Fortress, 1985). For the prophets in particular, see especially Gottwald, "Ideology and Ideologies in Israelite Prophecy," in *Prophets and Paradigms*, ed. Reid, 136–49.

60. J. David Pleins, *The Social Visions of the Hebrew Bible: A Theological Introduction* (Louisville: Westminster John Knox, 2000).

61. Ibid., 368–77. In contrast to Pleins, who traces these texts back to the historic prophets themselves, Philip R. Davies postulates that the prophetic books are actually scribal creations of the Second Temple period. Their political and

social critiques are presented as if they were from the mouth (and pen) of ancient prophets, but actually they are expressions of the scribes' own agendas and frustrations with the state of affairs in postexilic times. He does not deal specifically with Amos (Davies, "The Audiences of Prophetic Scrolls: Some Suggestions," in *Prophets and Paradigms*, ed. Reid, 48–62; idem, "'Pen of iron, point of diamond' (Jer 17:1): Prophecy as Writing," in *Writings and Speech in Israelite and Ancient Near Eastern Prophecy*, ed. E. Ben Zvi and M. H. Floyd [SBLSymS 10; Atlanta: Society of Biblical Literature, 2000], 65–81).

62. Pleins, *Social Visions*, 354.

63. Roy F. Melugin, "Prophetic Books and the Problem of Historical Reconstruction," in *Prophets and Paradigms*, ed. Reid, 63–78; idem, "Amos and a Hermeneutics of Transformation," unpublished paper presented at the annual meeting of the Society of Biblical Literature, Orlando, November, 1999. Also see his recent contributions to one-volume commentaries: "Amos," in *Harper's Bible Commentary*, ed. J. L. Mays et al. (San Francisco: Harper & Row, 1988), 720–25; "Amos," in *Asbury Bible Commentary*, ed. E. E. Carpenter and W. McCown (Grand Rapids: Zondervan, 1992), 735–49. Cf. Gene M. Tucker, "The Futile Quest for the Historical Prophet," in *A Biblical Itinerary: In Search of Method, Form and Content* (Festschrift G. W. Coats), ed. E. E. Carpenter (JSOTSup 240; Sheffield: Sheffield Academic Press, 1997), 144–52.

64. Donald E. Gowan, "Amos," in *New Interpreter's Bible*, ed. L. E. Keck et al. (Nashville: Abingdon, 1996), vol. 7:339–431. This quotation is from p. 341.

65. Gerhard Pfeifer, "Die Fremdvölkersprüche des Amos—spätere *vaticinia ex eventu?*" *VT* 38, no. 2 (1988): 230–33; idem, "Jahwe als Schöpfe der Welt und Herr ihrer Mächte in der Verkündigung des Propheten Amos," *VT* 41, no. 4 (1991): 475–81; idem, *Die Theologie des Propheten Amos* (Frankfurt am Main: Peter Lang, 1995). Pfeifer does not totally dismiss redactional insertions (he would allow that 1:6–12; 2:4–5; 3:7; 5:13, 26; 9:8b–15 might be later additions).

66. Jeffrey Niehaus, "Amos," in *The Minor Prophets: An Expositional and Expository Commentary*, ed. T. E. McComiskey (3 vols.; Grand Rapids: Baker, 1992–1998), 1:315–509; Stephen J. Bramer, "The Literary Genre of the Book of Amos," *BSac* 156, no. 1 (1999): 42–60; idem, "Analysis of the Structure of Amos," *BSac* 156, no. 2 (1999): 160–74. Bramer prefers the term "covenant enforcement document."

67. Paul, *Amos*, passim.

68. Paul, "Amos 1:3–2:3. A Concatenous Literary Pattern," *JBL* 90, no. 4 (1971): 397–403; idem, "A Literary Reinvestigation of the Authenticity of the Oracles against the Nations," in *De la Torah au Messie* (Festschrift H. Cazelles), ed. M. Carrez et al. (Paris: Desclée, 1981), 189–204; idem, *Amos*, 7–30.

69. See an introduction and survey in Paul R. House, "Amos and Literary Criticism," *RevExp* 92, no. 2 (1995): 175–87. A short literary reading of the book of Amos appears on pp. 181–85. House favors formalist approaches.

70. Stephen Dempster, "The Lord Is His Name: A Study of the Distribution of the Names and Titles of God in the Book of Amos," *RB* 98, no. 2 (1991): 170–89.

71. A. E. Steinman, "The Order of Amos's Oracles against the Nations: 1.3–2.16," *JBL* 111, no. 4 (1992): 683–89.

72. Robert H. O'Connell, "Telescoping N+1 Patterns in the Book of Amos," *VT* 46, no. 1 (1996): 56–73. In addition to the sources cited in the extensive footnotes, this article closes with a chronologically arranged bibliography on this literary device (pp. 71–73).

73. Jan de Waard, "Chiastic Structure of Amos V 1–17," *VT* 27, no. 2 (1977): 170–77.

74. Others include R. Bryan Widbin, "Center Structures in the Center Oracles of Amos," in *Go to the Land I Will Show You* (Festschrift D.W. Young), ed. J. Coleson and V. Matthews (Winona Lake, Ind.: Eisenbrauns, 1996), 177–92; Victor M. Wilson, *Divine Symmetries: The Art of Biblical Rhetoric* (Lanham, Md.: University Press of America, 1997), 157–80.

75. David A. Dorsey, "Literary Architecture and Aural Structuring Techniques in Amos," *Bib* 73, no. 3 (1992): 305–30; idem, *The Literary Structure of the Old Testament: A Commentary on Genesis–Malachi* (Grand Rapids: Baker, 1999), 277–86.

76. Dorsey, *Literary Structure*, 26–44.

77. Pietro Bovati and Roland Meynet, *Le livre du prophète Amos* (Rhétorique biblique 2; Paris: Cerf, 1994). A condensed version was published as *La fin d'Israël: Paroles d'Amos* (Lire la Bible 121; Paris: Cerf, 1994).

78. An article on Amos that does appeal directly to Greek rhetorical strategies is Y. Gitay, "A Study of Amos's Art of Speech: A Rhetorical Analysis of Amos 3:1–15," *CBQ* 42, no. 3 (1980): 293–309.

79. Roland Meynet, *Rhetorical Analysis: An Introduction to Biblical Rhetoric* (JSOTSup 256; Sheffield: Sheffield Academic Press, 1998). For the historical overview, see pp. 44–166; for his method and the examples from Amos, pp. 168–308.

80. Works that could come under this rubric, but that will not be discussed here, include, e.g., Pedro Jaramillo Rivas, *La injusticia y la opresión en el lenguaje figurativo de los profetas* (Institución San Jerónimo 26; Navarra, Spain: Verbo Divino, 1992), 181–233; Leland Ryken, "Amos," in *A Complete Literary Guide to the Bible*, ed. L. Ryken and T. Longman III (Grand Rapids: Zondervan, 1993), 337–47; Eric A. Hermanson, "Biblical Hebrew: Conceptual Metaphor Categories in the Book of Amos," *OTE* 11, no. 3 (1998): 438–51.

81. Karl Möller, "'Hear This Word against You': A Fresh Look at the Arrangement and the Rhetorical Strategy of the Book of Amos," *VT* 50, no. 4 (2000): 499–518. The thesis is "Presenting a Prophet in Debate: An Investigation of the Literary Structure and the Rhetoric of Persuasion in the Book of Amos" (1999). For a summary, see chapter 7 below.

82. In addition to the articles cited below, see Paul R. Noble, "Synchronic and Diachronic Approaches to Biblical Interpretation," *JLT* 7, no. 2 (1993): 130–48.

83. Paul R. Noble, "Israel among the Nations," *HBT* 15, no. 1 (1993): 56–152; idem, "'I Will Not Bring "It" Back' (Amos 1:3): A Deliberately Ambiguous Oracle?" *ExpTim* 106, no. 4 (1995): 105–9; idem, "The Literary Structure of Amos: A Thematic Analysis," *JBL* 114, no. 2 (1995): 209–26; idem, "Amos' Absolute 'No,'" *VT* 47, no. 3 (1997): 329–40; idem, "The Remnant in Amos 3–6: A Prophetic Paradox," *HBT* 19, no. 2 (1997): 122–47. In light of the earlier discussion of chiasm, it is worth mentioning that Noble, even though suspicious of too facile a jump to such constructions, also will see what he calls a "palistrophic" structure that stretches from Amos 3:9 through 6:14 ("Remnant in Amos 3–6").

84. Paul R. Noble, "Amos and Amaziah in Context: Synchronic and Diachronic Approaches to Amos 7–8," *CBQ* 60, no. 3 (1998): 423–39.

85. James R. Linville, "Visions and Voices: Amos 7–9," *Bib* 80, no. 1 (1999): 22–42; idem, "What Does 'It' Mean? Interpretation at the Point of No Return in Amos

1–2," *BibInt* 8, no. 4 (2000): 400–424; "Amos among the 'Dead Prophets Society': Re-reading the Lion's Roar," *JSOT* 90 (2000): 55–77.

86. Carroll R., *Contexts for Amos*; idem, "Reflecting on War and Utopia in the Book of Amos: The Relevance of a Literary Reading of the Prophetic Text for Central America," in *The Bible in Human Society* (Festschrift J. Rogerson), ed. M. Daniel Carroll R., D. J. A. Clines, and P. R. Davies (JSOTSup 200; Sheffield: Sheffield Academic Press, 1995), 105–21; idem, "God and His People in the Nations' History: A Contextualised Reading of Amos 1–2," *TynBul* 47, no. 1 (1996): 39–70; idem, "The Prophetic Text and the Literature of Dissent in Latin America: Amos, García Márquez, and Cabrera Infante Dismantle Militarism." *BibInt* 4, no. 1 (1996) 76–100; idem, "Living between the Lines: Reading Amos 9:11–15 in Post-War Guatemala," *R&T* 6, no. 1 (1999): 50–64.

87. A well-known scholar who also interacts with various disciplines to inform his readings of biblical texts is Walter Brueggemann, even though he does not use the method I am calling poetics. For treatments of the book of Amos, see "The Legitimacy of a Sectarian Hermeneutic," *HBT* 7, no. 1 (1985): 1–42 (reprinted in *Interpretation and Obedience: From Faithful Reading to Faithful Living* [Minneapolis: Fortress, 1991], 41–69); idem, "The Land and Our Urban Appetites," in *Interpretation and Obedience*, 261–89; idem, "Exodus in the Plural (Amos 9:7)," in *Many Voices, One God: Being Faithful in a Pluralistic World*, ed. W. Brueggemann and G. W. Stroup (Louisville: Westminster John Knox, 1998), 15–34 (reprinted in *Texts that Linger, Words that Explode: Listening to Prophetic Voices*, ed. P. D. Miller [Minneapolis: Fortress, 2000], 89–103).

88. Robert P. Carroll has helpfully surveyed the range of different reader orientations in "The Reader and the Text," in *Text in Context: Essays by Members of the Society for Old Testament Study*, ed. A. D. H. Mayes (Oxford: Oxford University Press, 2000), 3–62. While one may not agree with all of his characterizations, he has done a service through the breadth of his essay and bibliography. My next section will highlight only a few of the groups that have utilized Amos in a significant fashion.

89. For Latin America note, e.g., M. Daniel Carroll R., "Liberation Theology: Latin America," in *The Oxford Illustrated History of the Bible*, ed. J. W. Rogerson (Oxford: Oxford University Press, 2001), 316–29.

90. Gowan, "Amos."

91. Bruce C. Birch, *Hosea, Joel, and Amos* (Westminster Bible Companion; Louisville: Westminster John Knox, 1997). Birch has a long-standing commitment to Old Testament ethics. Note, e.g., his *Let Justice Roll Down: The Old Testament, Ethics, and Christian Life* (Louisville: Westminster John Knox, 1991).

92. Allen R. Guenther, "Amos," in *Hosea, Amos* (Believers Church Bible Commentary; Scottdale, Pa.: Herald, 1998), 228–370.

93. Gary V. Smith, "Amos," in *Hosea, Amos, Micah* (NIV Application Commentary; Grand Rapids: Zondervan, 2001), 203–418. His more technical commentary is *Amos: A Commentary* (Grand Rapids: Zondervan, 1989).

94. Ferdinand E. Deist, "The Prophets: Are We Heading for a Paradigm Switch?" in *Prophet und Prophetenbuch* (Festschrift O. Kaiser), ed. V. Fritz, K.-F. Pohlmann, and H. C. Schmitt (BZAW 185; Berlin: de Gruyter, 1989), 1–18 (reprinted in *The Place Is Too Small for Us: The Israelite Prophets in Recent Research*, ed. R. P. Gordon [SBTS 5; Winona Lake, Ind.: Eisenbrauns, 1995], 582–99).

95. Robert P. Gordon, "Present Trends and Future Directions," in *The Place Is Too Small for Us*, ed. Gordon, 600–605. This quotation is from p. 602.

96. One cannot avoid the impression that, at least to some degree, this sort of redactional work is being done primarily on the European continent (especially within German circles). Will this geographical concentration prove to be a limiting factor?

97. Note, e.g., Karel van der Toorn, "From the Oral to the Written: The Case of Old Babylonian Prophecy"; and Martti Nissinen, "Spoken, Written, Quoted, and Invented: Orality and Writtenness in Ancient Near Eastern Prophecy," in *Writings and Speech*, ed. Ben Zvi and Floyd, 219–34 and 235–71, respectively.

98. Helpful recent surveys are Hans M. Barstad, "No Prophets? Recent Developments in Biblical Prophetic Research and Ancient Near Eastern Prophecy," *JSOT* 57 (1993): 39–60; Robert P. Gordon, "Where Have All the Prophets Gone? The 'Disappearing' Israelite Prophet against the Background of Ancient Near Eastern Prophecy," *BBR* 5 (1995): 67–86. New editions of relevant texts are also appearing. Note, for instance, Simo Parpola, *Assyrian Prophecies* (State Archives of Assyria 9; Helsinki: Helsinki University Press, 1997).

99. Roy F. Melugin is an example of this move. Note, e.g., some of his recent work on Amos: "Amos," in *Harper's Bible Commentary*, 720–25; "Amos," in *Asbury Bible Commentary*, 735–49.

Chapter 3: Reading Amos from the Margins

1. For a helpful set of introductory and survey essays, see John Rogerson, ed., *The Oxford Illustrated History of the Bible* (Oxford: Oxford University Press, 2001), specifically the essays on "Feminist Scholarship" by Yvonne Sherwood, 296–315; "Liberation Theology: Latin America" by M. Daniel Carroll R., 316–29; "Liberation Theology: Africa and the Bible" by Gerald West, 330–42; "Liberation Theology: Europe" by Luise Schotroff, 344–55.

2. An African scholar who has done much work on this is Gerald O. West, most recently in *The Academy of the Poor: Towards a Dialogical Reading of the Bible* (Interventions 2; Sheffield: Sheffield Academic Press, 1999).

3. Cf. Michael Prior, *The Bible and Colonialism: A Moral Critique* (Biblical Seminar 48: Sheffield: Sheffield Academic Press, 1997). For another perspective that appreciates some of the positive long-term effect (even if unplanned) of missionary efforts in Bible translation, see Lamin Sanneh, *Translating the Message: The Missionary Impact on Culture* (Maryknoll, N.Y.: Orbis, 1989).

4. Note, e.g., R.S. Sugirtharajah, ed., *Voices from the Margin: Interpreting the Bible in the Third World* (London: SPCK; Maryknoll, N.Y.: Orbis, 1991); idem, *Voices from the Margin: Interpreting the Bible in the Third World* (rev. ed.; London: SPCK; Maryknoll, N.Y.: Orbis, 1995); Fernando F. Segovia and Mary Ann Tolbert, eds., *Reading from This Place*, vol. 1: *Social Location and Biblical Interpretation in the United States* (Minneapolis: Fortress, 1995); idem, *Reading from This Place*, vol. 2: *Social Location and Biblical Interpretation in Global Perspective* (Minneapolis: Fortress, 1995); Daniel Smith-Christopher, ed., *Text & Experience: Towards a Cultural Exegesis of the Bible* (Biblical Seminar 35; Sheffield: Sheffield Academic Press, 1995); Priscilla Pope-Levison and John R. Levison, eds., *Return to Babel: Global Perspectives on the Bible* (Louisville: Westminster John Knox, 1999).

5. For Africa, see Gerald O. West and Musa W. Dube, eds., *The Bible in Africa: Transactions, Trajectories, and Trends* (Leiden: Brill, 2000). For Latin America, note Leif E. Vaage, trans. and ed., *Subversive Scriptures: Revolutionary Readings of the Christian Bible in Latin America* (Valley Forge, Pa.: Trinity Press Interna-

tional, 1997). Vaage's volume is a selection of articles from *RIBLA*, a liberationist biblical studies journal.

6. Ruth E. Frey, "Oracle against the Nations (1992)," in *Many Voices: Multicultural Responses to the Minor Prophets*, ed. Alice Ogden Bellis (Lanham, Md.: University Press of America, 1995), 12–13.

7. Joel F. Drinkard Jr. "Thus Says the Lord," *RevExp* 92, no. 2 (1995): 219–33. This excerpt is found on pp. 222–23.

8. These lines are taken from King's speech, "The American Dream." The source is *A Testament of Hope: The Essential Writings of Martin Luther King, Jr.*, ed. J. M. Washington (San Francisco: Harper & Row, 1986), 208–16. The citation is from pp. 214–16.

9. J. Deotis Roberts, *Liberation and Reconciliation: A Black Theology* (rev. ed.; Maryknoll, N.Y.: Orbis, 1994), 96–98.

10. Some of the more prominent theologians would include Justo L. González, Fernando F. Segovia, María Pilar Aquino, Orlando O. Espín, Virgil P. Elizondo, Ada María Isasi-Díaz, and Eldin Villafañe. These come from a spectrum of denominational and institutional backgrounds.

11. Francisco O. García-Treto, "A Reader-Response Approach to Prophetic Conflict: The Case of Amos 7.10–17," in *The New Literary Criticism and the Hebrew Bible*, ed. J. C. Exum and D. J. A. Clines (JSOTSup 143; Sheffield: Sheffield Academic Press, 1993), 114–24.

12. Ibid., 116.

13. Ibid., 122–24.

14. Alice L. Laffey, *An Introduction to the Old Testament: A Feminist Perspective* (Philadelphia: Fortress, 1988), 151–67.

15. Judith E. Sanderson, "Amos," in *The Women's Bible Commentary*, ed. C. A. Newsome and S. H. Ringe (Louisville: Westminster John Knox, 1992), 205–9. Note, too, Phyllis A. Bird, "Poor Man, Poor Woman? Gendering the Poor in Prophetic Texts?" in *Missing Persons and Mistaken Identities: Women and Gender in Ancient Israel* (OBT; Minneapolis: Fortress, 1997), 67–78. The bulk of Bird's discussion deals with the book of Amos.

16. Sanderson, "Amos," 206–7.

17. Ibid., 207.

18. Ibid., 209.

19. Carol J. Dempsey, *The Prophets: A Liberation-Critical Reading* (Minneapolis: Fortress, 2000), 7–21.

20. Ibid., 7.

21. Ibid., 10–11.

22. Renita J. Weems, "Womanist Reflections on Biblical Hermeneutics," in *Black Theology: A Documentary History*, vol. 2: *1980–1992*, ed. J. H. Cone and G. S. Wilmore (Maryknoll, N.Y.: Orbis, 1993), 216–24. This excerpt is from pp. 221–22.

23. David J. A. Clines, "Metacommentating Amos," in *Of Prophets' Visions and the Wisdom of Sages* (Festschrift R. N. Whybray), ed. H. A. McKay and D. J. A. Clines (JSOTSup 162; Sheffield: Sheffield Academic Press, 1993), 143–60.

24. Ibid., 142–44.

25. Ibid., 147.

26. Ibid., 158–59.

27. Dempsey, *Prophets*, 17–18. Also note David Jobling and Nathan Loewen, "Sketches for Earth Readings of the Book of Amos," in *Readings from the Perspective of the*

Earth, ed. N. C. Habel (Earth Bible 1; Sheffield: Sheffield Academic Press, 2000), 72–85.

28. One example of this cross-pollination is Gerald O. West, *Biblical Hermeneutics of Liberation: Modes of Reading the Bible in the South African Context* (2d ed.; Pietermaritzburg, Republic of South Africa: Cluster Publications; Maryknoll, N.Y.: Orbis, 1995). One of the values of West's work is that he demonstrates the variety of opinions among those who use the Bible in the struggle for liberation in Africa regarding its possible ideological biases. Some will read the Bible as it is; others will question its stance and perspectives. In addition to the work just cited, note his "Gauging the Grain in a More Nuanced and Literary Manner: A Cautionary Tale concerning the Contribution of the Social Sciences to Biblical Interpretation," in *Rethinking Contexts, Rereading Texts: Contributions from the Social Sciences to Biblical Interpretation*, ed. M. Daniel Carroll R. (JSOT-Sup 299; Sheffield: Sheffield Academic Press, 2000), 75–105. M. Daniel Carroll R. explains why in Latin America those who work among the poor deal with the final form of the text in *Contexts for Amos: Prophetic Poetics in Latin American Perspective* (JSOTSup 132; Sheffield: Sheffield Academic Press, 1992), 140–75. Of course, there are those in Latin America who would also question the text. Mention could be made of scholars such as Jorge Pixley, although his work has not been in Amos.

29. Kris J. N. Owan, "Championing the Cause of the Less Privileged: Human Promotion in Nigeria in the Light of Prophet Amos," *Revue Africaine de Théologie* 17, no. 2 (1993): 37–57. This quotation is from pp. 37–38.

30. Ibid., 56–57.

31. Haroldo Reimer, *Richtet auf des Rechts! Studien zur Botschaft des Amos* (SBS 149; Stuttgart: Katholisches Bibelwerk, 1992). For his hermeneutical introduction, see pp. 11–27.

32. Idem, "Agentes y mecanismos de opresión y explotación en Amós," *RIBLA* 12 (1992): 69–81. This quotation is from the abrsact on p. 69.

33. Humberto Casanova R., "La época de Amós y la justicia social," *BolTeol* 50 (1993): 95–106. The quotation is from pp. 105–6.

34. M. Daniel Carroll R., "Reflecting on War and Utopia in Amos: The Relevance of a Literary Reading of the Prophetic Text for Central America," in *The Bible in Human Society* (Festschrift J. Rogerson), ed. M. Daniel Carroll R., D. J. A. Clines, and P. R. Davies (JSOTSup 200; Sheffield: Sheffield Academic Press, 1995), 105–21. The citation is found on pp. 120–21.

35. M. Daniel Carroll R., "Living between the Lines: Reading Amos 9:11–15 in Post-War Guatemala," *R & T* 6, no. 1 (1999): 50–64. This excerpt is from pp. 55–56.

36. Ibid., 59.

Chapter 5: Specific Topics and Significant Blocks of Text

1. This section is included because of the extensive war imagery in the book of Amos. This list is just a sampling of relevant and informative materials. Of course, much of the data for the eighth century comes from Assyrian sources. Although the Neo-Assyrian Empire's resurgence in Syria-Palestine comes a few years after when most would date the ministry of the prophet Amos, these sources do give us a glance into warfare in the general time period. If one dates parts of the book as later, perhaps references to the Assyrian defeat of Israel might be more direct.

Chapter 7: Doctoral Dissertations, 1985–2000

1. The doctoral dissertations abstracted here either have been read in their entirety or carefully reviewed. The summaries of dissertations that for whatever reason were not available through interlibrary loan have been based on the information provided by other sources (such as Dissertations Abstracts International and *Old Testament Abstracts*) and are placed in brackets.

Acknowledgments

The author gratefully acknowledges the following works of the scholars that are quoted in chapters 1–3: Francis I. Andersen and David Noel Freedman, *Amos: A New Translation and Commentary* (AB 24A; New York: Doubleday, 1989); M. Daniel Carroll R., "Reflecting on War and Utopia in Amos: The Relevance of a Literary Reading of the Prophetic Text for Central America," in *The Bible in Human Society* (Festschrift J. Rogerson), ed. M. Daniel Carroll R., D. J. A. Clines, and P. R. Davies (JSOTSup 200; Sheffield: Sheffield Academic Press, 1995), 105–21; idem, M. Daniel Carroll R., "Living between the Lines: Reading Amos 9:11–15 in Post—War Guatemala," *R&T* 6, no. 1 (1999): 50–64; Humberto Casanova R. "La época de Amós y la justicia social," *BolTeol* 50 (1993): 95–106; Robert B. Coote, *Amos among the Prophets: Composition and Theology* (Philadelphia: Fortress, 1981); Richard S. Cripps, *A Commentary on the Book of Amos* (reprint 2d ed.; Limited Classical Reprint Library; Minneapolis: Klock & Klock, 1981); David J. A. Clines, "Metacommentating Amos," in *Of Prophets' Visions and the Wisdom of Sages* (R.N. Whybray Festschrift), ed. H.A. McKay and D. J. A. Clines (JSOTSup 162; Sheffield: Sheffield Academic Press, 1993), 143–60; Carol J. Dempsey, *The Prophets: A Liberation—Critical Reading* (Minneapolis: Fortress, 2000); Joel F. Drinkard, Jr. "Thus Says the Lord." *RevExp* 92, no. 2 (1995): 219–33; Ruth E. Frey, "Oracles against the Nations (1992)" in *Many Voices: Multicultural Responses to the Minor Prophets*, ed. Alice Ogden Bellis (Lanham, MD: University Press of America, 1995), 12–13; Francisco O. García—Treto, "A Reader—Response Approach to Prophetic Conflict: The Case of Amos 7.10–17," in *The New Literary Criticism and the Hebrew Bible*, ed. J. C. Exum and D. J. A. Clines (JSOTSup 143; Sheffield: Sheffield Academic Press, 1993), 114–24; Donald E. Gowan, "Amos," in *New Interpreter's Bible*, ed. L. E. Keck et al (Nashville: Abingdon, 1996), vol. 7: 339–431; Hermann Gunkel, "The Israelite Prophecy from the Time of Amos," in *Twentieth Century Theology in the Making*, vol. I: *Themes of Biblical Theology*, ed. J. Pelikan, trans. R. A. Wilson (New York: Harper & Row, 1969), 48–55; Alfred Haldar, *Associations of Cult Prophets among the Ancient Semites* (Uppsala: Almquist &

Wiksell, 1945); William Rainey Harper, *A Critical and Exegetical Commentary on Amos and Hosea* (ICC, 18; Edinburgh: T. & T. Clark, 1905); Jeremias, *The Book of Amos: A Commentary*, trans. D.W. Stott (OTL; Louisville: Westminster John Knox, 1998); Martin Luther King Jr., "The American Dream," in *A Testament of Hope: The Essential Writings of Martin Luther King, Jr.*, ed. J.M. Washington (San Francisco: Harper & Row, 1986), 208–16; J. Lindblom, *Prophecy in Ancient Israel* (Philadelphia: Fortress, 1962); James L. Mays, "Words about the Words of Amos: Recent Study of the Book of Amos," *Int* 13, no. 3 (1959): 259–72; José Porfirio Miranda, *Marx and the Bible: A Critique of the Philosophy of Oppression*, trans. J. Eagleson (Maryknoll: Orbis, 1974); James Nogalski, "Intertextuality in the Twelve," in *Forming Prophetic Literature* (Festschrift J.D.W. Watts), ed. J.W. Watts and P.R. House (JSOTSup 235; Sheffield: Sheffield Academic Press, 1996), 102–24; Kris J.N. Owan, "Championing the Cause of the Less Privileged: Human Promotion in Nigeria in the Light of Prophet Amos," *Revue Africaine de Theologie* 17, no. 2 (1993): 37–57; Washington Padilla, *Amós—Abdías* (Comentario Bíblico Hispanoamericano; Miami: Editorial Caribe, 1989); Brian Peckham, *History and Prophecy: The Development of Late Judean Literary Traditions* (Anchor Bible Reference Library; New York: Doubleday, 1993); David L. Petersen, "The Book of the Twelve/The Minor Prophets," in *The Hebrew Bible Today: An Introduction to Critical Issues*, ed. S.L. McKenzie and M.P. Graham (Louisville: Westminster John Knox, 1998), 95–126; J. David Pleins, *The Social Visions of the Hebrew Bible: A Theological Introduction* (Louisville: Westminster John Knox, 2000); Haroldo Reimer, "Agentes y mecanismos de opresión y explotación en Amós," *RIBLA* 12 (1992): 69–81; J. Deotis Roberts, *Liberation and Reconciliation: A Black Theology* (rev. ed.; Maryknoll, N.Y.: Orbis, 1994); Theodore H. Robinson, *Prophecy and the Prophets in Ancient Israel* (2d ed.; London: Gerald Duckworth & Co., 1953); Leland Ryken, "Amos," in *A Complete Guide to the Bible*, ed. idem and T. Longman III (Grand Rapids: Zondervan, 1993), 337–47; Judith E. Sanderson, "Amos," in *The Women's Bible Commentary*, ed. C.A. Newsome and S.H. Ringe (Louisville: Westminster John Knox, 1992), 205–9; Milton Schwantes, *Amós: Meditaçôes e Estudos* (São Leopoldo: Sinodal; Petrópolis: Voces, 1987); Marvin A. Sweeney, *The Twelve Prophets* (Berit Olam; Collegeville, MN: The Liturgical Press, 2000); Renita J. Weems, "Womanist Reflections on Biblical Hermeneutics," in *Black Theology: A Documentary History*, vol. 2: *1980–1992*, ed. J.H. Cone and G.S. Wilmore (Maryknoll, N.Y.: Orbis, 1993), 216–24; Julius Wellhausen, *Die kleinen Propheten übersetzt und erklärt* (Berlin: de Gruyter, 1963 [German 3d ed., 1898]); idem, *Prolegomena to the History of Ancient Israel* (Atlanta: Scholars Press, 1994); Rolland Wolfe, *Meet Amos and Hosea, The Prophets of Israel* (New York: Harper & Row, 1945); Hans Walter Wolff, *Joel and Amos*, trans. W. Janzen, S.D. McBride, Jr. and C.A. Muenchow (Hermeneia; Philadelphia: Fortress, 1977).

Author Index

Scripture Index

Subject Index

African approaches, 67–68, 201 n.28

African-American approaches, 57–59, 189 n.133, 200 n.2, 3; 202 n.28

anthropology, 22–23, 41–42, 196 n.57

See also social science approaches

archaeology, 20–22, 39–41, 48–49, 170–71, 184 n.81, 185 nn.92, 93; 187 n.113, 187 n.113

asherah, 20–22, 40, 185 n.93 *See also* popular religion

Book of the Twelve, 26, 36–39, 173–74, 193 nn.29, 33, 34; 193–94 n.38

canonical criticism, 25, 28

chiastic structures, 26, 45, 198 n.83

See also literary approaches

covenant, 5, 15–17, 44, 169, 173–74, 181 n.54, 182 n.65, 182–83 n.66, 183 n.67, 197 n.66

cult, 5–7, 12–14, 16–17, 28, 174, 178 n. 16, 179–80 n.39, 180 n.43, 183 n.73

See also New Year Festival

Deuteronomistic redaction, 19, 32–33, 35–37, 40, 170, 192 n.21

See also redaction criticism

ecology, 66

ecstasy, 7–10, 13, 22, 179 nn.21, 38; 180 n.44

eschatological hope, 164–65, 167–68

ethical monotheism, 5–7, 177–78 nn.6, 7, 16

evangelical approaches, 29–30, 50, 57–58, 69–72, 189–90 n.150

See also liberation theology

feminism, 50, 61–63, 189 n.133

See also womanist studies

form criticism, 15–17, 19, 22, 39, 43, 180–81 n.52, 186 n.103

Hispanic American approaches, 59–61, 201 n.10

hymns, 20, 167

ideological criticism, 42–43,

64–66, 184 n.81, 196 n.59, 196–97 n.61, 200 n.3

intertextuality, 33, 36–38, 191 n.12

Israelite religion, history of, 4–8, 21, 177–78 nn.6, 7, 16; 179 n.38, 180 n.45, 194–95 n.48

See also asherah; popular religion

Kuntillet 'Ajrud, 20–22, 185 n.93

See also asherah; popular religion

Latin American perspectives, 27–30, 68–72, 164, 168, 175, 189 n.133, 189–90 n.150, 202 n.28

See also evangelical approaches; liberation theology

law, 5, 34, 165, 177 n.6, 182 n.61, 183 n.73, 191 n.16

liberation theology, 27–30, 47–48, 68–69, 164, 168–69, 189 n.137, 189–90 n.150, 200–1 n.5, 202 n.28

literary approaches, 24–26, 29–30, 33–34, 38–39, 43–47, 50, 164–67,

This index does not include sources from the bibliographic listings of chapters 4–6. For the categories within the bibliographies, see "Contents."

223